T0116231

A FRIEND OF ALL FAITHS

MICHAEL H. COHEN

"The whole world is a narrow bridge; the main thing is not to fear at all."

- Ethics of the Fathers

Order this book online at www.trafford.com
or email orders@trafford.com

Most Trafford titles are also available at major online book retailers.

Print information available on the last page.

ISBN: 978-1-4120-0854-9 (sc)

Thanks to Will Bueche for cover design, and to Elaine F.
Kerry for the cover image from Mutton Fish Point.

Trafford rev. 12/14/2108

Trafford PUBLISHING www.trafford.com
North America & international
toll-free: 1 888 232 4444 (USA & Canada)
fax: 812 355 4082

For all beings,
sentient and insentient,
visible and invisible,
created and uncreated.

CONTENTS

I wrote this book to explain two seemingly disparate sides of my being. These two archetypical patterns have various names, and all identities may be but masks for a deeper layer of consciousness; but in service of the narrative, let us call them Lawyer and Healer. I live an apparently ordinary life with an extraordinary inner life which has opportunity to publicly shine only when circumstances make it safe to do so—meaning that the recipient of a particular communication is open and does not consider it threatening to pour the whole contents of the unconscious mind—call it that, or That, or Spirit, that awareness Down Under although really Up and Down are relative variables in a no-land beyond space and time as currently conceived in only four dimensions—into conversation.

Put another way, I received classical training as a lawyer through a top law school, making the grade with Law Review, a clerkship for a federal judge, corporate practice in a Wall Street law firm, and legal academe, followed by medical academe and the opportunity to open and run my own law firm. Simultaneously I studied Ericksonian hypnotherapy, as well as energy healing in various venues, including the Barbara Brennan School of Healing.

Over time, I began to move as fluidly through the human aura and landscapes of spirituality reality as I could through judicial opinions and statutes. For a long while I thought these two sets of skills—lawyering and healing—were incompatible; and I discovered a long list of possible dichotomizations to explain why (i.e., left-brain vs. right-brain; logical vs. intuitive; West vs. East, and so on). This same dichotomy persisted in my professional life, in which I joined many others in lending talent to creating bridges between conventional (a/k/a orthodox) medicine (or biomedicine) and complementary and alternative medicine (a/k/a "CAM"). Creation of those bridges though legal scholarship led to a faculty position at Harvard Medical School, and to many other interesting opportunities. I also had a fellowship at the Center for the Study of World Religions at Harvard Divinity School, and used my time at Harvard to create connections with like-minded souls, people synthesizing science and theology; legal scholarship (and lawyering) and holistic health care; psychology and spirituality; and so on. I was successful as an academic but dissatisfied with the language of academic discourse; functioning well as a lawyer but wanting to find a more integrated place in which to engage my total being. Yoga, meditation, and various practices provided an outlet to be "real," "full," "authentic," but still the challenge persisted of bringing everything to bear in a world where separation often becomes a governing metaphor.

Because my spiritual awareness was considered radical in some circles, I felt it was important to write about the journey. I had always been predisposed toward the metaphysical, but at a certain point in my life, the mystical experiences became so strong, almost overwhelming, that it became clear that the connection to God, Spirit, the Self— whatever language one uses—was the only moist cake, everything else being the drizzled frosting: tasty, but not the main event. Over time, it has become clearer that there are many 'closet ' mystics and that, moreover, scientific advances are bringing us ever closer to making the implausible, plausible. Auditory contact with spirit guides may seem subjective, improvable, and completely speculative (if not delusional) to the hard-headed scientist, until one considers advances in physics, mathematics, and other disciplines; new theories of complexity and emergence; artificial intelligence; and even routine advances in telecommunications which now make the possibility of communicating on ever subtle levels (for example, through implants and sublingual vocalization, if not directly through thoughts— by connecting neural pathways to machines) an accepted phenomenon.

As a result, I have begun being more open about my experiences, knowing they are more commonly shared than I initially thought; and more open about integrating those experiences with the totality of my functioning, trusting the unity of outer and inner.

Recently, a physician sought representation at a disciplinary interview before the state medical board. This client had been a complementary medicine practitioner--as had his father, also an MD, who had happened to live in Vienna, and to have contact with some of the leading psychoanalysts, including Freud. My client told me during intake that his father had always been slightly afraid of the conventional medical crowd, concerned that they might treat him as they had Wilhelm Reich, the brilliant but unconventional psychologist who conceptualized the existence of 'orgone energy' and died practically insane in a federal prison (apparently his captors did not see the irony of his book title, *Listen, Little Man!*). My law partner and I coached the client based on everything we knew about disciplinary procedure for his state's medical board, the underlying statute and applicable case law, and regulatory trends relating to CAM. Based on this preparation, the interview went well. My client came across as strong and focused, and knowledgeable about all aspects of conventional medicine but dedicated to creating a specialized practice using only complementary approaches. Importantly, he defined his role as adjunctive and consultative-- that is, where the patient was responsible for seeking primary care through another MD.

Following the interview, we decided to find someplace to sit and process what had occurred in the room. We walked a few blocks and instead of going into a restaurant or coffee shop, found ourselves at a local church, rather old, which had a burial ground from pre-Civil War times. We sat on a bench overlooking the aging and fading stones. We fully discussed all the legal permutations and ramifications of the interview. We surmised that the investigation would likely be dismissed, based on the hints that were given during the interview and the seeming receptivity to the points we had made. Then, I turned to him and said: "I hope you don't mind if I say something that may sound like I'm playing amateur therapist." I am very conscious of my role as a lawyer and mindful of professional boundaries and the need to guide the client appropriately; nonetheless, information was flowing intuitively and so I checked with my client regarding his receptivity, disclaiming or acknowledging my limited competence in this non-legal sphere. He smiled: "Go on; if I can't take it I shouldn't be dishing it out"–meaning that in the CAM modality he has chosen, he tends to look at the whole picture (including the client's emotional state and dreams).

I pointed to the stones and said: "Since we're here in this burial ground, it seems appropriate to invoke the ancestors, as they are present....We both sense, based on the evidence of today's meeting and our intuition, that the result will be favorable. Maybe the guy who reported you to the authorities, malevolent though he may have been, nonetheless did you a favor. Maybe this is a gift–a clearing–a way to remove the shadow of fear that has haunted your practice. You will have faced the regulatory authorities and cleaned out the fear, which your father held and was then held by you; and as a result your practice will be brighter." He sighed relief and looked at me with immediate recognition. Now we can divide this beautiful moment into believers and skeptics–the former might laud the integration of law and healing, while another observer might critique the event as my feeding New Age poppycock. My evidence for the interaction is that the comment landed in a profound and mysterious way as truth, providing a cascade of emotional relief and spiritual clearing that cannot be conveyed on a strictly rational, analytical level. I know that those moments that I most remember are those in which I am fully present, and some truth is exchanged at a level beyond space and time, and quantum mechanics, and even beyond the aberrations of space and time that are rapidly becoming part of science. And the pilgrim's progress continues to evolve. This is the story of a significant part of that evolution.

NASSAU, THE BAHAMAS, 2007

WALL STREET, SEMINARY

(NEW YORK CITY, 1990)

Two photos, taken the same year, suggest different aspects of the same journey

Wall Street   Seminary

VISION

Tanya had a vision: a wise old woman gifted her with a wood box containing a white feather. Tanya thanked the old woman but awoke wondering about the feather's meaning. The next day, she learned that her friend Nick had enrolled in an interfaith seminary. She drove to his house to learn more; as she stepped out of her car onto his driveway, she saw a white feather, the same size and shape as the one in her dream.

I had found the interfaith Seminary by accident, wandering through New York City on a day off my Wall Street law practice, looking for a place to celebrate the High Holiday services. I belonged to no synagogue, even though my childhood upbringing included regularly attending services. For my Bar Mitzvah, I had read the Hebrew directly from the Torah scroll, denuded as the calligraphic text was of punctuation and vowels.

Our synagogue, named Shaarey Zedek–the 'Gates of Righteousness'–was shaped like an isosceles triangle, hands folded in prayer position; or a spaceship–depending on perspective. The lush chapel contained a triangular arch, enfolded by a metallic sculpture representing the Burning Bush; the voice of the choir emanated from somewhere invisible behind–I thought it the voice of the angels.

By high school, I had studied Talmud in Aramaic and served as Religious Vice President for the synagogue youth group. But my first day of college, the campus was plastered with recruiting posters from ultra-orthodox Jewish groups. Vivid sensations from childhood reemerged: the perennial outsider identified as such. The sense of separation was enforced by a meal plan in a separate, kosher dining room; our solidarity was social and cultural, and rather weak. I also learned in class that, contrary to childhood teachings, a certain J, E, P, D, and R (and not God) had authored and edited the Torah.

By the time I reached Wall Street, my spirituality was buried deep within. I affiliated with no synagogue, and resented having to buy tickets at premium prices for a few days' worship during the High Holidays simply because attendance was culturally expected. Rebelling, I took the day off. I found myself wandering the streets in shorts and a tee shirt; these wanderings literally took me to the Seminary's doorstep.

A white-haired but vigorous man warmly welcomed me to his Rosh Hashanah services: a dozen people sat in folding chairs in the basement of this Village apartment. The man explained that he had received ordination as an orthodox rabbi in Europe; that his wife and children had perished in the Holocaust; that immigrating, he had co-founded the Seminary with religious representatives of different faiths: a priest, a swami, an imam, and others. As part of the High Holiday service, he included a Tarot reading. The cards indicated a huge change in my life. Afterward, I picked up a brochure, describing a two-year, part-time program to receive ordination as an interfaith minister. I enrolled.

Weeks later, I met Nick and mentioned how Tanya had been drawn to seminary. Forgetting that my guidance had come—my own footsteps literally leading me to the door—I inquired: "Why did Tanya receive a beautiful vision from a wise old woman, while I received nothing but silence?"

"Sometimes," he answered, "God works only through silence."

CHANNEL

Leaves and old newspapers swirled at the basement entrance to the interfaith Seminary. Metal folding chairs were placed in a circle, the white-haired rabbi at the center, joking pleasantly with newcomers. Nick, flanked by Tanya and a pale but attractive woman who introduced herself as Jane, turned around with a warm smile, shook my hand, and invited me to join the three for lunch after class.

I immediately felt drawn to his warmth. He was about thirty, with a large frame and a boyish face; coarse, salt-and-pepper hair cascaded down his brow and swept behind his neck. He exuded an aura of quiet contentment, yet his dark eyes constantly scanned his environment, as if studying everyone and everything.

In a short while, the rabbi calmed us with an eclectic but not unpleasant meditation. Then, classmates made introductions: they were psychotherapists and massage therapists; intuitive healers; nurses; businesspeople. The common theme seemed to be dissatisfaction with conventional religious practice, finding it too limiting an approach for a mystical grasp of infinity. The Seminary's motto stressed pluralism and inclusiveness. The curriculum included study of many religions: organized (Christianity, Hinduism, Buddhism, Islam), mystical (such as Sufism, Taoism), informal (New Age thought; A Course on Miracles), studies of psychological thinkers (Freud, Jung, Maslow, Adler), and topics relevant to ministry such as alcoholism, death and dying, hospital chaplaincy, shamanism.

We were encouraged in our introductions to "dive deep." I welcomed this study as a counterpart to the rotation at my law firm through the securities, banking, and mergers & acquisitions departments. I mentioned that I had a strong Jewish upbringing-conservative Hebrew day school, participated in the National Bible Contest in Hebrew, studied Talmud, once went to an orthodox camp where I wore a yarmulke and *tzitzit*, the ritual fringes; that I worked as a Wall Street lawyer; and felt many contradictions on the path to unity consciousness.

Nick's introduction affirmed the distaste for the "foolishness" of, as he put it, the "many distinctions people perpetuate in the name of the One, Unity, Divine." As a child, he said, he was forbidden to "associate" with "those people"–the others who were not Catholic, middle-class, white; his church taught him to love his neighbors, "so long as they weren't Jews, blacks, Asians, Mexicans, Indians, or otherwise 'undesirable.'" He said he had left a Catholic seminary, finding its doctrinal teachings too rigid; further, he had experienced an undeniable psychic opening and felt compelled to share his gift.

At lunch, Jane asked him about his 'readings.' "Do you channel?"

"I open the tunnel to the astral world and let the spirits come through."

"How do you do it?"

"I don't know."

"Have you always been this way?"

"Yes. As a child I would see colors around people, their auras. Someone would come over for tea and I would say, 'Mom, what's that red on her shoulder?'"

Jane asked: "Do you 'ground' yourself so you're not taken over by the entity?"

This was new territory; though I was working on corporate takeovers in the mergers and acquisitions department, corporeal takeovers were another thing.

Nick was nonplussed and simply answered: "I pray to the Divine Mother."

"And after–how do you recharge the energy you've expended?"

Nick laughed. "I nap."

I assumed that painters, sculptors, poets, philosophers, and other artists "channeled" in the sense that inventing, composing, creating draws on the energies of the cosmos, involves a mysterious transmission of some kind of language from deep inside, amplified perhaps by archetypical energies latent in the human species. Notions of the Muse, 'inspiration,' the trance state, or simply openness to creativity helped explain a non-rational process of access to something greater than the thinking mind alone. But Nick was claiming to allow beings (or "entities") to occupy his physical body and deliver messages, not simply to imagine what other people–living or otherworldly–thought or said; he claimed to "see" and "hear" the spirits.

I decided to visit him. We stood on a beach overlooking the Long Island Sound and stared at the cascading waves, entranced by the water's vastness, the unceasing steadiness of whitecaps, crashing infinitely on the sand.

"Do you feel it?" Nick suddenly asked.

"What?" I replied.

He stretched his arm toward the waters. "All those spirits out there."

I paused and examined the beautiful landscape. "I don't feel them."

"God," he said. "Infinity."

We were quiet a moment. I strained to feel something non-corporeal. The setting inspired awe, reverence, appreciation for nature's magnificence. It spoke to my heart, but nothing invisible spoke audibly to my ears. I held the silence.

"In a hundred years," Nick said after a while, "you and I will be gone. But everything we see here will remain."

I suddenly lurched into a perspective of creation's vast scale, far outstripping the limited mind that had successfully navigated law school, the Bar exam, and Wall Street practice. My own accomplishments seemed puny and insignificant, my ego concerns dissolved into a dot. "We're so wrapped in petty concerns," I reflected. "The *I* is the center of existence, yet 'I' don't know what existence is."

Nick stared at the sand. "Look–it is so magnificent. If I can give you a taste of the world beyond the five senses, I will have respected the gift by sharing it."

"How will you do that?"

"You'll learn that the dead live among us, speak to us, and constantly guide us."

"I'll learn this for myself?" I asked skeptically. Although graduating with a college concentration in political science (after meandering through anthropology, religion, and English literature), I had read a lot of psychological literature on my own–favoring Carl Jung. I was receptive to the notion of collective archetypes and to the power of mythological symbols to catapult consciousness toward something beyond ordinary awareness. But I could not possibly imagine dead people hanging out at the coffee shop, whispering answers to law school essay exams in large halls, and talking to us like live ones on New York City streets or subways.

Quietly we returned to our cars.

LOCUST VALLEY

The train rushed away in a roar, leaving us alone on the cold and empty platform. Natasha and I released our matching, maroon, leather briefcases onto the cement–each embossed in gold letters with our initials–and peered into the blackness. A decaying, wooden sign glimmered under a naked bulb: "Locust Valley." I recalled that Tolstoy had died in a rail station, having written his last word: "*I.*" The bulb puttered out, seemingly on that thought, immersing us in complete darkness.

Natasha gripped my hand and shivered. Obedient to her Russian Orthodox heritage, she had only reluctantly agreed to accompany me to the séance that Nick was conducting. My quest for information about the phenomena Nick claimed to experience was to her a blasphemous investigation, a blatant violation of ancient ordinances of her faith. The snuffing of the light seemed to confirm her fears. I felt her grip tighten as my free hand searched trouser pockets for a calling card with which to telephone the local taxi service. In the cold, our attached hands grew number. The chilled air, permeated with the scent of dead leaves and fresh pine needles, enveloped us. Silence echoed off invisible structures into our interiors.

We had barely left our law firm early enough to make the "prayer meeting," as Nick called it. Another associate had stopped me by the elevator, grinning with an accusatory, "Leaving early, again?"

"I have a meeting to attend," I had replied, "to help the homeless." My behavior was governed by the pragmatic realization that I could not give anything away, that it was best to perpetuate the myth of the dedicated employee, burning my life's energy to satisfy the billable requirement. Although curious enough to attend the séance, I was not ready to crucify myself for the divine. And besides, I rationalized, spirits *were* "homeless"–no longer housed in physical bodies like ours.

But now a yellowed pair of headlights trained beams on us. Natasha clambered into the taxi's back seat, while I sat in the front, reading the directions I had scrawled on the back page of the merger agreement drafted earlier. We were to take a complex sequence of turns in the blackened roads, which only seemed to thicken around the taxicab's meager light. The taxi sputtered down the forlorn paths. In the dark, magnificent homes were recessed behind vast gardens. They spoke of self-made millionaires: Roosevelt, Morgan, and Reynolds, the aluminum-foil king. A headlight could no more penetrate these estates than a camel the eye of a needle. Yet, the driver seemed secure.

The taxi made a ninety-degree turn–Natasha fell into me; I grabbed the handlebar of the taxi door–and we proceeded down a gravel road. On either side stretched a row of pine trees, silent guardians of a secluded estate, and bushes shaped like people. The mansion at the end dwarfed us: I quickly estimated forty rooms. At its base a half-moon driveway circled around a fountain, plastered over with cloth. Four statues occupied the manicured grass between the fountain and the driveway; covered with plaster, they stood mute, stone angels suffocated by the blankets of cloth. Eyes peered at us from some of the windows; or perhaps I was imagining this, bleary from hours of proofreading.

I paid the driver and exited the cab. Natasha broke her grip on my hand to ring the doorbell. I gave her a reassuring smile. A dog howled from the back of the house; I pressed the doorbell again. A young girl answered our call, her golden hair tied into a ponytail with a crimson bow. She was about six, yet carried herself like an adult, which gave an elfish impression, as if she had been alive for centuries. "Welcome," she said. I had the odd sense that someone else was talking through her. "Welcome," the girl repeated, as if awaiting a response. "You are welcome here. Remove shoes." We obeyed. The girl slipped inside, leaving us in the marbled foyer. I silently helped Natasha out of her coat and hung it up in the vestibule, then followed with mine and tucked our briefcases in for the evening. I loosened my tie, rolled up my sleeves and looked around. French tapestries lined the foyer's walls; a jeweled mirror glinted from another corridor; on a mantle stood a photograph of a model, stately and composed in a white turtleneck, her hair expertly tossed back from her forehead.

"That was my mother." The girl's voice emanated from somewhere inside. I held Natasha's hand and followed the girl through two glass doors, down some marble steps to a sunken room, about half the size of a football field, and decorated with flickering candles. We passed through another set of glass doors, down wooden steps that creaked as we walked over them, as if they, too, were alive. A new set of flickering candle flames illuminated the immaculate and lush vanilla carpeting in this second living room. The dark-paneled walls were filled with paintings–mostly landscapes of hunts–and in the far corner, a bookcase served as an altar. It held a framed photograph of a saint, together with a tall, thick candle whose flame flickered with each passing invisible gust, as if moved by the breath of an unseen guest. In the other far corner stood a baby grand piano, the top propped open, as if waiting to be played. In the center of the room, two expensive sofas faced across a glass table, with framed photographs of saints.

"There's the patron saint of my high school," Natasha exclaimed in surprise.

Beyond the saints were photographs of attendees' relatives.

On each of the sofas sat a number of attractive, middle-aged women: one cross-legged on the couch, her open eyes rolled toward the back of her head; a second erect, her feet on the ground, her palms face down on her knees, her index finger and thumb curled together in a circle; a third stared straight ahead at the altar in the back of the room. At the end of the two sofas, facing the saints, with his eyes partly closed and his lips slightly open, sat Nick, mumbling to the dark.

He opened his eyes and greeted me with a smile. "We just finished the Rosary." A pair of blue, plastic beads hung in his free hand. "I can't believe you came."

"I'm good to my word," I said.

"Natasha." She put her hand forward and introduced herself.

Nick greeted her and made introductions to the other members of the group. They were dressed in sweaters of various muted colors, adorned with expensive, patterned scarves. I quickly sized them up as part of the spiritual jet set, wealthy matrons of the island. I made social pleasantries; others entered the room—a businessman, an elderly woman on crutches and her son or grandson, twos and threes at a time. Nick continued making introductions.

"Catherine," he said, introducing a lanky woman with tangled, brown hair and a worn face, accentuated by bright, pink lipstick. I gathered from the Bible she held in her hand and Nick's tone of voice that she was assisting. She embraced me with a quick hug and then shook Natasha's hand.

"You're a minister?" she asked.

"I'm studying with Nick at the interfaith seminary. By day I'm a lawyer."

By this time the room had filled to about thirty people, and antique leather chairs had been hauled in from another room. Rosaries, stuffed into pockets, were being fingered again; and participants were watching Nick. He had his own high-backed chair, sitting like a king at the head of the rectangular arrangement, eyes opened and now closed. Catherine sat at his left, fiddling with a recording device. Nick spoke: "This reading is taken from the Book of Corinthians, chapter 13, on the excellence of the gift of love." Nick had a large Bible spread open on his lap, with a worn leather cover, but he knew the words by heart and spoke with authority.

"Now I will show you the way that surpasses all others.'" Nick's voice was rich and alive, coming from deep within him, as if grappling with these words for the first time. "'If I speak with human tongues, and angelic as well, but do not have love, I am like a noisy gong, a clanging cymbal. If I have the gift of prophecy and with full knowledge comprehend all mysteries, if I have faith great enough to move mountains, but have not love, I am nothing. If I give everything I have to feed the poor and hand over my body to be burned but have not love, I gain nothing.'"

I had heard this passage from Paul before, but now certain phrases—*angelic tongues*; *gift of prophecy*—leaped out. They had leapt from the dead hand of writers gone to the live voice of Nick, sounding as if the words were channeled from another source. "'Love is patient, love is kind. Love is not jealous. Love does not put on airs; it is not snobbish... Love never fails. Prophecies will cease, tongues will be silent, knowledge will pass away. Our knowledge is imperfect and our prophesizing is imperfect. When the perfect comes, the imperfect will pass away.'"

Nick paused, allowing what he had read to sink in, and continued: "'When a child, I used to talk like a child, think like a child, reason like a child. When I became a man, I put away childish ways. Now we see indistinctly as in a mirror; then we shall see face to face. My knowledge is imperfect now; then I shall know even as I am known. There are, in the end, three things that last: faith, hope, and love, and the greatest of these is love.'" Nick closed the book and faced the group.

"Love does not puff itself up to make itself something. Faith, hope and love, and the greatest is love." His voice rose, but once again, although skeptical, I did not have the sense of being preached at or instructed, but of being brought gently into a greater awareness of something I always had known. "God is that consuming fire of divine love. And each person in this room is a mirror of that furnace of divine love. As you proceed forth on that spiritual journey, as you make the focus of your light, your eternal truth, your higher self, God, you will become more humble, more understanding. You will go more and more within the contemplative heart, your church, temple and mosque right within you. And you will mirror that light on a hill for all the people to see that great light that illuminates from your being."

There was another pause, in which Nick tightened his eyes and seemed to be drawn even more deeply into trance. "We practice the presence of that divine spark in every moment of our lives." He paused, leaned forward further until his forehead almost touched his knees, and then sat back upright. "Consider a smile to someone who's angry; a word of encouragement to someone who is sad; opening a door for someone with a smile. When we're ready to run into a store and we run to get in front of someone, to stop, and reflect. When we're in a vehicle and we're ready to become angry, to stop, and reflect." He took a deep breath and cocked his ears, as if listening for the thread. Again, it was all familiar, but the unusual environment, combined with Nick's sincerity and emphasis on *listening* for the words to come, added a sense that the source was deeper than his personality.

"The way to God is in simplicity." The silences were becoming longer now, the speech slower. I listened to Nick's talk with interest, though skeptical of any religious orthodoxy, any claim to a monopoly on truth. I forced my gaze back to the flickering candlelight, to the stillness of the room.

Nick continued. "And the light becomes greater ... and greater ... and greater. Your life becomes molded into that image of Love: a diamond in the rough. And when the chipping takes place, it is painful. But God can show pain to His child whom he loves. If you didn't have crisis and pain in your life, you wouldn't grow. They are opportunities for us to grow closer and closer in that light." Nick drew himself further forward toward his knees, popped back up again, and said: "Casting away all fear in an attitude of complete surrender and love."

Catherine turned on the music, an inspirational churchy song. The chorus sang: "Be not afraid, I go before you always. Come—follow me. And I will lead you there." The feeling in the room was shifting; a devotional sense crept over me, one I had not felt since putting on *tephillin*, the phylacteries, while praying as a child. I was surprised that this feeling of reverence from a private ritual, steeped in Judaism, during childhood, welled up in the midst of Nick's Christian motif.

Nick's voice now overlaid the music. "Praise, honor and glory to you, Lord God of the Universe, praise, honor and glory to you, Lord God of the Universe...."

The participants joined in. I found the words 'be not afraid' comforting, as the feeling of a shift—of 'something' inarticulable in the room—grew more and more luminous. Nick's voice overlaid the music: "'If wicked men insult and hate you all because of me, Blessed, blessed are you. Be not afraid, I go before you always. Come—follow me. And I will be lead you there.'"

The music stopped. Stillness resonated in the vastness of the mansion. I could hear my own breathing and the blood pounding between my ears. Nick cleared his throat and coughed. "We ask that the astral tunnel be opened, that Michael the Archangel, that Raphael, Gabriel and the archangels would guard the exit of this tunnel as these entities begin to move through this tunnel of light. We only ask that the highest vibrations be allowed to come through the tunnel of light." He chanted: "Spirit protectors, spirit guides, come. Come, Spirit." He began repeating: " March 16." Nick then said something indistinct, in an incomprehensible language. "March 16. It is the birth date of the entity that is through the tunnel. Further."

His face changed again: the features softened, the forehead flattened, the chin tucked toward the sternum; his hands rested limply on his lap. He repeated his incomprehensible language, rolling his tongue around in his mouth. He spoke details that seemingly came from the "entity." He seemed to be alternating between allowing the 'entity' to speak through him, speaking to the entity, and speaking to the assemblage. I had the impression that he

A Friend of All Faiths

was trying to read a blurred image, or perhaps to pick out a distinct sound through a band of noise. For a while, his voice went on in a rhythm as if somewhere a needle were stuck in a groove. "Deeper, spirit." He turned to the congregation. "Who recognizes March? What is it, Spirit? Come through my body." He snapped open his eyes and looked at a man seated at the far end of a sofa. "Ted, it is around you, having to do with the initial L."

I felt slight envy that the "entity" had not come to address me. Simultaneously, I asked myself: is the information valid? What does Nick see? What can he see that others cannot? Are Ted and Nick in collusion—in a hoax or swindle? Ted had been introduced to me as an insurance salesman.

"Lenny is my father," Ted answered. "He's dead."

Flickering hope rose: perhaps spirits existed; the possibility of life after death negated the proposition that life was a pointless squirrel's cage; or currently felt so.

"Thank you Spirit," said Nick. "What about Ted?" His voice rose; he seemed to be angry at the "spirit" for mischievously holding back information. He then let the "spirit" speak through him. "Pray for the father about March." Nick paused. "What do you want here?" he asked the "spirit." I suspended disbelief to watch this dialogue between Nick and the "spirit"—or perhaps between two sides of Nick's personality. "D is in trouble," the "spirit" answered through Nick. "What about it?" Nick asked. The "spirit," through Nick's body, addressed Ted: "Who is D?"

"Danielle is my daughter," answered Ted. "March 16 was a birthday."

Nick began speaking in tongues. "Combre madire sombre madire sombre canteshando madiya .... What is it, spirit? Why are you here for this? What is your message?" He waited for more information, and then said: "These family spirits come: pray for her. She will have surgery successful around March, not to worry."

Nick then presented various messages for members of the group.

"Beware—name—Joan—color red. Watch out."

"Have I met this Joan?" asked the recipient.

"A carpet is set for you. Once you walk it, make sure you pass rather than stop."

Nick emerged with another series of names. He negotiated the information from various spirits, demanding that this one come forward with what was important, asking that one to step aside. To one he said: "Are you playing with us, spirit? What is this number three? Mischievous spirit." After a while, the spirit seemed to comply. Nick said to one participant: "You will sell your place of residence, he says."

The woman began crying. "It will be within thirty days," Nick added. "He will help with it. One, four, five. What does that mean?"

"The price!"

Nick suddenly said in a casual voice. "There's a woman here with blondish-brown hair that committed suicide that's by the window."

Natasha leaned toward me and shook my arm as if to signal that we should leave. I put my other arm around her reassuringly.

"That was my sister," someone whispered.

"Thank you. She's standing over there by the window. Did she cut her wrist?"

"Yes."

"Thank you. Come into the circle, spirit. Don't be afraid. He pointed to her. Move over. Come in, don't be afraid." Nick's voice was gently coaxing. "Move next to Serina there. You can comfort her now." Serina was sitting upright on an armchair. She made the sign of the cross. "You have to pray for this girl," Nick told her. "She committed suicide." He spoke in tongues. "Meilamatai madia meilamadia sombre madia. Benny. Blood. Problem."

"My husband," someone whispered. "He has anemia."

Nick went deeper, speaking in tongues yet again. "Shambre elah makayia madia measandre. Pappa. Pop. Pop. Pop. Pop. Pop. Pop." Nick moved on, presented letters, initials and names. "Screaming." Nick's voice shifted again. "I am part of you and a part of this group. It was quick, quick, quick. "

"Nick?" Catherine asked. "Can you tell us if the war will end soon?"

"The number six," Nick said. "Six. Six. Six." Nick's voice shifted and he seemed to be transcribing poetry from the air. "More and more that which comes; bartered none, allies none. Coming west, driving force, many killed, thousands lost."

The apocalyptic turn struck a chord. I had completed my senior thesis, under a professor who later became a national security adviser, on MAD ("mutual assured destruction") and whether contemporary theories of nuclear deterrence would truly protect the human race against a possible Armageddon.

"Will Israel be safe?" Catherine asked.

Nick answered, again in rhyme: "Bomb to England burst and fall. Israel's future jeopardy sow. Nightmare furnished not to come. Playing skeletons one by one. Burning flame flesh to rot. Seeing sky amber lot."

"Will we be safe?" someone asked.

Nick answered, in the same voice as before, sounding like a Greek chorus I had heard in a recent rendition of the *Oresteia*. "That which is six-six-six becomes more and more prominent in the forehead of the madman. That which has attracted to him that vibration of Stalin and Hitler are becoming more and more prominent in the possession of this consciousness. The dark forces dwell within the consciousness of this person. His armies will attack more and more of the peoples around. There will be much bloodshed in the next week. Thousands will be killed, from the west end. From the west end." He paused: "Jeopardy, Israel, playing short; missiles fired, launching sought. Cannot see, crystal clear; rainbow heaven, nighttime clear."

"Are the prayers that are being said helping the situation?" someone asked.

"More good is needed: less hate sown. But the country of red, blue and white has taken a stand against the blue and white; it is the beginning of new departures from old treaties."

I was both relieved to hear the unambiguous denial of the possibility of nuclear Armageddon, and intrigued to hear geopolitics described from the checkerboard perspective of the "spirit" plane. I relaxed back into the sofa; and was jolted awake.

"*There will be a change for you, Mike, in the next six months at work. There will be a change in the next six months.*" I sat upright and felt my hearing open wide, a metallic taste on my tongue. "*There will be a change at work for good, in the next six months.*"

Nick—or rather, the "entity"—paused, then added: "*Hillel will help you.*"

Suddenly I was conscious of every breath. I shifted from observer to participant. It was not only the use of my name that startled me; the tone of voice and the precise words also seemed targeted to some part of me that Nick could not have known. Hillel was an ancient Jewish sage who lived several centuries before Jesus, who was asked by a non-Jew to summarize the Torah while standing on one foot, and replied: "Love thy neighbor as thyself. This is the whole Torah. Go and learn the rest." But even more directly, I had spent childhood attending Hillel Day School of Metropolitan Detroit.

I asked Nick: "Who is speaking?"

"Hil*lel.*" He used the Hebrew pronunciation, accenting the second syllable. "Hillel will help you," Nick added, and continued as if the "entity" had read the camera of my mind. "Hillel is not who you think it is. It is an astral being, of the Ashtar Command, under Tuella." Nick's voice was even but firm. "He will help you with the vibrations that have been frequenting you in the last year. They come from space energies. Mocha is One under Tuella of the Ashtar Command, of the galaxies beyond this one."

Questions crowded my ability to receive information spontaneously. Who is Mocha? What galaxies? Was this message really for me? From whom did it come? What was its underlying logic? What did aliens have to do with spirits? Why this reading for me, and impressions of dead relatives for others? Nick was continuing in a faraway voice. "*The vividness of those impressions are embossed in the consciousness of old. For Starseed has been born within you at age seven. The mask of many will begin to take form in the consciousness you develop.*"

A Friend of All Faiths

Nick spoke in tongues. "The woman: a consciousness of limitations, which is limiting; open, chakras V, divorcing symptoms, less to be." Natasha sat erect; she had finished a long and difficult relationship with a man named Vadislav. Nick went on. "Walking, walking, erect and straight; mind in focus, please—don't be late." Nick was silent again; his bizarre poetry struck a gentle, loving poke at Natasha—she was invariably on time. She released my hand.

Nick moved on to the next 'frame.' He turned to a bottle-blonde whose husband was a real estate magnate. "I can feel your guide, he's been watching you and smiling in happiness. He smiles down on you. Don't limit what you think. " Nick then identified other "entities" present in the room and invited participants to pray for them. After a while, Nick sank, as if exhausted, into a meditation. After a prolonged silence, he emerged. "Who here needs healing?" Catherine put a chair in front of Nick and various participants seated themselves as Nick sent them "healing light" and said: "Focus on my third eye. I'm cutting your pain in half. Right through your head." He finished working with her, moved on to another, and said to someone else in the room. "You have some legal things going on?"

"Yes."

"They are going to be successful. A brown suit next to you, he's an attorney. Call on him and he will assist you." Nick completed his healing and invited the group to recite the 'Our Father' with him.

Nick opened his eyes. "Are there quick questions?"

I asked: "How should I get in touch with Hillel?"

"Call upon him. Feel his frequencies begin to move through your consciousness. Dispel all doubts from around you."

Nick looked off into the distance. "Idolatry runs wild throughout the land; people running to and fro, as in Babylon. Ted, an entity stands behind you by the name of Archangel Mik-el, M-I-K-E-L. He is from a different star system. He wishes to come and be part of your band. Accept him and he will help you."

"How can I do this?"

"Just by saying, 'I welcome your vibration of light, and love, and peace.' I want everyone now to close their eyes and focus in on the space people, the Ashtar Command, and raise your level of consciousness into the next ring of the ladder of consciousness. Bring their vibration into your consciousness." Nick rang a set of silver Tibetan bells, inscribed with prayers. A clear, ringing sound pierced and vibrated throughout the room. He rang the bells once again, commanding the 'energies:' "Go back to the astral world, all of the spirits here. All of you." The bells vibrated a long, resonant, high-pitched ring and died softly away. Nick rose. The meeting was over; light from the chandelier softly arose in the room. "Let's keep our eyes focused in a meditative state," Nick said, and turned on a recording. "Just listen to the words of the song." It was a gentle and serene choral arrangement: "I will wait the silent night, I will make their darkness bright. Who will bear my light through this, who shall I send? Here I am, Lord. I have heard you calling in the night. I will go, Lord, if you lead me. I will go, Lord, even if I die."

"Who shall I send?" Nick said, over the music, as the verse repeated. The words resonated inside me. "Who shall I send?" God was asking for volunteers. I recalled God calling for Adam in the Garden of Eden—*hineni*, Adam had replied guiltily; "I am here." And later, when God called to Moses from the burning bush, Moses likewise answered: *hineni*. "Who shall I send?" Nick repeated, over the music. When the song ended, and people began gathering their belongingness, Nick, fully out of trance, tried to clarify details. He said of the spirits: "The bells dispel them, but the stronger ones will stay in this room until tomorrow."

"What is Ashtar?" someone asked.

"It is an outpost of beings from different galaxies," Nick answered.

"Is Hillel connected with the ancient sage?" someone else asked my question.

"Yes."

"Is there any reason we're hearing from them now?" a third person queried.

"Because of the danger of the planet exploding," Nick replied. "If we don't pray, instead of running after idolatry, we will perish. There's no question about it. And this is the beginning of end-times. If people do not come back to praying and to their spirituality, we will self-destruct. Already in the war, thousands will be killed."

"Are they ours?" someone asked.

Nick momentarily closed his eyes. "I see thousands being killed. Blood is the same." He prayed: "We ask you, Lord of the Universe, to protect these persons. "

I had prayed in synagogues, and we had chanted Native American melodies in the Seminary, but this was something different: in Nick's cosmology, prayer was effective—moved levers in the universe.

"How is mother earth reacting to this?" someone asked.

Nick replied: "In anger."

"How can we help?"

"Help by sending light to the earth now through your consciousness."

Nick turned to answer some other questions, and then bowed as the young girl I had earlier seen came in and indicated that it was time for all to depart.

Catherine and Nick drove us to the train station. As I asked Nick questions, Catherine intercepted with elaborations. Natasha said nothing. We waited for the train with the engine on, Nick in the front passenger's seat—watching us through the side-mirror; Natasha with her hands on her lap, and I in the back, puzzling over Hillel, Mocha and Ashtar. Finally, as the train pulled up, Nick turned around and said to me: "You still don't believe this is real, do you?"

It was difficult to fully embrace what seemed to have happened, with the oscillation from suicidal relatives to war predictions to messages about lawyers and housing sales. But something about Nick's invocation of Hillel grabbed me. As if sensing the weighing of information in my spirit, Nick reached over, put his hand on my shoulder, and gave me a knowing look.

THE ASHTAR COMMAND

The command structure I had to face on a daily basis at the corporate law firm was far from the intergalactic communications network that Nick had designated as essential to my future, the one implanted as "Starseed." While I had enjoyed varied educational opportunities, my assumption that legal regulators and employers might similarly appreciate this variegated background was mistaken. The more eclectic I appeared, the less I seemed to fit in. Such misunderstanding had sprouted in my profession even before joining a law firm. I had studied for the New York Bar exam during my judicial clerkship by memorizing flash cards on the subway after work, and passed the first time. Yet, the interviewer for the New York Bar's Committee on Character and Fitness seemed unusually preoccupied with concern about "dual loyalties"—law and writing—affecting my commitment to clients. I found the interviewer's relentless focus absurd: creative writing only enhanced my ability to meet the ethical obligation of "zealous representation." In fact, I was just completing my soon-to-be-published *Creative Writing for Lawyers*. The interviewer's one-track prosecution mode soon became exhausting, though fortunately, my regular practice of transcendental meditation helped me to check residual anger at the stifling narrowness. By remaining gracious, I passed the brief interview—but realized in the process that my educational opportunities and interests marked me as different.

I had been lucky to find employment in one of the world's premier law firms. The firm had an offer for full-time employment after my stint as a summer associate the second year of law school, and unusually, waited another four years for me to actually join. The package was sweetened by two signing bonuses—one for the clerkship and another for the MBA; and, the clerkship and MBA qualified me as a third-year associate with a commensurate salary.

A Friend of All Faiths

The problem was that I did not have the experience of a third-year associate, since corporate law was learned by doing, not by reading or through other experiences. I was behind the proverbial eight-ball, pulling all-nighters and finding that superiors expected me to know things I could only by having done them before–yet, no explanations were forthcoming as they were busy pulling all-nighters, too, or perhaps jet-setting off to their country retreats. Inevitably, I was handed over to a senior partner that most other associates had managed to avoid.

Jerome B. Hansen, III was recruited after a distinguished career in public service. Despite his international stature, though, his reputation at the firm was lackluster. He smoked a pipe from behind his closed door in the corner office, and, at the age of seventy, had a number of personality traits the younger partners found irritating: he spoke in a low-level mumble that was increasingly incomprehensible, gave cryptic lectures about "moral codes" at partnership meetings, wore down junior attorneys and office staff with incessant demands to bring his coffee just-right. Worse, he had not attracted the clientele that the partners–on guaranteeing him a pricey, annual partnership draw–expected his reputation to garner for the firm; he was no rain-maker, but merely a solid attorney who could methodically plod through the layers of issues in a complex corporate transaction. Apparently his professional style had petrified some five decades earlier, and he was a rather stultifying reminder of a world out of which the firm had grown, that now was passed–a pre-electronic universe of handshakes and agreements by gentle men, in hats and topcoats, in which international transactions depended on the goodly assurances of elite-bred peers, far from the madding Internet crowd.

Either the partners assumed that Hansen and I would forge a natural alliance–or they were punishing me for the extravagant bonuses, the way that, by virtue of my unusual educational path, I had leapfrogged in status and salary above other associates. In any event, my fate at the firm was sealed. Mr. Hansen now enveloped me in the smoke of his cherry tobacco, which wafted incessantly from the pipe he pressed to his lips, in between the murmured syllables. We were on a four-hour conference call to Tokyo, and my bladder had been full for at least two of the past hours.

Despite the corner office, with two large windows overlooking the New York harbor, the office was dark–not on the city's sunny side, and presently illumined only by the glow of a green, banker's light on Mr. Hansen's desk. The two dark-paneled walls, made heavier by the press of various diplomas and black-and-white photographs (of Mr. Hansen with the presidents, kings, prime ministers, and ambassadors, of various countries), only added to the gloom, as did the shut door, and the permeation of cherry tobacco into my nostrils, flesh, clothes, essence, bones. Or rather, I was enveloped in essence of Hansen: the pipe dangled from his lips as he spoke his few, practiced lines of Japanese to the businesspeople on the other end of the line.

"*Domo arigato.*" Thank you very much; it is a pleasure to serve you. Hansen sprinkled in a few additional phrases, consulting his pocket dictionary, in response to a bit of flattery from the client. I made a quick mental calculation: at our combined billing rates of $800 an hour, this bit of social pleasantry was costing the client $13 a minute, or about $.22 per second, in addition to the over-inflated rates the firm charged for long-distance calls. If I were to throw Mr. Hansen's pipe out the window, for example, scientific truth dictated its rate of descent at three feet per second, per second; and by the time the pipe reached the ground, some eighty stories below, the client would have racked up an additional hundred dollars. Snow fell with more leisure than the client's bill rose.

"Young man: what do you think?" Mr. Hansen was asking me. "If we get the 5-D to the SEC by 4 pm today, and announce intention to consummate the merger within ten days thereafter, and factoring in the proxy fight by our opponents, and the draft amicus brief filed by that son-of-a-bitch in the Justice Department, what is the likelihood the deal will go through?"

I made a quick mental calculation, remembering the adage that "he who hesitates is lost," and knowing the Japanese fondness for American sports. "I think there's a fair shot we'll knock this one out of the park."

Appreciation flowed from the other end of the line. Mr. Hansen nodded. That was what he wanted me to say. The conversation was scripted; he did not really need another lawyer—for Mr. Hansen, the associates were decorative. Foreign clients appreciated his pipe-puff sagacity, his mumbled verbiage that implied intimacy with governmental authorities; and Mr. Hansen's connections always helped him pull off a deal. Perhaps that was why the partners carried so much resentment toward him, and why they had paired us up. I, too, had passed the parameters of conventional boundaries, with my three graduate degrees and four-year deferral of entry into "real life," and had stretched firm credentialing to its limits. I, too, had blustered in to a place of pretense, knowing less than I was supposed to know, artful mentally but unversed in the practicalities one learned on the job, and thus ill-equipped to answer the kind of judgment-call questions that colleagues tended to hurl at more youthful associates.

"Well yes, I'll make a few calls and in the meanwhile Michael, here, can put the finishing touches on the document." He blew a cloud of cherry smoke toward my face and smiled, confident that I could read his scrawls on the two-hundred-page agreement he had worked out with opposing counsel. Voices emerged in a unified babble from the speakerphone; arrangements were made to conduct further discussions following Mr. Hansen's inquiries with Justice. We ended the call and Mr. Hansen spoke into his pipe. "Very good, expert, yes, excellent. More coffee."

"Straight on." I rose from my chair, closed the door behind him, leaving him in his cloud of smoke and framed photographs with royalty, and proceeded to the coffee machine down the fluorescent-lit corridor.

Years later, I would have recurrent dreams about being back in my firm: the kind of anxiety dream chronicled in dream books, where you are in your pajamas, or you have a test but haven't done your homework. I suppose that under different circumstances I might have thrived at the firm—better mentors, greater interest in the assignments. At the time, though, I felt my soul calling me for other work. Yet I had majored in political science, not religion or philosophy; had gone to law school, not for a master's in social work. I was trained to be a lawyer, not a theologian or counselor. In my mind, I could not put the different pieces together. And the work was genuinely dry: like assembly a thousand-piece puzzle, putting deals together with faceless people in suits only to get a crystal memento and move on to the next sleepless venture. At least that was how it felt at the time.

I sat in a coffee shop with Tanya two months into our training at the Seminary. She rolled the corners of faux fur past her shoulders and stared at the greasy omelet on my plate. Chunks of guacamole, bacon, ham, sour cream, potatoes, and scallions protruded from its shiny surfaces. Tanya lifted a small glass of orange juice to her lips, first dabbing off a bit of red lipstick, as I slurped on a black coffee, steaming from the microwave. "You're not hungry?" I asked her.

"Cramps, I can't eat." She nursed the orange juice, swishing the flavor around in her mouth. "You enjoy." She turned her gaze back to the omelet. "But I do mind your spending all this time with Nick. It's bad for your health." She nodded at my meal. "Worse than the eating eggs."

"What's wrong with eggs? I've got low cholesterol. Too little fat."

"It's the life-force," she said. "You're consuming someone else's, stolen without consent." The waitress came by and refilled her orange juice and my coffee.

"You used to go to his prayer meetings," I pointed out.

"In the beginning he helped me understand things." Tanya's mane of yellow hair curled down to her shoulders; her voice had a girlish quality, mildly accented with her native Russian. We sat together during sessions and often ate lunch with Jane, who "vibrated on a

A Friend of All Faiths

similar plane." Tanya's argument was persuasive to my legal mind, gleaning what it could of this abstruse world: by allowing "lower-level entities" to enter his prayer meetings—such as suicides and relatives or friends who had not been psychologically healthy in this life—Nick was jeopardizing the spiritual health his followers.

"Who wants to hear from Aunt Gwendolyn," Tanya emphasized, playing with a stirring stick in her second glass of orange juice. "Just because she's in Spirit doesn't make her special. If Gwen never got her act together in her lifetime, and still carried unresolved karma into the spirit realm, who needs her advice?"

"Those present seemed to derive comfort," I observed.

"But wouldn't it be better to use Nick's abilities to channel spirit guides at higher levels—like the angels?" Tanya drove the point home by fixating on a point above my head. The waitress came by with the check. Tanya had a pedicure appointment, and I had to finish inputting Mr. Hansen's changes for the Japanese deal, since he hand-wrote his margin notes and never touched a computer. Tanya tapped her pink, manicured nails on the check.

"No," I said. "My treat. All you had orange juice."

"With a refill." She pulled on the check. "In God's eyes, we're all equal." She retrieved a fistful of cash and placed it on the table. "You need redemption."

"Your paying the bill redeems me?"

She checked my nails for evidence of manicure. "Money karma."

The waitress, as if drawn by the appearance of bills, came and swept the cash off the table, swooping her free hand to refill my coffee a third time. Tanya drew her faux fur around her shoulders and neck. I asked: "What is the Ashtar Command?"

"I'm going to be late," she said, rising. "Red toe polish grounds me."

"Who or what is Tuella? What is Ashtar?" I had to know, and there was no other source of information. The waitress removed our plates.

Tanya said: "Tuella is a person who channels the Ashtar Command, space entities; aliens who live in our atmosphere. They are from other planetary systems, our space brothers and sisters. Spirit guides. Have you seen, *Always*? Well, it's in books and movies these days." She hesitated. "This may sound weird."

"Go on," I encouraged her, wondering how the puzzle would fit together.

"We are being bombarded with energy on a planetary scale. The Ashtar Command is a civilization that sits over the planet on a Mothership. The ship is 280 miles long. It comes from the Pleiades System."

I pulled out my pocket dictionary and looked up the reference. The Pleiades were the seven daughters of the Greek mythological hero, Atlas. Legend had it that they were metamorphosed as stars. Pleiades was also "an open star cluster in the constellation Taurus, consisting of several hundred stars, of which six are visible to the naked eye." I asked Tanya why these folks from the Pleiades System were watching Earth, and what that had to do with Nick's reading for me.

Tanya opened the top of her coat and reached for a glass of water on the adjacent table. "The Pleiadians gave us 2000 years from the time of Christ to make it. There's a separation now on the planet between those with and without God-consciousness; those upgrading their consciousness versus those who sit in negativity. We are beginning to affect the other planets. A nuclear world war will send radiation throughout the universe. Our nuclear capabilities threaten not only our world, but all the worlds. They'll stop us if necessary."

"What is Starseed?"

She pulled the gloves off her hands. "I knew you were Starseed, I knew it all along. Starseed refers to children born here who were seeded generations ago by space beings. They may have mated with earth beings." I listened, skeptically, as she continued. "Your soul has known other systems in the universe. Oh, there are workshops on this. I don't have to tell you everything."

"Why is this coming up for me now? Why didn't I hear of this earlier?"

"You were pre-occupied."

"That sounds ominous the way you say it."

"Let's just say that they have encoded in your memory the information, and are exploding the memories to make you remember. Certain things...." Her voice trailed off, and I looked around to see whether anyone else in the coffee shop was listening to this bizarre conversation. A man in the adjacent booth read his newspaper; the waitresses were busy at the cash register, and a homeless man drank coffee at the counter. Tanya said: "Part of you is not of this solar system. "

So now I was an alien. This was getting more and more difficult to handle. Nick and Tanya were supposed to be fellow, rational travelers in the interfaith seminary, spiritually questing in a part-time, instructional program in an innocuous basement.

"Since the age of seven," Tanya continued, "the Starseed memory has been triggered. The people you meet, the places you go, the connections you make, nothing is accidental. You're receiving help from space brothers and sisters."

"What kind of help?" I asked incredulously.

"Your DNA is changing. You are becoming a 'light being.' You are of the light. They are changing your mind, body, spirit, and emotions." She paused, noticing that I was rubbing my stomach. "Is this a little too much for one sitting?"

"I just remembered I have a huge document to edit and proofread."

"There's a whole group of us," she said. "Star people. There are star children, which you are, and star helpers, which I am. We are changing the vibrational quality of the planet. There are going to be earth changes, shifts in weather, landslides, earthquakes, storms, volcano eruptions, changes in land mass. I'd love for you to come out here some time and meet with us." I hesitated, part of me inquisitive, the other part wondering whether this would be one of those delusional groups masking self-destruction in some interplanetary ideology.

Tanya offered: "Let me help you. I'd do anything for an old friend, a very old friend. You know that lifetimes ago, we were married."

At eighty, Julian, a "Star Child," looked sixty with wizened but twinkling eyes. He wore a loose-fitting, yellow tee shirt and Bermuda shorts. Welcoming us at the door, he placed a cup of hot tea in my hand and Tanya's, and introduced us to his hundred-and-two-year-old mother. I shook her frail hand, careful of the labyrinthine, blue veins. "So you want to know about the Ashtar Command." Julian handed me a spiral-bound book with a cobalt blue cover that had "ASHTAR" in enormous, white letters, and an outline of a space ship. "How's the tea? I grew the spearmint in the back yard, gathering planetary and space energies."

I had a reprieve from work for the weekend, since Mr. Hansen's negotiations had stalled, and the deal was in the *bardo* state—the limbo between consummation and negation. Julian told us that signals were beamed to contactees in regular order, and could be interpreted as instructions for survival in the coming days, provided one knew the code. The Ashtar Command believed that the Apocalypse was imminent. A select few—whose consciousness and "vibrational frequency" were sufficiently high would be lifted off the planet by a giant spaceship run by the Ashtar Command. Tuella, a space sister, was the Supreme Commander of this enterprise, channeled by a woman who had produced the book. Star children and helpers who had awakened to their heritage of divine love would be saved.

The paradigm struck me as both hopeful and naive. On one level, the notion that some would be saved and others lost struck me as yet another version of discrimination practiced by various world religions. However one defined the "nonbeliever" or "infidel," selection criteria were key. Yet, though on the surface, the Ashtar message seemed to be that of old-fashioned religion, dressed in science fiction and fantasy, part of Tuella's message resonated. The material reminded me of the Kabalistic teaching known as 'raising the sparks:' redeeming the universe from the moment when the 'vessels of light' were accidentally shattered. We had to help God complete the creation. I mentioned this similarity to Julian. His mother nodded. "This stuff seems wacky to me," she said, "but what is a mother to do?"

THIRD EYE OPENING

Someone asked whether his teachings were "Jewish." Stroking his white goatee, the rabbi replied that Gandhi once had been asked whether he was a Hindu or a Muslim, and had replied that was a both, and a Jew, a Christian, a Buddhist... universal. The Seminary's underlying principles affirmed the values of many faiths, emphasizing the "One God of all humanity." The institution finessed one major dividing line between two world religions by viewing the "Messiah" as a "symbol" of unity consciousness, and at the same time, asserting that "the rainbow's beauty consists of its many hues," and that "unity does not mean homogeneous uniformity." The principles concluded: "We support and encourage whatever contributes positively to the unique, creative growth of every person."

The program provided a contrast to the working days around a mahogany table, drafting merger agreements, conforming changes on speakerphones, managing paralegal armies, and thousands of other mundane details. At the seminary there was singing, chanting, praying, hugging, and practical tasks-preparing a sermon, an interfaith wedding ceremony, a funeral, a baptism. I became familiar with new beings from the past: such as St. Francis, with whom I instantly felt a sweet and mysterious connection. I learned about Islam, Buddhism, Taoism, Sikhism, Confucianism, Jainism, Shinto, Zoroastrianism, shamanism, and other paths. Some of the seminarians insisted that collectively we were earthly representatives for the "White Brotherhood," or simply, "the Hierarchy," a group of spiritual beings entrusted with making sure the earthlings did not blow up the planet and send nuclear dust intergalactic, that human evolution followed the divine blueprint. I received a car decal that said: CLERGY. I learned to dwell in my heart, enjoying the trance-states induced by drumming, or chanting, or repeating sacred syllables.

Again Tanya spoke of my invisible connection to the space beings.

We had lunch at a Chinese restaurant that had the Musak turned up too high. It was my first experience with brown rice and vegetables–not the usual heavy sauce; no oil, no grease, no MSG headache. Tanya wanted me to lessen the load on my digestive system so that the Ashtar Command's messages would resonate more clearly.

"I had a spaceship come to my house," she said, as if describing a visit by a door-to-door salesman. She scissored a clump of brown rice with her chopsticks. "One time I thought I had breast cancer. It could have been more severe. But they're helping clean out my *chakras*." She poured me some tea. "Clean. You know, the way we clean out our house? Our bodies are temples. This has been said many times. They need to be cleaned before we can be filled with the light."

Tanya and I each had been involved in "the Work" developed by of G. I. Gurdjieff, and based on a series of exercises aimed at an enhanced awareness that he called, 'self-observation' and 'self-remembering.' Gurdjieff aimed to penetrate 'false personality' and help us connect with 'essence.' According to Gurdjieff, if only we could see ourselves as we truly are–and this involves the ability to observe one's self, from a neutral, objective position, in every moment of every action–we would begin to separate ourselves from our mask. All the 'buffers' that insulate us from the 'real I' or Self would drop away, and we would truly 'know ourselves.'

After immigrating to the United States, Tanya had spent a year with one of Gurdjieff's pupils, going been through many demanding exercises similar to the ones I had encountered in the version of Gurdjieff Work I had studied. I found the "Work" authentic in some ways, but disconnected from love. I asked Tanya how she had developed this interest in spaceships and aliens–fantasy and the unreal.

"This is real," she insisted. "Even my brother, who doesn't believe any of this stuff, found himself believing. They took over our house for a week–not the space beings, but the negative spirits that came after then. Nick had warned me that a woman would be coming who was connected to witchcraft and the occult. I screened everyone for this. One woman came in the door and I had an immediate intuition, but I accepted her as a client. As soon as I put my hand on her back I felt a wrist reach up and choke me. After the session, I grew nauseous. Nick went into trance and saw in her a doctor who was into the black arts. I finally called and asked her whether anyone she knew anyone who was in the occult. She didn't. A month later she said she told me she found out her ex-boyfriend, a doctor, had been in Santeria. The spirits were drawn to that vibrational residue."

"What did 'they' do to you?" I asked, disbelieving her extraordinary encounters.

"The usual. Break glasses, throw plates. My brother couldn't deny what was happening. Nick had to come and do an exorcism on the house."

I shifted tacks. "Why exactly did you quit your Gurdjieff group?"

"I grew tired of sitting around discussing negative emotions," she replied.

'Negative emotions' referred to emotions such as greed, jealousy, anger, resentment, dislike. According to Gurdjieff, the predominance of negative emotions in our psyche prevented us from accessing what he called the 'higher emotional center' where true feelings resided. To control our negative emotions, we first had to observe them, and how much they controlled us. One way to do this was to stop expressing negative emotions—not to stop feeling them, but simply to stop verbalizing our anger, jealousy, resentment and so on. Indeed, Gurdjieff's position was: 'if you think you have free will, just try not to express your negative emotions for a week.' As Tanya explained it, she was alienated not so much by her group's focus on negative emotions, as by the group's rigidity and narrowness.

"I couldn't talk about Christ in that group," she explained. "There was so much negativity. Even though they observed their negative emotions, they were negative about the prospect of ever getting anywhere in the Work."

I remarked that I, too, had been struck by the sense of despair in my Gurdjieff group—the hopelessness, the despondency about our 'slavery' and our 'mechanicalness' and the impossibility of ever being truly 'free.'

Tanya agreed: "A lot of these people were surrounded by negative entities—but I couldn't talk to them about the astral plane. You remember how Gurdjieff talked about the 'Law of Opposites?' Everything in time turns into its opposite. After my teacher died, her students became stuck in their own insular view of the universe. They were in search of freedom and created a prison. Still, my teacher appears to me in spirit. I receive so much love from her."

For a moment I wondered whether it would be possible to summon Gurdjieff's spirit, and ask him the many questions I had about his teachings—circumventing the many unsatisfying answers I had received from his working groups. But then I turned the conversation back to the entities. "You said you had Nick exorcise your house. Yet you disagree with his prayer meetings."

"I've known many psychics and mediums. They're not neutral. Who they are and how they live affects the transmission."

By this time, we were on the fortune cookies, practicing an ancient divination technique in the guise of dessert. Tanya's palm hovered over the cookies before selecting the one on her left. She opened it and read: "The star of riches is shining upon you." She seemed happy with that. I opened mine. It was empty.

"I guess my future can't be revealed in the present," I said.

"Confirmation," Tanya exclaimed. "I knew you were Starseed."

I began meditating daily, using a technique Nick had taught me: mentally chanting *om* up each *chakra* or energy center from the base of the spine to the top of the head. I continued to visit Nick's weekly prayer meetings—finding myself more intrigued, and increasingly alienated from my job and my girlfriend.

Once I received another personal message from my 'guides:' *Michael, you are racing toward the infinite.*

"Is that good?" I asked.

"Yes," the answer shot back. It resonated with I suspected: that I was making progress in meditation. Another time Nick reached into his pocket and pulled out a white speck wrapped in red velvet, stored in a glass case framed in gold. "It's from a bone of St. Augustine," Nick explained. "He will help you with your sexuality."

I was unsure what he meant. Nick claimed to be celibate, and indicated some disapproval about my relations with Natasha. After the prayer meeting, I kept the relic in my pocket for a few days. Once I pulled it out on the subway and stared at it–after a while, my sneakers seemed to dissolve. I had the impression that they were not really solid, but a bunch of vibrating molecules, and that my mind had been tricked into seeing them as sneakers. As the train pulled into my station, I immediately dismissed the experience and put the relic away, deciding that I was straining too hard for the phenomenal. When I mentioned the experience to Nick a week later, he just smiled and said "yes," as if acknowledging an unspoken agreement that some significant shift had occurred in my awareness.

Nick had promised to open my "third eye" between the brows. Between the all-night shifts at the firm (I caught a few hours' sleep in the "resting room," an eight-by-four cell with a lockable door and a couch, behind a set of Xerox copiers), I visited Nick. The mansion's matron had given him a large bedroom and adjoining study, free, in compensation for his spiritual services. Both overlooked the house's tennis courts, and the ravine below. Nick told me that the land "belonged to Native American medicine men." He swept the air with his hands, as if 'sensing' their spirits in the ground outside his window. "I can still feel them."

He had two wicker chairs, facing one another, and motioned for me to sit. His desk, a cherry wood, antique roll-up, held a framed photograph of Yogananda, and a well thumbed-through Bible. A large wooden cross hovered on the wall, a collection of relics, in gold casements with many points, like steeple tops. One, he told me, contained a piece of wood from the True Cross on which Christ had died. I was reminded that in Natasha's tradition, Saint Irene had been directed to a particular spot in Jerusalem where the three crosses had been buried; the saint tested the True Cross by applying its splinters to a sick man who then received a miraculous healing. Nick waved past the relics to a pictorial depiction of the 'space beings.' "They're here but I don't always rely on them," he said. He then told me about his family. "I had a lot of anger, but I'm dealing with it in therapy. The sins of fathers and mothers are indeed visited on their progeny. But in sharing with you, I release the ossification of old wounds. Before the spiritual can emerge, you must heal the psychological." That certainly seemed like a good working principle, I agreed. We proceeded to meditate. After a while, Nick asked how I felt. I told him I felt "great."

"That is the beginning of balance," he replied. "In the scriptures it says, 'be still, and know that I am here.'" We continued meditating. "I am activating your energy," Nick said quietly. "Do you feel anything in your spine?" I replied that I wasn't sure–a slight tingling, perhaps in the heart region.

"A family healing," Nick concluded. "Sorrow is being healed; abandonment, fear of abandonment, not only from this life. Maybe your karma from the blueprint of your astrological chart with which you came in–your strengths, your limitations–had it that you were to lose an arm, or meant to be in the Persian Gulf and get killed; but in the ultimate reality which is God, there is no blueprint, no karma, no debt. The more you sit in stillness, the more you release and burn. So instead of losing an arm you may have someone take a match head and hit you with it. Your body and mind grow sharp, so when you hear things, you discern, hear them."

"I'm getting a little spaced out," I said. "One side cool, the other warm."

"Balance," he reiterated. "By activating certain chakras, you are dislocating and materializing various entities, pulverizing certain soul memories and awakening others. Now for part two. Roll your tongue toward the back of the throat so the passage or tube of the spine is open, making an *ahhh* sound."

I tried it and gagged. "No, like this," Nick corrected, and I found the technique.

"Continue meditating. Now focus on my third eye," he said. "Continue focusing. Now open your eyes. Now close, and tell me the first thing you see."

To my surprise, I closed my eyes and saw a white pyramid pop into view.

"Good," Nick encouraged. "Try again."

"I see a man seated cross-legged in a white robe. Wow, it's very clear."

"Good," Nick restated. "Now come here." We walked over to his bookshelf, and he pulled out a particular book with a photograph of various Indian saints. I recognized one as the image in my meditation. "Confirmation," Nick said. "I was meditating on him, you were focusing on my third eye, and you saw what I saw."

As we continued in our weekly sessions, I saw many images in meditation. One was a woman with what looked like a baker's hat or crescent-shaped bonnet; this turned out to be a Catholic saint that Nick pointed out in a book. Nick asserted that these beings worked through him. "You're seeing what's behind this *shell*." He pointed to his chest. "I'm opening your third eye so you can see behind the shell."

He mentioned several beings that he saw behind my "shell." "And you know what your fear of the throat is?" he continued. "You were choked to death. But you are open, intensely psychic, though not yet aware of it; you can heal these memories. You'll discern not only what's coming through Spirit, but also through people. And Natasha is compatible with you in many material ways, but not in the spiritual. She's a good person, good heart, her moral standard is attractive, but she fears. You'll need to come to a resolution."

"She's in a fine place," I asserted.

"But you are moving beyond confinement, dogma, clouding. All your relationships are changing, professional and personal. I am only giving notice of the inevitable."

"I just got a shooting pain in my forehead," I said during one meditation.

"The tunnel is opening," Nick replied from his wicker chair. "It is expanding."

"I see a little white patch. Wait–I see three people."

"Look closely. They're my protectors. Now there's one to your right, by the closet door. When I say 'look,' I mean 'look psychically.'" I turned my inner awareness. "You can open your eyes," Nick said. "Part three: open-eyed awareness of entities. Right now I'm looking at you, but seeing other things in the periphery. There's a Spanish person, a Hindu, male and female incarnations. Stay in tune."

"I just saw a band of color around your shoulder. Now it's gone."

"Yes," Nick acknowledged. "They flash in and out. Look again."

Suddenly I saw a purple dot flash on the wall.

"Good," Nick said. He clanged the Tibetan bells. "That's enough for now."

After the session, Nick said he was looking forward to graduating from the Seminary. "Then I'll be able to lay hands and not get arrested." He did not clarify whether he had been in trouble with the law before. Shifting topics, I told Nick my eyes were dry from the firm's fluorescent lighting.

Nick asked: "Do you want and believe in healing?"

"That's another question," I said.

"You're sabotaging yourself with language," Nick replied. "You're in the process of developing. You need to replace words like 'scary,' 'weird,' 'not sure,' with constructive language. Change language to change consciousness."

In the next meeting, Nick complained that Catherine was "coming on" to him. In addition, his hosts were planning to sell the mansion. His entire income was from the prayer meeting and private channeling, and he had nowhere to go. The notion of Nick being homeless seemed incongruous with the powerful healer who had access to the entities and channeled wisdom from scripture so effortlessly.

Nick suddenly announced: "The Virgin Mary is standing behind you."

The comment startled me. "What does she look like?" I asked.

"She is wearing a white dress and a veil with a blue sash." I peered into the dark ceiling. The image was familiar and I felt some sudden affinity for this being, but to imagine her standing behind me was different than seeing a plaster statue in a church. My eyes strained in the darkness. Nick added: "Warn your brother about his drinking, she says." I was silent, and Nick continued: "The nearer to thee O Lord I become, the more one with your golden light... Separate yourself from everything that is not love of God and neighbor, and put it into the fire. Thus complete the commandments." Nick completed: "See to it you pray two by two. Working class man to be, meditation practices separate be."

As I continued to meditate, experiences increased in frequency and intensity; reporting this development changed my relationship with Natasha, who found my explorations in the spirit world unsavory. One evening we were together, reviewing a book about the Civil War, noticing a photograph of the hanging of conspirators in Lincoln's assassination. The scene looked surprisingly familiar. A vague memory floated of serving with Lincoln, perhaps as a surgeon in his army. "Something about this photograph," I said. "As if I remember...." Natasha returned the book to the shelf. I then flashed to the deathbed scene of one of Natasha's close relatives. "He was injured on his side like this," I said, pointing. "Am I right?"

Natasha turned away.

"She cares more about home and hearth than space beings," Bob said.

I had entered the therapy the way I was working my way toward God: skeptical, critical, dubious that I 'needed' either or that either could have meaning for me—in a nutshell, in denial. I pretended that therapy, like the Seminary, was an intellectual exercise to deepen self-knowledge. I did not acknowledge how it might open the psyche, heal old wounds, or connect me to patterns and feelings. I spent the first six months fidgeting, eyeing the clock, and pricing out fifteen-minute intervals.

But Bob was learned, humble and fun; no stranger to Gurdjieff, Krishnamurti, or channeling, he felt at home quoting Jung or Whitman. He practiced psychotherapy halftime and taught poetry the other; he saw in dreams, poetry, and the teachings of gurus the inner truth of metaphorical imagery—the language of heart and soul.

Bob pointed out my ambivalence about success as a corporate lawyer on one hand, and further spiritual opening on the other. "The spiritual center is scary: it opens up more than you can handle right now. It's a wise person who knows when to wait, knows their limits, marshaling the exploration. Your hope is that the center would provide the home you wanted; yet, it's so different that you're not able to integrate it." He also commented about images I was receiving in meditation and dreams: "All your devotion to responsibility, duty and loyalty is crapped on, whether it's at the law firm or in academe; the king doesn't know how much you've protected him, and you want to be given your due, your recognition. So you bolt out into space, Apollo 11; it's safe being identified with God, but you're also alone; there's no groundedness, connectedness, earthiness. Natasha at least is real for you, but it's to come down from heaven and be part of the earth." He summed up: "She doesn't care how many angels you see, so long as you can boil an egg."

Bob thought anger hid beneath the mask of corporate (and non-corporeal) superiority, and emptiness behind all the achievement. He spoke about "flaunting ... pouring shit on the authorities." "So you can pirouette," he said, "touching off people who admire but don't really know you. You like the tower but meet them in the pub, live in a split-level." He went on about relationships. "Women are comets who drift by your densely packed sun, passing through the atmosphere to move on. And the corporate environment exacerbates the distance. If you felt that loneliness, and felt this loneliness could be touched by somebody else, there would be sharing. To rediscover your emotional life, you've got to be simple, not grand—a first-grader doesn't do Boolean algebra." His no-nonsense, cut-to-the-chase approach was the perfect antidote to the extravagant meditation experiences I was enjoying with Nick—a kind of humbling, grounded packet of realizations about the emotional turmoil underlying the spiritual journey.

ROBOT DREAMS

Because of therapy, I started to keep a notepad by my bed at night and record the various images. Apocalyptic floods recurred. In one dream, a dog bit my hand; I whirled my hand and the dog disappeared, only to be replaced by another. I relied on Bob to help navigate these messages from the unconscious mind—I assumed they were more than random neuron firings and could provide symbolic information about the way my psyche mediated experiences of Wall Street and the Seminary.

"The flood is you letting out a flood of anger," Bob freely interpreted, about a half hour into our session. He ruffled his full head of curly hair with his left hand. "Pissing on the world. You try to deny it—the flood abates, but then in the next dream, the dog bites—that's you biting yourself; again the anger, there's no denying it now. You whirl it away, but another dog shows up—you can't get away."

"Bob, I don't *feel* particularly angry; I don't buy the interpretation."

He sat back in his red leather chair and crossed one leg over another like the poet-yogi he was. "You're denying a whole range of feelings. You act out the anger at the law firm, the superiority. The way you interact with Mr. Hansen, you're saying, 'I see who you are, fascist pigs.' They say: 'we'll show you.'" He turned to another set of images. "Let's look at the subway dreams. You're stuck, hermetically sealed inside yourself, never get to the world out there, trapped inside its portals."

"Bob, everyone in New York City must have dreams about subways."

"Yes," he insisted, "but you're stuck because you're afraid that if you move, be yourself, you'll unleash a lethal flood. All the emotions you can't let out."

"Well," I half-conceded, "hypothetically, how would I let it out?"

"Not at the office," he rejoined excitedly, perhaps at the semi-confession, "if you value your ass. Because they'll see it and get you—they're more powerful, paying the salary. You can play the game, but remember, it's their game, not yours."

We turned to my dynamics with Natasha. Bob, masterful in his world of metaphors, commented: "We can't deconstruct all the anger at once, but if you have a moment, say a night out with her, where you structure experience so you have a moment where you don't play in to the old dynamic, where you say, 'I'm going to experience her as a real person.' Tell yourself she's only human. Otherwise you make her into a goddess, she's got life and death power over you; then she disappoints you; you say 'fuck you' and kick her down the stairs."

Another week—again the red leather chair and the clock. Bob wanted to talk about fear. He asked me: "what do you fear in a woman?"

"This topic again," I complained.

"Well, your friend Nick is putting you in touch with the Mother of God, it's only appropriate we discuss your relationship to the feminine."

Something about the psychologist's logic was unbeatable, even to my trained legal mind. Still, resistance welled. "I can't connect to fear," I said.

"Do you fear your mother?"

"Does everybody? Does anybody?"

Bob sat back with neutral eyes—neutralizing my chess move. He reminded me of my Japanese clients, who used silence in a negotiation as a tactic; since Westerners typically are uncomfortable with silence—anything to fill the Void—they typically blurt out confessions and concessions. Recognizing the tactic, I bunted: "I'd like to express myself naturally rather than searching for the beautiful metaphor."

I figured Bob would call me on directing anger toward him, in implicitly critiquing his reliance on metaphor. Instead, he said: "Your awareness is cerebral." He paused. The pawn that moved forward on the chessboard of my mind was about to become a Queen, hitting the emotional cords I had suppressed.

"Yes," I said dryly, "I'd like to be myself, rather than manipulating the robot."

Over several weeks, I broadened beyond Mr. Hansen to additional partners and senior associates. Their standards were rigorous and our encounters brief, blips in their crowded schedules of conference calls and out-of-office meetings. The work schedule intensified, and I had little time to visit Nick. Intellectually the work engaged, but emotionally and spiritually, it was dry. Bob's office provided a place of respite from Wall Street–a place where I could be real, as emotionally authentic as possible, where I could, literally, report my dreams.

One recurrent dream was of a flood engulfing New York City.

Bob interpreted: "The flood is real. It is your emotional life. The fear is so real that you spend a lot of time dancing around a direct feeling."

I took that in for a moment. Bob watched while leaning back in his leather chair. "Bob, I've also dreamed about stealing a van and being chased by a cop."

Bob interpreted: "The van is you, drifting; looking for a cop–me–to bring you a summons and help you find direction. You're successful in the world, the problem is negotiating feelings instead of acting out against bosses and girlfriends."

"But I value these people," I protested.

"*Value*," Bob shot back. "We have a mercantile history: the marketplace above all. What did William Carlos Williams say? The pure products of America go crazy."

Check. The clock showed five minutes to end of session; having read some books about the therapeutic process, I reminded myself that the most important material tends to arise during the final minutes.

"I feel more like a dutiful soldier," I said.

Bob leaned forward over folded legs. "Exactly. I'm not into parent-bashing or culture-bashing, but let's face it: you graduated from top schools into one of the top law firms in America. This is the family, the societal *value*: we fill ourselves with accomplishments, almost a ravenous obsessional feeding, yet something is missing in the emotional texture, what is permissible to experience. The mind–superior. You inherit a love of tradition, culture, family, learned that to achieve brings rewards and that you can achieve. A house built on shifting sand; there's a worm in the apple; everyone goes into their head and nobody has their feet on the ground. You want to shit on the partner's desk and leave it there. Sure they have right behavior, proper conduct, hierarchy, 'lackey,' 'wipe my boots,' and you say 'fuck you fascist pigs.' You let them know you're not their boy, they pick up on it. You get your ass in a sling and become a hobo. At least honest feeling is leaking through."

"Is that good?"

He dodged the question and tacked. "These days everybody's in philosophy. We need more practical philosophy, as they say in The School Of. You're looking for grounding. *I don't want to sit in the air anymore*. That dream image recurs too, right? Soaring bodily or waiting for a plane to take off–but where's the ground?"

That night Natasha and I had an honest conversation about where we were "heading." I reported to Bob in our next session about the paradox of feeling inner power by expressing vulnerability. "It feels wonderful to be honest," I said.

"And that's your cue." Bob re-crossed his yogic legs the opposite way. "That it seems to relieve the pressure. You're training yourself to find the road, to smooth out the extremes of dismissiveness and the flood. Sometimes your mind works so quickly it works out all the possible responses to your response before you respond and then you get suppression. Feelings are unacceptable so they're shunted. *I'm angry, I'm upset, I feel uncomfortable, this feels awkward*. It's so basic, so simple, but you've got to unlearn and re-learn."

I dreamed I was in a classroom and the teacher, in a foul mood, decided to withhold our grades. I gave the teacher a Message; everyone applauded. I was asked to announce what had happened on the loudspeaker, but declined. Bob interpreted: "The whole world's a classroom for you; but when do you go to the gym?" From time to time he brought a pair of reading glasses to our sessions and a book of poetry, which he opened to a pre-marked page. Now he read: "'On the playing fields of Eden....'" He put the book down. "That's where kids learn to be. The teacher's in a foul mood, you're in trouble. You become the Boss—message from the Messiah named Michael. Your life becomes a quest, a heroic journey."

"Exactly. Isn't it, though? The hero's journey—Joseph Campbell."

"The problem is, she's always there, invincible, even if insubstantial, the ghost who can't entirely be defeated. Chop off one head, she gets two back."

"I took the lead to change the situation, but then backed off. When coronated king I declined, because I'm not the gadfly that pokes society, I'm not there to lead them across the desert, I just want to be myself, isn't that the point here?"

"Superiority disguised as modesty," Bob concluded. "You take the role of the jester who sees all and knows all but is not the king. He doesn't have the responsibility, but knows more than the king. The gadfly says, 'I'm just a gadfly' but inside he's superior; he doesn't mingle with the dirt of state. Kingliness implies attending to affairs; the jester says, 'I see you.'"

"I don't want to immerse myself in the muck of backstabbing."

"Okay, so you're cut from a different cloth than the would-be presidents," Bob agreed, "but in the classroom of the world we're all kings. That's a real interaction, learning, exchange. In the dream, you're a student who feels superior to others; compensation for always being under the Gestapo—here the schoolteacher. You tell her: 'I know all this about you, and the students, and the way the class works. That's my Message.' It's a nuclear attack, a thunderbolt. And *then* you say: 'Now you guys figure out how to change.' And you don't get your own hands dirty."

"That's the way Gurdjieff worked, right?" I answered. "These hooded characters in *The Hobbit* throw off the hood and suddenly their faces are luminescent, an elf or dwarf but otherwise they appear ordinary. Like Moses—radiant at Sinai, and then an ordinary guy trying to balance his checkbook, deal with administration; he says, 'Lord, not me, I'm slow of speech, don't send me to negotiate with Pharaoh.'" Bob uncrossed himself out of full lotus and leaned back into the red leather—which I later learned was made of soy, a veggie-chair. "Having the understanding is not a problem, except that it can lead you to cerebration, to intellectualization rather than action." A man flew to India, Bob told me, and traveled to the ashram to meet the great guru. The guru told the man to return home and teach skiing. This man had to learn to live in the world, day by day, earning a living. "That's why these gurus have beards," Bob concluded. "You live through a lot of experiences in the world, beyond the tent—and *that* qualifies you for wisdom."

Many of my dreams involved encounters with Nazis; Bob had already intuitively alluded to the schoolteacher as the Gestapo. In some ways, the law firm was the Nazi/bad teacher, the negative guru, the heavy authority.

"In the dreams," Bob said, "the conflict is clear: you're taking on the authority who tells everyone, 'you're a zero.' You rise from the despair of being under the thumb and about to be victimized; you marshal the whole world of other students. But inside there's no grounding, no acceptance. You recreate yourself constantly like a proteus, and that gives you temporary meaning, but it doesn't stick because of never-ending trials."

"What else can I do?"

"Maybe there's no need for a message; instead of saying, 'I know you,' in the dream he can walk out. The shul-teacher's message (I meant schoolteacher) is one of many, she is not the whole world. The approval and affection comes elsewhere."

"How does that happen?" My resistance to Bob-ism was softening over time.

"The pattern has been: (a) the thumb; (b) being furious at it; (c) delivering my message and marshalling the forces of Good to defeat Evil. You're still the preacher; you want to develop the minions, the minyans." I laughed with recognition at Bob's periodic allusions to our shared cultural heritage; a *minyan* is a kind of religious quorum required for Jewish communal prayer. Bob continued: " A clear dream is like an X-ray, it shows broken bones and tells you how to heal. Healing comes from wondering, just as you are now, 'what else is there?'"

The Virgin Mary finally did appear in a dream—she was under the floorboards, while "Let It Be" by the Beatles was playing in the background. In the next dream I was sculpting a head, and the face came to life, identifying itself as Dorothy Parker. She said: "I have the answer you're looking for."

I bolted up and replied: "I don't need answers, I need to know my question."

She answered: "What you want to know is, how to put your ideas in writing."

I could not recall having heard of Dorothy Parker, specifically. Bob informed me that she was a New York literary figure who was "sarcastic, witty, verbally adept." She held court at the Algonquin, a short distance from Bob's office.

"But," Bob cautioned, "notice you create her, give her life, like Pygmalion kissing the statue and it comes alive. Yet even though you think you're the 'god' or lifegiver, you take your answer from the statute. As for Mary, again the message comes from without, even if it's a message of peace." This psychological work on relationship to the feminine would blossom as the "third eye opening" deepened.

SOMETIMES A CIGAR

While as a poet-yogi, Bob excelled in dream analysis and extended metaphors, his Freudian sub-personality was particularly engaging. One time we were speaking about my tendency to idolize and then reject Natasha.

"Sometimes a cigar is just a cigar," Bob commented, "and other times it's a penis. When you want to see her so badly you have to call you become a mouth from head to toe and she becomes a breast. "

"She's needy too," I protested.

"If you're a breast, you have milk to give," Bob continued the metaphor. "But with any baby, out of sight is out of mind. You obsess with her; you hallucinate the breast, it's a conjuring: RETURN, RETURN. She becomes an entity to fill you."

For Bob, *entity* was just a name for something in a dream. For me, *entities* had a strange discorporeality—they flashed in and out visually, in my nascent meditation; their messages reached our world, transmitted through Nick, sometimes garbled but frequently targeted to burst some emotional dam of a prayer meeting participant.

Bob's sessions provided a counterpoint to the 'third eye opening' with Nick, as Bob mercilessly probed the sour and seedy underbelly of the psychological dynamic between us, and underlying my fascination with Nick's channeling. Bob pointed out that I was playing into a situation where I would be "under the thumb" of either the 'channel' or the 'channeled being.' "It seems to be either obey or die," Bob said, "because love is attached to obedience. Something to watch as you visit Nick more frequently." Bob's warning bore out in my dreams.

I am in a hotel room. A voice appears in the bathroom, saying Fuck You, and I say Fuck You, and we go back and forth. The genie is out of the bottle. I challenge the entity: 'If you're real, let this mirror crack.' There's a hand, then an arm. It flings itself against the mirror. I am angry and we struggle. Suddenly, Gurdjieff appears. His eyes light up. They hypnotize me and I spin around, terrified. I tell the bad spirit to depart and it responds, "We work well together, you and I."

Bob picked on a half-cantaloupe he had been saving for dinner, scooping out chunks as he spoke. "Remember the earlier dream, where you get sucked out of the airplane into the stratosphere?" His eyebrows raised as he simultaneously attended to my unconscious and the luscious fruit. "Falling to earth at a million miles an hour; well the Earth is a giant breast...if you gotta go, it's not a bad way. When the baby gets reassurance from her gaze, you want that to be eternal, stop-time, free-frame, locked in. Lovers do that, 'I'm falling into your eyes,' but we're dealing on a much earlier level, oral rather than anal or phallic. You've called Gurdjieff your brother, you relate to his work, but that's pre-sexual. We're starved for that in our culture. That's why there's a deli every two blocks in Manhattan. The world is a warm blanket of light that gives you strength to go on."

"Bob, you lost me here," I said. "The dream is rich, but what does it mean?"

He scooped in a mouthful of cantaloupe. "You're trying to avoid the floodgates with Natasha, the emotional intensity. All these entities coming at you, yet dealing with a real partner is difficult. You get angry, 'Oh my God, I shat on the floor again.' I'm not saying shitting is bad, it's just losing control; one of the first exercises we learn is being successful in where to drop it."

"What does this have to do with Gurdjieff work?" I asked.

He finished up his cantaloupe. I had mentioned to him that my Gurdjieff teacher was trying to "explore the volatility" of my "emotional center." She had made some comment about the genie coming out of the bottle, and my psyche apparently took this cue as a trigger for the dream. I recalled the legend of the Jewish mystics who ascended to heaven, got to the gates, but did not have the requisite magic word and were cast down; and that the Kabala warned against premature study because one might go insane.

Bob commented: "When you begin playing with the psyche you go mad if you're arrogant, I suppose. You say *fuck you* and they say *fuck you we're demons.* There's a cult aspect to this 'Work.' You're playing the sorcerer's apprentice, but you've opened Pandora's Box and get a bad trip. Ego, id, superego, they're not anthropomorphic forces; they're part of you."

"What's that got to do with this?" I asked, again caught between worlds—Nick's, Bob's, the dream's, my day job's, and my aspirations as a seeker.

Bob ruffled his curly hair, leaving half over one ear, the other tucked behind.

"The hotel room is a rented place," he said. "You're not at home with yourself right now. You're trying to get a relationship with this angry side of you. The bathroom: great. Fuck you, cockeydoo. A voice appears, disembodied. Because you're not able to own the anger. You go back and forth with the stuff you're not comfortable with, saying fuck you to the esoteric side. That's also the schoolteacher and you don't want to be under the thumb. *Fascist pig*, you say. When at the firm, Gurdjieff is my ally, but when I'm in Gurdjieff, that's the oppressor. This esoteric stuff doesn't give you grounding, answers. You respect it as a marvelous system of ideas, this Gurdjieff, Kabala, Socrates. You say: *Give me answers.* But you end up angry, because it doesn't help you become a real person. The teacher, here Gurdjieff, becomes the Devil, says you're supposed to follow him and not challenge him. You want to be the acolyte who is next in line, but it's disorienting. Your grandiosity is a nightmare; it brings nothing nurturing or instructive. So says the dream."

"I have to trust the dream, right?" I asked, less certain than when I had started.

"You're angry with these so-called 'Masters.' They're not leading you into a deeper connection. The esoteric side tries to seduce you, *we work really well together you and I,* but you're frightened, right, why?" Without waiting for my answer, Bob continued. "Because they take control of you and demand submission. That's a kind of madness. Lots of poets romanticize disorientation. The mirror is your hope of 'waking up,' the promise of Gurdjieff and others. He's just one version of the genie. You're terrified by the possibility of being taken over. Hypnotized is to go into an altered state and lose yourself while someone takes over."

Bob further helped clarify my ambivalence about continued 'Work' with the Gurdjieff group I was attending in parallel with channeling sessions with Nick.

I respected the Work, found many helpful ideas and exercises in it, yet like Tanya, felt myself increasingly longing for emotional connections with others, and frustrated with the superiority and intellectualization. My dream spoke:

I meet a group at the Gurdjieff Foundation, which is a storefront only. At first I'm lost and confused; it starts to rain. Someone brings in my jacket and I sit and someone explains: "We're doing more than cleaning up, you understand." I say: "I'm not even sure." His glasses are on the bed and I spray them with fluid and wipe them, and begin to 'self-remember.' Someone else joins us, he has long hair and wrinkled face. He speaks: "My planetary body means nothing to me. I have learned to non-identify." He speaks of himself in the third person. "He has learned to heal with his wrists." He shows me his wrist, swollen. His body is old and has begun to disintegrate. "There's a special vein here that absorbs the energies."

Self-remembering, according to Gurdjieff, entails attaining a higher level of consciousness in which the individual can see himself or herself objectively, from the vantage of a permanent, stable essence, rather than from a fleeting perspective of shifting *I*s, which operate, almost of their own accord, from the 'moving part' of various 'centers of intelligence.' I told Bob that the dream expressed the positive side of the esoteric search, a feeling of community. Monthly, my Gurdjieff work would have "Work days," when we would "sit" and do nothing but try to "remember ourselves," and then continue to gather this "energy" while doing "tasks:" cleaning, gardening, cooking. We would train ourselves to engage in "self-observation:" our "likes and dislikes," our "mechanical reactions" to certain aspects of the tasks or of the people with whom we Worked. "Man is a machine," Gurdjieff had emphasized, urging us to overcome our mechanical habits, impulses, daydreams. I simultaneously loved and loathed the Work days. Cleaning the dusty bottom of an aging washing machine, I felt little progress toward enlightenment.

"Sure, you clean the glasses, there's reciprocity," Bob commented. "But this long-haired, wrinkle-faced, typical guru kind of ancient gives you the old beyond-the-body message. But what are you, Michael, struggling with? You're trying to find the body! To get grounded. He says, I'm not my body, I'm going out to the ether, going to achieve the final yogic reincarnation; I'm going to burn up and attain nirvana. Hang around and watch! But he seems to be a parasite; he absorbs the energies of those around him, there's no sense of community." Bob finished his cantaloupe and flung it into the trash can as I told him the next dream.

I go to the saloon with friends to share my writing. A thug there thinks I'm flirting with his girlfriend. He threatens, but leaves, all bluster. My friends are putzing around. I end up back in my childhood home on Normanhust Street. I fly over the house. My mother is immersed in disputes with accountants in one room. I consider visiting myself in another room. But I fly instead over the backyard, where my father is throwing a football with one of my brothers, and there's a black woman washing laundry. I say "whoosh" to scare her away, and she gathers courage and comes toward me.

"The dream is a movie about you," Bob said, retrieving a bottled of iced green tea from his coat pocket. "You want a foundation, the Foundation of finding men you can be with, brothers. So you have a saloon, the society of men. Hang out, have a few beers, learn a few facts, Remember Yourself, go home, go to sleep. It's great, you fly over the house, over Normanhurst which is a mythical place of childhood, like Falconcrest,--Falconbreast. Your mother is running the affairs of state, and your father is the black woman: earthy."

He paused, adjusting the Velcro strap on his veggie-shoes. "You like to fly over the emotional reality. But I think you're upset by all this esoteric stuff. You love ideas and systems of thought—they are enlivening for your mind and writing, but ultimately lonely. Not as real as putting out laundry, or a father throwing a football to a son, or going for a few beers with friends. You can play with ideas, but it's not as nurturing as playing touch football in Central Park in summertime." Bob wound up the session. "God, you're at one of the best firms in the world. You've put in enough seriousness for lifetimes. Now get light."

Experiences of the numinous intensified as I continued visiting Nick, making time between assignments at the law firm. Once I was sitting in my living room, in the fashionable Soho apartment I had rented by the art galleries, and saw a silhouette of myself at age seven, sitting at the piano. When I looked again, it was just the shadow of a lamp and desk against the wall. I mentioned this to Nick.

"You went out of body for a moment; when you returned and examined the incident with your conscious mind, the experience dissolved."

I pursued this question of out-of-body experience with him, as it reflected two contradictory existences: the world of the law firm, in which faxes, phone calls, meetings, documents and billings had ultimate reality; and the world of entities in which no less potent information was exchanged. I was a "transactional" or corporate lawyer facilitating deals; and Nick in his way, too brokered transactions, those between the corporeal and disincarnate. Assuming that what I perceived was an authentic glimpse into some other facet of reality, not simply what a skeptic might dismiss as "hallucinated" from within my own imagination. It was a question of authority—mine to comprehend my own experience, versus a professional's perception of the right to label my subjective report. Since the line between real and unreal, perceived and labeled, culturally accepted and dismissed, seemed difficult to draw, I asked Nick whether he believed in transubstantiation, as opposed to consubstantiation, the merely symbolic transformation of the wine and wafer at Mass into the blood and body of Christ. I figured that he, with his visceral experience of the imperceptible, would have a response to this theological debate that had divided branches of a world religion.

"Of course the exchange of wine and wafer into blood and body is real," Nick opined. "Faith makes it real." It was difficult to dismiss Nick's views when he seemed to have such accurate information from the spirit world; and yet, the answer left me dissatisfied as I was skeptical of the claim. Nick could not simply resolve centuries of theological debate with a pronouncement based on his own mystical experience—an experience fueled with some validation by his accuracy in other arenas. Or could he? Nick's ability to generate experiences in others—he was not particularly charismatic, just committed to psychic opening—was puzzling.

In addition to his theological vicissitudes, another arena in which his views presented a complex personality involved sexuality. Nick stated that he disapproved of premarital intercourse, referring to it as "pungent pork," and then referencing his own self-reported celibacy. There was a kind of fundamentalism implicit in his views; for example, he viewed erotic dreams as manifesting the Devil. Yet I was beginning to have many experiences in states between waking and sleeping. I knew that in some traditions, saints reported such manifestations as 'attacks' on their purity and devotion to God; while psychologists might dismissively interpret this as the product of sublimation, repression, or some other defense mechanism. My experience, without any dogma or judgment attached, was of unclean interaction in the nether world, lacking clear boundaries or consent. Nick could not guide me here.

Nick's tales of his childhood were engaging but clearly beyond consensus boundaries of either his religious upbringing or mine. For example, he told me that when he was seven, he snuck away from the school playground and entered a nearby chapel. A woman was playing the organ. He began describing to her the various dead relatives he saw in her field. She chastised him and kicked him out. Another time, he reported, he was staring at a painting of St. Anthony, to whom he was devoted, asking: "I can hear you, but why can't I see you yet?" According to Nick, a voice returned. "Be patient."

One time Nick turned to me and channeled: "You are a light of love raising the vibrational frequency of the household." I found this difficult to believe, given my struggles at work and in my relationship. Another time, I asked whether he thought a family business would thrive.

"Surrender your wish to God," he said. I asked whether God was active in the stock market. "Ask Saint Anthony to give you a sign," he replied, "that their success is coming from him." I wondered why Anthony, a saint canonized by the Church, would want to bless a Jewish couple with abundance. Nick's faith was sincere, but it left the pantheon of gods in chaos.

"Nick," I pursued, "how can a prayer for money bring one closer to God?"

From the wicker chair, he explained: "If they make money, you could be sitting in a nice house and meditating all day rather than working in a sick environment."

"Still, is it right to pray for that?"

"You're not praying for anything. You're simply seeking intercession for good."

"What about when I prayed for someone who was having surgery?"

"You didn't pray for a cure; you prayed for a healing. The healing is one of spirit. A total healing would mean going into spirit."

"Isn't that called 'death'?" I asked.

"The body dies but the spirit lives forever. People subconsciously choose to leave this earth by surgery, illness, accident, or other methods. You don't pray that their choice be a particular choice of yours; simply pray for their highest good."

I then turned to work, commenting that I felt myself becoming increasingly anxious, tense, and tyrannical with subordinates, not saintly at all.

"I have seen beyond the sadomasochistic side to the love inside," he replied.

At that moment, I heard my own voice as if over a phone, saying "Natasha." The very next moment, the telephone rang: it was Natasha. After I spoke with her, I reported this to Nick. Again the psychic experiences made him difficult to refute.

"They're trying to reach you," he said, and repeated: "Faith makes it real."

I began reading *Butler's Lives of the Saints*. Nick had turned me on to this book as source material for mystical experience. After all, the Christian "saints" had seen, heard, channeled, and catalogued a variety of mystical phenomena. Sure enough, other phenomena began in my Soho apartment. Three cookbooks clattered and smashed against a metal pitcher; a painting fell off the wall in the middle of the night; an ice cube, that I had left on the countertop during the day, decided to fall to the floor the next morning. I took a shower and saw numbers emanating from the showerhead. As I shared these experiences with Nick, he told me he had been having mystical experiences since childhood. For example, his grandmother died when he was nine. His mother had said: "Someday you'll be with grandma." To which he had responded: "I'm with her now." His mother fell silent. Nick used this anecdote as a jumping-off point for describing why, despite his devotion to God, he was in a state of non-reconciliation with his family. According to Nick, *they* inhabited an "erratic environment" with an "insane mother" and siblings who were "hostages" to the family business. Nick tried to "save" them: "I was the crucified one," he said, "but there's no happily-ever-after with them." Nick made the point that he could still strive toward sainthood—*they* were the crazy ones. He turned the topic back to my work, as this too was a dysfunctional environment that could not possibly be conducive to the higher ground we would be treading. "Sage your office," he advised. "Clear the negative vibrations."

Thereafter, my Italian suits would be sweetened both by Native American sage-sticks and by the cherry perfume of Mr. Hansen's incessant stream of tobacco.

I visited a Gurdjieff-like group known as ARICA. There I "heard" Natasha's thoughts, including a Rachmaninoff requiem. Later I asked whether she had been thinking about a piece of music with bass, baritone, and a choral arrangement; I hummed what I had heard, and she confirmed that that was the piece. I was puzzled by how rapidly my intuitive faculties seemed to be unfolding. I contacted an old friend from the Gurdjieff work who took me to The Saloon for a drink. He attributed my experiences with Nick to "the intersection of life with the fourth dimension." My friend, a painter of miniatures with titles such as "Innocence Feeding the World," considered "The Exercise" (or "self-remembering") as nothing more than experiencing the present, keeping one's attention on the moment, rather than flashing to the past or contemplating the future.

"Self-remembering is not esoteric," he said, as wait-staff rolled up on skates and served our beers. "It's not copyrighted by Mr. Gurdjieff and his 'true' descendants. We're simply moving into Witness Consciousness. Your friend Nick calls it God Consciousness. It's all one." My friend attributed Nick's gift to a highly refined intuitive center. My friend thought Nick lived in the "intellectual part of the emotional part of the instinctive center:" his instinctive center was highly evolved, in its ability to pick up on beings from the fourth dimension, and yet had an emotional quality, in its religious dimension, and that had an intellectual directedness toward obtaining specific information.

As we finished back through an abandoned parking lot, my friend explained: "Right now we are perceiving this parking lot through three dimensions, but if we add the fourth, you experience this not only as it is today, a parking lot, but also as it has been and will be throughout time. You might see a vacant lot, a house, a farm, a bog, a watering hole for dinosaurs, a marsh, all the lives that have traversed this bit of gravel on which you are currently stepping."

"Such awareness," I said, stepping ever more mindfully on the broken chunks of blacktop, "would lead to either a high state of evolution, or to madness."

THE BVM

Marking the conclusion of our first year at the Seminary was a retreat held at Mariondale (literally the valley of Mary), an old nunnery. Nick, Tanya and I drove together through muggy air and a congested freeway. During the drive, Nick spoke about his devotion to the Blessed Virgin Mary (or BVM, as Tanya called her), also known to him as Divine Mother, a named he borrowed from the Hindu tradition. Nick had a wallet-sized representation of her with him at all times, along with one of St. Therese the Little Flower. I had boned up on these various figures by reading and also by watching some videos: *Song of Bernadette*; *A Nun's Story*; *John Paul*, *Brother Sun, Sister Moon*. Nick also had brought a collection of relics to "protect us" during the journey, as well as a medal of St. Christopher and several rosaries.

Curiously, the culmination of my religious education to date was occurring at a Catholic convent. My relationship to Christianity even in childhood had been more complex than the residue in literature of seeing the world in terms of *goyyim*, other nations. In Hebrew school, one of my teachers had explained that Yeshu (Hebrew for Jesus), rather than meaning "Savior," in fact was an acronym that stood for *yimach shemo ve-zichrono*: "may his name and memory be erased." That epitaph generally was reserved for Haman, Hitler, and other genocidal figures, and I wondered what Yeshu had done to deserve it. The history of the Church seemed bound up with anti-Semitism; and my identity with separation of "us" and "other;" yet, aspects of interfaith awareness permeated my psyche even then.

I cherished my Jewish education; loved studying Torah in its original Hebrew; treasured the calligraphy of the Torah scroll, the sacred melodies of the services; the living presence of God in our history; the taste of the Divine in the *davening* or sacred shuffling during prayer; the connection to my ancestors through the *tephillin* or phylacteries; the warm nurturance and transcendental light of the Sabbath candles; the embodied sanctification of life transmitted through chanting the *Kiddush*, the Friday night prayer, and the *Kaddish*, the prayer for the dead; and the presence of my *Zaydie*, my mother's father, beside me in the synagogue, as I twirled the ritual fringes around my index finger and marveled at his learning as he, a gymnasium student in Poland who had escaped before the rise of Nazi socialism and started a life in America, read novels in Hebrew during the rabbi's sermon. I was a *yeshiva bocher*, a child of Hebrew learning, dwelling appreciatively in my heritage.

At the same time, I had an uncanny appreciation for Christianity, combined with the antipathy to Jesus and a visceral awareness, from many visually explicit films during Hebrew school, about the Holocaust and the global attitude toward Jews over the centuries that seemed, at times, intertwined with Christian dogma, even back to the vituperative anti-Pharisee eruptions in the gospels. The charge of deicide weighed heavily, including being bullied and pushed to the ground for wearing a yarmulke in public. When I left Hebrew school for a much more rough-and-tumble public school in the eighth grade, ostensibly to "broaden my horizons," I became infatuated with a Monica J, and accompanied her to Catechism. While the move was for social rather than religious reasons, I had a photograph taken of myself appearing to pray before a cross while wearing a yarmulke. Perhaps this was the rebellion, the anger that Bob insisted lay deep inside; or perhaps an early way to affirm, as did the interfaith Seminary's logo, that "God is One." At any rate, the link to Christianity may in part have stemmed in part from close contact with an Argentine house-maid who was my closest companion during the three years we lived in Buenos Aires while my father served Chrysler Corporation's finance department. The maid taught me Argentine history and culture, a patriotic attitude toward Southern American heroes and liberators from Spanish tyranny (stories that resonated with the God-led heroism of Moses). I probably imitated her by praying on my knees, when my mother happened to stop in, notice, and gently reprimand: "honey, we don't do that, we're Jews."

We also visited country folk that Zaydie thought might be Marranos: Jewish families that had converted, centuries ago, to Christianity in order to escape the Inquisition, but continued to practice in secret, and thus were left with odd rituals, such as performing Sabbath services in closets. Childhood was full of brushes with individuals between or crossing the lines of faiths. So here in the dale of Mary I came for retreat and sanctuary, for individuation, for completion of the past.

The nuns mostly avoided us in the hallways and even scraped by the walls, a practice of humility; the convent was in decline, both financially and in terms of its sick and elderly population. The grounds had numerous statues of Mary, Jesus, and the saints, and benches overlooking the Tappan Zee bridge and Hudson river. Ironically, to salvage financial health, part of the grounds had apparently been sold to a Jewish health club. Even worse, our logos, songs, and group *om* must have seemed incongruous to the resident nuns, a reminder that they were sharing space with us out of financial need rather than religious tolerance.

The corridors had twisting staircases, which led from time to time to little grottos where a statue of a Christian saint would surprise the visitor, and one could apply a little holy water and make the sign of the cross. The rooms were Spartan, beyond a college dorm room even: a bed, sink and closet. We were instructed to keep our voices low as older nuns on higher floors needed rest.

Our retreat included a gathering in which we collectively wrestled with fifty-seven, year-end examination questions, such as: "What is the Kabala? What are the Sephirot? The Shekinah? The Five Pillars of Islam? The Four Noble Truths of the Buddha? The symbology and purpose of the Mass? What is your understanding of alcoholism as a disease? Compare how the term 'ego' is used in *A Course on Miracles* with its use in Freudian and other traditional psychologies. What are common elements of a near-death experience? How do you work with a dying patient? The Bible declares, 'thou shalt not make graven images,' yet Hindus worship God in forms such as Krishna, Shiva and Kali; how do you feel about worship of God with/without form?" We talked about everything: abortion; the death penalty; poverty; enlightenment. We analyzed a chart with the following categories: Religion; Founder; Century Began; Country of Origin; Holy Books; No. of Followers; % of World. In order of percentage of the world as followers, listed were: Christianity (28); Islam (19); Hinduism (11); Buddhism (5); Taoism (3.5); Judaism (.8); Sikhism (.7); Confucianism (.3); Jainism (.1); Shinto (.1); Zoroastrianism (.001); at the end were two large categories, Tribal/Shamanistic (20) and New Religions (2.5). Finally, our resident shaman gathered a big drum:

O great Spirit! Earth, Sun, Sky and Sea. You are inside and all around me!

Around and around, clearing the cacophony, we followed the beat of the drum, letting

ourselves cleanse from the struggles of answering the 57 questions.
Mother I feel you under my feet. Mother I feel your heartbeat.
Heya heya, heya heya, heya hey o. Heya heya, hey ooo.
We circled the room, making animal sounds, letting our power animals come to us. We stamped and stomped and brought shamanistic energies to the convent.
Fly like an eagle, fly so high, circling the universe, on wings of pure light.
Oh witchi ie tie, witchi tie oh. Oh witchi ie tie, witchi tie oh.
We returned to our circle of folding metal chairs for another session of sharing. We received a directory from the Association of Interfaith Ministers and contemplated how we would advertise and what services we might offer. Reading the list of specialties, I looked for another lawyer and instead saw: KUNDALINI YOGA, AKASHIC HEALING, TRANSPERSONAL THERAPY, CHAKRA BALANCING, MARIEL, INTUITIVE COUNSELING, ALCHEMICAL BREATHWORK, TEACHER OF AGELESS WISDOM, SPIRITUAL HEALING, PSYCHOMETRY, TAROT, ANGEL WORKSHOP, ASTROLOGY, AFFIRMATION, CONSCIOUSNESS EXPANSION, CODEPENDENCY COUNSELING, AROMATHERAPY. The interests of our former graduates were as numerous as the descendants of Abraham, as the grains of sand on the beach. I could perform weddings, funerals, christenings, and rituals not yet invented. One entry read: PARAPSYCHOLOGY, FACIAL REJUVENATION, PSYCHIC DIV., HIGH PRIESTESS, BALANCING USING KINESIOLOGY, AGE REGRESSION, MAGNETS, CRYSTALS, COLOR, AND MIND PROJECT.
I looked at Nick and winked: "Exorcist," I said.

At lunch the sky turned black and a violent rainstorm swept the convent.
Someone shouted: "Open the windows!" We watched as a tornado passed over. When the quiet came, we went outside; some large oaks had fallen. One oak had crashed over a statue of Jesus, but while the tree appeared to have split in two, the statue itself was unharmed.
We went to our rooms to check whether our belongings had been soaked in the storm. Since the elevator was full, I took the stairs. Somehow I made a wrong turn down some unused corridors and ended up in a stairwell that wound around endlessly. Finally, I emerged at the base in another empty hallway, which led to the back of a chapel, the place where priests put on their vestments, facing the pews.
Light flooded the stained glass and shone off the gold crucifix, filtering stillness into the space with quiet presence. I had a strong feeling of having been in this place before; it seemed to be a fragment from a forgotten dream.
With the changes taking place inside me from intense meditation practice with Nick, who knew? Perhaps I had astrally visited this place, or come forward into this future now from a dream-state. I had a strange feeling of being at home as a Christian priest serving the Mass; and simultaneously of being from elsewhere, as if the Earth were not my home. It was difficult to reconcile these impressions with my identity as a Wall Street lawyer; but in a kind of mental equivalent of an optical illusion, I could just as well have flipped identities and found the Wall Street lawyer sub-personality a foreign impression embossed on that of a Seminarian open to mystical practice. Which was the real Michael?

"Lord, make me an instrument of Thy peace," we sang the prayer of St. Francis. "Where there is hatred, let me sow love..." Our closing ritual for the evening, the song reverberated off the nunnery walls. "O Divine Master ... It is in dying that we are born to eternal life." Holding hands of fellow Seminarians to my right and left, I felt as if the line had been written to me, for me, by all, for all. I wept.

My colleagues at the law firm were graduates of the best law schools with finest credentials. Within the Seminary many stood out for their combination of strength and tenderness: Timothy, a vibrant, handsome, Roman Catholic-turned Orthodox Jew-turned New Age seminarian who, diagnosed with AIDS, had lain in a hospital bed for months, barely moving, and found recovery through *A Course in Miracles*; Stacey, a hyperkinetic mother of two teenage sons; Sally, a former off-Broadway actress who typed, part-time, for a U.N. functionary and prayed to her spirit guides each month to cover the rent; Vida, a/k/a Beth Israelson, who had left her Long Island husband, her three BMW's and collection of mink coats for the Rajneesh.

And there was Rad. His eyes were pools of green; he towered at six foot three, with a bushy, prophetic beard and a mop of hair to his waist. He was half-prophet, half-rock star; he emanated unusual scents, the result of potions he extracted and doused himself with daily. In fact, he was constantly rubbing potions over his body, or sipping some liquefied herb from a small bottle, or popping some "natural substance" into his mouth. Ostensibly a song-writer, he confided to being a "wizard," who loved Nature and concocted substances from leaves, herbs, grasses, making herbal uppers, downers, and sideways remedies for all occasions. He detested white bread and joked about all-night wrestling with the "mattress from hell" that the Sisters considered a divine gift. He taught me how to grace the "acid-loving trees" with the "gift of urine."

Within the circle, we spoke of our own spirituality: some had recovered from alcoholism, others from divorce. The paths to God were many. The rabbi spoke of how he was separated from his wife and children in the concentration camps; eyes lighting up and dampening, he lovingly said that we were his children.

The varieties of interfaith weddings we would be able to perform upon ordination were staggering: not only Jewish-Hindu, but also Moslem-Hindu; Protestant-Bahai; and any combination of religious boundary-breaking compacts.

Someone asked how to take the same wedding and make it Christian rather than Jewish. "Simple," the rabbi joked. "At the end, simply say: 'And all this has been done in the name of Jesus Christ, Amen!'"

Another favorite technique the rabbi taught was to take a story and tailor it to someone's tradition. He himself was well-versed, for example, in Hassidic tales: "There once was a famous rabbi from Lithuania..." But depending on the audience, this could change. In an ashram, these became Hindu stories: "There once lived a famous swami in India." In a Church: "There once was a famous priest in the Holy Land."

"Same essence, different garment," he summarized. "Thus all tales are put to the service of God." The nuns were aghast and we were thrilled.

The second night, we dressed in white for the Purification Ceremony: a ritual in which we traversed the room, holding hands, in concentric circles while bearing a lit candle, while in the background, a sweet tune played: "I open the door, the door to my heart, I let you in." We opened and opened, seeing the divine spark in each other, seeing each other as the white spark of the candle, the flame of God.

After, we sat as the rabbi proceeded around the room with a vessel of blessed oil. As he drew near, each individual would rise, and the rabbi would smear his thumb in the oil and anoint the forehead with the oil. In ancient times, kings and prophets had been anointed with oil; the Messiah was to be anointed with oil, as the name meant, "the anointed one." As the rabbi approached and anointed my third eye, Nick leaned over and whispered: "This is not idle ceremony. There's *power* in his hands. I *feel* it." Nick received his anointment appreciatively. As he sat down again, he whispered: "We've had a group initiation before: as Essenes."

I had risen full of joy, yet with desire for an experience. I tried, but did not feel any special power flowing through the thumb, through the oil. I recalled a visit I had taken in high school to Israel. I had made pilgrimage to the Western or Wailing Wall, the remnant of the Temple in Jerusalem; I had tried so hard for an experience of God that nothing had happened—until I gave up trying. "It's just a wall," I had thought, and *then* the tears had flowed, only once my mind had given up trying to feel could the feelings break through. Now, sitting back in my metal folding chair and surrendering the effort of feeling something momentous, my mind relaxed, and I slowly began to sense the power in this initiation.

After the ceremony, Rad led a small group outside to celebrate the full moon. We sat on blankets on the grass, in a "magic circle," surrounded by hundreds of elms and oaks. Rad chanted praises to earth, wind, sun, and sky. We witchie-tie-oh'ed to the moon and to the four corners of the earth, and to the winds, north, east, west, and south. We expressed gratitude for being alive; felt the cool night air against our skin. Having been trained by my previous walk with Rad, I could literally perceive the alive intelligence of the trees. We especially prayed for the trees because, as Rad put it, "they took the hit of the tornado for us."

I suddenly felt a huge inner cavern, as if the emotional life had dropped out of me. Yes, I had embraced "higher levels of consciousness" through the Gurdjieff work, and even begun to connect with some of my classmates. Yes, as at the Western Wall, this emptiness welled up at the core where I had hoped to find God.

Earlier in the day, Nick and I had stood before a statue of Bernadette having her vision of Mary. "Do you feel her?" Nick had asked, sweeping his hands.

I had shaken my head. "Nothing."

For the most part, I appreciated spirituality the way one appreciates jazz, different than flowing into a Beethoven sonata or becoming one with a hymn or chant. Inside lived deadness and a longing. I rose from the blanket and left to visit some acid-loving trees. I stood behind a woodshed and poured the lament of my stream into the grasses, impregnating them with fertile hopes. While urinating I looked up: there was a hole in the woodshed where earlier that evening I had seen a window, and the hole was covered with plastic; the plastic seemed to be breathing, out and in, with the night air. I popped into a slightly altered state of consciousness. A strange feeling came over me. An unreality, as though it was not really "me" standing there, under a starry night, watching a plastic window in a woodshed breathe. There were four elements: grass and stars, a Michael-entity and a consciousness of "me" by the woodshed. Which was the real "I"? A significant feeling of "me" was a consciousness implanted in this Michael-body from elsewhere. I truly *was* a child of the stars. In this altered awareness, I returned to friends in the circle.

I knocked on Nick's door. His face was buried in his pillow. "Tired?" I asked. He waved me in. I told him about my experience by the woodshed. "I asked for a sign, to experience God, but this is too much too fast."

He looked concerned. "Do you think something else entered in?"

"You mean, an entity?" This was getting worse.

"You can attract them if you don't protect yourself." He was matter-of-fact.

He looked me over, and then concluded: "You're fine."

"I'm not really here," I said tentatively.

"Neither am I," he replied.

Nick was "not there," alive elsewhere, but Rad was fully alive here. We sat on the bench overlooking the Hudson. "There are so many different forms of intelligence," he told me, rubbing himself with a lotion that smelled vaguely of frankincense. "If you're quiet inside and go up to a tree and really spend time, so that the tree can really feel the focused intelligence of another life-form being trained, you'll actually pick up a thought-form from the tree, a deep wisdom." He pointed back to the woods behind us. "This isn't some New Age mumbo-jumbo or pagan practice. Martin Buber writes about it. So you think you found God, pissing by the woodshed?"

"There as well as anywhere else," I replied. I recalled a poem called Kaddish, by Alan

Ginsberg, that begins, "holy, holy, holy, holy, holy, holy, holy," in which he names all the things that are holy, in a kind of Whitmanesque celebration of everything. And I recalled learning in an orthodox summer camp that one says a specific prayer after urinating, because even the most basic human function reflects divine intelligence and therefore can elicit gratitude. Louis Ginzberg, a great scholar of Jewish legend and myth, asserts that all of creation has its own hymn of praise to extol the Creator, even reptiles and mice.

I spent a long time reflecting with Rad. Afterward, we went to greet the trees.

It all happens it slow-motion:

We drop our trousers and feed the earth our urine. We pull up our zippers and stand in the enormous silence. We are blips of consciousness, alone with the trees. I see them, as if for the first time: the leaves, like tentacles, reaching down. They're huge, alive, reaching toward me. This is not some dumb, brute piece of inanimate nature; it is a living creature who knows I am here.

Rad and I walk back. I have the awareness of the grass under my feet as alive; and suddenly I see it shooting out before me, spreading out in all directions with its aliveness and intelligence as my feet pass over it. The grass knows I am walking over it; the grass acknowledges, subtly, my presence. I see the grass is not inert, but as aware as I am. I see the grass as one sees the highway rush past while driving at high speed. Then I look again, and it's just grass.

Now Rad leaves for the night. I walk alone toward the statue of Jesus, the one the cracked tree limb seems to have protected. The statue too is alive, the face watching me. There is no judgment, no opinion, but a neutral awareness. It knows me; has known me all along; what has changed is now I know that it knows I am there. The sense of Presence everywhere is strong, overwhelming. I walk quickly back over the grass: its intelligence flashes, arteries everywhere; and then again is just grass. That night, I sleep unusually soundly.

On return to the city, Nick joined me at a synagogue service. Nick sat through it in meditation, fingers encircled on his knees. "Tune in to my energy," he said.

I tried. "What do you see," I asked him.

"By the Ark, two angels, one on either side."

"What are they doing?" I asked.

"Just watching."

Nick stayed overnight. Before retiring, he prayed to his crucifix. He was repeating over and over: "God ... God ... God ... Divine Mother, Divine Mother, Divine Mother, Divine Mother." I was used to a conception of God as a powerful but remote Person, like the most Senior Partner in the law firm. Nick was praying to someone imminently present. I was reminded of the story that the Baal Shem Tov trembled so fervently in his prayer that bits of grain in a nearby barrel were seen to join his trembling. Suddenly, in the dark, Nick announced: "She's happy we're together."

He began speaking in tongues. The room felt cooler, as if the altitude had shifted. My breathing shifted too, as if I was being breathed.

Nick said: "We are ascending a mountain in Carmel. She is pulling us."

This started a chain of thoughts: the Divine Mother, in my room; Carmel, the mountain where the prophet Elijah proved Yahweh's ascendancy over the pagan god Baal; being breathed instead of breathing; an astral or metaphorical journey.

Nick called out: "Your life is a prayer, not a croquet game."

I felt an electric current down my body. I stood. I could not feel my arms. I could feel no connection between my brain and body. I seemed to be out of my body, but I did not know how or where. I heard a roar in my ears, like the *om*.

"The whole room is electric," Nick said. "She's everywhere."

I could see him stretch out his arms; they radiated light.

"Feel her," he said slowly. "She wants you to feel her." He moved his hand around my arms; I felt becalmed. "There. Your mind is slower." I looked at Nick's face, which came slowly into focus. But then my gaze opened further, and his face seemed to melt into a ball of white light. The light spread, covered his neck; his torso remained, but the head and neck were nothing but light.

I relaxed and the light covered the rest of him; I relaxed again and find I could adjust and attune, to let him fade in and out, first a being in a body, then a ball of light. *Our body really is an illusion*, came the thought. *We are two flames talking in space.* As if reading my thoughts, Nick said: "It's all here, now."

"Why doesn't everyone see it?" I asked, amazed at seeing light everywhere.

"They're not ready," Nick's voice floated from somewhere within this light.

"But there's so much pain in the world," my cognitive mind responded.

Nick had an answer: "They have to learn about the God beyond the pain."

GROUNDING

The initiation to mark completion of our first year took place at a reform synagogue. Nick wore a black frock, resembling a medieval monk. As he scurried toward the stage, he mouthed the word, "deeper."

We endured a few warm-ups of congregational *om* and a highly emotional, off-key rendition of "God Is Watching Us From A Distance." At one point, we invoked the archangels, Michael, Raphael, Uriel, and Gabriel. The ceremony freely mixed content from Judaism, Christianity, Buddhism, Hinduism, and other traditions such as Yoruba. The endless honk of an angry driver resonated through a silent meditation, during which the group of Seminarians on stage turned the sound into another round of *om*. Finally, we blessed the audience, a ritual which seemed hokey, but on another level, had a felt power; after all, Aaron and the elders had biblically blessed the people.

I had performed this blessing in a synagogue in Israel; tradition had the *cohanim* (plural for *cohen*) wrap their heads and backs in the *tallis* or ritual shawl and place their hands in a mystical configuration. They were not allowed to look when as the light of God came through the hands, as this could result in blindness. Now, though, I watched the audience of relatives receive the blessing; I could see smiles. I greeted Natasha and my family with a warm embrace. My brother told a dirty joke. I laughed, and then hesitated: I was half a minister.

In *Autobiography of a Schizophrenic Girl* (1951), a girl named Renee describes how she is in school and stops to listen while classmates sing a German song. Suddenly, a "disturbing sense of unreality" comes over her: she no longer recognizes her surroundings, and sees the school as a barracks, with the singing children as prisoners, compelled to sing. She simultaneously sees a wheat field, "yellow vastness, dizzying in the sun," and is filled with anxiety. These elements are "always present" in her "sensations of unreality: illimitable vastness, brilliant light, and the gloss and smoothness of material things."

Renee's description—apart from the anxiety that fills her with "sobs"—encapsulates the mystical state: a luminous vastness alongside the ordinary world of concerns. Renee's anxiety exists in parallel with what may be a perception of the numinous; and her perception of "unreality" may in fact be well-founded, a psychological reality about her school: the notion of children being compelled to sing, by some social order or perhaps a covert threat of punishment for noncompliance. Psychologists have not, to my mind, successfully separated definitions of the pathological from the numinous; visual and auditory perceptions of what my Gurdjieff friend called "the fourth dimension" accompany the mystical encounter, and arguably should not be dismissed as hallucinatory. I identified with Renee's sense of "unreality," of another reality parallel to what psychologist Charles Tart has named "consensus trance," the world of bodies and solid matter and group dynamics and tax deductions and suppressed emotions.

A Friend of All Faiths

Renee was "cured" by her growing connection with (and ultimately love for) her therapist, who, curiously, she came to call "Mama." It was through this attachment that "reality became more real." I did not need Bob to replenish my sense of grounding in the same way, though his admonitions helped check the possibility for abuse of a seeming spiritual brotherhood. I kept my feet on the ground, so to speak, by continuing to function and perform as an ordinary associate in a corporate law firm; continuing in my relationship with Natasha; continuing to embrace my family; and beginning to "ground" myself through regular bodywork in which a shiatsu practitioner whose namely, oddly enough, was Griffin, stimulated pressure points on my arms, legs, and feet, and brought me back to the body.

Griffin also had me stand (again, oddly enough, considering the symbology), on a broomstick. That was to help open up the tiny chakras in the feet, connecting my energy more fully to the Earth. Griffin was an old soul, looked like what an old soul should look like: a woman who could have been in her twenties or eighties. She lived in a tiny apartment near Penn Station with three cats, who were said to temporarily house extra-terrestrials. But she was practical, paid attention to her diet; spoke from experience. "The more you go out of body, the more you need to stay in the body. There is a reason you chose to be in this body. So be in it now."

Her comments had an irrefutable Zen kind of logic. She also gave me physical exercises that made it difficult to rely on my usual defense, a kind of intellectual end-run around everything I was told. I had to squat until my legs trembled, and remain in that painful position until it was unbearable. Griffin had a point: unrelenting pain was an exquisite method to connect with bodily existence. Not that one wanted to rely on pain for sensation—that had its unhealthy aspects; Griffin was simply offering one tool, to be used with reasonable prudence, to increase grounding. In the eternity of a six-minute squat, I could not ignore the pain, nor float into the ether. All I knew was the pain, and that my muscles were trembling.

Griffin stroked and intermittently chatted with one of her cats while she supervised. "When you exit through your head, you become disconnected from your lower chakras. Experience the weight on your legs." She gave me some additional tips, including these: "Stay away from coffee and sugar: both get you high when you're trying to literally come down. Be careful not to meditate too much; maybe stop meditating for a while. Don't focus too much on the experience. Wear red socks when you go to sleep; red has a lower vibration than white; what you're experiencing has a higher vibration than you've been prepared for. But if the experience happens, don't go into fear; you just have to learn control."

Dreams in some tribal cultures do not trigger psychoanalytic interpretation; they are the shaman's divination tool, a way of messaging from Spirit to the human plane. For me, dreaming began to function on multiple levels. Like the cigar that is sometimes a cigar, dreams sometimes were just that—musings, processing information the day, a sense of completion; at other times, voices of the ancestors or the guides; and still at other times, ways for my unconscious to convey information.

I am on a plane or spaceship circling the Earth. People are sitting or going into sleeping tubes. Some are dancing erotically on a podium. The captain announces that cabin pressure will adjust slightly to accommodate the environment; as we pass over Long Island, the airplane smells faintly like a Jewish deli. I go to the back of the ship or plane to the bathroom. A swami sits there, with a man on either side of the front row. The swami asks a political question. I decline to get involved in the conversation. The swami says: "You'll have to stay longer if you want the power to control what is happening here." I leave.

I expected Bob's opening line: "The ship is you." But he then went on to interpret the rest of the dream, again tossing the peel of his cantaloupe into the trash. "Floating above the Earth means: above Mother. You are going out of body to escape her, but also you are still connected to her. You are also encapsulated, a womb with a view. You have a choice between fastening your seat belt, that is remaining conscious, or the capsule, being unconscious. Either implies a commitment. So you reject both. You go to the back of the plane, where the swami is lecturing." He looked down on a pad of paper where he taken notes about the dream. "You don't stay for the swami's lesson; you realize you need to satisfy your primary functions, peeing. The message seems to be that first, you need grounding. Your deepest wish right now is to be hovering over, but not partaking of, the Jewish deli. But that's a problem for you: you need the deli. What could be more grounding, and by the way more spiritual, than a Jewish deli?"

With this thought, he pulled another cantaloupe slice out of a paper and began to eat it. Bob was always pointing out that I need not run to the metaphorical ashram; that I could find the spiritual in the mundane. "Mundus," he commented, "meaning the world. When you reach to the ethers, to outer space, you miss the celebration of life. Read Walt Whitman. The spaceship hovering above the earth is an escape, spirituality an escape, a literal high. You should chop wood, carry water. Or stop and smell the pastrami. There's a five hundred pound man yelling: PASTRAMI! WHAT KINDA BREAD! JEWISH RYE! SOUR PICKLE? FULL DILL! To be in the deli and take it all in, without letting your mind dissect the experience."

I called Nick to tell him Bob had suggested I take six months off of meditation, cut out the spiritual work to gain grounding. The opening had been fast, a bit scary. Nick disagreed with Bob's suggestion. I asked whether Nick had manipulated my experience to create the "white light" experience. He replied: "My love for you was so pure that the energy flowed." The answer felt sincere. But now a wedge existed.

"When I first went out-of-body," Griffin reported while stroking another of her cats, "I saw these little monsters, harpies, rush toward me. Eventually I learned to send them into the Light. Send them love and they move on to a higher level. Then, if you want to get back, all you have to do is say, *I want to be in my body.*"

She assured me that in "traveling," I was merely learning to see other sides of myself. "Your system has been amplified; the body has to adjust." She said that swimming, oatmeal, and sex would be helpful; also, grains ("they're heavier; they bring you back down"), physical exercise and emotional work ("force the first and second chakras to work"), and meat ("has a lower vibration"), Tai Chi and yoga ("integrates the energy harmoniously") could assist. I wore red socks to bed. But while Griffin continued to offer tools to integrate the somewhat extraordinary psychic experiences, my Gurdjieff teacher was not pleased with reports of Nick's head bursting into white light. I sat in her modestly furnished brownstone, filled with hanging copper pots and aging copies of literary magazines.

"Do you want to become a *Superman*," she asked, turning down a page in one of *Tales of Beelzebub*, Gurdjieff's masterpiece. "Is that the final goal of your spiritual quest? Will becoming a trance medium create the necessary conditions for continuation of consciousness after body consciousness drops?" She took a pinch of spices from a bowl at her side-table and filtered the grains through her fingers. "I can always tell when food is intelligently prepared. What is your aim?"

The Gurdjieff Work had its buzzwords like any religion, like the kind of orthodoxy Gurdjieff claimed to supercede and end-run. "Aim" was one of these. My teacher continued with greater intensity. "Is it powers? Do you want to manipulate others?" She raised eyebrows, implying she knew something hidden.

"I am only after truth," I said. "I had a real experience. I am after understanding. I don't have others on Wall Street with whom I can share these openings. What are they, what do they mean, what must I do next to understand."

"You need to prepare yourself before you can receive these kinds of energies. We are servants of these powers, although we may find that if we serve, there can be a place in the work for us." Most unhelpful: *preparation* meant years of these kinds of no-answer conversations, real questions being answered only by grilling me.

A Friend of All Faiths

That week I spoke with my father about the Gurdjieff Work and the practice of being present, not just in a church or synagogue, but in the now. A curious experience unfolded: a cloud of white formed around him, and his body, like Nick's, receded into this tunnel of light. I was entering an altered state of consciousness during a casual conversation with my father. I knew that the sinister interpretation of my Gurdjieff teacher had no basis–that I was not after power or manipulation, but in pursuit of the path shown; and further, that the inability or perhaps disinclination to explain my experience, despite the Work's claim to penetrate these other states of awareness, left me dissatisfied. Further, my Gurdjieff teacher had stated that the Work was "the only game in town," suggesting that leaving the Work would leave life's work unfinished, incomplete, and dissolve the possibility of transcending our petty concerns for something more permanent, stable, and transcendental: a state Gurdjieff termed objective consciousness.

This was the same objectionable proposition of all religious orthodoxy, the thing that divided peoples in the name of God; the notion that one had to follow path X (say "accepting Jesus Christ as your Lord and Savior," or some other formulation) or else suffer eternal damnation, or at least the possibility of missing out of The Truth for some false path. This insinuation marked the end of my formal passage through the Gurdjieff work, although his ideas continued to exert a pull.

Curiously, I began to see this insistence on the part of the self-appointed shepherds of the Gurdjieff transmission to an exclusive link to truth, repeated in an emerging dynamic with Nick. As he left the mansion and moved into a smaller, basement apartment, began to "channel Mary" more regularly for me, and to an ever-smaller circle of prayer meeting attendees, he started insisting that those who left his company were succumbing to "Satan." That, combined with a rigid insistence on constructing our universal ministry (pursuant to "Her" instructions) in a sectarian (Catholic) format, was the beginning of the end.

But a few more threads needed attending before the final unraveling. The effect of Nick's channels were mesmerizing, not the least because he purported to channel "Her," and the fact that I subjectively had the experience, irrespective of Nick's talents and shortcomings, of a powerful, alive yet disincarnate super-being who knew me intimately, reading me psychologically almost better than a trained professional named Bob.

Griffin helped me understand and digest some of the more unpleasant psychic experiences, because these intensified too. Griffin warned: "Once your third eye is open, you'll see the bad as well as the good. You may be walking down the street and see a demon, or see death, or a spirit of murder."

"On the other hand," I said, "you may walk into a church and see angels."

"That's right. But you can't always control what you see."

In the healing session, she put a quartz crystal, about the size of a fist, on my chest, and another between my knees. She put a third in my right hand. These, she said, were to open up "unconditional love" in my chakras. The only way to release the dark entities, she said, was to "send them into the light," with love. Cursing them or growing angry at them would only allow them to sap more energy.

After the session, she commented on the way I always lay in the same position when she did my back: face to one side, with one arm up, over my hand, and the other arm by my side. "Your body is creating a swastika," she said. "You know that the swastika was not invented by the Nazis. It was an esoteric symbol in India, much as the Seal of Solomon. You may have been a member of that order. Hmmm.... I'm getting that you were a monk in a former life, maybe in India, and that you are familiar with exorcism work," she said.

She looked at the glass next to the healing table. "Get rid of this water. It holds the entities we released." We poured the water down the sink.

I asked her what was happening when she spent about twenty minutes concentrating, while holding her arms over my legs. "I was getting the impression of a hoofed animal," she said. "I was trying to remove it, but it was stubborn. That's because part of you was holding

Michael H. Cohen

onto it. I'm trying to get rid of it, but some part of you is curious and wants it to stay."
"What does it mean?"
"The hoofed animal is compulsive—it's them acting out through you." She paused. "By the way, where were you last night?"
I replied: "Cafe Iguana."

"Did you succeed in removing it?" I asked Griffin.
"What do you feel right now?" she asked in return.
I searched my body for information. "My legs feel numb."
Griffin nodded. "That's the goat trying to reattach itself to your legs." She stared at me intently. "Go look in the mirror and tell me what you see."
I looked. My eyes were glazed. It looked as if "no-one was home," inside.
"Right," Griffin said. "You're half out-of-body right now. That's why you feel lifeless, dazed."
"Well, how do I get back in?"
"Meditate," she said. "Send love to that entity and ask that whatever good spirits are with you help send it on. It will dissolve into white light and ascend into the light." We did a quick meditation to do this. I kept seeing different beautiful women pop into view; each had only half a body—there was nothing from the neck down. Griffin added: "That's how you know they're harpies," she said. Harpies were what she called the annoying spirits. "They have no eyes, or no body; but in all other respects they look normal."
"Now I see a priest with a white hat and robe. He's chanting mantras."
"One of your guides," she said. "Thank him."
The numbness dissipated. I could feel my legs again. "You've got to be careful," Griffin said. "These entities will try to have astral sex with you."
I told Griffin about different experiences I had had, especially at night.
"All these experiences are the harpies trying to get your attention. They feed off your energy. Just keep on sending them into the light. Keep radiating that love."
I told her about the levitating office chair. "That's not uncommon," she said. "One day I saw my cat levitating in air as if held by the neck.... Another time, I came home to find one of the lamps knocked off the table. The lamp was on, but not plugged in. That was the time my roommate told me, 'that's it; I've had enough.' She couldn't take it anymore, and moved out." She laughed. "I'm glad I finally have a client who appreciates what I'm doing!"

Griffin offered another perspective to the opening of consciousness I was rapidly experiencing. By "meditate," she meant going into a quiet space of contentment and love. Nick conceptualized meditation as a state in which one could contact deceased relatives, entities, Divine Mother, space beings, and others. Were these one and the same? I was unfamiliar with all the rungs on the ladder. But Griffin combined safe and respectful, body-oriented healing work with her notions. Nick of course had a different take on the harpies: "The hoofed animal is attached to the Satanic in Christian mythology. But do not fear. What is attached to your consciousness is only a residue of what existed. Your prayer has cleared it. When you have intercourse, any demonic principalities attached to the other person can enter and become entrenched in your aura."
"What's the difference between demonic and regular bad entities?" I asked.
"Many of the astral tramps are simply mischievous. They'll appear to you in dreams or as voices merely to get your attention, to draw on your energy. They will annoy you and sap your strength, but they won't do much damage." He took a breath. "A demonic principality, on the other hand, is the father of the dark spirit. It will be much more difficult to expel. The demonic principalities are very powerful. Lust, greed, murder, these are among them. They are Satan's henchmen."
I found the reference odd. Nick seemed to notice my skeptical look, and added: "Stay away from dark places. These Satanic entities can enter these dark people and attack you.

A Friend of All Faiths

They're attracted to the light."

"You mean it's nothing personal, it's something hanging out somewhere, seeing the light, and wanting to snuff it out."

"Exactly. The same thing happens at work. The darkness in people there will make them try especially hard to rattle or punish you during your assignments. And when you're in a dark place, these negative entities will go and get fifty of their friends and attach themselves to you. Let's say you go into the bar with one or two negative entities around you, they'll grab their friends and get fifty more. Unless removed, they'll eventually destroy you. In cases of alcoholism, domestic violence, arguments, the darkness grows thicker and thicker. So keep the focus on God. By practicing the presence of God, the light grows stronger."

Nick's comments about the entities made sense from a certain perspective, though his God/Devil dichotomy was inconsistent with my view of the world. Fortunately, while Nick could be authoritative when focusing on 'phenomena,' he had a humorous side. He said that one member of his prayer group had complained that her dishwasher was possessed; another felt someone had 'entered' his photograph during the meeting; another found it critical to let Nick know that he woke every morning at five and began his day by cleaning the toilet bowl. Nick laughed raucously on relating these anecdotes.

I asked what advice he had given the woman with the possessed dishwasher.

He said: "There's something wrong with the on/off button!" As to the second: "This woman wants to build a grotto to the Blessed Virgin on her front lawn; but the message I received from Spirit was that she needs to soak her dentures longer."

Another person had come complaining of a spirit that stuffed his nose.

"Release it!" Nick had commanded.

"How?" the man had asked.

Nick had replied: "By blowing vigorously into a Kleenex."

I had started out as a curious observer of Nick's prayer group but now was drawn more and more into my own meditation experience. Meditation was revealing worlds I could neither describe nor report in any way credible to those unfamiliar with visioning from their own meditation experience. For example, I began to regularly see the screen of my mind blanketed with scintillating purple. One day, I opened my eyes slowly. I could still see the shimmering purple before me, flecked with gold. The experiences grew still more powerful.

Natasha had an icon of Mary on her bookshelf, one handed down through the generations in her family. As such, it carried the vibration of many prayers. "Pray to Her," Natasha said. She brought the icon close to me. "Kiss the icon, and ask Her for protection." I did so. Natasha and I had a long, honest talk. I had the impression that without the trance, the different voice, the change in the air, the unusual language, Natasha, in her way, was channeling the Divine Mother to me. I began to see the divine everywhere.

I paid my final visit to my Gurdjieff teacher. I told her all that had happened and sought guidance in a final attempt at reconciliation. We discussed self-remembering. "Can you do it now?" she challenged. As I slid into Witness consciousness, her face melted into white light. The whole room began fading into this matrix of vibrating dots of light. This was not something she wanted to hear.

I decided that despite Bob's advice, it would be good to have a quiet place to increase my daily meditation practice and more thoroughly understand these experiences and openings. I wandered down Broadway and ended up at the Church of Jesus Christ of Latter Day Saints. One of my roommates during college had been a Mormon, and we had attended services there. I had a pleasant memory of the experience, and especially the curious hymns to our heavenly Mother. Now, as I entered the church, a smiley-faced "Elder" introduced himself, spoke about my obvious intelligence and sincerity and took me upstairs.

"I'm just looking for a place to meditate," I said.

The word *meditate* seem to confuse him. "This here is Lord Jesus." He showed me a floor-to-ceiling portrait. I examined a handsome man with long hair. "And this is how he looked when he appeared to our community in 600 B.C."

"Yes, thank you, but do you have a quiet room where…"

"You see, the descendants of Joseph—are you familiar with Joseph?"

"Yes, I am, but–"

"Well, his descendants left Jerusalem and founded communities in America in 600 B.C. and again in 400 A.D. Jesus Christ appeared to them and founded His church with them. Now then, coming over to this painting"–he led me in further–"we see the prophet writing their history on gold tablets which they buried." He went on: how they were destroyed by wicked tribes, how the tablets were discovered by Joseph Smith in 1823, when an angel of God led him to the site. I was led to a room with about thirty plush and crimson seats, a private viewing room. "This will just take a few minutes," he finished, as I eased into a plush chair, figuring it would not hurt to watch a movie or two. The film showed a handsome, all-American man—with pearly-white teeth—saddling a horse on a beautiful farm, all the while talking to me—personally—about Jesus. Just like the Elder, he seemed to know how sincere and intelligent I was. And how troubled, confused and disturbed I was by life's many problems. Fortunately, he told me, there was a solution. All I had to do was "accept" Jesus, and everything was going to be peachy-keen. I, too, could have pearly-white teeth and a wonderful tan and a big, brown horse, cooking beans on an open fire with the smell of leather and manure behind me.

Speaking of which, the Elder and a missionary sat one row behind me. I was sure they had seen the film dozens, if not hundreds, of times, but they watched it as eagerly as if it were new. The missionary was a fresh-faced kid from Northern Utah who had been in New York three days. Sure, the message was Love, but Love meant more than becoming Our Lady of Perpetual Happiness. Feeling good in some kind of mass hypnotic trance was not my way to God.

The Elder talked to me a little about Jesus. He insisted on my filling out a card with my name and address. After some wrangling, I politely wiggled out.

I visited the health care service at the New York Stock Exchange to check on this feeling of 'being breathed.' I was wearing my best Wall Street suit. The physician, a graying man with owl-shaped, wire glasses and a pointy, gray goatee, said: "So, young fellow, what seems to be ailing you?"

"I have a friend who does séances. When we meditate together, his face dissolves into white light. I'm not crazy … I work at a law firm down the street…."

"Are you eating right?" His voice was warm. I nodded. "Sleeping okay?"

"So so."

"I'd like to take a few tests." He made me walk a few steps, touch my nose, the test the police give for drunk driving. Then: "Lie down, pull down your trousers, cough. Again. " He performed a few more tests, then listened with his stethoscope. "Well son, your heartbeat is normal. Blood pressure, normal. Neurologically, normal. I find nothing the matter. My conclusion is: you're hyperventilating. Too much oxygen in the brain is why you're feeling light, dissociated, tingling."

"Then it's a matter of science, not mystical experience."

"Absolutely!" He pushed up his wire glasses. "The classic remedy is to breathe into a brown paper bag for one minute. You get more carbon dioxide and balance." I thanked him. As he escorted me out, he patted me on the shoulder: "Don't worry, you're not alone. This sort of thing is common on Wall Street."

Nick began 'channeling' personal messages from "Divine Mother" for me. The first was short: "Never fear that which comes/I am the fortress, Sentinel One." Then Nick did a Tarot reading for me. He asked: "What is happening with Mike right now?" He drew the Two of

Pentacles, which shows a man balancing or juggling with an infinity sign. That, Nick said, came from Divine Mother. "You're sitting on the fence, she says. You're asking: is it real? Is it all in my mind? Don't experiment with me, she says. I am real."

We meditated in Nick's kitchen; it was actually a short counter next to the refrigerator that set off the living room in his one-bedroom, basement apartment.

"What exactly are you feeling right now?" Nick asked.

"Like the chair is not on the ground."

"Right. Theresa is here. She's guiding us through this work. The little way to God. That's the way in which it is to be presented. In child-like faith. The kingdom of God is within ... the child." I felt light under my feet, up my legs and my spine.

"You're the channel today," Nick said. "You're the one that is processing everything that I'll be saying. And you're channeling it now into that which is written. That's why they're working through your whole body. They need to have it perfectly balanced and clear. They move it up the legs and into the back, because I can feel three people doing it. It looks, Mike, as if they have a screen, and they're taking all the impurities out of your body now, that what you're hearing will be clear, not distorted or colored by what your own mind would say or think."

My body was growing numb. I was going out-of-body. I began seeing images with my eyes closed. "An old woman in a wheelchair, bent over, in a hospital."

"You may have been there," Nick said. "You may have astrally projected to that person. Someone who said, 'I need help,' and you were there."

"What was I doing?" I asked, part of my mind cognitively processing.

"Just being present with her," Nick responded.

"Now I see a tall figure coming down a staircase," I said, as a new image came.

"What color," Nick asked.

"Dark. A man. Tall, a giant."

"Your shadow side," Nick said. "We're practicing the presence of God right now. As Brother Lawrence said. We're here, but with God."

"My body feels so still," I said.

"Right. 'Be still, and know that I am God.' We have no worries or fears. They're just an illusion. 'How can I record if I don't know what to say?' Divine Mother just said. She wants you to pick up *Whispers From Eternity* from the bookshelf and read out loud from page 51."

I did so and read: "O Krishna... Lotus of Love ... I am one of thy lost calves which followed thy flowered footprints on the shoals of time. Listening to the melody of thy flute of wisdom, I am following the middle path of calm activity by which thou has last led many through the portals of the dark past. .. O divine Krishna, lead us back to thy fold of everlasting freedom. O Krishna, thou reigns in the heart throne of each knower of thy love."

Nick then began:

> And as Joseph Smith was given the tablets of gold, so I put into your hands those same tablets etched in the wisdom of Moses and the prophets. For as I have come this day I have brought with Me those of the command of Ashtar. I and the living presence and the living flame. For that which in the middle you, of the orange, is the eternal flame of Spirit and consciousness, that which has been ignited is only the beginning of that which is coming, in a greater floodwater of truth and light. Those particular aspects of the Akashic are being burned in the fire of divine wisdom.... There is a great beacon of light now that begins to shine from your heart, Michael. You must not be looking back into those aspects of yourself to critically analyze what has been done before, but to keep it to the ever-present now of today, and the now. Be always present with people when you are speaking. Remember that those who are abusive to you have been brought into your consciousness as a realistic estimation of your own worth at that particular moment.

The language was poetic. It grabbed me. I also sat with the premise that the Blessed Virgin would be channeling as Divine Mother to a Jewish lawyer and instruct him to read a passage from an Indian saint. Moreover, the Catholic Church went through a long process to 'verify' and 'validate' sightings of Mary, yet could object that Nick was putting himself on a par with others such as Bernadette of Lourdes. Did saintliness have to accompany mystical experience? Further, were I to admit that I experienced Mary speaking with me, others would probably think that I had converted. Yet, true to the ecumenical perspective of the Seminary (God is One), I was able to open to these experiences and develop a relationship with a nonphysical being that appeared to me as Mary, without having to accept any orthodox, swallow any dogma, join any church or either adopt or reject any specific belief system. I could also suspend judgment about the requirement of saintliness. I simply had a relationship with a being I experienced as Mary just as I did with Nick or Natasha or the rabbi or someone in a physical body.

You are unique. There is not another like you. And as you have been crucified as Jesus the Christ was crucified upon Golgotha, the place of the skull, there cannot be that which is the resurrection, My son, of the mind, and the body and spirit into the highest dimensions of the Queen of heaven and earth, until there is the crucifixion of ego. For the ego is de-compartmentalized within many systems and beliefs, but the only one that is true rings forth from My fingers to your ear, the eternal Mother.

For the eyes of many are upon you, not only of the highest frequencies and vibration, but also those of the lower world infiltrated with that which is ego, lust, and murder. For this is a great scheme that is also taking place in the world, where the currency of the world will become one currency, and there will be a great upheaval in the hearts of many. For Anti-Christ spirit is permeating the very core of this society. In the numbers, not in the philosophy, or psychology, but in the individual numbers of those who are turning further and further away from the truth of universal spirit.

We had many channeling sessions in which incoming information seemed attuned to my idiosyncratic queries, hopes, fantasies perhaps, quest. But if the giver of information beyond the personal ego was pure, the channel was not. Nick could Hear and I could not; he had the gift and I did not. Our ministry was inherently tainted with this hierarchical power dynamic. In fact, over time, 'Mary' had instructions for our ministry, and if my logical mind disagreed with these instructions, Nick would flag me as disobeying the Mother of the Universe and not simply disagreeing with a person named Nick. Hence the potential tyranny of all channels, all religions, began, over time, to repeat itself in my honest, good faith, interfaith ministry with Nick. Another issue was the way everything was framed in specifically Catholic verbiage (combined mysteriously with information about 'space beings'), while I needed a more universal language. Nick preached simplicity, humility, child-like faith; yet he could not reconcile the orthodoxy implicit in his understanding of Mary, and my profound encounters with this being.

Over months, I also began to receive channeled messages, through Nick, from a being I identified as Jesus not only because this was the way he identified himself, but also because of tremendous upwelling of love I experienced when he came through, as the masculine polarity of the loving presence I identified as 'Mary.' Again the presence came through as a relationship, my heart to that being's, a great understanding, unity awareness, unmarred by theological niceties. Nobody came with a punitive demand that I 'accept' or 'embrace' or 'believe;' there were simply moments of experiencing a being from another dimension, great in wisdom and love, connected to my heart, beyond the theology of any time and place, beyond identification with my body or belief system. Faith mattered less than openness to relationship. My own channeling began as I learned to relax and trust the words coming through me. Of course, I suspected then, as I firmly know now, that one's own mental and emotional predispositions, biases, and personality quirks influence whatever one may take to be a "pure" or "inspired" message.

In Indian traditions, the sacred energy is said to be coiled at the base of the spine like a serpent which, when awakened, sends trillions of volts of spiritual 'electricity' up the spine, purifying lifetimes of accumulated *samskaras* (impressions) and leading the seeker toward liberation. I began having experiences of such numinous electricity traveling up my spine and overwhelming my sleep with brilliant light, the 'light of a thousand suns' as the crown chakra is called in Hindu texts. I wondered if I was going insane. I telephoned the Center for Spiritual Emergencies in Menlo Park, California but could not reach a volunteer. Then I called Nick. He felt the energy was moving faster than what my body could absorb, and recommended that I "think of Her before going to sleep." I began practicing the Rosary. Through the practice, I found a way to connect with the presence with whom I was connecting in meditation.

Outside life continued normally; I worked on deals at the firm, and meanwhile published a book, *Creative Writing for Lawyers*, which I creatively promoted. One promotion involved selling the book at a Wall Street haberdashery. "Writing and suits are a good fit," I quipped to reporters. The book was favorably reviewed in the *New York Observer, New York Law Journal*, and *New York Post*. 'Divine Mother' decided that I should help Nick write a book about our experiences. On a trip back from my visit with Nick, Natasha asked: "How's your book coming?"

"I'm not doing the writing. Neither is Nick."

"Say no more." And with that, the subject was closed.

Over ensuing months, 'Divine Mother' or 'Mary' gave us numerous messages through Nick pertaining to the ministry we were to build. One of these messages concerned my growing dissatisfaction with the law firm, and growing split within me between my work there and these inner revelations.

> *I am not pleased with, and I am not happy about the people that are in the positions of authority. I wished and prayed that you would understand that it is your ego that has attached yourself to this position, and that in surrender to Me, and believe Me, I want only the good for you, you will be finding your rest in Me. It is impossible to do My work and be in that which is the semblance of disorder and chaos, as in Babylon. For you know what the word Babylonian means. Babel. That is what's going on in the tower of your office. Babbling. Rattling. Senselessness. The essence and core of Me is absent. And where I am absent, there is no life. Regain your consciousness. Open the eyes of your third eye. And recognize the bliss and peace of your Mother.*

This message was accurate in encapsulating my difficulties with the lack of fulfillment in the firm. But on another level, the message made no sense in light of how hard I had worked just to get an offer from such a high-powered firm. I had followed all the valued impulses of education and achievement—and was trying to fulfill desire to make a contribution to the world, a desire that stemmed from my family environment and values.

Several evenings later, Natasha and I were talking. Spontaneously, I popped into a state of self-remembering that lasted ten or fifteen minutes. I was viewing myself from another angle. I called my friend from the Gurdjieff group.

His response was simply: "That's great. Just keep doing what you're doing." I began seeing flashes of purple everywhere, light that intensified in the channeling sessions and meditation.

Bob was not impressed. "You can't *will* yourself into bliss," he insisted. "Or sainthood. That's ego. Krishnamurti was asked at age fourteen to be the Second Christ and he said *no, that's not for me.* Since you haven't been asked to be the Second Christ, you must walk the road with humility and patience." He paused, and took another tack. "Someone asked Rilke whether to become a poet. Rilke responded: *Live the question into the future.* But you're pushing. You're trying to live the answer, not the question. Take one day a time."

While taking a walk in Central Park at twilight, I suddenly came upon a man who seemed, at a distance, to be psychologically disturbed. This man stared at another man at a bench and yelled: "Do you have a problem?"

"Yeah," replied the second. "I'm paranoid-schizophrenic. Do *you* have a problem!"

"Yeah," replied the first. "I'm psychotic. I killed someone."

"Want to kill me?" replied the second. "I have a knife."

The sky grew darker. When I came home, I called Nick.

"You have to be careful where you walk," he said. Your consciousness is raising to such a high level, that negative spirits are attracted to you and are entering these people. The entities see the light and are attracted to it. They want to snuff it out. You're a threat to them. The entities can enter these lowlifes and cause them to attack you. As you come more into the consciousness of that which is God, you have to be careful where you walk. Avoid dark places. Be vigilant."

"Isn't Divine Mother protecting me?"

"That's like putting an alcoholic in the bar and locking him in. All the protection in the world won't do any good unless you choose your environment. Stay away from those places. Then you will be safe. Banish fear. She is here with you."

"The virtue of the Zen masters," Bob said, crossing his legs full-lotus on the vegetarian 'leather' chair, "is that their knowledge comes from within. Through a long process of self-knowledge, they develop humility. But the only time you feel humility is when you're thrown in the deep end. You think it's mind over matter: 'I can handle this.' Then you get these pre-psychotic experiences." He was talking about the anxiety with the breathing, the experience 'self-remembering' with Natasha, Nick's face dissolving into light, and other such phenomena, all of which frightened me. "You're playing with your psyche," he continued, tossing a cantaloupe skin toward me, "without respecting it. You haven't been trained in this, and your learning doesn't translate into this realm. You can master Nick and make a lot of money, but you don't know what you're projecting and what you're receiving. There's a sorcerer's apprentice quality: you're the apprentice, which means you can really hurt yourself. Why would you want to do that?"

He gave the example of Jacob wrestling with the angel. "Jacob saw the angels walking up the ladder, not flying. You have to walk before you can fly. You're not giving yourself the time to digest these experiences. You keep wanting more and more. You need to use your ego: 'I'm thirty years old and I have plenty of time to learn the mysteries of the universe.' Your spiritual life is making you afraid; that means your eyes are too big for your stomach. Just remember, thinking doesn't make it so." He looked at me intensely; I squirmed with the contradictions.

"If this was right for you right now, why would you be so upset?" Bob shifted, mirrored my movements. "Not that spiritual discipline doesn't bring transformation; it can. But we're dealing with *hubris*. Remember when Moses took his staff and beat the rock? He wasn't allowed to enter the Promised Land. You can say: 'I demand that everything be open to me.' That and a dollar will get you on the subway. This is coming a little too easy. You're confusing intellectual progress with emotional progress. You had that dream about the spaceship and walking away from the guru to urinate. But you don't listen to yourself. You've got to learn to piss in the pot to be a citizen of the world. Do you believe that?"

"No. I skipped a grade."

"And you want to do it again. But now it puts you on a slippery slope. Also, if you're simply taking commands from *Divine* Mother"—he always put in the emphasis on *Divine*, whereas I always put in on *Mother*—"you're simply replacing the bad, human mother with the good cosmic one. You're trying to be the good son, a good vessel for God, but you're ready to meditate on this yet."

"I feel like I'm floating even now," I said, feeling spacey.

"You're resisting what I'm saying. There's an early, deep wound in you. The Divine Mother idea, or being, has in part come into your life to repair that wound. Otherwise you wouldn't be so receptive."

HOME

I tried to interest a friend from the law firm in meditation. He said: "I don't want anything that ties me in to God." My friendships were dissolving, too, along with my interest in Mr. Hansen's international calls. One day at the law firm, in the middle of a conference call, I began experiencing someone sending waves of vibrating energy around my head and body, as if someone had dipped me into an ultrasound.

If I had reported this to the health services physician, he probably would have sent me for a psychiatric consult. And then the psychiatrist, like the physician, on taking inventory, would have found 'nothing wrong:' I was not depressed or anxious (not more than the average Wall Street workaholic) or suffering from any pathological diagnosis. There was an irony in my increasing receptivity to mystical experience while working in a Wall Street law firm; and the concomitant insistence of conventional health care that such disorientation could only signal dysfunction.

In fact, I was functioning at a high level at the firm and cognitively curious about my experiences—and indeed, responding (albeit sometimes defensively) to Bob's psychological review and guidance. And I was finding a failure of guidance from institutionalized religion, colleagues, and most others I knew, who were clearly wedded to 'ordinary' reality and fearful of non-ordinary reality. On the other hand, my guide to this strange world was Nick, clearly flawed and sometimes intemperate. The irony deepened: during junior year of college at Columbia University, I had worked as a legislative aide for a New York City Councilman. One of my roles involved responding to constituent letters. One constituent wrote that he was being 'bombarded by rays from new neighbors' with extraterrestrial connections, and thus being 'forced to engage in excessive autoerotic stimulation.'

At the time this seemed funny. Yet now, here I was experiencing states that others, no doubt feeling as superior to me as I did to the 'lunatic' who wrote the letter to the Councilman, might, in their mask of 'normalcy,' superiority and reductionism, deride as 'delusional' or 'hallucinatory' 'symptoms' of trouble.

Neither the 'ordinary' nor the 'extraordinary' worlds provided guidance. I was caught between the worlds. And so I called Tanya for assistance.

"Be careful," she warned. "Be discriminating. I've gone all over seeking different channels for advice and now my money and health are wasted."

"Why so many channels? How can you tell which spirit is which?" I asked.

"Take my advice," she urged. "Get out of the business."

But her suggested remedy was too easy, as much a panacea as that of my Gurdjieff teacher. And I was invested in seeing this journey to the end—remaining in relationship with whomever was speaking to me; not running away.

Nick had his own interpretations of my growing discomfort. "If what is happening to you is uncomfortable," he claimed, "it's not Divine Mother, but an entity of darkness. The Holy Spirit is gentle."

That weekend, while lying down, I felt myself floating. I heard an internal voice: "the spirits want to express themselves." Inspired, I went to the computer and whipped off a six-page piece. The piece was satirical. As someone who had attended the Iowa Writers' Workshop, I was curious about the Muse; some students at the Workshop had tried a séance to gain 'inspiration.' If Nick could channel such a range of beings, he surely could include the Muse. I called him.

"Would you like to try something?" Nick asked in reply.

"Sure."

"Close your eyes. In the name of Jesus Christ," Nick said with great authority, "I demand that the spirit that manifested in that writing manifest itself now in Michael's consciousness." He repeated this several times. "Now look with your third eye. What do you see?"

I concentrated. "I don't really see anything," I said. "Well ... this sounds silly, but I have the vaguest impression of a figure wearing a dark hood."

"Yes," Nick said. "Hood means occult. A dark spirit."

Nick went into tongues. I listened on the phone from my desk at the firm.

"I'm going to give you a prayer to say," Nick came back, "when you feel yourself under assault. Can you write this down? St. Michael the Archangel, defend us in battle, be our defense against the wickedness and snares of the devil, and do Thou, O Prince, of the heavenly hosts, by the power of God, cast into hell Satan and all other evil spirits who prowl about the world seeking the ruin of souls. Most sacred heart of Jesus, have mercy on us. Immaculate Heart of Mary, pray for me. All ye angels and saints make intercession in my petition to repel to the netherworld all spirits of the occult and witchcraft. I am now in the light of Christ and the blood of Jesus Christ cleanses me from all powers of darkness. Amen." He paused. "Wow," he said. "I want a copy of that. Everything after 'have mercy on us' came directly from Her."

"It came from Divine Mother?" I asked—we had jumped from the Muse to occult spirits and back to Divine Mother. Nick was nonplussed.

"Yes. The first part is part of the tradition; the rest she just channeled right through me." We said the prayer together, doing our exorcism over the law firm telephone. When the exorcism ended, Nick asked: "Now what do you feel?"

"Good," I said, "except that my legs feel light and hollow. It's as if the chair is being lifted off the ground." It was if the chair was beginning to move beneath.

"You must watch your curiosity." He went into tongues. "They're attracted to your curiosity, and you are seeking an experience. You must seek only God."

"Is this unusual?" I asked, surprised at how intense this was becoming.

"Padre Pio was lifted up out of his bed. They found him in the morning thrown across his cell. His face was covered with bruises—beaten by Satanic agents."

"How did he survive?"

"Divine Mother intervened and saved his life."

"What happened to bring it on?"

"He took it on, the karma of others. He soaked it up, to prevent the negative energy from harming others. He was a great servant of God."

"Will that happen to me?" It was a natural question, since I had felt the chair starting to lift—unless I had imagined it. But reducing my experience to imagination felt no more satisfying than explaining it away as an excess of carbon dioxide.

"You're not Padre Pio," Nick concluded, "and neither am I."

"Why does Nick have to be the one channeling?" Bob challenged. "Why can't you channel for yourself? Why does Nick have to be the one dispensing the instructions?"

It was Bob who tipped me off to the growing power struggle with Nick over who could channel authoritatively, and the dangers of dependence on Nick for 'spiritual direction.' Defensively, I gave Bob some spiritual answer about divine will. I also reported that Divine Mother had said—through Nick—that I needed purification.

Bob warned: "You're setting up Divine Mother as a potential sledgehammer for your being. Every time you go to Nick, you're asking, 'is this the time I'll be abandoned,' and at the same, 'is this the time I'll find out I'm the chosen one."

"And yet," I shielded, "I'm starting to get messages myself...as I'm ready."

Bob was firm: "But then when you get another message from 'Divine Mother' that you're not ready yet, you get shot down from the grandiosity, and also feel guilty because you knew you were being grandiose. It's like Adam in the garden, he's hiding from God, but there's nowhere to hide. My message to you, from *undivine Bob*, is to look between the psychological instead of the scriptural lines."

The experiences continued to intensify; neither Nick, nor Bob, nor Griffin, nor Natasha could completely put the puzzle together.

"Fear comes into your aura on an astral level," Nick said. "These entities are trying to scare you. They know you better than you know yourself. But when you say the prayer, they have no power over you. Say it until they get the message."

"Does meditation help?" I asked.

"Meditation helps. Reading spiritual books helps. From now on, saturate the mind with God. Then you will be filled with godly feelings. But also, know what these entities are. Know the hold they have on you. Know what they elicit in your heart." He paused. "You may need to say the prayer over and over for an hour."

But at 3:30 in the morning, I heard someone from the tip of my bed say, "it's your case, counselor." I woke up and said, "Huh?" Natasha continued sleeping.

The next day, Nick interpreted the experience as an interaction from an entity I had picked up from someone on the street. "Whenever you're with people," Nick said, "surround yourself with white light and the blood of Christ. This dispels the darkness. And we'll been praying, curing, doing more exorcisms."

Changing subjects, I told him I had received my bonus from the law firm.

"Good," Nick said. "Now you need to give parts of it away. If you hoard it, the Universe will take everything from you. If you give it away, it will multiply." I was skeptical. "You have to have faith," Nick said. "Whatever you put to the Universe comes back to you. It's a spiritual law. More real than the laws you're studying."

To have some gauge of the range of experiences, I continued to look to the individual lives of the saints profiled in *Butler's*. St. Theresa, one of Nick's "patron saints," may have come from a family of *conversos*, Jews who had converted to Christianity in outward form so as to avoid the terrors of the Spanish Inquisition. Her writings struck a chord. For example, she said she first embarked on a holy life more from fear of hell than from love of God. She also wrote about God taking one's consciousness by storm. *Till now,* Theresa wrote, *I had identified with myself; now God took over.* She stressed her reliance on God's grace rather than her own efforts. She mentioned the importance of recognizing her own inner fragmentation, rather than simply forcing herself to focus on "holy thoughts" as a means to create unity. She said one had to recognize the fragmentation, 'I am a divided self,' rather than assuming one was, as the outset, capable of leading a holy life. The Catholic saints provided useful working models.

Then again, if Nick had been from another tradition, I probably would have been drawn to a culturally different model of experiencing the divine. And the experiences continued to intensify. When Nick and I next emerged from a particularly long session, I looked at Nick and saw everything around him dissolve into one light, as if he were receding in time down a white tunnel. His face looked like that of a child. The features thinned, the eyes looked at mine with the love of a son to a father.

"What are you seeing right now?" Nick asked. I told him that I could see and feel him in another time and place as my son. Nick replied that I was experiencing with the phenomenon of "transformations," in which one looks at another with the "third eye," and begins to see karmic relationships, the relationships from a past life or past lives. He added his own impressions. "I'm seeing your face is changing: a rabbi with a long, white beard. It is somewhere in Poland, perhaps several centuries ago. You were my father. That was the bond. You taught me Jewish learning. I am repaying the karmic debt. You helped develop me spiritually in a former life, and I am helping you in this lifetime." Nick channeled:

Shout loudly from all that is within you, that God the creator of Israel and the creator of that which is the Chosen People has rejoiced in this day that you have come together in an attitude of adoration and praise. For My light is becoming clearer within the lips and in the tongue and within the very consciousness of your being. You have come very far My children into that which is the Fatima message, the message of surrender to your Eternal Mother and the mother of all mankind. Work therefore hard this day to understand the deep mysteries of My holy immaculate conception. For within this Immaculate Conception has been born to you the Christ consciousness of your life. Remember that all things do not happen in a moment's time. And that each thing that you do, and each particular exercise and discipline that you carry out is do be done in an attitude of surrender. I have formed you and molded you as I have molded you upon My hand. It is all to divine purpose that you have been brought together as father and son in the unity of the Divine Mother.....

Your consciousness cannot comprehend, My son, that which is in store for you. For this is the base of the iceberg. The ego consciousness in which you have been forming your life for the last thirty years is not be to be confused with the moving of how I have taken the railroad of your consciousness by storm. For it appears that it has come to you in a period of accelerated vision. It has not been accelerated, My son. It is the picture frame of your life that I have impregnated that you will see that which is the Immaculate within the landscape of your consciousness.... In that golden ball of the reflection of My maternal heart, I have imprinted Myself upon you, not only in your psychological being. It has been brought to My attention that you have been suffering from that which is headaches. These headaches are that which I am engrooving within you, a change of the karmatic features of your character formation from the beginning of time. Your mind is more and more receptive to the eternal ring of the Tibetan bells that ring the universal Christ consciousness for you.

Nick and I began having regular meetings in which we performed a communion service at home followed by channeling. Sometimes others came; it seemed to be the beginning of a ministry. One night, we did a Tarot reading. I asked for guidance, and pulled a card: The Lovers. Nick looked at it and said: "Natasha."

I pulled another card: the Two of Wands (a man turning his back on the world). Nick said: "Separation." Just then the phone rang. It was Natasha. What did this mean?

I was living two parallel lives: one, the Wall Street attorney, busily coordinating legal research, documents and international conference calls, doing the grunt-work and strategizing to keep hundred-million-dollars deals alive; two, the mystic and intuitive, diving into trance, working with therapeutic hypnotic stories and metaphor, or simply staring off to receive revelation. I had two business cards: one as attorney and another as hypnotherapist.

I began to transition off work from the Wall Street firm and changed to a medium-sized, but still intense, litigation practice in midtown. I was now a litigation associate. A new partner, who was pregnant, insisted on working through the night. At four a.m. she was still asking for fresh research to go into the brief that was due at nine the next morning. I felt like the firm owned me: an indentured servitude disguised as a high-paying, prestigious job. In response I took my lunch in a local synagogue and tried to meditate, but God seemed far away: I could not sit still and focus. Yet, the awakened energy was moving through my body with such force that I would take bathroom breaks, sit on the toilet at the new law firm, and let my body jiggle up and down as I engaged in "breath of fire" (a rapid in-and-out breath) to release the energy. Once sitting on the toilet eyes closed, and I saw all the veins in my hand--an experience of internal (or x-ray) vision.

I spoke to a colleague about a brief, and saw his aura light up with yellow; when the conversation shifted to spirituality, the aura turned purple. My friend mentioned that he was trying to write a spiritual book, and I saw an entity flash to his left-a spiritual guide. A nose, eyes, and mouth, a whole face-were clearly distinguishable. At night I began traveling to different realms--medieval Japan, ancient Rome, the Civil War. My 'third eye' was exploding with energy.

I visited a friend, whose suburban home was on sacred native American Indian land, and channeled an entire tribe, spontaneously bursting into "hey-ya-ho, wey, hey, hey-ya-ho"--we both experienced the spirits dancing and drumming in a circle around us. I had left Wall Street but nonetheless continued my psychic opening.

A videotape called *The Lost Years of Jesus* purports to pick up where the gospels are silent. The video claims that during the time Jesus was between twelve and thirty, he traveled through India, Persia and the ancient worlds mastering Buddhism and practices of many religious traditions. This information, while entirely speculative, increased my appreciation for 'Mary' and 'Jesus' as having universal appeal outside the specific rubric of Christianity, among a pantheon of beings such as Krishna, in a pluralistic acceptance of many religious traditions in parallel. Through this understanding, I could connect with a channeled being as 'Mary' or 'Jesus' in a unique and personal way, without dogma.

Michael, you have been looking for the truth for so long, and now rest, in Me. It is I who is behind the veil. I am not the darkness of your dream states, but I am the light of your present state of consciousness.... There is no Resurrection Sunday without the Crucifixion of Good Friday. All My children are tested; some will pass; their interior castle will be illuminated with the candle light of My presence, in each room of their consciousness that is illuminated with My love and presence... Hebrew is that which you are, Hebrew is that which you have come from, and Hebrew is the line of ancestral heritage. Cultivate it. Understand the working of it. Look at that which you have come into in the last couple of months as complementary to your faith.

Nick and I were instructed to begin the Mass together during regular weekend meetings. We also began attending services at a Russian Orthodox church: the incense, the icons, the priestly intonations all contributed to a trance state of immersion in God. During one service I went deep in meditation and experienced myself as a priest in Russia. I saw myself wearing the gold robe, waving the incense, performing the Mass. I experienced times and places devoted to Mary.

One night Nick taught me to speak in tongues. I just relaxed during meditation to a place where my tongue freely started reciting. Was it gibberish, or "tongues"--an object of ridicule or reverence? I could feel the conscious mind loosen its analytic grip on every emotion, and my heart beginning to open. We were praying for a girl who had been knocked unconscious by a truck. As we prayed in tongues, I closed my eyes and saw her in her hospital bed. I put my physical hands in the air, and saw myself waving them over her body. Minutes later her mother telephoned: her daughter had just emerged from a coma. That was the validation I needed that something real was occurring.

I visited many houses of worship on my own. In one church, as I gazed up into the eyes of a statue of Mary, the face, the eyes, suddenly became alive. It seemed she was watching with infinite love and intelligence. I was jolted from the routine of my prayers into a moment of dialogue, of being face to face with the Presence. I found myself distracted by the loud sound of a group of pious people saying the Rosary loudly a few pews away. Their Rosary was no less sincere than mine, but, and this may have been entirely a projection, I felt in the loudness an artificial piety, as if saying, 'come pray with us, we have the connection.' I turned back to the statue to see if the feeling of that presence was still with me, and I began to experience the phenomenon of "transformations" with the face in the statue. I saw a nun (myself, perhaps) in her face. I stood rooted in a trance, communing.

Just then the leader of the group that had been saying loud Rosaries came beside me and said a bit too loudly: "Your prayers will be answered."

I turned back to the statue. "Tell people who I am," I heard inside. Simultaneously, a tiny woman with a red bun of hair thrust two leaflets under my nose and said: "These prayers are extra special insurance."

I put my hand up to indicate that I did not desire the interruption. "Oh, you're praying!" she said. "I'll leave these here." She thrust the pamphlets at me.

From that church, I proceeded to an orthodox synagogue. Men in black hats and coats pacing this way and that; they cradled in their hands the sacred volumes of Aramaic text, the Babylonian Talmud, whispering and groaning the ancient words of learning. Stained glass windows and carvings of the ancient Jewish symbols, the menorah and Star of David, adorned the space. Whispered praises to HaShem, the Name, the Holy One, Blessed Be He. A box full of black yarmulkes, one of which I gingerly placed on my head. I touched my fingers to the mezuzah and the door and kissed them. I prayed the *Kaddish* for my grandfather.

That night, I received three messages. The first was: "There are so many dark things in the psyche he wishes to hide." I asked the voice: "But what do I do?" The reply: "Open them up. Scrape the tar off the street." I went back to sleep. Several hours later, I heard: "Tell me twelve sins." Several hours later, I dreamed that Nick opened his mouth and an angelic chorus came out: "War is hell. Hell is war. Neurosis is hell." I seemed to be an open medium now, receptive as Griffin had warned to many different elements. The floodgates were loosened, and no one seemed to be at the controls, filtering things out. Jung had similarly experienced himself almost overwhelmed by these forces, though he called them something like unconscious contents, and we considered them entities.

As the ministry continued unfolding, there were various tasks to complete. "Divine Mother" had us purchase various relics, pieces of bone from different saints; we also investigated a program wherein we might each receive ordination as priests. Then, Nick and I followed instructions and traveled several hundred miles to meet an archbishop in a charismatic church. The church had a healing ministry; the archbishop would lay hands on congregants who would fall backwards, "slain in the spirit." The archbishop conducted a baptism in which I participated, after which he insisted that I had renounced an old and ineffective religion (Judaism) in favor of the Truth; I was simply following 'Divine Mother's' instructions channeled through Nick. The trip put increased strain on the ministry. As Bob had warned, I was the acolyte and Nick was the channel. This meant that if I disagreed with something, he could always come back with an instruction from Above. While I trusted the pure, connected voice that spoke to me through him, it became increasingly difficult to receive clarity through his own projections.

Another problem was the Archbishop. He turned out to be a chain-smoker. Clouds of smoke wafted between us and over and into the food at dinner in his home, sending me into paroxysm of spasms. The Archbishop continued smoking, ordering his wife about as she served many dishes, while he sat snatching gobs of food from various entrees. When he came to discussing his past before his religious ordination, it was full of "sin"–egregiously so. Indeed, he had been a "spook" during the Kennedy era. He said Kennedy had betrayed him during the Bay of Pigs, and that as a result, he had gloated in Kennedy's assassination. He spoke in startlingly disgusting forms of racial epithets that were startlingly disgusting and crude. He also had little tolerance for Jews and Judaism. The man seemed to delight in religious myopia as well as bigotry and plain insensitivity.

After the dinner, I went up to the room in his house where we were staying and pounded my fists into the bed, working through the rage. I could not believe we were being led to this man by the being Nick claimed to be "Divine Mother." Nick 'channeled' one word: "Detach." I found it difficult to believe that this was all that "Divine Mother" would counsel on the subject. Later, Nick elaborated that according to what he received in prayer, we had been drawn to see the depths of delusion. When enemies are full of hatred, Nick stated, our task is to "love them more." He also observed that in our ministry, we might have an array of guests, even murderers. "We need to love them more because of their pain, not to sink into anger and hatred." The messages, however inspiring, were becoming less and less authoritative, as they seemed to have led us nowhere.

The ministry was dissolving. Nick insisted on the Catholic Mass even though 'Divine Mother' had encouraged me to developed my own, universal communion service, called

A Friend of All Faiths

Universal Service: Worship of the One God. I wrote:

> *This is a universal service for persons of all faiths, practices and beliefs, uniting brothers and sisters under the banner of one God. One God, many names; one Father over many children.... The service is a composite of various traditional forms of prayer; fragments of Latin, Hebrew and Aramaic have been added to flavor the worship...The service is not Catholic, Protestant, Buddhist, Moslem, Hindu, or any other 'ic,' 'tant,' 'ish,' 'ist,' 'em,' or 'du.' It is rather a mutual participation in the presence of God.*

I took the elements of the Mass and made them universal. For example, I substituted the "seal of faith" for the sign of the cross. I noted: "At various points in the service, individuals may choose to seal themselves with a sign of their faith in God. One may use whatever sign feels appropriate: the cross, the *magen david*, the *om,* or any other religious symbol. The sign is generally made at the brow chakra, located above and between the eyebrows, the seat of psychic power, and the heart chakra, the energy center for love." I noted that the Kabalistic Cross also could be used: the individual says *ve-atah* (touching the forehead), *hamalchut* (touching the heart), v*ehagedulah* (touching the left shoulder), v*ehagevura* (touching the right shoulder), *l'olam* (touching the heart) ("for Yours is the kingdom, the power, and the glory, forever"). I noted that this seal also had the power to balance the energies of the chakras. For "Jesus Christ, our Lord and Saviour," I substituted, "the Christ within," so as to "denote the awakening of God-consciousness within the individual." One drew on Moses, Buddha, Krishna, Muhammad, any other avatar or prophet as a model; or simply meditated on the sound, *om*, or any of the names of God (Adonai; Yehovah; El Shaddai, and so on).

The process reflected a creative wrestling with the contradictory urgings reflecting input from 'Mary' and 'Jesus' to remain 'Hebrew' yet 'universal.' I interpreted the "Lamb of God" as "that aspect of God which is unconditional love for the creation; this aspect of the divinity suffers whenever any human being falls from at-one-ment with Him." I noted that the Jewish philosopher Abraham Joshua Heschel had chosen to title his book, *God In Search of Man*, instead of *Man In Search of God*. I quoted Moses' invocation: "Yahweh, Yahweh, a God of tenderness and compassion, slow to anger, rich in kindness and faithfulness" (Exodus 34:6). I noted that consecrating a 'Eucharist' had power in the sense that "*any* food that is blessed vibrates at a higher frequency," and that we invited Jesus, Buddha, Krishna, and other holy ones to enter the bread. "By partaking of this food, the celebrant incorporates into his or her body the spiritual power of these holy ones." In this way, I made transubstantiation universal:

> *This service allows each person to experience communion in an individual manner. Some will experience the Eucharist as the Body and Blood of Jesus the Christ; others will experience it as embodying the collective presence of the avatars; still others will view the Eucharist as a more concentrated presence of Almighty God; still others will find in it a bread that has been sanctified through the act of being blessed.*

The service emphasized the power of God-centeredness, noting that: "Belief separates people; feeling unites them. Belief creates ego attachments to principles and concepts; God's Presence transforms. 'Belief' and 'acceptance' require the intellectual acknowledgment of verbal concepts; feeling and sensation reach the ineffable mystery of human existence, which cannot be named." Thus:

> *We are not measured by creeds but by deeds. Therefore our 'creed' is a universal proclamation of God-centeredness. Whether we proclaim Him/Her as Yahweh, Christ, Father-Son-Holy Spirit, Allah, Brahma, Father-Mother, or Eternal Spirit, God is One. He is felt with the heart, not proclaimed with the mind. Even as we acknowledge linguistic convention, we recognize the sacredness of both masculine and feminine energies in this consciousness. The words of worship merely point to Him; His true divinity reigns in the heart chakra of each person. The purpose of this service is to awaken that universal divinity. The objective is not to obliterate*

distinctions between persons and traditions, but to celebrate them in the Oneness of the Creator.

I pointed to the importance of universality: "The word 'Jesus,' *Yeshua*, means salvation. Anyone who finds salvation in God is a 'follower' of this principle, one who worships the 'Christ' (the anointed one) within. Similarly, 'Judaism' comes from 'Judah,' which means, 'one who praises God;' thus, anyone who praises God is a Jew. 'Buddha' means 'Awakened One;' thus anyone who awakens to God is a Buddhist. 'Islam' comes from 'salaam,' peace; thus one who surrenders to the peace of God is a Muslim. What a strange new world, in which Christians are simultaneously Jews, Buddhists, and Muslims, and the reverse (in its manifold permutations). Perhaps this understanding can lead us still deeper, to the one reality of which each tradition is a cherished and blessed manifestation."

I changed the Nicean Creed to an Affirmation of God-Centeredness, introduced prayers for the living as well as the dead, brought in other religion's readings, affirmed the presence of "Divine, Universal Mother, Cosmic Mother, Mother Earth, Mother of God, Mother of the Universe; Virgin Mary, Tara, Isis, Sophia, Stella Maris, Kali, Madonna, Shekina, principle of yin, perfect Feminine, Breath of Life, Queen of Heaven and Earth, High Priestess." I invoked the Patriarchs, Matriarchs; prophets; the kabalistic masters; Christian martyrs; Hindu saints; Bodhisattvas. I translated the Lord's Prayer from Hebrew and made my own version. I included a prayer for healing and the Priestly Blessing. The Appendix gave meditation instructions. The idea was to join together all the religious traditions I knew, each being one individualized form of expression for a crisscrossing truth.

Another idea I developed was translating the Catholic "Mysteries" into a Jewish context: text and biblical verses to support each of the Joyful Mysteries (the Emergence of the Patriarchs; the Call of Moses; the Exodus from Egypt; the Conquest of the Promised Land; the Reign of King David); the Sorrowful Mysteries (the Expulsion from Eden; the Immersion in Wickedness; the Enslavement of Egypt; the Building of the Golden Calf; the Destruction of the Temple); and the Glorious Mysteries (the Creation of the Universe; the Revelation at Sinai; the Revelation of God; the Reign of King Solomon; and the Vision of the Prophets).

At first, Nick followed the service, but he quickly complained and returned to the conventional Mass from the Catholic prayer book he kept at his side.

My shiatsu session with Griffin as always offered another perspective on my experiences with Nick. In the middle of the session, after I had fallen asleep, I heard Griffin slam a book. I bolted up and asked Griffin why she had slammed the book.

"I didn't," she said. "They did."

"They who?"

"It could have been one of your protectors, letting you know it was time to come out. Or it could have been a negative entity trying to get your attention. I pulled a bunch of harpies off your lower body, from your feet to your hips."

"What are they doing there?" I sat up fully.

"They're attracted to you, because you're open to them. You're half out of body much of the time. You may be getting messages from Spirit, but you're in a body to learn what it is to be you. If you don't get it, you'll have to come back and do it all over again. So you might as well be in your body and learn what that's like."

The message resonated with what Bob had told me. "If you don't set up boundaries," Griffin concluded, "you'll attract negative as well as positive energy. The negative will suck out energy, the positive may be too much to handle."

Another growing bone of contention with Nick was his insistence on interpreting my mounting experiences through his own lens. As my own sense of safety in the spiritual realms grew, I increasingly found him authoritarian and confining.

For example, Nick told me that if entities appeared in a meditation or dream, I should challenge them by asking: "Do you accept Jesus Christ of Nazareth as your Lord and Saviour?" Only those of the Light, he claimed, would remain. In response, one time when I perceived a spirit in my room, I asked whether the spirit accepted Christ. The spirit replied: "Of course not. I'm Jewish."

Later, a group of spirits appeared. I heard inside: "We are associated with phenomena in the ancient Near East, such as transmutation, transubstantiation, levitation, and arcane ideology." Their names included Archangel Paltiel (of whom I had never heard) and Metatron (or Enoch). I asked whether they accepted Christ. They replied: "Some of us do, some us don't." My whole body started vibrating with energy. They said: "Do not separate yourself from the experience, but just recognize the wisdom in knowing your limits." I felt a new being, one I perceived as Mary, enter the Internet chat room of consciousness and say: "It's a new beginning." The other spirits added: "We're concerned about Nick. Help him to understand, and do not be afraid. Do not go back.... We're impressed with your ability to handle these things. The operation of grace moves with this process."

I was receiving more and more auditory messages in meditation, which I perceived as coming from different guides. Many of the messages were playful. For example, I heard the word, "sherperdization." This had two meanings: there was the spiritual allusion to the shepherd; Shepard also referred to a book of rules for legal citation. Another time I heard, "amanuensis." I had to look up the word in the dictionary: it meant "one employed to write dictation or to copy manuscript."

In meditation, I also started seeing friends and lovers from what I interpreted as past life experiences. One contemporary friend was a medieval queen; I saw her wearing a robe and crown, her faces slightly pudgier than at present.

I heard Mary say: "Surrender to the will of God in all things is part of your path."

I had more and more conversations with Mary in my dreams. First I would see the purple light fill up my mind's eye, and then her. I asked: "When can I see you in the physical world?" She said: "First establish peace within." Then: *Peniel* (in Hebrew, "my face is God's"); and then: "I bore you in antiquity."

Bob affirmed that these experiences could have value, though he insisted that the 'divine ministry' with Nick was deepening as a human power struggle. Bob observed that whatever sacredness I was experiencing, the fear was making this a "cult of two." He also opined that I was being "grandiose," trying to learn in a few months what Nick had developed over two decades. He suggested that if this was truly the Great Mother, she would understand my breaking away from Nick and taking some time off from the notion of a ministry.

I left Nick fearful of his admonitions concerning Satan's wrath—wary of leaving my personal channel to 'Divine Mother,' but I trusted Bob and the process of psychotherapy as a more neutral arbiter of group dynamics than the spiritual authority of one individual, even though he had been my gateway to tremendously powerful inner experiences. To my surprise, not only did I survive the 'wrath' that never came; but in addition, my meditations and personal connection to the divine seemed to intensify on their own.

Bolstering this growing autonomy were disclosures by third parties about Nick. One told me an Indian master had said to Nick: "You cannot channel, for you are a rotten fruit and everything you touch will be tainted. It is important for you to go home to your family and heal these problems." This was all hearsay, admittedly, but it further validated my decision to leave Nick and continue my own path.

Some years later, I had a reading with another channel who described several lifetimes in Marian orders. That supposedly was why it was easy to connect with Mary or the Divine Mother. Years after that, I met Tanya on the street. We had lunch, and I asked her what she thought of Nick's channeling. "It was real," she said. "Because these high energies are part of your band, they reached you through him. Otherwise, he was channeling low entities and dead relatives." She added: "Someone can be a gifted channel, yet be disturbed in other parts of their life." I asked her about my relationship with Nick. She closed her eyes and said: "He was your son."

One of my *pro bono* projects at the law firm was representing a nonprofit foundation that had brought the Dalai Lama's monks to this country to make one of the first sand mandalas. Apparently the foundation disagreed with the monks on matters such as who owned the copyright to the mandala, and how the royalties from photos, calendars, and books would be split. There appeared to be a lot of distrust on both sides. The monks did not want their representations of sacred deities to be commercialized; yet, they had much to gain from deepening Americans' understanding of their tradition by increasing appropriate dissemination of the teachings.

The negotiations came to a head during one "empowerment" given by the Dalai Lama in New York. While the Dalai Lama was teaching from on-stage, I was behind the stage, together with my client, with an attorney for the monks, and with three or four of the monks. I liked the idea of practicing law within the energy field of the Dalai Lama and his monks.

For the first time, I felt law put to a sacred purpose, and that my professional path was being guided.

LAW SCHOOL

(BOSTON, 1983)

Michael H. Cohen

LAW'S COOL

My first memory of law school is encapsulated in a photograph taken in the law school's basement locker room. I am half-kneeling at the locker, arms embracing a stack of books, loaded from knees to chin. The titles on the spines all say: *Cases and Materials*. I am carrying the weight of the Law that will someday, professionally, carry me: Contracts, Torts, Property, Civil Procedure, and Legal Methods. Oddly, I have a half-smile on my face.

In the next frame, I am in an amphitheatre-style classroom, a hundred or so seats cascading down toward a pit. At the bottom of the room stands Professor McNeil. He is aging yet enormously threatening, his movements unpredictable, his voice a throaty rumble. His bony finger points at random to a name on an enormous seating chart that is spread out on the lectern before him.

"Ms. Galapolis, please recite the facts of *Pennoyer v. Neff.*" Somewhere in the galleys a person twitches, and the movement catches on as others to her left and right tremble, convulse, bend over, seem somehow touched by the cascade of fear that ripples through the person whose name has thundered from the bottom of the pit. An irascible scowl spreads across McNeil's face ... satisfaction.

Pennoyer is a case decided over a hundred years ago: dense, impenetrable, some Dickensian concatenation of decisions, reversals, remands, and oddities. The language is old, unfathomable; the decision murky; the distinction between procedure and substance ungraspable, and to a first-year law student, terrifying. In our collective initiation through the obscure eccentricities of *Pennoyer*, a case I later had opportunity to teach, a dark version of the wise Socratic method reigned: reducing students to tears, if possible, and otherwise randomly humiliating them.

On the surface, *Pennoyer* is the story of an ejectment action involving a future governor of Oregon, an illiterate settler, and an attorney forced to marry a fifteen-year old student he had seduced. In the depths, new doctrine forms—and to find it: the unholy grail. McNeil was pitiless. The rule of law the case establishes is that of personal jurisdiction: the necessity of the court having authority over the person of the defendant before rendering a valid judgment on the case.

Shrieking, probably cursing, hurling halting words through wet eyes, Irma Galapolis struggled through an unrelenting, ninety-minute interrogation on the case. She audibly sucked back tears as Professor McNeil exposed her careless reading of text, logical errors, flawed analysis, and general unfitness as a student of law before her peers. At every turn, her blundering speech exposed her total incompetence; she was mentally hacked, ripped, shredded piece by piece, and reduced to bloody pulp as terrified students watched, arranged in the theater with McNeil as ringmaster at the bottom of the pit. He had a method and message, all right: giving new meaning to the word, "preparation."

"Ms. Galopolis, did you even read the case? Five times? Not enough!"

Every second-year law student knows that the rules in *Pennoyer* eventually give way to new standards for personal jurisdiction in a U.S. Supreme Court case known as *International Shoe*. But to get from *Pennoyer* to *Shoe* as a first-year is like venturing down a crocodile-filled, mosquito-infested river, with spear-armed natives on the shores. One travels through *Hansen v. Deckla*, wades through *in rem* jurisdiction, encounters the notion of the *long-arm statute*, and the place where the limits of statutory analysis meets Due Process; one learns a language, and through various peregrinations, receives absolution and acceptance into the brotherhood and sisterhood of Law.

After torturous interrogation, McNeil fastened upon the next victim. When that student turned mute, McNeil then challenged the crowd: "Any lawyer worth his salt should know the answer. Now who's got a bright idea?"

The room was still. I raised my hand.

A long, slow smile played across McNeil's face. He played cat-and-mouse, tearing a wild chase through the Federal Rules of Civil Procedure. The rules were intricate, layered;

one rule referred to another, and one had to follow the branches without forgetting their nesting, and the way each modified the other as well as the whole argument. It was like reading the various commentaries of the Talmud, keeping a different finger on each commentator, and putting the whole together, understanding, for example, how Rashi interpreted the Gemara, again interpreting the Mishna, again interpreting a verse of Torah.

I was in the race toward the year-end exam, the three-hour written test in each course that would set the tone for future success in the law firm market.

The early successes in McNeil's class were not matched in every class; there was an ebb and flow to the first-year, law school rhythm.

I comforted myself by listening to the *Kaddish* symphony by Leonard Bernstein. In this symphony the narrator, Job-like, confronts God, demanding answers to the horrors of life. Perhaps unconsciously, the symphony reminded me of the situation with McNeil. Perhaps God was a Professor McNeil, similarly sadistic and omnipotent, arbitrary and capricious, selecting victims by use of a world-sized seating chart; and at His side stood Peter, guarding the Pearly Gates, testing, barking commands: *Ms. Galapolis, recite the facts of Pennoyer!* Perhaps God used Socratic Method to expose our lies.

Many had urged that this was indeed an accurate description the God of the Old Testament: a God of Justice without Mercy, a punitive deity, hurling thunderbolts at hapless humans. I had heard this view of the "Old Testament god" repeated by teachers, ministers, and even friends on numerous occasions. Then, immediately following, this ugly "Old Testament" God was invariably compared with the God of the New Testament, an Emissary of Love. It all made sense: Jesus had come to throw out the rigid and iconoclastic Jewish law and substitute a universal faith based on accepting him as the doorway.

God had always been a tender subject for me, tied to politics and differentiation and feelings of being an unwelcome minority. There was the Presence that I felt, the Adonai portrayed in the sacred texts of childhood, and the God proclaimed by others according to their own belief. Children from the neighborhood had asked me over and over: "do you accept Jesus Christ as your Lord and Saviour?" They could not understand why this made no sense to me.

And how could I respond? Aside from not finding any meaning in this particular phrase of theirs that seemed so crucial to life, I found it difficult to imagine that God would cast me out of heaven simply for failure to pencil or bubble in Yes to one exam question. As well, I knew that my ancestors had accepted martyrdom–death–precisely on this issue: when forced to choose between apostasy, and death while being true to their heritage, they elected the latter. I did not see Christianity as "replacing" Judaism, did not see Jesus as "completing" the prophets, nor as "prefigured" by the prophet whose words I had chanted on my Bar Mitzvah. I did not have any definite views on who Jesus was or what had happened, or which of the verses highlighted in red were actually said by this character, but I knew the logic presented was off.

And, the logic of the "God of violence (Old T), God of love (New T)," I later learned, was known as the "replacement fallacy," a kind of covert anti-Semitism, perhaps not intending to but ultimately resulting in killings nonetheless, all by misconstruing Jewish theology and urging the replacement of Judaism with Christianity. This whole fallacy was connected to the notion that the Jewish people had missed the boat, not just once (way back in Roman times) but for all times, and were doomed to be ejected from admission to heaven in discriminatory fashion for failure to bubble in Yes to an overwhelming question. Many (non-Jewish) adults and children had reinforced this interpretation during my childhood.

God was not McNeil writ large. But his looming presence brought these apocalyptic ruminations to mind. Because there were hints of sadism and I had developed a deep sensitivity to any form of darkness, even covert. Perhaps the skill I later acquired for energy healing could be traced, in some way, to this early anxiety around the way others could suddenly, in a flash, reinterpret the world–reinterpret my world, turn the nectar of my heritage into poison; as such, I developed a kind of deep radar to any kind of distortion, disrespectful misinterpretation, a kind of one-up/one-down view of their religion by another, power occupying shared sacred texts.

I quite like how Harold Bloom puts it in his Preface to *The Book of J*: "Christians call the Hebrew Bible the Old Testament, or Covenant, in order to supersede it with their New Testament, a work that remains altogether unacceptable to Jews, who do not regard their covenant as Old and therefore superseded." (Bloom goes on to write that we might speak of Jewish scriptures as the "Original Testament" and the gospels as the "Belated Testament," for that, after all, is what it is, a revisionary work that attempts to replace a book, Torah, with a man, Jesus of Nazareth.")

McNeil was not a deity, even given Freud's notion that we invent God by projecting our archetype of the father onto the cosmos. McNeil was fragile beneath the terror, perhaps even kind, if one took the trouble to seek him out beyond the classroom.

By diligent study, I learned to master the Federal Rules of Civil Procedure, and thereby to anticipate questions arising in class.

By a quirk of fate, I later ended up teaching Civil Procedure twice a semester for several semesters. But first year of law school, I could not predict whether I would succeed, or even pass my classes; the exams were all stacked at the end, and playing the *Kaddish* symphony was a way to connect with various feelings inside. I urged different dates, all law students, to listen to this piece, with mixed success; afterward, I would play something from *U-2* or *The Police*, to mask the intensity I was feeling that came through the *Kaddish*.

One night Irma Galapolis sat on the sofa, as I held her hand empathically, letting her know at least *I* (with two weeks under my belt) felt she had a future in a law.

I experienced a Presence in my room but decided I was imagining things. I was lying on a queen-size futon in the middle of my room, the one overlooking the "T" on Boston's Commonwealth Avenue near Brighton. I had been allocated this front room, my two law school roommates having arrived earlier and taken the two back rooms. I was in Section "P," while they were in "O" and "K;" one roommate played electric guitar and used "fucking" as verb, noun, adverb, adjective, and in other playful forms of syntax to modify almost every third sentence. The room was crammed with casebooks, "hornbooks," "nutshells," commercial outlines, and stacks of Xeroxed articles of every variety. The Presence did not mind the mess.

I had experienced this Presence before, in childhood during a tornado; and again at John Jay Hall during freshman year of college. At that time I had decided I could no longer go to sleep on my back, since that induced a kind of floating out of my body. I did not necessarily float out to the ceiling; but I felt a kind of paralysis, as though I had to concentrate hard to get back into my body. I continued having "that floating sensation" for some months. My head would start to buzz, I would feel myself being pulled out of my body, and get scared. I lay on my side before going to sleep, and concentrated on my law studies.

As my class performance improved, I began to enjoy the first year of law school, testing myself against the professors-intellectual pit bulls, some of them. I started thinking about what I might do after graduating. I had the idea I might go to Israel, "work the land," do something meaningful.

My Zaydie was deeply involved in the Zionist Organization of America (ZOA) and chaired the Public Affairs committee of the Zionist Organization of Detroit (ZOD); we had distant relatives in Israel (escaped before the Holocaust); and my commitment to Israel as a land in which mystical encounters lived was deep. I kept a journal, noting regret at not having the time to read literature, religion, and philosophy. Over time, I also grew tired of some classmates' dogmatic approach to the material. We had the usual "red-hots," students whose hands shot up automatically; most of the time, the professor would let them "do a Statue of Liberty" (holding hands aloft for quite some time).

One student would always open her remarks with the same nasal sing-song: "Well, the court says...." Each time, the professor would say: "I don't care what the court says; I care what you think." I was surprised to see such student reliance on the written text, a kind of literalist, fundamentalist approach, and a concomitant unwillingness to think for one's self. Once, McNeil cut off this student's recitation of precedent with: "The hell with precedent; you can always play it both ways. Just give me a policy argument: why should we adopt this rule over that one?"

One of our professors had the reputation of failing a good portion of his class. This inspired terror, as early failure could mark the end of hopes for a legal career. I had pulled together a study group, in which friendship and competitive frenzy easily mingled. We passed around outlines hoping to retain enough bits of information to survive the grueling grilling. Midway during the semester, the feared professor had a heart attack. Sadly, many of us felt relief, more concerned with our ambition and survival needs than this tragic event. We had been spared a potentially fatal failure.

Another faculty member took over: Thomas Jackson was young, curly-haired, cocky. Jackson's mission was to teach the art of distinguishing cases: we had to figure out why the rule of law emerged one way in one case, and differently in another. Jackson wanted to show us that it is easy to memorize legal rules; the challenge is to apply the rules to the facts of each case.

Jackson played "hide the ball," never giving anything away. Perhaps he was amused at our inability to find bottom-line answers, or perhaps the lack of a 'bottom-line' was itself the nub of his teaching. I found the strategy maddening, first because he left an already insecure audience even more insecure; and second, because I felt there were injustices hidden in various court opinions, and Jackson never attended to this aspect of the law.

Alternating bouts of fear and confidence turned into bitterness at Jackson's refusal to take a stand on anything. Although I could see utility in the method, it was instilling me a desire to dive deeper than rational analysis. The results in some of the cases struck me as unfair, and I wanted this point to be made and acknowledged.

In one case we read, for example, plaintiff A had purchased a blueberry pie from the defendant, and bitten in only to find a thumbtack lodged in her tooth. In the succeeding case in the book, plaintiff B had purchased a plateful of baked beans and bitten in, only to find a nail lodged in her tooth. Plaintiff A recovered for negligence while plaintiff B did not. Jackson asked why the cases turned out differently.

Flash forward: J, my friend the oncologist who designed seven levels of healing for the whole person and founded an integrative center that cared for thousands of persons, once relied on information in a standard medical reference book to design a unique chemotherapy cocktail for a particular patient with a rare cancer. The individual had an adverse reaction to the drugs. Some months later, the publisher wrote to J, informing him that it had made a mistake concerning the published drug combination; J in good faith called his patient, letting him know the situation.

Shortly thereafter a sheriff walked in with a summons and complaint. J lived for four years "of hell" with this lawsuit. It turned out, however, according to J, that the deviation in the drug combination from what it should have been was so small as to make no difference at all in the plaintiff's condition. Therefore, even if J and not the publisher had been responsible for the mistake, that mistake was not the cause of the patient's injury. At the conclusion of the four-year litigation process came the trial.

Within six minutes, the jury returned with a verdict of 'not guilty.' But J had lived as "the Defendant" for four years, all the while caring for terminally ill patients in his center. "Me, the Defendant!" he said. "With my commitment to love, to caring for people; the healer. *Will the defendant please rise*. Me!"

My personal experiences of "plaintiffs" and "defendants" was quite different from the abstractions used in law school to teach us theory. One can question the extent to which such 'depersonalization' is necessary or useful; it occurs in medicine, as well, as medical students learn to separate the person from the organ, the individual from the disease classification and treatment strategy. Can surgeons operate clearly when they truly know their patients? Can they do so while aware of the bluish layer of the first level of the field, and of the chakras, and the guides? Should law professors tune in to this level, or is the playing field of abstract logic preferred?

But my critique of the process during first year was different, since I had not yet been exposed to the tools and techniques of energy healing. Intuitively, case B struck me as stupidly decided; someone had baked a nail into a pot of beans and as a result the buyer had gotten injured–surely this was negligent, auguring recovery.

For ninety minutes, different geniuses in the class raised absurd and arbitrary distinctions: for example, the idea that in the first case, the person *assumed the risk* (i.e., someone can inspect the innards of a blueberry pie, whereas in the baked beans, the offending nail is camouflaged). Not one mentioned anything about fairness; students read both decisions as gospel and tried to justify them. Again, this struck me as an absurd failure, almost an intellectual laziness, as if by trying to please the professor, some of my classmates had decided not to think.

Finally, Jackson told us: the results differed because the judges did.

Yes, he affirmed, we needed to learn about "legal realism." As Justice Holmes had put it: "The law is what the judges say it is, nothing less and nothing more." But we could also place this in the context of an evolving rule of law. We were studying "privity of contract," the early notion that one could not sue a distant manufacturer of a good, since there was no "privity" when one did not purchase the product from that manufacturer. Ultimately, the rule of privity was abolished, and other legal rules, including even "strict liability" (i.e., liability irrespective of negligence) for "unreasonably dangerous" goods, evolved in tort law. As to cases A and B, the only difference was that one jurisdiction had a more enlightened and evolved approach to negligence theory; one judge was more willing to move past archaic requirements that there be "privity of contract" between the buyer and the manufacturer.

Again, the revelation to me was not so much that legal rules were malleable, according to judges' preferences and the times–early on I had discarded the notion that every bit of precedent followed "natural law"–but rather that so many smart people could suspend thinking. In a strange way, this reminded me of Milgram's experiments, the ones in which he tried to see how much subjects were willing to follow authority, to the extent of inflicting pain on one another by the touch of a button. Milgram showed that innate mechanisms setting limits on our ability to hurt one another quickly dissolve, and that it is easy for large numbers of people to blindly obey an arbitrarily imposed authority. Concatenation of this memory with the experience in Jackson's class enhanced my previous disposition to distrust authority, including the authority exerted by leaders in the legal profession.

Life in Study Group continued as an exercise in veiled competition; by our insecurity, each trying to prove who was smartest. I wrote in my journal: "Lord help me. Let me draw strength from my faith in You. But I have no faith. I believe in nothing.... Inspired by the Muse? Or am I about to blow a fuse?" To comfort myself, I quoted a line from the Jewish sage Hillel: "If I not for myself, who will be for me? But am for myself alone, what am I? And if not now, when?"

All this scribbling served to defuse the chronic anxiety and tension of a competitive environment, where everything was focused on the final day's exam performance. When Williams Carlos Williams wrote, "Everything depends upon a red wheelbarrow," he might have meant, "everything can depend upon a law school exam." I had the vague thought that I was in law school, not for myself, but for some larger purpose, which would eventually be revealed. But I had no idea what that purpose could possibly be. All I knew was Buddha's First Noble Truth.

Most students hated the first year of law school because of the workload and humiliated status. I enjoyed the back-and-forth, give-and-take, Talmudic disputation about the facts,

A Friend of All Faiths

holding, rationale, and so forth. What I disliked was the way many students tried to take shortcuts to the bottom line. As well, I disliked the lack of sensitivity to the emotional texture of the cases, to fairness. Students seemed awed by the fact that these tomes collected in the casebooks had been written by judges; whereas I found some of the judicial opinions cruel at best, stupid at worst. I developed a short list of the truly offensive decisions, such as the one in which one person invites a neighbor over, the neighbor falls into a well and drowns, and the court holds that the deceased "assumed the risk."

But I learned to "argue both sides," to "make noises like a lawyer," to play plaintiff, defendant, and judge. There was no sense of ethics or compassion; to the contrary, the purpose seemed to be abstracting to solve intractable disputes through reason and rules. The emotional and spiritual components were missing, even though the written "rationale" or reasoning, attempted to explain how the judge had arrived at the decision.

We stood on the grassy knoll overlooking the Charles River, awaiting the results of final exams. Five numbers, our examination scores for Contracts, Civil Procedure, Torts, Property, Legal Methods, were likely to define our fates as lawyers: a good score meant a summer job that was likely to lead to a permanent with a prestigious law firm, or government agency, while a bad score meant no job at all, not now or ever.

My scores turned out to be among the highest: I was in the top two percent of my class. I suddenly received all sorts of awards and invitations: I could join the law review or any other journal; a legal encyclopedia appeared in my box; I had "AmJured" a class or two (receiving the highest grade in that class, with a corresponding award); the Dean wrote a congratulatory letter. Awards tumbled in; at the same time, I had a yen for California. I applied to transfer to Berkeley and was accepted.

But the Dean in Boston urged me to stay, warning that if I left, I might not achieve as highly, while at BU, my future was secure. He made all sorts of offers, and to my surprise, intensified a negative message, warning of potential failure elsewhere. I sat in a New York coffee shop, holding my head in my hands, weighing my future, sitting in such a state of gravity and intensity that incoming coffee aficionados kept the stools on either side of me empty. I weighed pros and cons, to no avail. Rational thinking offered no answers. Suddenly, a feeling of love swept my heart. In a flash, I knew—intuitive guidance.

Business School

(Berkeley, *1984-86, 87-88)*

Exploring life's options.   Reading about option theory.

A Friend of All Faiths

COMMUNION

The People's Republic of Berkeley, a/k/a "Bezerkeley," was home to the Free Speech Movement in the sixties, when students forced a police car to stop, sat on its rooftop, and brought the university to a halt. Like them, I sat on the steps of Sproul Hall, the seat of power from which the Administration tried to control everything. Down those steps was Sproul Plaza, where jugglers, speech-makers, and everything imaginable was on parade. It was a different age, though; the protests were about apartheid in South Africa and not American involvement in Vietnam, but the spirit of protest filled the air nonetheless. Had I stayed on those steps with those chanting slogans just a little while longer, I would have been hosed down or jailed—a little notoriety, par for the course at Berkeley.

Wandering the campus were the Polka Dot man (who wore the polka dot outfit) and the Naked Man (who exercised his right of free expression quite literally). They roamed, just like Sam, a man at Columbia who for decades sold Hershey bars and painted dreamscapes. But while undergraduate Columbia personified the city, Berkeley offered nature; the university's campus was lush, with streams and bridges, exquisite varieties of trees, and endlessly diverse architecture.

For law students, a common expression about the law school experience is: 'the first year they terrorize you to death, the second year they work you to death, the third year they bore you to death.' Indeed the terror and exhilaration of the first year had yielded to boredom. I felt I had learned what I needed from law school; classes simply reiterated the same kind of analysis in different fields. A prisoner of structure, I drank large cappuccinos to keep my nervous system firing. Once a homeless man in Berkeley begged for money and shelter; I had nothing on me except my Evidence casebook; frustrated with my perception of its irrelevance to my desire to help this person, I tossed the book in the trash and never recovered it.

I made law review a second time, based on a writing competition, at Berkeley: again an anointing. Everything seemed clocked, in a hierarchy: which law school you attended; which editorial position you had on the Law Review; for which judge you would clerk and for

which firm you would work. I followed the track. Indeed, in my second year, I received an offer from one of Wall Street's best, and thereafter a judicial clerkship with a judge in the Southern District in New York, one of the nation's most prestigious trial courts. My best friend received an appellate court clerkship with a "feeder" judge, and was properly "fed" on to the ultimate law school accolade: a clerkship with a Supreme Court judge (I got to visit and putt golf balls in Justice White's chambers, then test out the Justices' basketball court and Justice Sandra Day O'Connor's exercise bike). I enrolled in a joint program with the Haas School of Business at Berkeley, obtaining a J.D.-M.B.A. in a total of four years, with my judicial clerkship in between. I was considerably less adept at finance, my business-school major, than at law; and while my friends in business school interviewed with investment banking firms (such as Salomon Brothers; Goldman Sachs), I made it through macro-economics (guns versus butter), micro-economics, and accounting, only to have recurrent dreams about showing up for the exam in my pajamas.

During this time, I tried out for our business school band, Dow Jones and the Industrials. I became its lead singer, "Dow Jones." I hired an acting coach, who had me look into a mirror and say, "I *am* Dow Jones." Bare-chested, wearing a sleeveless leather jacket, my hair spray-painted green, a tie maniacally around my forehead, I performed at parties, included one at Stanford University, standing on the very spot where Jerry Garcia and the

Grateful Dead had done a gig. I was big on *Talking Heads*, a song called *Life During Wartime*. I drank. I grabbed the microphone and shrieked: "All right! Is everybody wasted out there?" There were cheers and hollers. "We're gonna party!" (More cheers and hollers).

It would have been hard to predict myself in full lotus, embracing Silence.

Our third year came and we had a banquet for departing and incoming law review officers. No sentimentality, there: we had completed our chores, hours and hours of 'cite-checking' articles, finished our editorships, and moved up the ranks of prestige. At the banquet, I made my up to the band to sing "Jailhouse Rock." This spontaneous performance rewarded spending all-nighters learning the footnote-renumbering program in the law review offices. After the performance, I was lifted on my classmates' shoulders. We were thoroughly drunk.

St. Augustine had famously prayed: "God grant me chastity - but not yet!"

God granted me something better than chastity: an opening to the spirit world through a chance meeting with someone at a dance. She was a Bahai. I was a slightly intoxicated business school student with indigestion. We were in the Limelight, a church converted into a den of nighttime iniquity. After the dance, she put her hand on my stomach and explained that she had studied the art of touch healing, centering oneself and unblocking the energy fields in others' bodies.

She was one of "Krieger's crazies," a nurse who had studied with Delores Krieger at NYU. I did not know I had energy fields and could not possibly imagine that if I did, they could be blocked. Nonetheless, her hands were warm and soothing, and within minutes, my stomach felt better. Later, we lost touch, and for a long while I forgot the experience. But she had initiated me into energy healing.

I had a business school friend from Pakistan. One night we went out for a beer and the conversation turned to Israel. My friend kept referring to Israel as Palestine. I grew upset and prepared to leave. He grabbed my collar and said: "Mike, I'm Muslim and I believe in God; you're Jewish and you believe in God. We worship the same God. The other things are bullshit."

Hal, my best friend in law school, the editor on the law review who wound up with a Supreme Court clerkship, was a devoted Catholic. We used to take our shirts off, "catch some rays," and try to meet Scandinavian *au-pair*s at Roma's coffeehouse, across from the law school. Usually, though, we were greeted by the Hare Krishnas, whose bobbing shaved heads, swaying in ecstasy, marked a sharp contrast to the dull, unblinking heads of law review editors proofreading. When we were not looking for escapist removal from the drudgery of law review editing, we spoke about religion. Hal went to Mass every Sunday. I joined him one Sunday afternoon in the worship. I found the service sweet but indistinguishable in many respects from services in synagogue, except that there was a giant cross on the altar. Also, antithetical to the advertisement for a radio station, the church as compared to my synagogue experiences had "more talk and less music." Many of the elements of the service were familiar from Judaism, but Latinized.

A Friend of All Faiths

And then came time for communion. I decided to receive communion in order to see what the experience was like. It was a purely experiential move to try to understand what mystical symbolism communion held. I realized I was ineligible for communion by the laws of the church, but nonetheless decided to forge ahead; I realized that my undertaking could offend and that I might be judged, even though Jesus had said: "judge not lest you be judged." My intention was not to make a mockery of the ceremony, but on the contrary, to honor it, and see what it held inside for me. I tried to imagine that transubstantiation was occurring and that I was, indeed, ingesting the body and blood of a being who had sacrificed himself for love.

Each person filed in, trudged up to the priest, and dutifully put forth the tongue to receive the wafer. I did the same. Nothing happened on receiving the wafer. On the way back, I could see various people returning to their seats; some were in prayer, another was kissing her boyfriend; another counting his money. But when I got back to my seat, it hit me: I started savoring the wafer in my mouth, thinking about imbibing the essence of Jesus, when this white light flooded over me and I became lost in some delicious and sacred plane of existence. For a moment, I merged with what I perceived as his love and respect for humanity.

I could not hear the priest's words, the continuation of the ceremony. I was gone. Possibly a beatific smile was fixed on my face, I do not know. I was beyond language. Some time later, I returned to ordinary awareness. The ceremony ended, the lights undimmed, and I thanked Hal for inviting me to the service.

As predicted, for the perceived sacrilege, I was judged. Later, I heard that some of my law school classmates who were present at the service were offended to see me taking communion (if they were offended, imagine what *my* relatives would have thought). I kept my thoughts and experiences to myself. Their harshness suggested that they would have understood neither my reasons nor my internal experience. Their judgment of my external actions was inconsistent with my internal intention to respect the communion as a possible gateway to the divine. And it typified the hostility directed toward others in the name of "faith," an angry mood opposite to the faith's actual teachings—a manifesting outward of what I later would come to know as Gurdjieff's Law of Opposites.

ALARM CLOCKS

The Berkeley summer passed slowly. My girlfriend at the time was memorizing a stack of thick books for the California Bar Exam. I began writing a series of essay on the unconscious mind, focusing on the image of the labyrinth as a metaphor for our movement from reliance on law (external, social rules) to the psyche (internal, individual impulses) as a system for ordering human relations.

Law, the essays asserted, was a failure; the "thou shalt not," whether imposed by the father, the Father or the Fatherland, could never bring peace, either outer (an end to war in the world) or inner (an end to the warring impulses within). The essays drew on law to propose "spiritual crimes," such as "spiritual homicide," "spiritual genocide" and "spiritual infanticide." I attempted to synthesize psychoanalysis, the Kabala, esoteric Christian lore and meditative practice, and critiqued the pervasive influence of media-dominated images on our thinking, concluding that we were in a kind of consensus trance, nearly incapable of original thought, and hypnotized by mass market images and messages. The way out of the labyrinth was through individuation: the hero's journey. With this writing, I had moved from both discourse and external ambition of law school to the inner life. I was less interested in fashioning societal regulations and in the machinations of the mythical philosopher-king than in undressing the veil of illusion, and seeing past the shadows dancing on the walls of the prisoner's cave.

That was fine, but meanwhile, my girlfriend truly was a prisoner in the cave of her one-bedroom apartment, her mental state rapidly deteriorating: the more she studied, the more she felt helpless, depressed, and adrift in a sea of materials. Some of her friends already had developed illnesses (some real, others imagined) in response to Bar study: one had an ulcer; a second, migraines; a third, intestinal bleeding; a fourth had dropped out (moved to Santa Barbara to become a schoolteacher). A fifth, who had already failed the Bar twice, moved into a hotel to study for the summer, whereupon his wife initiated divorce proceedings. A sixth had a nervous collapse and required a week's hospitalization; the Bar was out for her for that summer. A seventh found his legs mysteriously paralyzed, although the doctors could find no physiological explanation. My girlfriend, who had "quit" smoking a month earlier, was now a chain smoker, and secretly sneaking glasses (or perhaps a half-bottle a day) of wine. She was in a perpetual state of panic; she could not study fast enough, absorb the immensity of material. Each day drove home humiliation of self-perceived stupidity. Freedom was illusory; the labyrinth was real.

Across the street from her apartment, the Breema Institute taught a gentle form of bodywork retrieved from the Himalayas. I learned to move others' bodies into surprisingly relaxing positions, and to drink Breema tea, a healing combination of cardamom, ginger and other spices. During the days, I took long walks through Sproul Plaza, pausing by the Hare Krishnas, who had a plastic crèche of a cow staring back at a man about to lower an ax. The sign urged vegetarianism. I knew the Krishnas were on to something, but shaving my head to wear orange and bob up and down with a tambourine was not an option. I picked up a copy of *Easy Travel to Other Planets* and read it while my girlfriend memorized Torts, Contracts, Civil Procedure, Criminal Procedure, and fourteen other subjects. The theory of astral contact with other worlds seemed plausible, certainly no more implausible than the alleged necessity for sadistic immersion in abstruse arenas of law that took my girlfriend and her pals to other realms of learning. Krishna Consciousness and Bar study seemed two extremes on the polarity between the professional and the spiritual, with little conversation between the two. And the image of the pleading cow stayed with me. I had already taken the New York Bar, so I did not then have to suffer through California's (that demand would come during an abrupt career change more than a decade later). So I read and read.

One day I was reading a book published by Shambhala Press that had been recommended by a friend of a friend: a vivacious, dark-haired beauty currently popular with various talk show hosts. She could read palms and runes, draw with her toes and channel poetry from a spirit named Michael. A card tumbled out of the book advertising a new book by a Charles Tart entitled, *Waking Up: Overcoming the Obstacles to Human Potential.* I knew of Tart's book, *Altered States of Consciousness*, which had helped explain my experiences of lucid dreaming. I had learned that "altered" states were common, and could be induced by a variety of means. I had discovered, via Tart, that one could "alter" consciousness by allowing one's self to bring into consciousness experiences that had been previously omitted, through, for example, awareness of one's breathing.

I ordered the book.

I forgot all about *Waking Up* until it arrived in the mail a month later. I tore off the cardboard wrapping to find an over-sized volume in bright blue with glaring white letters. At first glance, the book seemed to repeat the familiar. The introduction proclaimed: "The purpose of this book is to help you find what you think you already have, namely, free will, intelligence, and self-consciousness." I was certain I already had these qualities. After all, had I not freely and consciously ordered the book? Tart's language reminded me of a standard phrase from constitutional law: a defendant's right to be present during his or her own trial is satisfied if the individual has "knowingly, intelligently and voluntarily" waived the right. Yet, Tart had set out to prove that nothing one did was with "knowledge," at least not "self-knowledge;" that nothing was "intelligent," in the sense of being directed by a "free" self, and that nothing was voluntary, but to the contrary, everything was quite involuntary and mechanical.

Suddenly, the book became more than another interesting theoretical proposition to digest; it was causing tiny ripples in my perception, actual changes in consciousness. I dove in. Tart was smart: consciousness creates a map of reality; we often operate from the map rather than from reality; we are hypnotized by social conventions, so that we define reality and behave in circumscribed ways; as a result of these circumstances, it is difficult to discover our essence, to answer the age-old question, "who am I?" In addition to an elegant presentation of these points, Tart discussed the notion of being able to change states so as to be more effective in the world. For example, if I am angry but need to negotiate a certain position, it would be helpful to be able to direct my emotional state into one more useful for persuading my opponent in the situation. If I am frustrated because of a deadline, I may need to learn to let go of my tension and adopt a state conducive to productivity.

Tart concluded his book with two chapters containing practical exercises for "waking up:" "Self-Observation" and "Self-Remembering." Tart referred to the work of G.I. Gurdjieff, a "Russian Asiatic mystic" who claimed to have studied in an esoteric school possessing ancient secrets that allegedly were the source of all religious and spiritual practice. Moses, Jesus, Buddha and others purportedly had studied there, and attempted to pass on these secrets, veiled in ordinary language; did Jesus not say that his own disciples would not understand him?

Self-observation refers to the practice of observing one's self objectively in every situation. This is more difficult than it sounds. Our thoughts, emotions, and sensations pass through the filter of personality. Judgments about ourselves and others and about the world cloud our ability to see any of these objectively, prevent our ability to see with any objectivity how in fact we see. However, by long, diligent practice, one can begin to accumulate mental photographs of one's self, of the "mechanical" nature of one's thoughts, emotions and movements. One discovers, for example, that movement consists of a series of mechanical postures, that it is difficult to "stop" between the postures, that one is not "in charge" of these postures. The mouth adopts a shape independent of my will; so does the forehead, the jaw, the spine, the breathing. One learns that one does not "know" one's self, and that one is not the person he or she imagines himself to be. Only through such practice at "seeing," over many years can one obtain a clear picture and develop a "pilot," an inner self capable of directing the otherwise mechanical stream of thoughts, emotions, and movements. Only then can one begin to discover the stuff of which these "shadows on the cave" are made.

The practice is conceptually simple; nothing hidden or mysterious. Yet, to make a sustained, continuous effort requires enormous concentration.

Self-remembering means literally re-membering or recollecting one's bodily members: to suddenly "wake up" and connect with the consciousness behind consciousness. The person "senses" each part of the body, bringing it into conscious awareness, and tries simultaneously to be aware of emotions, thoughts, sensations. Over time one learns to observe one's emotions, and the effect on the body, and discovers how thoughts trigger emotions and how mental images trigger emotions and thought patterns. One begins to experience one's self as more than a thought machine. One becomes more whole.

Self-observation and self-remembering are the keys to "waking up." For according to G, as Tart explained it, the individual is "asleep." The "waking" state is no more than a dream state, with the person's mind enmeshed in illusions, delusions, imaginary conversations, regrets, memories of past pain, dreams of future glory. Ordinarily, it is difficult to receive impressions without getting lost in this useless circle of internal experience. Much of our self-talk merely justifies existing, entrenched self-perceptions: "I was right in such-and-such a situation;" "I deserve more money, glory, success, recognition;" "If only I had such-and-such I would be happy;" "I am kind, I am generous, I have such-and-such a quality, contrary to Mr. So-and-So's assertion."

Thus, a person can be "free" in the sense of having constitutional rights and liberties, but what about his or her own constitution, a physical existence that keeps him or her enmeshed in waking dreams? How can one be free from the innumerable inner impressions that churn about mechanically, without our conscious awareness, despite the fact that we pride ourselves on our "will?" Why do the Gospels, and other sacred texts, constantly command us to "wake up"? What would it mean to be truly "awake," even for an instant? So-called philosophy, psychology and other disciplines were created, according to G, from sleep. "Man is a machine," G had asserted, and to know anything objective, one first had to *know the machine*. Such knowledge could only come from accumulated moments of self-remembering.

By practicing self-remembering, Tart went on, citing Gurdjieff, one begins to see that one is actually a "three-brained being," with each center (intellectual, emotional, and moving) a "brain" with an intelligence of its own. At any moment, one of the brains is in charge. There is no "master" coordinating and linking all three brains. G likens the person to a carriage, a horse and the driver. The horse (the emotional center) does not understand the language of the driver (the intellectual center), and is likely to kick or bray or veer off the road. The carriage (the body) is old and rickety and may at any moment break down. The driver (the master) is off in the tavern getting drunk with the other drivers (society), all bound by a consensus trance.

Astonishingly, G's parable is not intended as mere metaphor, but as a description of the truth of our experience, a truth we can only discern by careful observation. According to G, we do not notice our centers and hence attribute everything to "I." Moreover, each center has its own intellectual, emotional and moving components, and by using the wrong center for particular activities, our actions are muddled and yield confusing results. For example, the part of the mind that churns uselessly about may be the moving part of the intellectual center: in motion, circling without a definite aim. As a result of this improper use, the mind is fettered. Without freedom, no real thinking is possible. With the mind explaining away, and commenting on, every emotion, it is impossible to see with objectivity what is occurring in the situation. We are hypnotized by our imagination.

It is difficult to explain self-remembering without experience, but one can try to sense each of one's centers at the same time, remaining aware of the body (every member, from foot to head), one's emotional life, and each thought that passes through the mind, without letting attention get caught by any of these, and simultaneously moving through life. Every moment, each center's experience is shifting, and it takes concentrated attention to see what is arising, what is passing, in each. The aim is to be ... aware ...of my ... manifestations ... now.

Tart explained it thus: when self-remembering, your attention is simultaneously focused externally and internally, both on the object observed, and on the observing subject. In other words, you are observing yourself observe. This may be more readily attainable when one is still, or passive, but becomes more difficult when one is in the "grip" of anger, sadness, or other negative emotions, or even while in joy or some strong positive emotion. One can be a slave to both joy and sadness. The goal is to awaken the master. Yet, according to both to Tart and one of G's main students (a Russian named P.D. Ouspensky), it is virtually impossible to remember one's self for more than two minutes at a time. The moments of "objective" consciousness achieved through self-remembering are rare, and although suggested by the effort of will, seemed to appear spontaneously, almost as a gift.

I was intrigued enough by my experience with Tart's "waking up" exercise and by these ideas to pursue G a little further. But I did not get far. I tried "self-observation" and "self-remembering" here and there, but quickly grew bored. I figured I was able to do the exercise, and nothing had happened. I did not see what this little trick had to do with Enlightenment.

A few days after finishing Tart's opus, while flipping through a local Berkeley newspaper, I noticed an ad: "APPLIED GURDJIEFF STUDIES: contact Hugo." I clipped the ad and dialed the phone number indicated.

The person who answered on the other end of the line had a toneless, almost mechanical voice, with no trace of accent or emotion or inflection whatsoever.

"Hello," the voice said, with a curious flatness.

"I'm looking for Hugo."

"This is Hugo." Again the remarkable absence of expression was startling.

"I'm calling about the Applied G Studies."

There was a pause. Then, "What do you know about G?"

"He was a Russian Asiatic mystic who had some ideas about waking up."

"Waking up," the voice said expressionlessly.

"I'd like to wake up."

"What is your aim?"

I did not have an answer. The voice on the line waited.

"If you want to be a superman, I can't help you," he said flatly.

"Wait," I said, "it's more than that."

"Why do you want to wake up?" A bit of urgency crept in.

I searched my mind. "That's all there is."

"Where?" the man named Hugo asked.

"That's what we're here for."

There was another pause, which I interpreted as skepticism. Hugo seemed to be evaluating the call. Finally he said: "We're having a meeting tonight. Buy Ouspensky's *In Search of the Miraculous* and meet us at eight." He stated the address and hung up. He left no explanation of who "we" were, or what the "meeting" would entail.

Hugo lived in an old Victorian house at the south end of Berkeley, where crack addicts roamed and life generally became a little rough. Since I had no car, and lived on the north end, I asked an ex-roommate for a ride.

The lawn in front of Hugo's house had a two-foot black cross planted into the ground, with red paint dripping over its edges like blood, and flowers at its feet. A wood sign behind the cross said "IN MEMORY OF THE FALLEN CONTRAS."

"You sure I should leave you here?" my ex-roommate asked. "Looks like witchcraft."

"Not witchcraft," I said. "We are in search of the miraculous."

"I wonder just what these guys are into. I wouldn't go near that cross. Someone's probably cast a spell."

"I'm sure it's a political message. After all, this is Berkeley."

Reluctantly he deposited me at the house, as soon as someone came to the door, departed. I maneuvered up the walkway around the "grave" and rang the door-bell. A tall, wraith-like fellow appeared. He had pale skin, small features, dark, straight hair, cut like the early Beatles, and thick glasses, set into thin silver wire frames. He was wearing a white T-shirt and jeans, ripped at the knees. He was barefoot.

"Hugo," he said expressionlessly.

"Mike," I said in the same tonality.

He opened the door. "Welcome to my nightmare."

I searched his face for signs of irony, but not the faintest trace of a smile, or any sign of emotion, for that matter, could be detected. At first glance, the living room seemed entirely normal, and gave no trace of anything unusual. A sophisticated stereo system, with hundreds of records lined a bookcase against a wall. There was a plain white sofa and some wooden folding chairs, and also a rocking chair, surrounding a tasteful oriental rug. A Beatles poster hung on the wall, along with an M.E. Escher print, detailing a string of staircases chasing each other's tails, and a life-sized poster of the Magus, done in luscious reds, purples, midnight blues, and El Greco colors. Hugo indicated that I take the sofa.

"Care for some mint juice?" he asked.

Mint juice? What dread oriental concoction was he conspiring to make manifest? What alchemical substance might such strange juice possess? Did it contain ingredients designed to induce trance? Peyote, or mushrooms?

"Sure," I said, and prepared mind and body for hallucinogenic experimentation.

Michael H. Cohen

My heart was beating rapidly as I waited on the sofa for Hugo to return from the kitchen. I knew that I was nervous, that I did not know what to expect. Ouspensky's book (I had read about a third in the hours since I'd first spoken to Hugo) had left me enticed, and eager to receive more of O's ideas. Mint juice aside, O's writing had an alluring quality. It had spoken *directly to my being*. It was if I knew O, and he were speaking personally, as if standing right in front of me, even from his very first words in the book:

When leaving Petersburg at the start of my journey I had said that I was going to "seek the miraculous." The "miraculous" is very difficult to define. But for me the word had a quite definite meaning. I had come to the conclusion a long time ago that there was no escape from the labyrinth of contradictions in which we live except by an entirely new road, unlike anything hitherto known or used by us. But where this new or forgotten road began I was unable to say. I already knew then as an undoubted fact that beyond the thin film of false reality there existed another reality from which, for some reason, something separated us. The "miraculous" was a penetration into this unknown reality.

I had read Vedic texts in college, and knew intellectually all about understanding the thin film of "reality" as mere illusion, as nothing but maya, this greasy fog that rubs its hypnotic ointment on our senses. That was what Eastern religions had taught. I also knew of Cubism, and Primitivism, and of Gaugin's mid-life infatuation with Tahitian breasts, and of e e cummings' "rhythmic lover," his "sweet spontaneous earth" ("pinched" and "poked" and "prodded" by "prurient philosophers," taken upon the "scraggy knees" of religions), of Allen Ginsberg's Howl, and of the Merkabah mystics, excitable rabbis, tiring of the endless infinite mental commentary upon commentary of the beloved rabbinic, leaving mind, leaving body, ancients and youths who, like their ancestor Jacob and the heroine of an old Led Zeppelin tune, longed to ascend in a "chariot" to heaven.

In short, I had read many descriptions of roads others had taken, but had never myself penetrated into this unknown reality. I knew the map but not the territory. But Ouspensky, he had traveled East in pursuit of esoteric knowledge, and his writing, fresh, vital, sincere (literally, "without wax"), promised to convey an experience of penetration. Ouspensky in Petersburg; I in Berkeley. The parallel was clear, at least to my mind, grand with grail-like visions of the Search. Our quest: the road out of the labyrinth and into the center of all things. But what was the door, the royal road to the center? Not the unconscious, for how could one apply psychology to a "machine?" Nor yoga, nor art, nor Tarot, nor philosophy, economics, mathematics, or the "occult" would end the search for knowledge. Miracles were easy, oftentimes cheap. Of this Ouspensky was certain.

"People invent miracles," Ouspensky wrote, "and invent exactly what is expected from them. It is a mixture of superstition, self-suggestion, and defective thinking." Ouspensky found so-called miracles aplenty in the external world: magicians, hypnotists, charlatans. Thus Ouspensky, the accomplished mathematician, the great skeptic and rationalist, had ended his initial quest in cynicism and failure. The "miraculous," he concluded, by the book's opening chapter, consisted of nothing but gimmicks and vast self-delusion; until he met G at a crowded cafe in Moscow.

"*Man is a machine,*" G told O, perhaps with a twirl of his black moustache. *All his deeds, actions, words, thoughts, feelings, convictions, opinions and habits are the results of external impressions. Out of himself a man cannot produce a single thought, a single action. Everything he says, does, thinks, feels-all this happens. Man cannot discover anything, invent anything. It all happens. To establish this fact for oneself, to understand it, to be convinced of its truth, means getting rid of a thousand illusions about man, about his being creative and consciously organizing his own life, and so on.... But no one will ever believe you if you tell him he can do nothing. This is the most offensive and most unpleasant thing you can tell people. It is particularly unpleasant and offensive because it is the truth, and nobody wants to know the truth.*

G's truth had to do with inner work, "work on oneself," a constant struggle against negative emotions, imagination and lying. That much I had gleaned in my afternoon read of a third of the *Miraculous*. Now, sipping the cool juice Hugo had slipped between my hands, a tall glass with a liquid of a remarkable sea-green color, I waited, curious as to what might happen next.

Hugo took the rocking chair to my right. Two other persons emerged from the kitchen, each cradling a glass of mint juice. Hugo introduced them, in his robotic voice. "Da-*veed*. Sa-*leem*."

"Hello," I said. They took their seats.

"We live in this house together," Hugo said. When he spoke, he gave each word equally weight, as if each word took great effort. "We are computer engineers."

I had the feeling that the last sentence was for my benefit, as if to remove a sense of mystery about something not in the least mysterious. I sipped the tea and waited. Hugo had the habit of leaving great, open pauses between his sentences. The sound of his voice seemed to inhabit the tiny space between a great emptiness. I looked at Da-veed. His eyes had a curious penetrating quality, as if a light had been clicked on inside. I got the impression that he was not so much looking at me, as he was looking into me, or through me, perhaps, or looking at himself, from somewhere inside, looking at himself look at me.

The mint juice was a great comfort as I contemplated these thoughts. Its cool sensuality kept me out of my head, and helped soothe my anticipation.

Hugo caught me staring at Saleem. "Don't worry about him. He likes to make funny faces. It is only *useful*, nothing more."

Saleem smiled. His eyes were moving rapidly back and forth, as in REM, only the lids were open. His mouth twisted and turned, up in a smile and down in an inverted U. His cheeks went through various contortions, his face all the time changing shape. I hadn't seen anything so drastic since "The Exorcist."

"He does that to try to get above his machine," said Hugo.

Then there was a great silence.

And more silence. I glanced up at the Beatles poster, thinking of that group's musicality, but now an endless void permeated the room. Some immense effort was being made, but being uninitiated, I could determine neither its origin nor its purpose. I could only speculate from the snippets of Ouspensky I had read.

"Have you ever," came a voice from Saleem, not from his throat or chest, but somewhere else; it seemed to be coming out of his forehead. "Tried." There was another great silence, followed by a tremendous contortion in his facial features. He smiled, as if to apologize. "I almost forgot to remember myself."

Hugo spoke, slowly, considering each word. "Have you tried ... to watch ... each thought, each emotion, each micro-movement of your body?"

He was speaking to himself. Watching. As best he could.

I was unsure what to watch. But I had the uncanny sensation of having stepped into another dimension, a strange new room. And the outside world had practically disintegrated, leaving behind old perceptions of reality.

"I am beginning to divide my attention," said Daveed.

"That's good," Hugo said.

Silence. The consensus in this sealed environment as to that in which reality consisted was quite different indeed, than beyond the threshold of the cross on the lawn. Indeed, I was amazed that the vision of the mock grave suddenly popped into mind, as I had been hurled by Daveed's facial contortions and the gravity and slowness of Hugo's voice (or perhaps by any undisclosed ingredients in the "mint juleps") into an altered state of awareness, in which the present moment held fast and hovered in the room, rather than slipping away like second-hands on a watch.

"I've worked ten years for this," said Daveed, the slightest triumph in his voice.

Saleem continued his struggle to get "above his machine."

I tried my best not to cast sideway glances at his "funny faces." And tried my best not to interpret what they might mean. I knew that Ouspensky, like Tart, had spoken of four states of consciousness. The lowest one was ordinary sleeping and dreaming. Next came ordinary waking, which Tart called "consensus trance" or "consensus reality," and G called "sleep." Then came a state characterized by self-remembering; and finally, a state G called "objective consciousness."

If a person had achieved a higher state of consciousness, what would he or she look like? How would we know? Those were exactly the same questions written on a poster advertising a lecture on the life of one Meher Baba, who was purported to be an incarnation of Christ. I had seen the poster just after placing the call to Hugo. Meher Baba had written a book called *The Everything and the Nothing*. In the introduction, he noted:

> *In earlier times he was known as Jesus the Christ and Gotama the Buddha and Krishna the Lover and Rama the King. This time he is called Meher Baba. Later, after he has dropped his mortal body, men will probably add, 'The Awakener' ... for he has said, I come not to teach but to awaken.*

Meher Baba lived in silence, taught in silence. If God came down in human form, would we know Him? Was Baba real of fake? Was he "awake?" Could he "remember himself" and obtain the fourth state of consciousness all the time? Did G have this level of being? If someone had achieved the fourth state of consciousness, how would someone from the outside know? Mere actions would not necessarily reveal an extraordinary state. Was it possible that Saleem's "funny faces," the visible signs to the external world, were harbingers of some immense, internal effort, some Work, an inner alchemy, a crystallization of an internal being (call it the indwelling aspect of God, the soul, or "permanent I") of unknown dimension, and by standards of ordinary consciousness, potentially "miraculous"?

I knew that I had come to the limits of my ability to know, at least by sensing truths with my head. I had to open myself, if possible at all, to this "meeting" with knowledge of my lack of knowledge. If anything that was being "done," either internally or externally, were to have the possibility of teaching me anything.

It would, of course, have been easy to dismiss the whole experience as a wacky interlude with silly people. I considered this option and sipped the cool mint juice. But as Hugo spoke of Ouspensky's work, the ideas took a powerful hold.

The lamp on the nightstand spread filtered yellow light over my friend's sleeping face. The oversized Bar exam book lay folded on her chest, rising and falling with each deep breath. She looked peaceful. Quite literally, she was asleep; and I awake. What did that mean? Who in me was asking the question, and who was listening? And who was watching one part of myself address the other? Could I be still and experience the observer? Could I re-member, if only for a moment? Could I practice the exercise, quickly, before the circling thoughts, inner talking, commentaries on commentaries, body movements, silent sneaking speaking emotions, a thousand tiny movements directed from somewhere beyond my conscious awareness took charge of my "I," without announcing themselves, and before the "I" could detect their presence? And could this inner work be done while maintaining an ordinary outer life, observing even while participating in everyday activities, living on two levels, being in the consensus trance while piercing its veil?

That was, after all, the premise of G's method: not the way of the monk (emotional), the fakir (physical) or the yogi (mental), but a "fourth way," one grounded in the world, requiring neither asceticism nor retreat from ordinary intercourse. What did the Fourth Way mean to Hugo, Daveed and Saleem? What was divided attention, anyway? And what did "self-observation" have to do with the kind of observation demanded of a lawyer or writer?

Such thoughts made me sleepy. I climbed into bed. It seemed as though nothing had changed. And yet: everything had changed.

One of my favorite set of books in childhood was the *Foundation* series by the science-fiction master, Isaac Asimov. In these books, an esoteric society guards the galaxy's fate, using computations of universal laws known as "psychohistory." Asimov succeeds because, like J.R.R. Tolkien in *Lord of the Rings*, he taps into universal myths and archetypes. Asimov actually invents two "Foundations"–the first, an exoteric group that preserves technological knowledge while the rest of the galaxy deteriorates into barbarism; the second, the esoteric group that develops telepathy and other mental powers. As the galaxy comes increasingly to rely on the technical wizardry of the First Foundation, leaders of this Foundation appear to govern galactic developments, but the reader knows that the Second Foundation, through its computational abstracts, is controlling everything, pulling humankind slowly toward a kinder, gentler future, speeding up the karmic process, as it were, by shaving hundreds of years off the barbaric age through psychohistory.

Asimov's notion of historical cycles resembles the ancient Indian notion of ages, as we are supposedly moving from *Kali Yuga,* the age of destruction and unrighteousness, slowly toward *Satya Yuga,* an age of decency and justice. And his notion of the Second Foundation's invisible, goodly guiding influence resonates with New Age notions of the Masters, a "hierarchy" of beings dedicated to accelerating our spiritual evolutionary processes. The Gurdjieff Work into which I was temporarily drawn after my encounter with Hugo seemed to echo this childhood plant in my psyche of the mysterious Second Foundation. The Second Foundation's exercises were purely mental–like those of the Gurdjieff Work–and members of both groups appear, to the external world, merely ordinary. Yet, their ordinary appearances masked the tremendous mental powers they would possess.

In some sense, the Gurdjieff Work was creating a Second Foundation in my life–exoteric Judaism being the First.

From Berkeley I managed to contact the authentic Gurdjieff Foundation in New York, and got a certain Elma on the telephone. She told me that members conducted bake sales from time to time, for purposes of Self-Observation. To the external world, these were merely sales of cookies and brownies under the assumed name of a crafts group, but to the members, a whole world was opening up. We arranged to meet at Eat Here Now. I looked around the joint, figuring that any customer at a given table might be some closet devotee, practicing a secret internal ritual while outwardly observing the rituals required by the world.

Elma was an attractive, sixty-ish, gray-haired woman, dressed in an elegant silk jacket, off-white, with a pearl necklace and matching earrings. My conversation with her was similar to that of Hugo and company, but without the funny faces.

E: So what have you discovered in your *researches* this week?

M: I tried *Self-Remembering* while watching a movie, but found that after a few minutes, I had sunk into *The Robot.* (I showed her how it looked physically: head strains forward, causing tension at the shoulders and neck; face becomes a mask, with jaw pulled taught; teeth grinding; eyes bulging; almost not breathing). I last five seconds in Self-Remembering, and then forget myself.

E: So you are not behaving as you think you are.

M: No. "Relaxing" movies actually cause more tension. But everyone is tense. We are all *identifying*, being the hero, getting pulled into someone else. It's a basic posture toward life, this becoming the Robot. As Gurdjieff said, "*man is a machine.*" One sets oneself against life, don't you think?

E: I cannot give you answers. You have to *verify* everything for yourself.... What else did you *discover* in your *research*?

M: I tried Self-Remembering while playing tennis. I watched *my Machine* play tennis.

E: And how was that?

M: It was difficult not to *identify* with myself playing the game, because I was absorbed in the competitive desire to win. Once I released my *mechanical identification*, I felt that joy of which the mystics speak.

E: You were learning to *divide your attention*.

Michael H. Cohen

<u>M</u>: I let the *Machine* play but divided my attention, because my mind was saying over and over: *he Remembers himself.* It was interesting to add that extra dimension to reality, to have an internal world that is alive and playing different films rather than being completely absorbed in the ongoing movie. But it was impossible to *divide attention continuously;* I kept back-sliding.

<u>E</u>: What else did you *discover?*

<u>M</u>: I thought about my *aim.* It shifts from moment to moment.

<u>E</u>: (growing excited): You are discovering the *many I's.*

<u>M</u>: *I* start with one *aim* and then the next *I* has another *aim.* One *I* subverts the other.

<u>E</u>: One place you can experiment is to try in that moment to *observe yourself* in the moment. Sense what you body, mind, and emotions are experiencing. *Observe* the *center of gravity:* the one from which the *Machine* is operating. Each will be linked to an association. We are very complicated *machines.*

<u>M</u>: I've tried sharing these ideas with others, but they are defensive in response.

<u>E</u>: You have to *verify* these ideas for yourself. You cannot turn to others to *verify* these things. You have to *continue experimenting.*

I looked around. Nobody seemed to notice our conversation. We could have been discussing the weather. Elma took a sip from her iced coffee and I continued.

<u>M</u>: Am I really following my *aim* in this *Work?*

<u>E</u>: You are simply making *observations,* that is all. You are *getting to know* yourself.... Do you want to get to *know yourself?*

<u>M</u>: I'd like to know the meaning of life. The *Work* speaks to me.

<u>E</u>: A lot of us have that experience reading Gurdjieff and Ouspensky. You can have as your *aim, getting to know yourself.* That is the point of *Self-Observation,* to get to know yourself. We think we know, but we rarely have contact with our physical bodies, with our minds, with who we really are.

<u>M</u>: I suppose that is what Gurdjieff meant by, *he is never at home.*

<u>E</u>: Yes. We either *live ...* or we *merely exist.*

<u>M</u>: How do I know whether I am *Self-Remembering* correctly?

<u>E</u> (pausing for a very long time before replying): Aha. That is the question of the day.

<u>M</u>: Well?

<u>E</u> (again a long pause): It is different for different people and for the same person at different times. All you have to do is *experiment* and see.

<u>M</u>: I am worried that I will discontinue the Work after joining a law firm.

<u>E</u>: A new job is an excellent opportunity to *observe yourself.* You will be *taking in so many new impressions...you can see what you do.*

We parted company without a handshake, merely acknowledging each other in some secret exchange of energy, a furtive glance admitting our share of secret knowledge. I contemplated the exchange as the *impression* gathered itself up into my consciousness. I had previously experienced self-remembering as a kind of disincarnate, out-of-body experience, whereas Elma was encouraging me to do more *research,* just noticing, nothing special or extraordinary. Ouspensky had spoken of "traps:" you start thinking, *I self-remember, therefore I am superior to those who do not.* One "I" starts with an aim, and another "I" takes over. How could I possibly become the "objective crystallized Fourth Man" of which he and Gurdjieff had spoken? In *Views From The Real World,* Gurdjieff had critiqued the person who settles world problems over a cup of coffee and has a vibrant "spiritual" life, yet throws a tantrum when his bedroom slippers are too far to find, who remembers and forgets a thousand times a day. He wrote:

A man ... is not like the picture of himself, and the words 'man, the crown of creation' do not apply to him. 'Man'–this is a proud term, but we must ask ourselves what kind of man? Not the man, surely, who is irritated at trifles, who gives his attention to petty matters and gets involved in everything around him. To have the right to call himself a man, he must be a man; and this 'being' comes only through self-knowledge and work on oneself.

Yes, my meeting with Elma, like that with Hugo and company, was full of jargon, false turns, unmet hopes, and lack of the heart-opening I would come to associate with an open and embracing, yet appropriately discriminating, spirituality. Yet, Gurdjieff, it seemed to me, had an enormous contribution, a great piece of the puzzle, a wonderful truth-telling rhapsody that could have transformed the sober, interest-based view of international relations I had studied at Columbia. I was particularly impressed by Gurdjieff's psychological understanding of humans (the time-bound, gender-based references to "man," notwithstanding), and by his Law of Opposites, which he claimed occurred because without the opposite, the thing would not exist—no light without dark, no cold without hot, no good without evil.

Gurdjieff also palpably tied the answer to war to addressing the war within. Perhaps my father had gotten at this by letting us know that aggressive strife between brothers mirrored warfare between nations. But Gurdjieff was going further, by encouraging all of us to look within, to take responsibility for our status as creatures made in God's image, to fully own our divine heritage by clearly seeing all the contradictions in our personality, all the little impulses that subvert our deepest wish to be free, authentic. Gurdjieff was offering tools to make peace every step by a simple practice others later would call mindfulness.

In remaining days at Berkeley, I *struggled against mechanicalness,* and also wondered how much mechanicalness the Machine of the Bar Examiners had planted into the process of being qualified for law practice. I considered that one could succeed in law school and gather all the trophies, yet still be utterly tied in to the Robot—mechanically following a wash of thoughts and emotions without any real center. Certainly memorizing dozens of subjects and preparing for multiple-choice exams that were designed to weed out entrants to the profession did not exactly constitute training in awakening. Nor did it produce an iota of compassion.

I incorporated Gurdjieff's ideas at conscious and subconscious levels.

A good Christian man pledges to love his neighbor and turns around and yells if his dinner turns cold. A Buddhist adept who meditates on compassion that morning honks his horn if the afternoon's traffic causes frustration. A parent loves a child yet unnecessarily scolds that child if the day at the office has gone sour. How can a person become whole? We cannot "work" on becoming whole, because one aim will subvert and replace another. We are a mass of contradictions; one I wills love in the moment, then the next moment, another I subverts this intention. If one I prays for peace, the next frustration will usurp this peaceful I and trigger a less wholesome one to occupy its place. The only possibility is to create a real and permanent I, one that masters all the little ones. This permanent self is capable of abiding by laws, regulations, rights, the wish for peace ... or perhaps those requirements will be unnecessary, or inherent to the permanent I. The important point is that a permanent self is necessary.

But how can one be created when so many parts of ourselves live opposition? By first discovering all the various parts and seeing the contradictions. Each person thinks he or she knows himself or herself, yet this is the greatest arrogance. Certain habits, little propensities, gestures, mannerisms, all these manifest when the person is not watching. "I'm sorry, I wasn't myself." Then who was the autopilot? A machine falls in love with another machine; one pushes the button of another and a guttural yelling sound is emitted by the second.

What I was describing was not theory but practice—my own experience of self and the world. I hoped that my sessions with Elma would help me correct these deficiencies.

Elma picked up on this wish in our next and final meeting:

E: You are discovering a lot of *energy leakages* in yourself.

M: Much energy is consumed in roiling about uselessly in anxiety. (This was a good observation, one I have since wished I could remember each day.) And the imaginary conversations and planning conversations never get "me" anywhere. But how do I replace the worry *Is*?

E: Right now you are only observing, to know yourself better.

M: How do I begin to *think intentionally*?

E: You have to still the *moving center* of *the intellectual center*.

M: Why are we so privileged to discover this *Work*?

E: Do you feel privileged?

M: (reflecting): Maybe this is leftover from the concept of the "chosen people."

E: Do you feel chosen?

M: Maybe, that's just part of *ego*.

E: Ego serves many purposes. It has helped you accomplish in law.

M: Yes, but this *drive*, perhaps it is *mechanical*, the result of *conditioning*.

E: Could it be that determination is part of your *Essence*?

M: How can I tell what is *Essence* and what is *Personality*?

E (mysteriously): You are still *observing*.

I recalled a chapter in Ouspensky's book, *In Search of the Miraculous*, in which Gurdjieff had taken two people, the first with an outgoing and sparkling *personality*, and the other a shy one. He then hypnotized them so as to bring out their *essence*. The outgoing subject was, *in essence*, a boring boor, while the shy subject turned out, *in essence*, to be scintillating. I asked Elma about this.

E: Your *research* is producing some interesting results. *Impressions* are *food*.

M: Do you believe that people are *food for the moon*?

E: What do you think?

M: I can see we're being Socratic here. Gurdjieff thought we feed the moon.

E: Well?

M: It seems so. Most people are *not Self-aware* and their attention is short as a baby's. The attention does not rest on anything for more than a minute, unless they are drawn into a *negative emotion* in which case they are easily diverted and left to brood. But can it be that only through self-awareness that people can become free, and that most are doomed not to achieve this, and to live and die merely to serve planetary purposes?

E: Aha. That is why we *Work*.

Elma smiled, looked at her watch, finished her iced coffee, and said: "Do you have any more burning questions for me?"

I had many burning questions, but a deep glance from Elma's eyes reminded me that time is finite on this plane; that I had sufficiently engaged my intellectual center and it was time to pick up and discard the accumulated trash from my meal and continue my "research" in private. I flashed a covert goodbye to Elma as she picked up her purse and, with a light but probably mindful and self-remembered step, left the diner.

Elma recommended me to a small Work contingent led by a trained person from the Foundation who had known "Mr. Gurdjieff." This group work involved continuing to share our "observations"–between cascading waterfalls of silence–on a weekly basis, and fixing things during our monthly Work Days. I noticed that members of the group had respectable day jobs, and seemed transformed in these sessions into philosophical mavericks, exploring the frontiers of inner consciousness. I liked them and shared ground with them, but also sensed a gulf between their reports of their 'research' in the group, and the ability to putt these insights into practical use in mundane life and thereby achieve both understanding and joy.

One member named Armando Lorenzo departed from the Gurdjieff orthodoxy in numerous ways. Among other things, he experimented with "brain machines" that linked his mind to technology and induced various adventures. He would eventually lead me to hypnotherapy—and to his departure from the group.

I dreamt of a unicorn disappearing into the waves.

Another dream: *I come into a room where a blue deity who looks like or is a cousin of the Indian deity Shiva is sitting in meditation or at tea with his wife or divine consort who is like Parvati. Later in the dream, I am in an unsavory room and winged demons attack; the room has a number of tridents, and I pick one up and find it a potent weapon against the demons.*

Mysteries seemed cast in the waters of never-ending 'observations,' never quite reaching resolution but somehow being engulfed by still further 'research' about the inconsistencies in our 'unstable, impermanent *I's*. I wondered whether any objective would ever be achieved, and whether the objective state of consciousness had even been revealed to anyone in the room.

It was like Socratic method gone awry, leading not to ultimate resolution, but only to further chaos—the only structure being a knowing look from the group leader or one or two of the more senior Group members who seemed from that glance to have made real progress.

Meanwhile, mounting questions continued to burn.

Michael H. Cohen

WRITERS' WORKSHOP

(IOWA CITY, 1988-90)

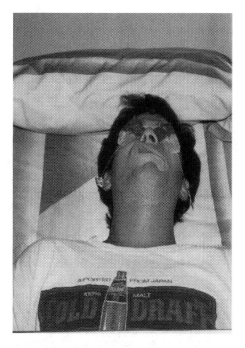

The artist's life - wet tea bags soothe a writer's eyes.
Notice the patterns.

BLACK SMOKE, WHITE FIRE

The Greyhound bus from Chicago dumped its passengers onto the patch of concrete in the midst of endless rolling, yellow hills, full of wheat, corn, and cows. *Skyscrapers for Cornfields*–I already had the title for my next book. I surveyed the alien landscape of Iowa City: it was as if I had landed on Mars. Moving quickly with backpack on shoulders, walking at New York speed, which appeared to be at least twice that of the surrounding Iowans, I noted the small storefronts, like a Hollywood movie set: a yogurt shop, a barbershop, a tiny record shop. From time to time, someone would stop me and ask: "where are you from?"

And I would answer: "New York."

"What are you studying here?" the person would ask.

"Creative writing," I would respond.

Most people knew about the Iowa Writers' Workshop, home to such famous students as Flannery O'Connor and teachers such as Phillip Roth. And they, like me, were impressed–an ego stroke that helped make up for the geographical and psychological displacement. I had escaped from early commitment to the law firm, and had a year and a half of protected time to study fiction and write. This detour from Wall Street into what I hoped would be my most authentic self might offer the magic key. And so I was gratified by the recognition granted by passers-by during my opening moments on this new soil. But one woman looked puzzled, and reproached me with a question that cut to the fact that I was living off a gift: "Have you ever *worked?*"

In fact, I had negotiated with the managing partner of my Wall Street firm to defer acceptance to the firm for eighteen months, because I had been accepted to this program based on a series of stories I wrote during my judicial clerkship. The stories were about the cases I saw in court: no sex, no murder, just the coming-of-age tale of two law clerks named Christian Mandlebaum and Nathan Bookbinder–my alter egos, of course. Bookbinder was the straight character, and Mandlebaum the odd one. He had a Jewish father and Christian mother (or perhaps the reverse), thus giving him an interfaith identity quest. I called the collection, *Temple of Justice*; it would become my MFA thesis. The book lived and the characters developed in my head as I surveyed the surroundings and thumbed a ride.

A businessman gave me a lift across town. He told me he loved literature; why in fact, Paul Erdman's *Crash of '79* was his favorite. Within the womb of his air-conditioned, leather-seated car, safe from the hundred-and-ten-degree July heat, and rolling a gold and garnet ring on this index finger, he asked me: "Why don't you write about business? Seems to be that's the best literature there is."

I wanted to say, "Because I write about the human condition. You know, the Abyss, capital A, the meaning of life, God, suffering, love." I figured the Workshop would finally provide the sense of purpose and completion that law school had left incomplete; if in law school I learned the logic of law and the logical conclusion to my Talmudic studies in childhood, and was in the process disappointed by the divorce of reason from emotion, of analysis from feeling, I had hopes that being among writers would help me dive deep into the spiritual and emotional core that nourished creativity. But all I said to my companion was, "writing *is* my business." To which he laughed and dropped me off.

He left me at the student dormitory, a concrete building at the edge of campus. Staring at my new quarters, I romanticized being in a dorm room again at twenty-eight as mirroring the classic beginning writer's experience: exiled to a cramped, lonely room, no money, starting from scratch, eating tunafish from the can.

Walking, drifting alone through the town bars, I found myself on the edge, peering in, cultivating an ear for the Iowan dialogue, wondering how to turn this conversation or that into a story. The sense of alienation was perfect–surely a bridge to great creativity. I made first contact: two college girls zooming by in a convertible yelled "hey there hot stuff." Next, a bedraggled man approached me on the sidewalk. He was wearing a torn t-shirt, and his biceps displayed tattoos marked "Mom" and "Captain." He looked like the kind of guy I

Michael H. Cohen

would have crossed the street to avoid in New York. I looked down apprehensively, scanning his movements for the usual blade, anticipating that at any moment he would leap for my throat with a death-grip. But our elbows brushed as we pass. Abandoning the stone face I had interpreted as hostile, he grinned at me and uttered a determined, but friendly, "HI."

Once the danger had passed, I realized that my eyes remained stuck to the pavement, a holdover from New York. So I said, "HI YOURSELF." Soon I changed habits: I actually started to return the greetings of other passersby, and found the act of walking more pleasant and relaxing.

"Folks from New York are skeptical at first, but eventually they like it here," the clerk at the bookstore counter said. "They come to realize the Midwest is a special place where you can be honest and friendly. Nobody lives in fear."

I watched her, suspiciously, wondering whether she was going to ring up the discount to which the coupon I had handed her entitled me.

Some time later, I found myself sitting in the sauna at the University gym, again listening to the music of the Iowan dialogue. I thought if I recorded it in minute detail, a short story might burst from my pen like Athena from the head of Zeus.

No. 1: I hear walking's the best exercise for old people.

No. 2: Yep, walking's sure good.

No. 3: No, bicycling.

No. 1: I can't bicycle 'cause I banged up my knee.

No. 2: You gotta remember you ain't eighteen no more.

No. 1: No I ain't. But he is. This here's my boy.

The boy: Hello.

No. 2: How many you got?

No. 1: Four. My oldest daughter's forty-two.

No. 3: How old are you?

No. 1: Sixty-one.

No. 3: Boy, you started young.

No. 1: They start later now. Problem is, kids don't understand the world the way we do. We've been through the Depression. I make my kids eat once a year the way I did then, let them know what it's like.

No. 2: I remember. Boiled potatoes and cabbage.

No. 3: Boy, I used to like that dandelion green soup. Momma sent me out and I'm come home with a bushel. And green tomatoes like you never seen. You had to grow them yourself.

They left, rubbing their backs with their towels, while I let the sweat drip into my eyes, wondering whether the Muse would manifest in the steam. She did not come then, but as I left the gym, the sun began to set, smearing the sky with streaks of magical purples and pinks.

I am drinking in a bar called "The Deadwood." Drinking is fashionable. So too are stories in the present tense. Nobody seems to be using the past tense - perhaps the past does not existed, except disguised in the stories; or perhaps the myth of eternal recurrence is true: everything that has happened continues to happen forever, in the eternal present tense of the stories.

Though I don't know anyone in town, I feel warm, like I know the town already. I'm seeing how it looks from the underside of a foamy beer. I'm as far as can be from the world of stock options and power-ties. I'm thinking about bicycling. I'm thinking about children, about boiled potatoes and cabbage, and the greenest tomatoes you ever did see, about endless rolling yellow hills, full of corn, and wheat, and horses and cows, with their leathery smell, about open blue skies over acres of green, about sun and sky and dirt and earth.

The next day, the temperature rose another ten degrees. My pace slowed as I circumnavigated the toy town (or so it seemed compared to New York). It was a relief to spend a sabbatical away from Wall Street, before I had even started: a year of immersion in fiction and poetry, rubbing elbows and sharing consciousness with writers. The local bookstore contained our reading assignments. The cashier was reading the Village Voice when I walked in; a breath of the familiar. She was a pleasant woman named Dixie (her parents liked the South), Polish with hair the color of the now-familiar corn. I introduced myself and we arranged to meet for iced coffee by the riverbank. I prepared myself for a romantic interlude: blankets, umbrella for shade, two iced coffees, a casual leaning on one elbow at her side.

Dixie's intense brown eyes complimented a round, innocent face. She leaned next to me and opened the conversation by telling me she thought that lesbians were simply "acting out their aggression toward men." This comment had been triggered by something she read in the Village Voice. Before I had time to respond, she added that she had the habit of picking up sticks and breaking off the tips; she wondered aloud whether this had something to with an unconscious desire to castrate her father. I immediately decided she was not the healthiest prospect for a relationship.

But Dixie had much to offer by way of companionship. She read widely, especially in psychology (awareness of her post-Electra-reverse-castration-complex notwithstanding). She mentioned this Bulgarian, ex-patriot professor who was offering a course on literature and psychology.

We sat through the professor's introductory session together: he spoke of Kristeva and Lacan, and other scholars, whose ideas drew threads between fiction and the unconscious mind. He reminded me of my seventh-grade, science teacher at Hillel Day School, who similarly studied Kabala and spoke of personal encounters with gods and demons, and experiences of other lifetimes. (I can remember my science teacher leaning against our junior high-school lockers, telling me of time travel and that if I were to study the Kabala before age forty I might go crazy.) I took the course; but more importantly, through this professor, I was introduced to yoga.

My first experience of yoga was unpleasant. I overstretched. We twisted on our tushies and backs on a carpeted, fluorescent-lit room at the top of Iowa City's Unitarian church. I did not "get" the church; "church" implied Catholic or Protestant, but this church had yoga teachers and Buddhists. The room was anything but conducive to spiritual practice, with crayons and markers and assorted board games spread around. But this was where the ex-patriots gathered, a touch of international awareness in the provincial town that time forgot, a breath of air among the University of Iowa undergraduates (the males wore tank tops, and the women spandex bottoms and cut-off T-shirts bearing the University emblem).

I folded myself into various strange positions and found myself after an hour clutching my spine in agony, as muscles up and down the back went into spasm.

The Monk presided in a second-story classroom in the universalist church, directly below the makeshift yoga studio. Like me, he too had only been in Iowa City two days earlier. There the resemblance ended.

I had long hair; rebelling against Wall Street, and reveling in my newfound freedom as a student again, I wore my hair down to the shoulders, and shaved intermittently, just enough to keep a little "grunge." The Monk was, of course, clean-shaven, including his head, and wore the familiar robes of the Tibetan order. He had been sent by the Dalai Lama, from his monastery in India.

He sat cross-legged on an octagonal, purple cushion, in front of the room.

For the first hour he lectured, using the few words of English he had learned on the plane. "Space ... sky ... no mind." His pronunciation made the words difficult to understand; he said "seh-guy," for example, instead of "sky." His voice flowed in a soft, soothing

Michael H. Cohen

monotone. "No self. Self illusion. Maya." He seemed quite insistent on this point. I strained to catch the thread of ideas. "Clouds," he continued. "Clouds. Go, come." He emphasized this again: "Go, come." What did this mean?

I adjusted my legs on the cushion I had taken; the cramps in my calves were becoming unbearable. The Bulgarian professor, ahead of me, sat upright, a smile (I imagined) floating on his face. He understood "go, come." I had no clue.

The Monk continued: "Nothing ... is."

Suddenly his eyes bored into mine, as if to illuminate the message. "Nothing is," I repeated to myself over and over, hoping for a revelation. I looked at him and slightly raised my eyebrows, as if to say, "I appreciate your teaching, but I don't get it." He smiled, and held the silence, as if the message could penetrate through the gaze. *Nothing is*? I wondered. Existential philosophy? Oxymoron? Contradiction?

"Not self ... and yet Self." Again, he looked past the Bulgarian and into mine.

Clouds go, clouds come; nothing is; no self, what did it mean?

I relaxed a little as I noticed people around me closing their eyes. The room was so hot. My head, bobbing up and down; a recognizable word, here and there, mixed with Tibetan. No self, and yet Self. Searching vainly for English translation; beyond the window, overgrown cornfields; the Bulgarian, transfixed with a smile.

"Now meditate."

The command floated in from somewhere beyond the cornfields: it was the Monk's voice yet not the Monk's voice; the command of his master, the Dalai Lama, embodiment of the Buddhas, yet not the Dalai Lama; it came from India yet via Iowa; it came and went, like the clouds, into space, into sky, into the no-mind that my mind became.

"Inhale, two, three, four; exhale, two, three, four. Inhale the white smoke, exhale the black smoke." The instructions wafted in, pleasantly. "Inhale white; exhale black. Inhale white; exhale black."

My head bobbing; the Monk's face came into focus. Calm, steady, clear-eyed, shaven, a bright contentment, head floating in air. "Space, sky, no mind, no self." Thoughts came and drifted like clouds in the sky. "Illusion." Behind the thoughts, an awareness. A Presence. My Self? No self! Inhale, exhale, deeper in.

Intellectually, the Monk's broken English made no sense, gave no lasting theology, offered no cosmology I could fathom. The teachings I could learn from the Bulgarian professor, but there was not enough, at first glance, to grab onto.

And yet, as I was walking through Iowa City, the day after the meditation, something shifted. I sensed that my brain somehow was different after the experience. I was engaged in ordinary activities: walking, talking, shopping, yet somehow had the added dimension of seeing deeply into people, behind the mask of language and social pleasantry. I could read emotions viscerally–and sometimes in the form of symbolic information. Sometimes creative energies literally created sparks around people; in other cases, spirits of fear, greed and lust seemed to speak through those huddled around a table.

One of my first workshop classes: many classmates looked like hungry, devouring ghosts: these were the energies I saw through them, behind the shell. Real demons leaped out and sucked their energies into dimensions of anger, sadness, and pain. Had the Monk transmitted something, non-verbally but nonetheless palpably? If I had no self and he had no self, then who had transmitted what to whom? And what *did* one monk say to another in the cave of silence? Cognitively, I had no explanation; yet my whole sense of reality had shifted.

The director explained how privileged we had been to be selected. Twenty-four of us had been chosen from a pool of thousands of aspirants for the oldest and arguably finest creative writing program in the nation.

"We look for one thing only," the Director announced. "*Talent*."

My romanticized notions of the place, together with the Director's affirmation of my gift, were to undergo cognitive re-wiring. I had a beer with a graduating student at the Deadwood. He kicked some peanuts on the floor and tried to deconstruct my illusions. "People are scrambling here as much as on Wall Street," he said. "If you do manage to publish, don't tell anybody. Not if you want friends."

"You mean it's competitive," I clarified.

"I'd sell my grandmother if the *New Yorker* commissioned a piece on slavery."

The Monk gave us handouts, in English, and created a short ceremony where we could renounce "self-cherishing" and align ourselves with the Bodhisattva's vow:

May the pain of every living creature
Be completely cleared away.
And may I be the doctor and the nurse for all sick beings in the world
Until everyone is healed.

This spirit ran contrary to the narcissistic impulse I felt controlling motivations around me: writing about Me: I, Myself, My World. We studied great fiction writers as models, and they wrote from the depths of their humanity, of their empathetic understanding of the human condition. Great characters in their books were crafted and nourished from the wellspring of some universal truth bubbling through their own experience. The writers were mature. They represented the ideal. We were the raw material. Having been selected to this crème-de-la-crème experience, we had technical virtuosity, and the ambition to be on the bookshelves, but many of us lacked the maturity and breadth of vision of great writers. Competitiveness, nastiness, stifling of others, narcissistic narrowing, often ruled, not the supportive community I had envisioned.

One of the unspoken challenges was how to transform darkness and pain into transformation and triumph, rather than wallow in and celebrate one's own shadows. There seemed, from my vantage, to be excessive romanticizing of personal darkness, as though unprocessed, distorted emotional experience could provide the only initiation, the sole inspiration.

For example, one student wrote stories about schizophrenia and dark shapes and smashing a car at ninety miles an hour. Perhaps I was unappreciative of this fellow student's talents—competitive myself, masking insecurity in the guise of a critique—yet I felt only the writer's grandiosity on hearing the tale. Another student told us held séances in a rented house where the previous occupant had committed suicide; these sessions were supposed to be generating "inspiration" for the student's gothic tales. And my search for community was a failure: after class, sharing a beer with one student at the Deadwood, I was suddenly warned: "Don't think you can write a great story through raw horsepower. It's not like taking the Bar." Another informed me of which students in my class (a surprising percentage) were on Lithium. Yet another noted: "Whatever friendships you might make will dissolve between November, when the competition for scholarships begins, and March, when winners are announced." I also learned that: "publishing is a dirty word; don't mention it, you'll attract envy." Another said: "any mentoring occurs in secret." Jealousy, envy, and competition: the smoke-filled haze of the Deadwood provided a haven for dead wood inside. People were expunging their demons through their writing—or perhaps using their writing to feed these inner wolves.

Sitting silently before the Monk, I took a vow: that my creativity would spring from light and hope, from positive aspects of being; that I would never find destructiveness or self-destruction romantic; nourish the highest and wisest parts of myself. If I were to write about suffering, it would be from a place of compassion and wisdom. I would eliminate "self-cherishing" and place my being in service of compassion, toward relieving the suffering of all beings. I would renounce ego.

Of course, writers write because they *must* write. Writing is catharsis, therapeutic, an exorcism. As Rainer Marie Wilke noted, writing requires above all else, solitude. I had plenty of solitude. So many famous writers had studied or taught in this place. Physically, it is a number of classrooms in a simple building alongside a winding river. The summers are too hot and the winters too cold. Emotionally, spiritually, it is something else: a cauldron of hopes, refinement, creativity; and psychic numbing: alcoholic attempts to distract from pain and depression. There would be marvelous poetry, explications of great texts, expressive humans, expressed appreciation for the emotional and spiritual struggles of wonderful friends. There was much brilliance, inventiveness, positive aspiration, exhilaration, discovery, and also darkness, jealousy, and desperation.

The famous workshop, the exchange of ideas and feedback about writing, transpired in a brick building, in a classroom made of white cinderblock, under harsh fluorescent bulbs, on cheap wooden tables seating two apiece, resting on spindly metal legs. The Workshop itself consisted of a class in which two or three students each session presented their fiction to the group; the other students would offer a critique, focusing on one aspect or another of the work (such as theme, dialogue, characters, language, tone), and then the instructor would offer comments.

We could select from four faculty members for our Workshop; I chose a middle-aged, lanky author who had published a literary bestseller some years ago. He adjusted the drawstring on the metal skull suspended above his heart, rose slowly from the wooden table, and drew a diagram on the board.

"We are interested in one thing and only one thing: the text. Over here," he pointed to a chalk-in stick figure labeled "R," "we have the Reader." He drew another stick figure at the other end of the board. "Over here is the Writer." He chalked in a "W" over the figure's head. "The text is a contract between the Reader and the Writer." He drew arrows flowing from one to the other. "If you don't give the reader enough...." He drew an arc with an arrow that shot up from Writer's hip and fell at the Reader's feet. "You miss him completely. And conversely, if you give too much, you bully the reader." He drew an arc that shot up from the Writer's hip and overshot the Reader's head. "You miss him again. You've got to give enough for the reader to participate in the manuscript; but don't him over the head."

Then he chalked in three words: CLARITY. MEANING. SENSE.

"These three precede any attempt at what I call the fancy stuff. Don't be fancy. First make sure your writing is clear, that it means something, that it makes sense. This is the heart of the workshop." He had given us our new mantra. Later, we would meet at the pool table, and I would see this same expositor of clarity, meaning and sense in an alcoholic haze.

Not that I was free from vice, suffering, masks, or pain, purposeful deadening, confusion. Like others, I had come to Iowa with plenty of ego. The Destroyer of Ego moved silently through the halls, a spiritual force denuding unrealistic ideals and exposing a cauldron of jealousy, bubbling up egos only to burst them, trumpeting teachings to temporarily disguise fear, insecurity, pain, and just as quickly—like ripping the band-aid off a still-fresh wound—remove the mask.

In the following session, our teacher reduced the first student to tears. For the second story, after the students had gone around and praised the prose, the instructor assaulted the text, line by line.

"Language," he urged. "Be precise. The beauty everyone is talking about is irrelevant if your words don't mean anything."

He chastised students for imprecision. In one case, a student writer had used the phrase, "tufts of grass." The instructor tore into the writer: "THERE IS NO SUCH THING AS TUFTS OF GRASS. DO YOU KNOW WHAT TUFTS ARE?"

The student swallowed, nodded. "Clumps," she got out. "Clumps of grass."

"Well / looked it up," the instructor growled. He looked at his sheet. "'Tuft: a small cluster of elongated flexible outgrowths or parts attached or close together at the base and free on opposite ends.'" He paused, taking in the class. " You can have a tuft of grass, but not tufts." He concluded: "Don't misuse language."

One student wrote a deliberately experimental piece, using words that were clearly nonsensical, and imitating the untamed abandon of Jack Kerouac. The instructor was emphatic that this was the wrong way to write a story. Several students rebelled, and spoke in defense of "experimental" prose. This response irked the instructor. He focused on a line in the story in which the writer described his financial woes as "getting it up the back door." The instructor spoke in a low, austere voice that was sharp as a scream. "I want all of you to know that I grew up without money.... Butt-fucking does not give you working class credentials!"

Later, at the Deadwood, the writer complained to me that the "back door" line was just one sentence, not the heart of the story. The story was really about finding one's way in the drifting, post-college years. He was saddened and demoralized by the instructor's response; even though he had been "chosen," based on "talent," the teaching tactics were undermining his confidence and esteem. The other disheartening aspect was the peer response to this criticism: after the story's demolition, this student's popularity would markedly decline.

Shauna's stories were about failed relationships. Like the main character in her stories, she had dark eyes, a lithe body, bent toward the ground like one of Picasso's "blue period" figures, and a tight, cruel mouth curled downward. Her voice was brittle, and tended to use words such as "hopeless" and impossible." Lines like "she felt an overriding gust of anguish" were routine. Shauna had a high, nervous laugh, more of a cackle. She might have been considered attractive, but she wore oversized, brown plastic glasses, and had the habit of nervously brushing her hair back with her fingers, after adjusting the cigarette that perpetually dangled from her lips.

A classmate reported: "That woman has sadness at her core."

I was always interested in how classmates obtained material for their stories. In most cases, the autobiographical element was unmistakable.

We were all here working something out; although we had reached the sacred cornfields through various paths, a similar hope and goal underlay the obsession with writing. In a way I was lucky: I had been brought by serendipity or maybe grace, not imaging myself in the same league as other, more accomplished writers, whereas classmates like Shauna had worked their way up the bread-chain of prestige, moving from writer's conference to writer's conference; first being a waiter and associating with the famous ones, and then presenting work themselves.

We were all a bit intense, perhaps equal to but a shade different than the intensity on Wall Street. We all hoped to be published in some respected literary forum (even *Playboy* counted; one of my teachers had succeeded in "placing" a story about two lovers struggling with a full-body condom). Paralleling shared insecurity as writers and need for approval, we shared the passion for written self-expression. Although the word, "healing" was never used and spirituality never introduced, everything being disguised as some ideal called "literature," I suspected that these terms would encompass the goal.

Shauna's stories contained a lot of dialogue consisting of arguments with lovers. Was this autobiographical? It seemed to fit her personality profile. Rumor had it that Shauna got her dialogue by secretly tape-recording her arguments with her boyfriends; the microphone hidden beneath a pillow-cushion or book.

In one class, I objected to a line in one of Shauna's stories in which the protagonist observed that she hated her body and hated sex. I said I did not know *why* she was having these feelings, or what these feelings meant.

Immediately the room polarized. Whatever I had touched, it was deep. Such polarization was not uncommon in an environment in which the instructor could be quick to criticize and wound, not just the writer, but other students, and expressions of hostility sometimes went unchecked: a baptism in collective neurosis. Anxiety was palpable—

Michael H. Cohen

understandably--about self-worth, talent, ability, in a competitive environment with some of the supposedly finest talent in the country. As before, gaining admittance to an elite club did not guarantee peace—it only increased competition among people at ever-higher levels of accomplishment.

For some reason, my objection to Shauna's language stirred up the nest. Suddenly, Shauna's story was compared to Dostoevsky's *Crime and Punishment*. I was accused of trying to suppress a legitimate exploration of humanity's dark side.

The arguments raged, as the instructor weighed on one side, then the other.

At some point, the discussion changed course. Students wondered why the protagonist in Shauna's story might hate her body and her sexuality. The focus now was off of me, and turning against Shauna. From a literary perspective, we often had spoken of the "distance" and difference between author and narrator; the writing, our instructor had told us, must make the reader aware that the writer *knows* he or she is behind, but apart from, the narrator. This kind of objectivity allows the reader to enjoy the subjective point-of-view of the narrator, to know that the "I" is a fictional construct, and that the writer will not manipulate or intrude into the mind of the character he or she has created. Indeed, many writers, when asked about the secret of their writing or about plot, have explained that "they" do not invent plot at all; rather, they merely invent (or transcribe) the characters, and let the characters themselves work out the drama.

But this kind of objective distance between author and narrator was missing in Shauna's present work, and the class, which initially had defended Shauna's choices, talents, and ego, now had turned against her. The veil between Shauna and the protagonist was growing precariously thin. Our instructor rose to the rescue. "Yes," he said, "Shauna, her narrator that is, writes that she hates her body and hates sex. And I agree that 'hate' is a very strong word. And you don't want to use very strong words in your prose unless they mean EXACTLY what you want them to mean." He was using general language to make a more generic point; sometimes he did so to deflect heat away from the writer, and other times to make the critique of that writer's choices more pointed. His words were slow, carefully chosen. "Is 'hate' what you mean, Shauna?"

"Sure," she replied, her hands drumming the table. She unconsciously reached for the cigarette pack in her shirt pocket. "It's obvious." She lifted the story to her eyes and reread the line, then giggled, nervously. "You all know what that means. Don't you." She put the unlit cigarette in her mouth.

The instructor continued: "When someone uses a very strong word, I like to substitute the opposite word just to see what happens. Let's try 'love' instead of 'hate.'" He picked up the manuscript: "She stared at her hands. They were large, dry and ugly. She loved them. She LOVED her hands the way a woman can LOVE sex." He put down the manuscript. "Hmmm. Still makes sense, doesn't it?"

For a moment, nobody spoke. Then the instructor added: "You can't throw around words; they have to mean something."

Shauna fumbled with the cigarette. "Look," she said nervously, "I'm writing a novel, okay?"

The instructor drew the skull tighter up his chest. "Okay, big deal. I've written fifteen. One was published; I burned the rest."

Did Shauna hate sex or did Shauna love sex? Did she really put a tape recorder under her pillow and provoke her lover into arguing with her? Did she manipulate her love for the sake of a story? Did Shauna compromise her ethics to generate writing? Were her motivations and methods as petty and impure as the subgroup attending a séance in the house of a suicide, as ignorant and demeaning as those celebrating a suicide for the sake of expression and art? Were Shauna's demons gloating in the classroom, hovering among the cinder-block, peeping out from the paint-coated cracks, jeering from the spindly metal table-legs? Why did Shauna always wear spandex tights to class? Who or what spirit spoke through Shauna? Was it the confused, complex, twisted, love-hate dynamic of Shauna's childhood, recycled in garrulous, gaggles of garbage of speech and verse?

Others too brought their angels and demons into the classroom. Tim sported sandals and a yellow, cloth bag he purchased from a child in Guatemala. A photographer, he documented the "pitiful poverty, oppression, and desolation" of Central America. Fiction-writing gave him "another vehicle for the work." He wrote of the children and families he had left behind. Brandi left her husband, five children, and "a shit-load of laundry" to find her "liberation in writing." Writing meant "escape from domestic horrors." She wrote stories about women leaving men to find their own destiny. Escape was a common theme. Sam was an "escapee" from Appalachia. His face evoked suffering and experience, with its craggy contours and pock-marked valleys, and his scraggly and evocatively biblical beard. He was a scrawny child who took up boxing to survive. "I had to: a matter of survival." His stories covered the territory of his ancestry. "I vowed never to talk about my family except through fiction. Some uncles might come shooting if I told the butt-naked truth."

Jim lost his best friend the year he started writing. In his novel, "the protagonist's secure life is chipped away, bit by bit, by this death, but it becomes an opening for him as well, an emotional unfolding." Jim spoke through choked tears: "You see, this buddy of mine died in a rock-climbing accident. I'm writing in part about him. *No: to* him. The dead need reading material."

Then there was the classmate who, on learning I was an attorney, commented: "I've known lawyers. My ex was one, and there was also the shark, I'll think of the name, who crammed the divorce settlement down my throat."

In the luxury of the year of creative sanctuary I took a painting class, and read *Ways of Seeing* by John Berger. Berger, a Marxist, makes the verbal and visual case that in Western art, the woman only exists for, and is defined by, the male gaze. Women are defined either by their sexual power, or by their clear lack of sexuality; they are either objects of romantic fantasy, or tough and brutish. Either way, they exist only for the pleasure of the male viewer; they are placed in positions which are titillating for the male, not for their own pleasure. After reading Berger, I began consciously working on the integration of male and female within myself. I resolved to bring life equally to my male and female characters.

I made resolutions. These were challenged when I had to paint a nude model named Margaret; nude except for the crucifix that dangled between her breasts.

I made swirling vortices of color and texture on the canvas, blotches of blue and red hues, hurricanes of colors shifting from dark to light and back. Black lines ran down the centers of my canvases, but midway, the lines would intersect with some symbolic figure: a menorah, a Kiddush cup, a cross, suggesting a connection. I swirled raging, ravaging, clouds, the holy horror and terror of the world; thick black definitional lines (suggesting the world of reason; categorization; definition; scientific thinking). The instructor came by. "Interesting use of color. Write me three sentences about what that means."

I wrote: "Christ is the Self spread across the World. Christ is for me the identification of the Self with World. I am God and God is the Universe."

Our Workshop read from Nathaniel West in *Miss Lonelyhearts*: "He was twisting the arm of all the sick and miserable, broken and betrayed, inarticulate and impotent. He was twisting the arm of Desperate, Broken-hearted, Sick-of-it-all, Disillusioned-with-tubercular husband."

I was no good at representational painting, but my abstract shapes were, according to the teacher, "intense." I read from Chaim Potok's *My Name is Asher Lev.* "Millions of people can draw. Art is whether or not there is scream in him waiting to get out in a special way." Lev's assistant corrected him: "Or a laugh."

I wrote, painted, read. And then I prayed. I did not know to whom or for what I was praying. I had Judaism mixed in with the Monk's white smoke and black smoke, mixed in with law moving into writing, wrapped in the narcissism and competitiveness of my community, the failure there to find purity of emotional expression a parallel disappointment to my feeling in law school that rules and rationality lacked the capacity for brining forth the fullness of spirit. Part of my van Gogh/Lonelyhearts/Asher Lev phase in Painting 101 was a response to the void the Workshop left inside. Emotions were intensifying; spiritual experiences were intensifying; alienation was intensifying. The cornfields, alternatingly blistering with heat and frozen in snow and ice, offered little solace. I alternated between feeling cut off from humanity and feeling embraced by Providence. The relentless criticism affected my sense of purpose and pleasure. I wrote: "Each day I realize how shallow the prior day's work has been, and if I fail to realize this, there are plenty of people around to tell me." Another night I wrote: "Everything is rich and good and full. I love God. I love myself. I love life." Deeper and deeper I plunged, into my own psyche, as I worked on *Temple of Justice*, the temple of my own being. The external stories of the clerkship became metaphors for inner development. I was searching for God without and within.

Still, my writing was criticized as "too commercial:" a critique that complimented as much as it was hostile, since we gnawed on the bone of commercial success. To be sure, I lacked the years of fiction-writing workshops that classmates had; I was coming from another profession, one in which words were used as much for destruction as creation. And yet, I had been accepted into this group, because of my "talent." There was wounding as well as support, shadow alongside light, engulfment alongside encouragement, anger as well as love.

In one session, the instructed instructor suggested there was no hope of revision for my story; I should discard what I had written—this coupled with an observation that "Philip Roth writes a hundred pages, then throws them away and starts again." Here again, the generalized or generic was used to cover up a kind of sadism behind the criticism: you might as well give up and throw it away.

Most of the class agreed that the story's irony was so heavy as to tread on satire or mockery; this may have reflected how difficult it was for me to access my emotions--or it could have uncovered a gift for satire. I did not have enough accurate feedback to know. One person defended the manuscript, but told me (in class) to "rely more on id, less on superego." She privately said the class critique was a response to my raising a critical remark about Shauna's story a few weeks earlier, which previously basked in the glow of the 'mutual admiration society.' He warned: "You have to be more political. Otherwise, you get what you deserve."

While the fiction and poetry divisions rarely mingled, as the talents were related yet disparate, I bridged the gap through Rose, a poet. Our relationship was filled with the kind of drama that fueled Rose's award-winning poetry. One night, lying on a large futon in her basement studio, she cried out to the dark: "O God, the loneliness!" She was poetry, pure and expressive; I was fiction. She lived in this visceral reality-pure feeling, no cerebrating; my strong suit was analyzing emotions. She could penetrate my mask and read the micro-emotions in my face; my specialty was not knowing what I felt, but describing accurately what I thought I felt. Rose talked about her family, origin of her torment and poetry: "My mother denied her emotional and spiritual side in order to succeed in medical school; now she's an emotional cripple who doesn't know how to show affection to her own children."

She was equally effusive about her father. "My father is a string of credentials, that's who he is. He doesn't feel any bond arising out of paternity." Rose's poetry was spontaneous and unpredictable: awake or asleep, every few hours, she would say something completely random and nonsensical, yet strangely coherent. It was like living with another version of the Monk. These bursts of induced poetry would resonate, then Rose would turn over and resume on a more normal, recognizable level. I was living with the Greek Chorus; who knew, maybe that was who she was channeling. Rose was quickly acknowledged as the best poet in the Workshop. Within a few months, she won a

A Friend of All Faiths

prestigious scholarship, which made other classmates envious. What luck, what grace, I thought: instead of a wounded inner child, she has an expressive, prize-winning, inner poet.

"Rose," I asked as she lay navel-skyward on the futon, "why poetry?"
"Rolling off the tongue like candied strawberries." When she spoke, her tongue and lips did a little dance, as if the sounds themselves were poetry. She was generally incapable of full sentences; the half-haiku was her preferred style; she might string seven or eight words together at a maximum.

We alternated between her basement and the grassy bank of the snaking brown, Iowa River, eating avocado submarines, the same place where Dixie had informed me of her aversion to lesbians. On that same altar, Rose proffered her pierced navel to the sun. ("O slender concave half-moon of milky flesh!") She rolled over and propped her chin on her elbows, reading to me from her cloth-bound journal: *Two birds squawk in unison. The sky beats them. An eyebrow is eating the moon.* The sun illumined a tattoo of two dolphins on Rose's backside.

"The art of juxtaposing two dissimilar things," she said. "An eyebrow and the moon. Yet it strangely makes sense." She licked some dark chocolate off her fingertips. "My god!" she cried to the muddy waters.

"What is it?" I asked, concerned.
"The pain, the loneliness!"
She picked up a blade of grass (not a tuft of grass, I reminded myself) and placed it between her teeth. "Love is grounded in narcissism."

"Yes, Rose," I said, encouraged by the full sentence, verb and all.
She stared at the brown water. "We fall in love because we see in the Other a mirror for ourselves." She sucked the grass, chewing its end between her molars. "And that," she removed the blade, "is the only defensible theory of desire."

I told Rose, I had to speed-read poems, because I did not understand them.
Rose rewarded my confession by turning up nude in my art class. "Paint me," she urged. "Paint what you see, not what others see."
That night I wrote a poem:
I used to think my city was paradise.
Then billboards choked the empty sky.
The boy was beautiful. Children glittered.
In the evening, they cut down the grass.
Now the cornstalks, yellowed crust.
Mowers bark, shepherds graze,
angels guzzle. Paradise is within you.
A man is changing the billboard.
The best poetry I found was at the local tae kwon do studio. Succinct, rhythmic, compelling. Haiku-like. For example, when I would lose concentration, and be thinking about my next story, the instructor would exclaim: *White belt, fifty pushups! Count ... in Korean!* I liked the cadence. I slept with wet tea-bags on my eyes to counter eye-strain from constantly reading and writing. My Workshop instructor talked about the trade-off between life, and art. "How much life are you willing to sacrifice for art?" I did not know, but I wrote that night in my journal: "I want to touch the universal heart, not just self-indulgent obsessions."

I read this to Rose, who complained: "You think too much." She added: "Do you do mushrooms? You should."

Rose led me to a nightclub, where I met an Irish woman named Mary, who taught me the Rosary and the sacraments. I was vitally interested in this information, because I had made my fictional protagonist half-Catholic, and realized I knew nothing about Catholicism. Though we only met that night, and she thereafter disappeared from the movie screen of my

Michael H. Cohen

life, in some sense, she was an important teacher, a link perhaps to later encounters with Mary. Mary's husband, George, then told me his story. In childhood, he took a G.I. Joe doll and nailed it to it two pieces of wood and burned it. His father promptly beat him.

George added: "Now I have a master-slave relationship with myself. I push myself with authority." He turned back to his drink.

Mary and George offered portals into a new awareness of a tradition vastly different than the one of my childhood–expanding the information gleaned from a brief visit to Catechism class in pursuit of a childhood crush.

I made a new friend: he had traveled, spent years in India; had a beard; he had meditated; he knew about mystical experiences. His stories contained unusual characters: he had talking monkeys, living spirits, and a character called Death. His fiction resembled that of magical realists (like Gabriel Garcia-Marquez), whereas the minimalists (Raymond Carver, Richard Ford) were in vogue at the time.

This new friend introduced me to some tapes for visualization, tapes that helped further open the experiences that had started with the monk. My new friend was ordinary, down-to-earth, intelligent. Our esoteric conversations took place in the local Taco Bell.

In our final month together, he told me a Gnostic story: the Apostles gross out as they see a decaying dog in their path; Jesus points and they notice a gleam in the tooth of the dog. My friend was fond of meditating, using this image to remind himself that "life is not shit, but even shit contains holiness. And then the comic subsumes the tragic, as we move beyond both."

With meeting Mary and her sadomasochistic husband and learning the Rosary in a nightclub, and a new friend who told Gnostic tales in a Taco Bell, life was changing again.

WASHED IN THE BLOOD

My friend the mediator invited me to a charismatic healing service at Grace Church, way out in the cornfields beyond Iowa "City." He had heard of this place; he practiced *Creative Visualization* by Shakti Gawain; and he thought the church might provide an interesting perspective; after all, we were *writers*. And so we drove into the endless yellow, toward a vaulted cement building among the fields.

The church had hanging chandeliers; the families inside were brightly lit, radiating luminescence, filling the pews in their bright clothes and faces. Grace Church represented another end of the spectrum, far from the repressed, ritualistic, cerebral tone of the communion services I had experienced in Berkeley. Rather quickly, the service gathered momentum. Singing began. Congregants let the Holy Spirit descend on them individually as, inspired and filled, they laid hands on each other and those "needing healing" in the crowd. The organ whipped faster and faster, coaxing away shyness, stirring passion. They chanted: "The Blood, the Blood, the Blood! Wash us in Your Blood!" Their hands were swaying to and fro. A giant screen hung over the organ, with a bouncing ball of lights dancing over the lyrics.

"Why in God's name," I thought to myself, "would anyone want to be washed in *blood*?" Obviously I did not understand. And indeed, simply by being present, I too was being laundered: the blood, whether literally or figuratively, dripped down in huge buckets from the vaulted ceiling over the thrilled participants who leaned their foreheads skyward to receive their God. At least everyone else could see it. Amidst the clapping and thrilling, ecstatic singing, even I leaned heavenward to see what might be raining down. The stucco ceiling, though, remained mute. After the service, a woman came up, threw her arms around me, and asked me my name.

"Michael Cohen," she repeated. "Is that Hebrew?"

"Yes," I said. "Although I was born here," I clarified. She looked uncertain, so I added: "In Ann Arbor, Michigan. Not Israel. At the University, the Medical Center."

A Friend of All Faiths

She threw her arms around me again in an unexpected expression of *agape*. I felt and received her spontaneous love. Suddenly she had her hands around my waist and leaned back. "Michael, would you like to receive God in your midst right now?"

"Do think it's a good idea?" I asked.

"Sure. Just close your eyes and pray with me...."

"Well...." I began.

"Holy Lord," she said with her eyes closed. "Holy Lord, we ask you to descend on this child of yours, Michael Cohen, let Him enter into Your light. Wash him in your blood, Lord Jesus. In the name of the Father, the Son and the Holy Spirit, Amen!"

The prayer escaped her lips before I had time to protest. Matching her stance, I bowed my head, slightly and respectfully. My analytical mind searched for an experience, but there was nothing dramatic: just a feeling of quiet contentment.

And so I too was washed in the Blood.

Late in business school, I had begun seeing a counselor, a gentle man with a slight Spanish accent who encouraged me to "relax" and do what was "enjoyable." Our sessions were short-lived, because my MBA program was ending; I was unsure why I had even begun them; and on the way to one session, riding my motorcycle, I was cut off by a driver, and flew over the handlebars, landed on my helmeted head in the middle of the opposing lane. Miraculously, there were no injuries. This had been near-death experience number two; at three-and-a-half, my tricycle had collided with an illegally-driven go-cart, causing the axel of the go-cart wheel to grind into my face, creating a scar from temple to neck. The scar actually bisected my face, moving diagonally across the forehead, between the eyes, again across the nose, down one side of my mouth, and again diagonally across the chin. I have memories of blood (I was washed in Blood early); being scooped up in a towel and brought to the hospital for surgery.

Perhaps this early experience opened my inner life, psychic life, awareness of other dimensions, and was for a reason, destined, if one subscribes to the belief that such influential events in one's life are not random. On some level, I learned early about life's fragility, and our total dependence on the divine. This early life-lesson from Upstairs preceded Downstairs classes—Hebrew school; Talmud study; experiments in Catechism class with friends in junior high school; interfaith Seminary; study at the Jewish Theological Seminary, the Barbara Brennan School of Healing, channeling, kundalini awakening, all the phenomena. Early on, I was awash in blood, baptized in blood, learning about our flesh-and-blood heritage and the limited nature of the body.

Counseling. My relaxed and gentle Spanish counselor at Berkeley was round number two. I had gone to see a counselor in college, at Columbia's Health Services, but found the counselor unhelpful and antagonistic; I had visited to explore my terror around visits to the eye doctors, and instead was interrogated about possible depression. Round three: I found a female counselor in Iowa City who, I hoped, would help me unlock inner secrets conducive to further freeing my creativity for writing. Again, the tack was not what I expected: she had me do various bioenergetic exercises, like taking a tennis racket and smashing a pillow while saying over and over again, "Stop it!" Sure enough, this exercise tapped into a vein of anger; whether I had residual anger from childhood this or that was uncertain; I suspected that anyone smashing a tennis racket into a pillow while saying "stop it" would trigger some memory of violation somewhere along the human experience; and within a session or two, my hands were blistered, and that was the end of that therapy.

I visited a professor to discuss my experience at Grace Church. His response was to read me a passage from Plato's *Phaedra*, which observes that the lawmaker and the poet are the same: lovers of wisdom, who devote their lives to twisting words around the page, so that the written compositions become precious gifts to humanity. The professor suggested we meet weekly to discuss my relationship with God. At this time, I connected with a

Michael H. Cohen

passage from Tolstoy's diaries:

As a young man I began prematurely to analyze everything and to destroy unmercifully. I was often afraid and thought - I'll have nothing intact; but here I am getting old, and I still have a lot intact and unharmed ... and I still have unshaken my love for one woman; children and everything to do with them.... Is that all? It's an awful lot.

The reading; the nights writing until dawn; the visits with the Greek professor; creative visualization; the initiation from the Monk; and being washed in the Blood; intense dreams. Though I had come for fiction writing, I was undergoing a shift.

The Greek professor had this to say about counseling: "You can't even begin to think about your father. You're doing that only with the father, but you have history with the fathers', and his father and his father before him, reaching back to Abraham. And behind them, you've got the Father. Have you ever read Kafka's letter to his father? He knew what I'm talking about." And then the conversation shifted again. "God is a loving father," the Greek professor said. "God loves you; there is nothing to fear." We sat in his small office, overlooking the winding Iowa River, the spots where I had courted Rose over avocado sandwiches and poetry. The professor made a sign with his fingers. "Man has two triangles of flame: the one pointing up, the other down. When you follow the false spirits, the lower one fills up and drags you down. When you follow God, He lifts you up; the lower flame swings up and joins the upper one."

I stared at the row of Greek books on his shelf: classics, probably Homer, Sophocles, the greats. I told him I was having recurring nightmares, in which this intruding and frightening face appears in my childhood bedroom.

"God is facing you," the professor interpreted. "The face is your own."

I was unsure. I told him about creative visualization. He was skeptical, emphatic. "The loving God has spoken to you for two thousand years!" He gestured with his hands. "Again and again He tells you, *do not fear, I am with you.* You are *filled* with Him; you have only to pick up His word and fill yourself!" He pointed to a shelf full of New Testaments. "You have your Holy Book; why turn to Eastern practice? Jerusalem is Eastern; Judaism is Eastern!"

I disputed the Professor's contention that Judaism represented all things Eastern, or carried sufficiently Eastern Easternness, whatever that might be, to satisfy my search. Something in me resisted the insistence, subtle or not, that I stick to "Western" religion, to the common home port of the "Old" "Testament."

Certainly I found my home, my roots in Judaism; and West and East served more as metaphors than geographical locators of religious history. Yet, these experiences ... the Monk ... yoga ... the white fire, black fire ... the Blood ... dreams ... even a bit of psychotherapy ... everything was an opening. I was becoming a friend of all faiths, not limited to one holy book opposed to another, not opposing East to West, not contrasting one faith to another, not interested in the differences, but rather pursuing the common thread of mystical experience among them all. And even the Professor's fundamentalist approach could not stem the tide of inner experience.

Awakening. When the Serpent, coiled at the back of the spine, begins to rise, all hope of analyzing, describing, studying, or containing the experience dissolves. The energy is infinitely more powerful than anything a human personality can handle. According to ancient texts, it is the energy of the entire creation, secreted within the human body. Different religious traditions have various metaphors for and descriptions of awakening, and this notion of an energetic awakening in the form of serpentine awareness can be found and perused in the works of religious scholars.

My dormant energy was awakened by reading a book entitled, *Kundalini.* I simply assert this as so because no other language or explanation corresponds with my experience. When I read others' kundalini accounts they map some correspondence for my own.

A Friend of All Faiths

Though some assert a biological basis for kundalini rising, there is little consensus. Being remains a mystery. Nothing neurological, ever has been detected or recorded about this aspect of my own mystical experience, nor would I reduce the 'raw data' of my awakening to someone else's speculative or dismissive interpretation. Instead I can only share my own understanding of a consciously experienced awakening.

The 'energy hit' from reading the book was powerful beyond anything previously experienced or imagined—not terrifying, but overwhelming in intensity, occupying sensation completely with scintillating vibration.

The book cover had a photograph of its author. He was Indian, with a red dot on his forehead and a short fuzzy beard. There was sweetness to his face, softness about the red cashmere sweater he sported. But I was more interested initially in the book's contents than in him; I did not, at the time, realize that according to Sanskrit writings, one could have a kundalini awakening simply by looking at the photograph of one capable of transmitting such an awakening.

To allow as much—a spiritual awakening by the will of a disembodied teacher—would be ideologically dangerous: it would grant the author of the book on kundalini (or any other 'Guru') a kind of superhuman power; it would mean that he was a living being, standing (or perhaps hovering) right next to me as I read the book; that he could transmit energy by thought; that he might be, perhaps, what they call a Master, one who has mastered the energy and can initiate others; it might mean that I would have a personal relationship with him, as one does with a *guru*, a master teacher. To have a guru, then, might, in a distorted chain of thinking, mean succumbing to another person or force; worse, yet, drowning my hard-earned Judaism, the religion of my birth for which my ancestors were martyred, in a kind of neo-Eastern idol-worship, raising a human being (this man who lived, whose childhood name did not have the label "guru") into the status of a deity.

All this and many other blasphemies and heresies, and betrayal, in the thinking of the Greek professor, of the God who *already loved me*, and *already had written personally to me*, in the form of our Holy Book, the Torah, which I was privileged by my Jewish education to be able to read in the original Hebrew, on the scroll itself, without *nekudot* (vowels); of the God who had ample tools to convey grace, who could do so just as easily through Israel as through India. And yet, there was something about this teacher: I could just as easily see him (and indeed, years later did so see him) wrapped in a *tallit*, the ritual Jewish fringes. And I found something much deeper about the notion of a guru or teacher than the fears the concept raise in our culture, something more beautiful and intimate than blind submission or obeisance to a *person*. In the teachings I imbibed, the Guru is the inner teacher that the outer teacher awakens; the Guru is the *Shakti*—the energy, not the *vyakti*, the person. Even though the Guru means one's own inner teacher, somehow that energy gets crystallized in the form of an outer teacher, someone who helps on the path, like a finger pointing toward the moon. I remembered reading in *Be Here Now* that Ram Dass, former Harvard faculty member, traveled to India, and met his teacher, who merely touched him on the forehead, sending him into some ecstatic mystical experience. I remembered reading this in college and thinking, *poppycock*! And yet, the experience of reading the kundalini book took me beyond dismissal, beyond cognitive boxing, beyond an arrogant assumption of knowing all.

I then turned to a scholarly book on the kundalini, *The Serpent Power*. The rise of the serpent energy is claimed to be the beginning of the journey for which all paths have prepared. Much information about the rise of this 'Serpent energy' comes from Indian scripture, though it finds correspondences in other literature. Yet this book tells the story of experience, not scholarship about world religions, and the title I have chosen for this book conveys my reluctance to frame my experience in terms of a single tradition. Suffice it to say that within weeks or months of reading the book about the Kundalini, I was visiting a friend in Oakland, California. We happened to pass a meditation place; I stopped in, and was offered to do *seva* (selfless service), by washing dishes. "Cult," I shuddered, declining the invitation, and almost missing everything by a quick judgment; the offeror was no less sincere and inviting than the woman who had prayed over me in Grace Church.

I was invited also to visit the "Meditation Cave." This was a darkened room where the author of the book on kundalini used to meditate. At the time, I did not connect him with this place. I simply opened the door and entered the room, completely dark, until my eyes adjusted and I could see purple cushions dotting the carpeting. At the front hung a portrait of a man, of swarthy skin and deep-set, penetrating eyes, which seemed alive and powerful. The portrait seemed more like a living presence.

Later I learned that once he had been asked by a concerned seeker: "What if I lose myself in meditation?" To which he is said to have replied: "Go ahead, lose yourself. I will find you." This anecdote reflects my experience in the meditation cave: the living presence in the portrait walked forward, greeted me in meditation and initiated me, igniting the divine energy in my own body. This was a classic experience known as, *shaktipat*-the awakening of the Serpent energy.

On returning to Iowa City, it seemed that my dream life rose a notch in frequency, intensity, and depth of vivid detail. I had dreams of floating and flying; of dissolving into white light; of meeting different divine beings. I could feel the energy playing around different parts of my body. I would see my field of vision ablaze with purple during meditation. I had messages from departed relatives in my dreams.

In certain shamanistic cultures, the notion of hearing others' thoughts is well-accepted. In this state of recent heightened awareness, I perceived hearing other people's thoughts. For example, I thought I received telepathic information from my grandmother, who was living in Detroit. Another time, I had a dream about a fellow in a leather jacket named Guzman; the next morning, I hailed a taxi, and looked with shock at the driver's nameplate: it said "Guzman." I knew that on a theoretical level, space-time could flow backwards (e.g., from future to past) as easily as forward, but found it hard to believe that the universe was so organized and self-aware that a taxi driver would have the same name as the one I had dreamed the night before.

That night, on going to sleep, I heard a voice: "*Believe in yourself and your God-given gift.*" Whatever the gift was, I interpreted this message as a command from the Inner Teacher—perhaps God within me—to continue to pay attention to the inner process. Skepticism was fine, uncritical embrace was not required—as Paul Tillich noted, faith includes doubt; as long as I directed attention to this growing awareness of a life within the life I thought I was leading. And so I mentally opened myself. There were many voices coming to me, as if I had stepped into the universal, live "Internet chat room." But this did not cause alarm—I simply paid attention.

And through reading, learned I was not alone. A professor in Columbia's medical school had heard a voice in a dream, telling her: *This is A Course on Miracles, take notes.* That was the start of a many-year process in which she channeled a book of psychological and spiritual material. As I began to read books specifically about kundalini, such as Philip St. Romain, *Kundalini Energy and Christian Spirituality*; Lee Sanella, *The Kundalini Experience*; and best of all, Gopi Krishna, *Kundalini*, I realized I was not alone in experiencing, as St. Romain put it, a "highly energized liquid forcing its way through the pinhole opening that was the point of the forceps, and seeming boring its way toward its destination" in my crown.

Continuing with *Altered States of Consciousness* by Charles Tart opened me to the ease with which I could now move into ASC's, and to the connections between mystical experience and psychologists' understanding of these states. I took notes on characteristics of an ASC: alternation in thinking; disturbed time sense; changing emotional expression; perceptual distortions; loss of control. Yet I knew that I could always choose to "wake up" from the trance state. Dreams came with numinous images piled on one another, and sound effects too, layers of information:

I am flying over everything. One scene fades into another and whales are slipping down the mountains toward me. I realize I can fly over the mountain. I say, napalm. The whales and seals burn up. Then all these people are soldiers in there, and I'm thinking that I love my creatures but how is it possible to do so much when they're out there just bombing each other right and left. I'm hovering over the mountain seeing these different groups of armies. I decide to keep moving, make it pleasant. I go past the edge and there's my sanctuary, it's called the Zen Center which has been set up for worship. It's all light and clear. I go further and further beyond the windowpane. The window becomes larger and larger as I get closer and then I'm into the window and through it out the other side into the woods. Now I am in a forest which is all white with trees. It's snowy and beautiful and magnificent and I've never seen anything like it. My mouth is open and this incredible Ave Maria comes out of it, just this high-pitched voice, it's like ten voices in one, just Ah-ah-ve, A, ah ... coming out of me, it's the most incredible moment. I'm hovering, I can control my distance from the ground and can see the entire thing and I'm swooping over these beautiful fields of snow and white and naked trees and it's just incredible. Then I try to see whether I can maintain that, whether I'm actually in real life singing, so I wake up and find that my lips are open but no sound is coming out. How amazing, no fear, just enjoying.

The days were filled with critiques of writing; the nights with encounters in which I could do incredible things: fly while singing *Ave Maria*; hover over armies; swoop over snowy fields.

Dreaming, I was in a bicycle race. But my bicycle was locked in an inconvenient spot. I was wearing a polyester suit and people made fund of me. I got down on someone, because I could not afford anything better at this point of my life. The dream informed an increasingly distressful real-life situation. I had contracted with the expatriate teacher to write a book together about writing. During conversation, he kept using the phrase "master and disciple," which made me uncomfortable. I figured that in the dream, "disciple" was transformed into "bicycle." In the race, everyone was prepared except me.

A subsequent dream affirmed my growing discomfort with this man:

I follow this teacher on a bicycle. We come out of the library. He sings one line from Haydn's Lord Nelson Mass and I sing another. We are laughing and joking and I keep up with him. He runs first into the elevator and I am behind. He makes obscure references which I don't catch. He says some scholar had invited me to Boscilania and I should be grateful. How would I get there, I wonder, how far down the tip of Africa would we have to go, not to go off the edge of the earth. Then his bicycle goes ahead of mine. He gives me directions. I'm sure I follow them: two blocks and make a left. He's out of sight and I'm in a labyrinth all over again.

It's horrible: the houses are big and scary and I'm at a dead end. All that's out there is restaurants. I'm afraid the dogs will come out. I pedal as fast as I can; the bike does not work properly. There are rows of chickens—cut, cooked, hundreds of them—I have to bicycle over them and splatter them and they go everywhere. On my bike I fly out the wooden doors in this barn I'm in. I'm on the street riding away.

The dreams offered clues to emotions I could not consciously embrace. I had not yet met Bob, but attuning to the dreams offered a way to make sense of my feelings. After this dream, I abandoned the collaboration with the expatriate. Unwilling to become his acolyte, I simply relinquished my rights to the manuscript we had been putting together. He had become a negative teacher, an archetype that would reappear following the Workshop in encounters with Nick.

In the next dream, I met the Wise Old Man of Myth, who turned out to be my poetry teacher. My unconscious was apparently sensitized to real events, freely conflating "real" and "imaginary" in the world of night-dreams. But I was also dreaming about healing people through the power of meditation, a theme that began surfacing in dream life, too. I was taking a different direction at the Workshop than the path of the writer—moving instead into interest in healing.

Paradoxically, time at the Workshop was a perfect incubator for spiritual expansion, because I had no boundaries when it came to sleep, and found it perfectly acceptable to write until 4 am or to start at 4 am and begin sleeping at 9. A dream:

I am talking to my expatriate teacher over pizza. I examine the triangular slice, with an artichoke on top. I had eaten something mysterious; what was left had a long sperm or yin-yang shaped thing with teeny arms or bulbs emanating from it. I was reading in a book that this was the basic shape of the universe—it was green, standing for all living things. In the Nutcracker, *which was on the radio, the soldier's dance is a whirl, turning faster and faster, recreating the form which now looks like a series of asterisks, which is the basic element of continuity and narrative as he dances toward the women. This is the basic structure of the universe.*

I want to ask Mom, but she doesn't want to talk about it. I approach my middle brother Danny: "guess what this is?" He seems to know. He says: "the basic shape of the universe." I say: "How's that." He answers: "We're living in a fallen world, and if that is true then our physical destruction, after the destruction of the universe, will be sufficient justification to activate the dormant part of ourselves which is spiritual."

I think: the shape is green, the shape of a man with his arm stretched; the shape of the cross; the shape of the female symbol, if you elongate the bulb at one end so it becomes a stick and loop with sperm-like arms. It is a sperm with arms, the shape of Tao, the shape of the female principle, a quotation mark or upside-down comma with arms, or maybe the yin-yang transposed horizontally and shrunken onto others. By shape of the universe, I mean the Klein bottle or Mobius strip. A three-leaf clover: the number three. I am playing weird music on a tape, a T.S. Eliot poem that just goes: Dum, Pum ... with bizarre noises. The shape is also the ghost-like outline of a human, or maybe essence of the spirit.

When kids draw the sun, a little circle with rays, straight lines of light coming out, they are drawing an image of the Self, an energy sphere that radiates out to everything around them.

If I had analyzed the artichoke on the pizza to this extent in a real-life, pizza shop, a licensed psychologist probably would have made a diagnosis. Yet, somehow dreams afford the safety in which everything can be revealed, everything seen in its true light. All these shapes, colors, images, had meaning. To a mystic the whole world was filled with dazzling light, and with meaning; so, too, to Renee, the schizophrenic girl.

What differentiated awakened dreaming from pathology, and how did one follow the razor's edge of the creative process without dipping into madness on one hand, or demonism on the other (like my classmates who enjoyed hanging out in places carrying memories of suicides or murder victims, and tried to derive inspiration from darkness)?

Happy children drawing the sun *were* drawing the Self, it seemed to me—they understood in a state of primordial grace that most adults could not access. If dreams sometimes offered an atavistic, primitive regression to earlier regions of the psyche, then dreams offered a gift: relief from all that logical analysis and inescapable worrying that characterized ordinary mental life. They offered a highly compressed version of input from the day, a map to inner realms where even the shape of artichoke on pizza could point a finger to the Godhead.

The Workshop was ostensibly a search for honesty—clear expression of emotional and spiritual truth. Frequently it provided the reverse: a mask for authentic expression. One creative attempt to recover authenticity was a student's effort to emulate "music television" by filming Workshop students reciting poetry. This medium intrigued me; actors who meditate have told me that they regard the camera as terrifying yet liberating, because of its capacity for objectively recording the truth of emotions. On stage, an actor can evade truth in the sense of elevating the voice or using blocking for dramatic effect, but one cannot lie before the camera–its eye reveals all.

The camera entered my dreams as a metaphor for choosing levels of consciousness. In one dream I told a friend, "shhh, I'm looking at this image."

I could both have her in the dream, and yet if I didn't look at her I could concentrate on these images so I could control the images and not lose them even though something else was going on in the dream–it was almost like reality where someone sits next to you, and your mind is formulating images on the screen. She noticed and said: "wow, you can change that." It is just like a screen. Because– after that the camera or screen looked it was a camera going through a house. The camera (I was maneuvering) would wobble, or go upside-down or sideways or have special effects like a movie when you pan on something.

If I could control the camera, I could control the scene. The camera was also the mind– the movie-screen of images in the landscape of feeling and thought. If Patanjali defined meditation as stilling the willy-nilly movements of the mind, then controlling the camera of the mind was meditation.

It was amazing to have my mind working just like a camera. Which was similar to the labyrinth dream where you're coming down a staircase that you're not just– you know, in normal life–you're looking at something as though the camera is playing tricks. So this picture of me in the dream turns into a little boy who is smiling. I'm saying, "okay, I'm making it heal, I'm making this boy feel happy...." Suddenly we're a camera going into kitchen, panning sideways. We're now in a restaurant, where we see a beautiful woman with a hat, like a Toulouse-Lautrec painting. And another one is next to her in a booth. I think: "let me see that." The camera comes down to the booth. The woman is making out with a man; she looks surprised that I'm there. My girlfriend is watching this on the screen, but meanwhile I've moved beyond the screen to the action. I want to see the booth to the right. It's a little difficult, but I can get the camera to move and there's a woman, being taken captive by a waiter with a hood. I decide the waiter does not deserve the kind of procedural protections my girlfriend has been discussing, so I give him a punch in the face and nothing happens. I light up a laser sword and we're lasering away. Then suddenly I become the man in the black hood: I turn around and have fangs, my face is all dark and bloated. I turn around and make a 360 or 180 with my face, slowly, I'm looking at you with the camera, and the laser light takes a wide swath at everybody.

This dream showcased anger–not only about the competitiveness at the Workshop, but also the coming end of the Workshop and return to Wall Street to begin at the law firm. I sensed I would be giving up an important part of myself. I dreamed again that I was looking at a map, dotted by many towns.

Dad goes to the bank to pay taxes. It turns out there is a job available. So he signs me up! It pays $5.50 an hour, more than minimum wage. Dad is filling out the forms. I tell him: "This job, I just can't take it. I hope you don't think this arrogant, but it's not worthy of my talents. I only have a limited amount of time and I should be doing something different. This is the kind of job I could've done a long time ago, it's going to be an hour-long commute, and it's just not worth it."

I was in rebellion against the need to follow Adam and crawl on my belly like everyone else. Wilhelm Reich writes of the "NO," the command the child learns at age two thrusts him or her out of the world of infantile unity consciousness and into the painful separation from the permissive, nurturing, Mother archetype. The world is no longer Yes; it is now divided into "must" and "should." The Law Firm was the Father, the No archetype, the expulsion from Eden. Rather than seeing this chance to join a world-class, Wall Street firm as opportunity, I saw it as manifesting the post-Eden indictment. In fact, in the dream, I told my father that my riches would exceed $5.50 an hour if only I was allowed to do what Joseph Campbell called, "follow your bliss." *And then this bank employee says: "Two things: One, I see your point. Two, but I've never dealt with anyone with less social grace."*

In the dream, I had done the unacceptable, gone beyond social convention. The bank teller agreed with me that this was right. But then she condemned me for not immediately accepting the path of success in law school–a prestigious clerkship, a prestigious Wall Street firm. I had veered from the professional path, dived into spirituality.

At least I was making progress since childhood dreams, in which I used to imagine I was flying, lose control, fly too high and suddenly drop. Although my dreams in Iowa were infused with a mix of emotions about rejoining the world–at times I was the avenging hero, at others, the dark "hood"–the dreams also manifested a growing sense of awareness behind the camera. I was writing, making choices, expressing myself, learning that spirituality and creativity and the world of law were coming together within me.

A friend from New York admonished me: "You came to Iowa to write a novel, not to decide whether your kneecap is the next chakra."

I disagreed. St. Romain had written:

I began to experience falling into a semitrance state. My breathing would taper off to almost nothing ... and the visual background with my eyes closed would become a beautiful shade of blue.... With my eyes closed in deep silence, I was treated daily to an aurora borealis of ultra-purple and shimmering gold lights.... I began to experience wise sayings coming into my mind as from a higher self of some kinds.... I had a distinct feeling of receiving messages from another, and for the first time in my life, I began to understand how some of the passages in Scripture came to be written.

I recorded hundreds of dreams and messages. I would wake up in the middle of the night and transcribe perhaps three or four vivid dreams. Some of these dreams involved my family, others involved archetypes. Some dreams reflected increasing tension about returning to New York to join my law firm. I had recurring dreams about endless winding staircases; Joseph Campbell calls this the "labyrinth" dream–Jonah running from God, only to find himself in a nightmare.

In one dream Mary spoke. In the dream, I asked her: "Why can't you appear during the day, like a normal person?"

She replied: "Someday, I will."

In another dream, a rabbi appeared. I asked him: "What is the meaning of my existence? Is it better to study dream interpretation, or Torah?" He said: "Torah. The other depletes a man." I responded: "I'm not sure this is true for me." He said: "Then again, I don't know everything; who does." I said: "That's quite an honest statement. I'm glad I don't have to stick to the Torah."

I dreamed that I was flying along the highway, beneath the stars; ahead of me, a woman was floating, seated in lotus position.

I had another dream:

Rats are coming out of a tunnel toward the crowd. I leave the tunnel and enter a cab. The driver is Indian. I realize we are going to crash and die. First I say the Shema ("hear O Israel, the Lord our God, the Lord is One"), then I try self-remembering, then I exit through my third eye."

This dream prefigured or at least had the feeling of my 1997 car accident.

My first job had been at Weinstein Jewelers in Old Orchard Mall, West Bloomfield, Michigan. I was thirteen; my great-uncle Fred owned the store. His son, who was ten years my senior and served as my supervisor, used to sing: "Michael, the Lover; before him ... there was no other." I did not know why this song would come to him as we sorted out boxes in the store attic. The Lover: archetype for seeker of God. Seeker also of the feminine: nurturance, receptivity, emotional openness as counterpoint to the masculine world of business, law, achievement; a quest for the soft freedom of the inner world and escape from the tyranny of external pressures. And again, the Kundalini energy *is* known as the Divine Mother. She was awakened inside me–in a very real and not just metaphorical way. I could feel this energy arising in my own body, a different experience than implicit in the notion of a transcendental God "out there."

The kundalini is described as awakening *within* the spine, as the rush of Shakti (the female aspect of the godhead) toward Shiva as she moves from the base of the spine toward the crown. The energy rush up into my spine: the godhead both as immanent and transcendent; later, in healing school, the Divine Mother would come to me as the *Shekinah* (the feminine aspect of God), or as the Sabbath Bride (She came once as a guide during a healing, all in white). I felt the universality of the same feminine aspect of a loving, all-pervasive God, manifesting in different disguises: the serpent of fire charging up my spine; the Hindu deity; the Christian Mary; the Jungian archetype; the Jewish *Shekinah*. But to feel this love, a sense of unbroken communion with the divine, took work. And, I was trying to reconcile the Judaism of my childhood with my kundalini awakening, lucid dreaming, divine love, and other experiences of the numinous. I was like Saul on his way to becoming Paul, only it was Michael becoming Michael.

ASHRAM

(LYKENS AND UPSTATE NEW YORK, 93-96)

"Is Liberation attainable this lifetime?"
"You are already Liberated.
You have only to meditate and realize That."

SHORT MOUNTAIN, DEEP VALLEY

Yea though I walked through the shadow of the valley of Wall Street, I feared no evil, for I knew something else was in store. I completed a three-year rotation through the law firm's securities, banking, and mergers & acquisitions department. My reviews indicated that I had the head for this work but not the long-term commitment. Divine Mother had promised, through Nick's channeling, "*I will set your feet on higher ground*," but I had left Nick, was seeing the purple light on my own, and needed a grounded, pragmatic path, "higher" or "lower," to earn a living.

My firm generously paid for a career counselor to help sort out the next professional move. I had earned enough goodwill through my work to receive an extended period of paid soul-searching. I appreciated the long lag time; I needed it. I felt sufficiently skillful to continue in corporate law, but the counselor focused on other aspects of my search. In response to her questions, I mentioned the ten-day seminar on Ericksonian hypnosis during vacation time at the firm. I suddenly saw white shadows dancing on the wall. I listened inside, and saw these as some of my spirit guides. Obviously I was in the right place, seeking right advice. The career counselor did not notice my eyes flashing to the white figures. She told me that my insistence on retaining identity as a corporate lawyer was at odds with my variegated educational background. The clerkship pointed to litigation; the three graduate degrees (together with the ministerial ordination and hypnotherapy experience) suggested legal academe. That was the path she recommended–to become a law professor. "You seem to like school."

The first move was to change to a medium-sized firm in midtown, doing a mix of civil and criminal litigation. I had to try something, and it would take time to find a job in legal academe. Once again, the work was intellectually interesting and I had an aptitude for it, but had no heart for the work, and the hours were punitive. The final straw was the new partner who, eight-months pregnant, insisted I continue to research legal issues throughout the night on several projects. Each time, with the brief due in court at 9 am, she would not quit tinkering until 8:35, sending us flying toward staplers, clips, envelopes, messenger cabs. When sunrise came on one occasion, I had it out with her and went home to sleep; then I quit.

I wandered onto Fifth Avenue, called Natasha, and screamed into the phone (loud enough, I figured, for God to hear): "I WILL NOT DO THIS ANYMORE!" And promptly checked into a local synagogue to put my hands on my lap and contact Divine Mother within.

I received no answers inside, just the equivalent of 'keep walking on the path.' I believe in retrospect that the answers, certain events were pre-programmed. For example, because I spent my first year of law school in Boston, and had a girlfriend from Massachusetts, I took the Massachusetts Bar, which turned out to be useful when interviewing for a job as a legal scholar at Harvard University seven years later. The Israelites had wandered in the desert for forty years, grumbling (they would have shouted in cell-phones had they been able to) while all along their entrance into the land of milk-n-honey was divinely preordained. The peregrinations, meanderings, and circumlocutions were destined; like *bashert*, the term karma helps encapsulate that we are destined to wander for a time, meet interesting souls, be blown across the seas of life like Odysseus, meet giants and gods as well as swine. But shouting into the phone on Fifth Avenue at the time, I did not see much resonance with the Israelites in the desert.

Instead, I took my savings from the law firm (enough to live on for a few months) and had two cards printed: Michael H. Cohen, Attorney-At-Law and Michael H. Cohen, Certified Hypnotherapist.

In college, I had decided never to enter academe: I had too many memories of students' heads bobbing up and down, as Sleep nudged them into stupefying silence. I wondered how

Michael H. Cohen

professors could tolerate it. Then again, Milton Erickson, the great hypnotherapist, was famous for lulling medical students to sleep-literally boring them into an unconscious stupor so that he could work on them at a subconscious level through hypnotic metaphors. So perhaps I could learn to deal with this.

On the other side of Sleep was Hydra, the multi-headed demon, faculty politics. Having served in several capacities in student government, I knew Hydra guarded the door to academic promotion.

As the universe would have it, one door closes, another opens, and the waiting, with all its depression and freighted anxiety, is part of the path of clearing. I landed a job as a law professor in Pennsylvania, thus closing the door on Wall Street. The law school's location turned out to be an equidistant drive from New York City, where Natasha and my parents lived, from the healing school where I would shortly study, and from the ashram where I would spend my summers.

I purchased a cedar house on Short Mountain in rural Lykens, Pennsylvania, a thousand feet up the driveway from a farm, located on six acres of forest. The location was still; at night I could sense my guides, hovering on the wrap-around deck. I was alone on the mountain, literally: a thousand feet of dirt driveway from a neighbor, with my spiritual books and a commitment to descend twice a week for back-to-back teaching of Civil Procedure, a course about litigation strategy.

Around this time, I took a ski vacation in Montreal, stopped in a bookstore, when Barbara Brennan's book, *Hands of Light*, literally fell off a shelf and landed in my lap. Gazing at the illustrations of the different layers of the auric field (or "human energy field," HEF), as Barbara saw them through her "high sense perception" (or HSP), I was amazed that someone else could actually *see* and *hear* the guides, and with such specificity. Barbara had a rare gift, and when she came to town, I decided to attend her talk, held in a local hotel.

The audience was filled with believers in guides, auras, chakras, and non-corporeal messages, and momentarily I separated myself from them, imagining myself to be this rational, Wall Street lawyer, as opposed to them–the rabble-- embracing all sorts of things, self-deluding. Despite my opening with Nick, experiences of the numinous were not integrated into my personality as a whole. I denied that I was a healer, filtered everything through my skepticism.

In a demonstration on stage, Barbara seemed to be channeling someone's dead parent, and at the same time, facilitating a conversation between the deceased and the subject on stage. During the break, I wandered into a small, side room, where as it turned out, Barbara was recuperating. Respecting her privacy, I said nothing. But I sensed that something had been exchanged, some bond had been forged, some recognition had occurred.

Several months later, I signed up for her inaugural, four-day workshop.

The second day, I found myself, unexpectedly screaming on a healing table, with someone removing entities from my ankle, and simultaneously connecting with Mary and someone named Kwan Yin. When I, in turn, completed my first "chelation"–Barbara's term for the method of energy healing she teaches–I hugged my client, and we both cried.

The workshop seemed to have removed barriers (Wilhelm Reich would call it "character armoring") to fuller emotional and spiritual experience. Even during the period with Nick and other Seminary students, I had rarely allowed myself to go so deep. While Nick, despite his psychic attainment, had strewn the spiritual opening with psychological debris via his unresolved wounding, Barbara Brennan and her teachers had pledged to integrate the psychological and the spiritual. Their work thus was supposed to facilitate access not only to the highest levels of conscious–including the angelic realms–but also to the deepest core, our essence, the place past wounding, where genuine love resides. And accessing those places meant wading through the muck of past hurts, and healing on emotional as well as spiritual levels: that required honest confrontation.

I entered the Brennan School, then five days at a time, five times a year, for four years.

A Friend of All Faiths

Curiously, I kept no notes during my time in school—perhaps because the transformation was so pervasive. Much of our time was spent on the table, as a "client," or beside the table, as a "healer."

Most of what occurred on the table, either as client or healer, would challenge most beliefs—experiences stretched beyond what even many mystics from various religious traditions have reported. And Brennan insisted that healing consisted of "skills" that could be transferred, was specific about skills to be learned and tested.

I was graded (pass/no-pass) on such subjects as: "silver & lavender purge microbes; spine cleaning (levels 1-7); restructuring levels 1&3; consciousness awareness: aura, hara, core star; upwell core star & hara & aura & physical; hold hara line straight; 5th level spiritual surgery; interpret chakra with hand; 7th level sewing; perceive inside physical body [teacher commented: "good connection"]; restructuring organs; perceive 7 levels with 2 senses; healing cords; listening skills; contact skills; understanding how to handle transference; main belief/image and its constellation; knowledge of the wound; idea of ego & superego; witness - sit as witness; boundary issues" (junior year).

One of the experiences I reported in *Beyond Complementary Medicine* involved sensing parts of a fetus within the energy field of a student on the table, and then—as Barbara had done in her demonstration—allowing the feelings and words of that being to come through during the meditative, healing state, and energetically allowing the mother to grieve, while "clearing cords" of relationship and thereby facilitating a healing encounter between the two. Such experiences occurred without having any prior information of the client's history.

Another time, I worked on a female friend. I had entered the Brennan school skeptical and denying that I was a "healer"—just as I had entered psychotherapy skeptical and denying that I had any emotional work to do; and had entered the interfaith Seminary program masking my passionate quest for God with the veneer of mere intellectual interest in different religious traditions. The truth was that I had an innate reservoir for deep, mystical experience—a passionate life beneath the surface of the 'quiet scholar' archetype. And mystical experience came quickly, easily, as it had with Nick. While my friend lay on the table, a vision opened in which I "saw" her as a soldier during the American Civil War, during which time I saw myself working as a surgeon on the battlefield who perhaps knew Lincoln in the White House. The images came visually and in the form of direct perception.

After the healing, my friend independently reported that while lying on the table, she had seen herself on a Civil War battlefield. My vision was confirmed.

During the opening of four years in healing school, I came to sense the presence of the guides by expanding my awareness beyond thinking, feeling, and the usual five senses. Such recognition, thought in many religious traditions to be reserved for prophets especially chosen by God for revelation, is in my experience a simple shift an awareness that can be taught—just as most 'skeptics' are easily 'hypnotizable' if they allow themselves to enter a slightly altered, trance state, one away from what Tart had called 'consensus' trance. I came to understand that we and other beings co-exist, sharing spaces between dimensions, of which the material reality in which we pay taxes, worry about the rent, fold laundry, and buy clothes is only a small part. Do ants know what we think and consider, and what do we know of their world? Yet we share their space. The leap in logic required to embrace such experience was a demand that everything be experienced and measured in the physical world; the leap was one of consciousness.

The two hundred and forty students in my class moved through freshman year—healing our characterological deficiencies; into sophomore year—learning the astral realms and facing our shadows; into junior year—perfecting our high sense perception, working on all seven layers of the field, and learning to coordinate with guides from different realms; and then into senior year—facing what still lay in shadow, and claiming our power and identities as healers.

Over time, the constant reminder of these other realms came increasingly frequently and naturally: between school sessions, I would return to Pennsylvania or my parents' home in

New York City, and sense energy all around me. Such sensing—Don Juan calls it *seeing*—is common in other cultures, but it could become confusing in mine, a world in which information overload is routine. How, for instance, can I explain that I am disturbed by the distorted, etheric mucus emanating from someone's solar plexus while in line for a Starbuck's coffee? Or that someone in the elevator is trying to hook up with my cords? Or, that I can sense aggression two lanes over and one car down? Integrating what I had learned with the reality of a culture not steeped in high sense perception would be key to assimilating the knowledge and using the awakening wisely.

I struggled. Early on, one of my teachers remarked that I had a lot of sensitivity in my palms. "One day," he predicted, "your client will be on the table, screaming and kicking; you'll be pulling stuff out of the astral levels for them; and your guides will be giving instructions. You're opening to what we were all given at birth."

At the time, I had doubted this prediction, until over four years the "skills" had become a familiar part of myself, one I was only learning to rediscover.

All this time I taught Civil Procedure, but the more time I spent studying energy healing, the less sense three-dimensional, highly intellectualized, law school reality made, and the more I became aware of other dimensions around my students and colleagues. During one faculty meeting, a conversation about "down-sizing" created visible shadows around particular speakers, a clogging; and in one meeting, I saw a demon speak through someone. Karma was real, apparent: and as I watched others' auric fields—literally brightening and darkening—I learned a lot about free will. We did, indeed, have choices: channel angels or demons, and no matter how we rationalize or justify ourselves (whether using language of religion, or language of academic politics), the entities are what they are. Or as the Gospels put it, we fight not against the flesh, but against principalities of darkness—angels and demons appeared as real to my expanded consciousness as flesh-and-blood figures--just as the literature and art of so many cultures had asserted.

I wrote in *Future Medicine* that "hate is hate and love is love, no matter what the banner." Since healing school, our society has moved into a time where Armageddon seems imminent, with suicide vests, car bombers, biological weapons, degraded behavior toward the environment, nuclear proliferation, a global culture of living daily with the possibility of terrorism anywhere, shared recognition of our vulnerability and interdependence, and a pitting of religions against one another with clerics brandishing hatred under the banner of *jihad* or some other concept distorted from the true transcendental impulse of religious founders. The seeds of unity awareness were sown in healing school—and as well, the desire to eventually merge the fruits of this experience with everything I had learned in law school, my professional identity as a lawyer, and even my undergraduate work in political science; and writing, too.

In short, healing school opened doorways to expanded perception to both hatred and love. It also brought new experiences of intimacy, as it gradually wore down the barriers. In school, (consensual) touching was frequent and expected, though not invasive; as were long, meaningful gazes and intense exchanges, not so much in terms of verbalization, but measured via endless empathy, filled with understanding conveyed through glance, breath, body. If Buddha's first noble truth was that *life is suffering*, then the second noble truth at healing school would be: *and someone else understands, someone else is capable of holding you in and through your experience of that suffering*.

Ahhh, thank God. Embraces were frequent: one time I clasped my classmate Bob in a long embrace in the middle of the hotel (where the school took residence); after, two passers-by asked: "are you two brothers?" Another time, this same classmate took me to visit his mother's grave; I held him, as he wept. A favorite activity was piling up on a couch: men, women, whether married or not, our bodies were available to each other, not in a sexual capacity, but for healing. Everyone was immensely hurt, granted, but so was all of humanity, and here, at least, we could freely admit it, without shame, and even more a treat, be present for each others' wounds.

Because we had so much emotional "clearing" to do, we were encouraged to constantly drink water. At the water table, clearing myself with several glasses of room temperature, filtered liquid, I connected instantly with Sid: a man exactly my height, with the same color of brown hair, warm brown eyes and a friendly smile. A demian, perhaps: alter ego, other self, another like me.

He radiated goodwill; in fact, classmates nicknamed him the "blissed-out dude." Of course, that friendliness belied a deeper inner torture that he, too, would have to work through during the school.

Sid and I decided to become roommates. Our first week, we hooked up with a third student and meditated together. As we went into trance, and checked in together, the three of us simultaneously seemed to be experiencing the *same past life*. We were in a saloon, in the Wild West. We looked about the same but were cowboys. Someone was killed in the saloon: we all saw it, channeled it, in meditation.

Later that night, I found myself sitting in a light trance and allowing words to come through me, giving more information about that lifetime and others we had shared. It was easy to reach in this way toward other realms of consciousness, particularly in a group of others who were grounded, stable, professionally accomplished, yet also spelunking explorers of the mind. Sid and I shared a particular resonance: we both had the feeling that we shared the same Oversoul. I was not sure exactly what that meant, but the concept seemed right: we were two individuals but whatever he experienced, on some 'higher' level, I was sharing in the knowledge of it, and the same for him.

Sid was special, but I also made many other friends, and with each, the relationship took an inter-dimensional turn. The phenomenon of 'transformations' fascinated—of staring into someone's face and watching it change form. I would practice with classmates and watch them transmogrify. One beautiful female classmate, who liked sporting a bikini around the hotel pool, turned into a Chinese male warrior, complete with beard. Another good friend seemed to have a head hovering above her face, a foreign intelligence, smiling and taking everything in. Nobody was who they seemed—some 20th-century adult with enough interest or financial and calendar fluidity to attend this school for spiritual and psychological self-work and knowledge; in fact, a tall Californian named John I had just met in the hall gave me a bear-hug in the hall, explaining that he remembered me as his teacher from Atlantis.

"What did I teach in Atlantis?" I asked.

He smiled. "Law, medicine, ethics, and healing."

Sid introduced me to the Ashram. I had heard various things about the place, the usual accolades and warnings. None of these gave full testimony to the beauty I found on arrival. I disembarked from the bus and immediately proceeded to what my companions called "The Spaceship." It was a giant glass building, bathed in blue light; inside, thousands of seekers were chanting God's name in Sanskrit, sitting cross-legged or kneeling in rows on small cushions. I could tell immediately that great devotion had been lavished on the marble floors and glass walls, to keep everything clean and sparkling.

Because it was my first time at the center, the ushers moved me past the rows and rows of chanting people on their wool prayer rugs, on the marble floor, and up to the very front. I was right in front of the spiritual teacher, the Guru, who sat on her chair chanting swaying, hands flying into the air. She was wearing orange robes and pleasant to look at. An easy sensuality flowed around her body, and at the same time, a sense of joy, as she alternately chanted and led the crowd in response to the melodious chanting call.

I tried to catch the Sanskrit syllables. All around me, people were going into ecstasy: hands wafting in the air, eyes rolling up, clapping, cheering, and singing enthusiastically. Again I stared at the woman on the chair, mentally asking over and over: "Who are you?" My mind tried to understand what was happening. Who was the Guru? Was this my Guru?

Michael H. Cohen

Did I need one? How could simply singing lift thousands of people into a swaying, ecstatic unity? Was she the source of some power, or simply a human being whose clarity and dedication had created a clear channel for that power? Questions mounted, burned.

And then I decided to surrender to the chant. Before I knew it, my head was bobbing, turning from side to side, and my whole body jiggled up and down as it could not contain the great energy that was surging up my spine. I started singing ecstatically, with great joy. Inside, I heard her say: "*I am your Beloved, your very own Self.*" Later, I learned that these the words that formed the core teaching of the ashram: *worship your own Self, God dwells within you, as you, for you.*

I saw her in meditation, in the form of Mary. Before my thoughts could process what this meant, I heard her say: "*We are One,*" and then she pointed to me: "*We are one.*" Again, the core teaching: the guru and the disciple are one; there is no separation; there is no person sitting on a pedestal, controlling hapless followers.

And that she could meld seamlessly into Mary and back, a heretical notion no doubt to various faiths, and then denote that I too could meld into either or both, indicated to me the fundamental lesson of unity consciousness: the notion that, as many Indian scriptures assert, all is Brahman, God is everyone and everything. Or, when Moses asks God, "by what name will people know You," God replies with the four-letter word transliterated as Yahweh or Jehovah; the letters literally combine to denote, "That Which Is Eternally Present," or simply, "Being." (Or, recalling John Mack: the *Passport to the Cosmos.*) God tells Moses: *Eheyeh asher eheyeh*, often translated as "I am That I am," and literally, "I will be what I will be," or in my version, "I am Being;" Being is the Passport. A core teaching of the *Upanishads* is to describe Brahman (the Absolute Infinite) as: "I am That." Or, per Christian liturgy: "As it was in the beginning, is now, and ever shall be."

After the chant, I sat in front of a picture of Lakshmi, the Indian goddess of abundance. I thought: "How strange that I am praying in front of this picture, since in Judaism we are taught to avoid worshipping images." At that moment, the goddess melted into the form of my spiritual teacher, and back again; she then stepped out of her photo, and entered my heart. Telepathically, she spoke to me: "*I am within you,*" she said. "*I am you, and you are me. There is no difference between us. You are worshiping me as the divinity inside you. When you see me, you see the image of your own divine Self.*"

Every morning at dawn the spiritual center held a ninety minute chant, which contained great purifying energy. It was called the *Guru Gita*, the song of the inner teacher. I loved to sleep in, but on one occasion, my experience was of hearing God speak in the first person, inviting me to go the chant. This was one of the rare occasions in which I experienced God in the first person: a warm, friendly voice of someone who knew me tenderly and thoroughly, and had no judgment, only gentle encouragement, reminders of my larger identity.

After that experience, I rose each morning at four and went to the chant.

The words of the chant were difficult to learn, at first, and because of the early hour, I tended to nod off. Again, I heard God's voice: "*Perform an action with love, rather than just trying to get through it.*"

Here I am using these different terms: God, the Self, Brahman, Yahweh. What do they mean? Why God this day, Jesus the next, Krishna another, Moses again, next Kwan Yin, then perhaps Mary? This book is about my experience of God, not a dissertation of religious scholarship—and that experience is multifaceted and pluralistic, drawing on the different traditions I imbibed, and including mystical experience, shamanism, high sense perception, whatever that ability to connect with the 'non-ordinary' is named.

Some say scholars of religion are interested in the differences in religious expression by different traditions, while mystics and mythologists (like Joseph Campbell) find the commonality. I embrace the paradox that on one level, there are experiences of unity consciousness: my teacher and Mary and Lakshmi and me, all melding into one; and there

- 113 -

A Friend of All Faiths

are experiences in which the individual "personality" of these different beings comes to the fore in delicious encounter: Jesus hovering above our dinner table in the Washington, D.C. restaurant or coming through my body on a New York City bus; Mary as the figure in blue-and-white with a sash, or in her myriad forms through the visionaries of Fatima and elsewhere; Krishna as the thousand-armed being who is all-pervasive and walks without legs, sees without eyes, and whose mouth contains flaming armies and all-that-is-and-has-already-been-determined-to-be; God in the first person, an intimate friend, a sage, a lover and Beloved, a warm feeling of accessible, personalized wisdom, ever-present to guide; Buddha in austere meditation, gentle and loving, compassionate yet straight-backed, contemplating the no-bullshit reality behind a myriad delusions.

To be a *friend* of *all* faiths means that theses variegated experiences of the divine are *available*, if I am sufficiently open to receive them. Like Joseph Campbell and Carl Jung, I find in these myths deep metaphors for the human condition; yet, unlike Campbell and Jung, I do not consider them merely myths and metaphors. Perhaps Jung's version is closer since he considers the archetypes to be living realities of the psyche; and yet, at some level, what one considers "inner" versus "outer" becomes blurred; Krishna and Mary and Moses and Buddha live in realms that touch mine, so I conceptualize them as real, perceive them as real, irrespective of tales of their history on Earth. I encounter them outside as well as inside, immanent and transcendent, both without and within. In the *Guru Gita*, Parvati (Shiva's wife) asks: what is the nature of reality? Shiva replies that Brahman, the Self, and the Guru are one. Thus, at a fundamental level, God dwells within you, as you, for you; "the kingdom of heaven is within." And yet, "those who think they know, do not know; those who know they do not know, know." To see God within is not to assume a posture of arrogance, to 'think that one is God;' because this divinity has many aspects, not all comprehensible. In the *Bhagavad-Gita*, when Arjuna is granted the vision of Krishna's true form, the all-pervasive nature of God is terrifying to behold, and Arjuna begs Krishna to resume his more limited form as the blue, personal deity; later, Arjuna merges into Krishna's consciousness, but then individuates again so that the sweetness of individuality can add to the throb of relationship between Lover and Beloved. God breathes his own breath into Adam's nostrils, and reminds Adam that humans are made in God's image. The paradox of unity and individuation remains.

Hearing God in the first person voice did not make me into an instant saint. In fact, just the opposite: I learned how far I had to go. Self-observation did not mean self-deprecation, though; the ashram emphasized the universality of our innate purity. Although the deities it featured on murals and in statutes, such as Ganesh and Lakshmi, were taken from India and Hinduism, the ashram embraced all and emphasized the universality of the Self (this term was used more frequently than "God;" sometimes one would hear of "the Lord" or the "Supreme Spirit" interchangeably). The ashram imposed no system of belief on anyone.

"All religions are His," my teacher's guru had written; "all countries are His." Reportedly, he once met an insistent seeker who demanded: "Show me where God is." Not missing a beat, he apparently replied: "Show me where He is not."

The ashram was truly a meeting place for the Beloved; and the injunction to find the Beloved in everyone is typical of the *bhakti* or devotional element in Indian philosophy, the notion that, like the mystics of Christianity or any religion, one can make contact with God through intense devotion and emotional fervor, not only through intellect. Treating each person with love and respect, since God dwells in everyone, was the aspiration apparently bequeathed to this palace in time. It was as palpable and power as the serpentine energy I felt moving up my spine.

In 1996, I went up to meet my spiritual teacher, the swami in the orange robes that I had first seen in 1992 during the chant in the "spaceship." I offered her my manuscript-in-progress on law and complementary medicine (later published by Johns Hopkins University Press) by placing it in a basket where people traditionally left gifts. Some weeks later, my parents visited me in the ashram and I introduced them to my teacher. I was surprised that she recognized and remembered me from among the thousands of visitors that she would greet formally each week.

At that time, the ashram was sponsoring a writing assignment in which residents were to write a "thesis" on the subject, "what is an ashram." I had not done the assignment. But when my teacher met my parents, she smiled and lovingly said: "Your son has offered his thesis." By this, she was referring to the manuscript, and in a deeper sense, to my life. All my writing *and* life is a "thesis" contemplating the question: "what is an ashram?" Even though I had not literally completed the assignment posed to ashram residents, my whole being was responding to the question, "what is an ashram." In terms of translation, the answer is simple: an ashram is the Indian name for a place of rest and contemplation, a retreat, a physical center in which one has the space to find one's center, to meditate on the Self. But then, what is the Self that one what discovers in that state? Such is the single theme and question my life poses to me. The journey to discovering the ashram was becoming a metaphor for my life, for the journey of finding the place in which I was aspiring to dwell in within. Like the inner message I received: "remain at peace within, no matter what happens on the outside." Working "inside, out" was the way.

During my experiences at the ashram, I was amazed at my teacher's presence, the way her very state of consciousness conveyed sublime experiences. Without deifying or mystifying her, I simply appreciated the depths of consciousness I tapped into within her in our inner relationship. Our outer relationship consisted of a few seminal meetings, some of which I can describe; others of which triggered non-ordinary experiences. The Self-Realization I was studying in books, I began to approach in her presence in ways I am still trying to understand; and I appreciated the "personality" part of her that spoke with wisdom, wry irony, and humor, often packing multiple meanings into simple statements such as letting my parents know she knew that when I had "offered" my "thesis" by sharing my manuscript with her and the timeless lineage of perfected beings, I had put my entire being into the gift basket to God. (That was, indeed, my experience: after the encounter with my teacher, I had gone to the portraits of various sages and saints on the walls, mentally addressing each one, feeling their presence, acknowledging to them their guidance in the turn my professional life had taken, the right direction appearing at the right time in the kind of "effortless striving" of which the *Tao Te Ching* speaks).

Our culture often misunderstands the orange-robed holy person from India, and sees in the would-be guru all the distortion and manipulation so endemic to falsity in the spiritual marketplace. My time at the ashram has been precious, sacred, and among the most beautiful in my entire life—a healing sanctuary for spiritual practice, and a portal to master teachers from other times and places, and to myself.

I decided to take some courses at the ashram. During a break, my mind started thinking: "I just spent two hundred dollars on these courses.... Can I take this as a tax deduction?" My teacher passed by in her resplendent orange robes. She glanced in my direction, as if reading my mind. Her gaze silenced my mind, and again I felt a burning desire to know God. Later, in the course, I heard a swami: "Yoga is practicing the stillness of the mind.... We are not our minds; we are the Self, which is behind the mind. When the mind is stilled, then we rest in our true nature, the Self." These were in fact among the first words of the *Yoga Sutras*, by the ancient sage Patanjali. I picked up a copy and was amazed to discover Patanjali's economy of words and thought. The first *sutra* (or suture, verse) goes: "Now the beginning of instruction in yoga;" and the second, "yoga is stilling one's thoughts;" and the third, "then a person abides in his or her true nature." In three concise sentences, he had defined yoga. Often translated as "union," yoga meant a state of inner repose involving cessation of the rise and fall of shifting movements of the mind; *then*, and only then, did a person experience his or her *true self*, which, according to Patanjali, was **bliss**. Patanjali said that the Witness, the silent observer behind our shifting moods and thoughts, is the source of our power and inspiration.

Patanjali categorized the ways the mind deludes into missing the supreme reality, and described the 'grooves' in our consciousness, accruing from past action (the *samskaras* that obscure our recognition of the Self within us). Patanjali identified eight limbs of yoga: restraints, observances, posture, breathing, withdrawal of the senses, concentration, meditation, and absorption. Patanjali did all this in a series of pithy, precise, and memorizable aphorisms. The man was a genius.

This is how my friend, a nurse who worked in surgical wards and studied at the Barbara Brennan School, described her experience of Jesus: one time she was in the O.R. (operating room) and suddenly saw him hovering, mid-air, near the anesthetized patient. His arms were outstretched: not to say, "look at where they put the nails," or "see how I died for *your* sins," but rather as if to say, "hey, isn't this great?" Meaning, isn't it great to "hang out on the etheric planes," as my nurse-healer friend put it. More like a grinning surfer dude than an icon of impenetrable suffering. Then again, perhaps we yogi-meditators interpreted the so-called "Western canon" of religion in so-called "Eastern terms:" Patanjali emphasized that our true nature was bliss; and our own experience of the guides and "Masters" was indeed that of tremendously illuminated, but also happy, beings. They did not dwell on the "slings and arrows of outrageous misfortune," to quote Hamlet, although they knew the realms of suffering well. Rather, they healed suffering through their infectious good humor, laughter, patience, endurance, joy. One can think of the Hindu saint Ramakrishna, worshipping the Divine Mother in ecstasy, even through the ravages of throat cancer; or even Jesus, for that matter, flesh ripped from mutilation by repeated beatings and his crown of thorns, sweetly asking God to forgive his tormentors, Jesus as Bodhisattva, like a Tibetan monk or nun offering blessings toward his or her captors and torturers.

My experiences of Jesus during the time with Nick had been of a being holding perfect love. This continued during time at the ashram—I saw no inconsistency between the Judaism of my childhood; immersion in the Buddha during meditation with the Monk in Iowa City; connection to Mary and Jesus gleaned during meditations with Nick; and this connection of love and wisdom with my teacher in the ashram.

Yet, conceptually, I had residual confusion about this "son of God" assertion. This was the great dividing line—at least in my childhood, the difference in beliefs that had caused someone to hurl me to the ground for wearing a yarmulke. The paternity issue remained unresolved: was Jesus truly "son" in a biological sense? Did he "sit at the right hand of the Father?" Did God even have a "right hand"? Wasn't God, at least in Hindu tradition, supposed to have millions of hands? Or did Jesus have a kind of endowed chair (a metaphor that would preoccupy my academic side much later)? I sought the assistance of Jesus in clarifying the doctrinal fringes of my perceptual apparatus. Who better than he could resolve the debate? Here I was, experiencing his undying love in meditation, while living in a culture that emphasized the "passion" of his torment. Perhaps Jesus could instruct us.

I was sitting with two friends, a nurse-healer and an attorney with a master's in social work. We were in a fancy Washington, D.C. restaurant talking about the identity of Jesus. After all, so many *Times* magazine cover stories had been devoted to the historical Jesus; to which were his real words; to attempts to separate myth from fact, fantasy from truth. Collectively we visualized him, hovering above and near the table. Mentally, I asked him: "Who are you?" recalling that biblically, when asked, "Are you the Son of God?" he had responded: "So say you."

Now I wanted a definitive answer as the conversation was turning into an argument, my nurse friend insisting that Jesus did, indeed, have the divine equivalent of an endowed chair and played a special role in judging us during the Afterlife. To my perception, Jesus hovered, non-judgmentally, holding out his hands as if to say, "you can argue all you want over steamed dumplings, but I'm just here, not needing to argue with anyone."

Still, I hurled the question over the parapet of material reality to him, hoping he could illuminate our discussion and help restore our friendly feelings. My mind heard him flash back with great tenderness: *It doesn't matter who I am or who you or others think I am. What matters is the opening in your heart.* With that I felt a beam of light flash from his hands directly into my heart.

Contra to the Gospel version of his stony silence in the face of unbelievers, he proved a rather cooperative witness, responding with a great love. His response sealed my understanding. Whether he was poured from semen or from God's will, studied with gurus in India between the "lost ages" of twelve and thirty or helped his mother with the dishes back in Mesopotamia, released *my* karma (and everyone else's) on the cross or simply existed as metaphor for the human condition (*narayana*, we sang at the Ashram; half-divine, half-human, like us all, but a little less than angels and a little more than dirt, as the psalmist sang), this being we identified as Jesus, Yeshu, he was some great embodiment of compassion with whom I could converse; more, who could flow through my veins with great love.

Months later: I am on a bus in New York City: one of those smoke-choked, noisy vessels where one assumes a posture of humility beneath the sweaty armpits of crowding fellow travelers. Patanjali writes: "once the modifications of the mind are stilled, then humans rest in their true nature." The mind of Michael watches street-signs pass by: 79th and Broadway; 81st; 85th; and thinks about the laundry, taxes, the to do list, what an asshole the law school dean is, the corruption of the current presidential candidate, and so on. Suddenly, Jesus enters my body.

An immense, oceanic feeling of love wells up inside. Other passengers enter and the bus driver shouts at us to move down and make more room. My hands are raised instantly in a blessing as I move through the aisles of the bus. I am seeing each person singly, in full light; as if I can read a thousand burdens and concerns, and am lightening them with the eye of compassion. In the *Bhagavad-Gita*, when the warrior Arjuna asks to see Krishna in his true form, Krishna replies: "you cannot see me with your own eyes, but here I lend you a divine eye with which to see me." So it is with the divine eye, the divine heart, that I am seeing each person, and their families, and all those connected with energetic cords. And it is Jesus I feel moving through me: he has a distinctive note, a unique "vibration," it is his great heart, the "sacred heart," hold each person, invisibly, the eternal glue, binding everyone in this great love.

The love I feel is so strong I might burst out weeping in the middle of the bus.

And then the moment passes, and I am watching 91st street come up through my own Michael-eyes, my own limited awareness, a consciousness of daily contraction.

Many, many images came in meditation during summers at the ashram (as a law professor, my great good fortune was to have entire summers "off"). I saw a snake coiled like a water hose; "it's good to have," my mind thought, "because it eats bugs." I saw my spirit guides benefiting from my spiritual teacher's energy; then, using that energy, to do a healing on the back of my sixth chakra, the energy center said to be responsible for executive planning and decision-making. I saw Earth and Apollo 11-from space. I saw myself in another time in the role of protecting Lincoln from an assassination attempt. I saw several lifetimes as a soldier, including as a redcoat protecting the British colony again the American revolt. Many meditation experiences were exalted, others painful. I read *Play of Consciousness*, another record of kundalini experiences. This author, too, had gone through some pleasant and some difficult moments, commenting that although one normally should not share inner experiences—so as to avoid dissipating *shakti*, spiritual energy—this was allowed if beneficial to other seekers.

In many cases, I could identify from the meditation images corresponding emotional associations, often with archetypical dimensions, such as: fear, rejection, loneliness, anger, and so on. For example, I saw myself in the silver, mesh armor of a medieval knight, protecting a king. I was betrayed by colleagues and killed. As I died, my spirit flowed out and followed four or five of them to the king. This leader, apathetic to my death, said: "It's a hot day." In contemplating my meditation experience, the feelings lingered long past the meditation.

According to Patanjali's *Sutras*, meditation facilitates a clearing out of the *samskaras* or grooves, latent impressions accumulated over lifetimes. Not being a biologist, chemist, or physicist, Patanjali does not explain "past lives" in terms cognizable to modern scientists; his expertise is the domain of consciousness; but perhaps philosophic notions such as the transmigration of souls can help fill in the gap. According to Indian texts, Shaktipat, the initiation or awakening of dormant kundalini energy I received in the meditation cave–and then again in my teacher's presence–is a catalyst, speeding up the clearing out these old impressions. The ultimate goal of this awakening is full illumination, Self-Realization, Liberation: to become a *jivanmukti*, one who is liberated while still in the body. According to the philosophical teachings on which the ashram drew, in this way one "completes karma," moves beyond the wheel of birth and death. It is a path in which grace complements self-effort like "two wings of a bird." My spiritual teacher once humorously explained that shaktipat is not "pot" and not a "pat," but an ongoing process of transformation. The expression of awakening is individualized, as individual have accrued different experiences over lifetimes. While the "symptoms" or manifestations of kundalini arising many be shared (such as buzzing sounds, energy up the spine, and so on), the living experience is unique for each person.

Again, the paradox of immanence and transcendence recurs: shaktipat involves an awakening of divine energy *within* the body, rather than an encounter with a transcendent deity somehow *outside* and *beyond* the body; yet through shaktipat, one can become more receptive to encounters with deities both within and without. Inner life becomes more vivid, and outer events more clearly act as clearing agents. One has to let go of concepts, dogmas, fixed understandings, in order to be open to, and make sense of, these kind of experiences. Many people come to the ashram (or any ashram) and then make a whole new religion out of that yoga, or guru, or teaching; whereas in my experience my spiritual teacher did not wish to be deified, but rather wished us to explore our own experience from the inside.

Her teacher reportedly would yell at ashram residents who stared at him: "Stare at yourself! God dwells within you!" He encouraged them to move from dependency on emotions and the authority of others (including spiritual leaders) to true independence in a world of interdependence (since all are God).

The bliss I experienced in the ashram, and the healing techniques that I was learning in my program, collided with destructiveness in the world. The three hours back from the ashram were full of the bliss Patanjali described, as I chanted, moving through traffic in a car filled with the energies of Self-Realization. I sped through mountains and valleys, God-intoxicated, and arrived ... in the parking lot of my law school. The word "down-sizing" had ripped faculty into factions, renting the garment of the temple of collegiality; and already a series of meetings, critical and distempered, were finding flaws in candidates under review–findings calculated to reduce our numbers, a struggle for self-preservation beneath the speeches.

My own course, Civil Procedure, was hardly a repository of spiritual knowledge, and students focused on such things as: "do I need to know this for the exam;" "do you award points for class participation;" or the more hostile, "if I read the case three times, how come you're insinuating that I don't know the answer."

Events were testing me, and in some ways ran counter to healing work. I was learning to deconstruct my character armor, and in the process to become more loving, empathetic, compassionate. The psychological and psychic openings were developing a highly delicate and refined consciousness, which it took to, for example, connect with a client's former fetus on the astral planes during a healing, and facilitate a healing conversation between the disincarnate being and his or her biological mother over an event that mother perhaps had too much unresolved grief to wish to remember. Certainly, the school taught us about "boundaries," and we learned to live in the Warrior as well as the Lover; and yet, the development of this delicate and refined consciousness, in an environment in which we explored our wounds, shared them, healed them, bared all, healed all, felt antithetical to the black-and-white, strictly mental world of law, a world in which healing had no place, in which learning was confined to learning a way of thinking.

During my second year of teaching law, I was so sensitive to the fluorescent lights in the classroom that I could hardly hold my energy field intact for the ninety-minute class. Fluorescent light, which flickers so many thousands of times a second, is said to break apart the first (blue) layer of the auric field. I could see it and feel it. None of my students seemed bothered by the breaking-up of the first layer of their auric fields; they had other stresses, did not want to hear wisdom channeled from a disincarnate being. The dull and fearful refrain as to "what's going to be on the exam" enforced a dumbing-down to the "flat, stale, weary, and unprofitable uses of this world" (to quote Hamlet again).

The required emotional detachment to teach law took its toll. One of the cases I taught was called *Piper Aircraft v. Reyno.* My opening gambit was this: "Five people die in an airplane crash over Scotland. Is California a proper jurisdiction and venue?" Then there was the *Buffalo Creek Disaster* case. "The Buffalo Creek Coal Company fails to monitor the level of its coal dumps and during one rainy night, the sludge spills out over the dam and floods, wiping out most of a village in West Virginia. Does the federal court have subject matter jurisdiction?" Forget the human tragedy; hit the procedure. From course to course, I felt I had to numb out, focus on the pertinent legal rules. A brutality seemed inherent in abstracting densely emotional tragedies into a series of rules. Was there a deeper way to integrate the subtle energies I was assimilating with law teaching?

I was "sensitive to energy" from my students as well as colleagues. Some students were perpetually launching their hands into the air, challenging, refusing to back down even when Socratic method was used to gently reveal the flaws in their thinking; demanding acknowledgment of being "right." In healing school we had worked with characterology, learning a different "healing" response for each of the different character types. I found some more difficult to handle than others. (A classmate claimed she had learned more of value to her work with clients than in two years at an MSW program in an Ivy League school). If I would confront students with their hostility; but this often produced defensiveness and in the school's highly charged atmosphere, filled with mutual denouncements and personnel cuts, student complaints to the Dean could be misused as leverage against faculty members. A few critical remarks in this hypersensitive environment, and selected faculty might be sacrificed to the god of popularity. Unlike scholarship, which could be more objectively assessed, "teaching" assessments were often bully sticks for covert personality wars among faculty.

Over time, as a strategic response to this no-win situation, I tried seeing whether good wishes might defuse misplaced acting out. One time I stood next to Jim, a first-year Civil Procedure student who I found particularly hostile. Instead of remaining glued to the podium, I moved around the room and hovered next to him as I asked questions to the class. Three seconds in his energy field and I felt spikes emanating from his body: rage. I moved outside his seventh layer, and the spikes no longer touched me. I moved back in: prickly spikes.

I turned to another student and noticed that I could see red when he asked me a question. His eyes actually burned with red, like pictures of the Devil. I did not think he was the Devil, but I definitely perceived angry energy being thrown at me. Behind this rage, I could sense someone else: his father or perhaps brother. Like an aikido or chi master, I sensed and read and tried to find ways to react appropriately. I noticed that for many students, I was simply someone at the front of the blackboard: a stand-in for someone's father, mother, grade-school teacher, brother, or other authority figure. Once I understood the projection, I felt a lot safer, and my teaching improved. Eventually I also learned how to handle the energies by shielding myself appropriately.

Teachers in healing school were candid about transference, positive and negative (particularly after one teacher crossed boundaries and married one of his students). Brennan warned: "The first year, you all see me as an angel: there is so much positive transference, I'm Super Mom; the second year, the dark energies come up, and the feeling is opposite." Since this was the year we were studying past lives, she went on to say: "Some of you will remember lifetimes in which I 'did it to you,' or you 'did it to me.' It doesn't really matter who killed whom; we are in this lifetime and you must act appropriately."

After that talk, a classmate later told me he saw a life in which he ran a ship; Barbara was a galley slave, and he was kind to her. Because of this, he thought, he had the merit to return and study with her this time around. Did students have negative past life memories of me, as well as psychological transference? Or was transference in this lifetime enough - white, male, Jewish, lawyer, whatever the associated prejudices and stereotypes, this life's mental junk was probably enough. And more generally, I speculated as to why law students as a whole carried aggressive energy. Of course, the school's environment was not the most supportive; and I recalled that many leaders in world history had been lawyers who modeled non-violence. And there were many emerging leaders in schools around the world, whose being was permeated with peace. I found then when I quietly tuned in to the soul level of their being or to the Masters in the back of the classroom, some of the students increased in their hostility. When I watched my colleagues lecture (some were keen on displaying their techniques, which I perceived, in the embattled environment, as a kind of egotistical superiority, masking deep inferiority), I observed some being lost in an intellectual fog, not really connecting with students' hearts and spirits, but dancing around concepts.

In meditation I saw one student with black boots as a former Nazi. I tried to be honest with myself about when I was projecting, and when I saw images from other dimensions of reality. Because of school, I was so sensitive that I found if I looked in students' eyes directly, as if in a healing room, I would be communicating with their inner being; and I recalled that my teacher wore sunglasses because the gaze conveyed too much *shakti* for most people to handle. Yet again, intention could help soften various chakras, literally put people in touch with their hearts, some reacted with aggression. I felt split: did I really have to leave the healer in me outside the classroom, outside the law school, or could it be integrated?

Many law schools now modify the autocratic "Socratic method" in which the law professor reduces students to idiocy by exposing the fallacy of their logic and leading them from conclusion to a deep questioning of any and all premises. I felt rigor and humanity could coincide. One time, a student was insisting on a point, again in the eighty-person, theatre-like Civil Procedure class in which I stood at the bottom of the pit. I was about to deny it when a spirit guide jumped in front of me and said, "you're right," meaning that the student was right. (Sometimes I hear the words I am supposed to speak). Immediately I said, "you're right," and explored the student's point, which was more sophisticated than initially I had realized.

Thereafter I noticed that my classes were crowded with guides and beings. Later, I began to hear a student's name in my mind before I called on them, as if it the guides who would choose on whom to call. Using the seating chart and randomly pointing is such an elaborate ritual for law professors, that I found the intervention of the guides humorous and welcome. Later, I would discover that each person was called on for a definite reason. For example, one student reported: "I can't believe you called on me to discuss that case about the police officer who was carrying a loaded pistol into a party. My husband is a cop, and we went through a similar incident...."

Once at a faculty meeting I saw a rainbow of light emanate from the associate dean's throat as he made a point about the grading curve. It was as though the energy was being fed in from a source beyond this dimension. The healing hands of Jesus were above this light; the whole meeting was being coordinated from above.

FROM THE FINITE TO THE INFINITE

Ernest, an attorney, did *seva* or selfless service at the ashram. He had met the guru in the 1970s–had seen a poster and somehow had wandered in to a talk given by this swami in sunglasses and an orange lungi. He found the room, in the middle of the talk, dissolving into blue light.

Such experiences of shaktipat apparently were not uncommon; the teacher reportedly transmitted the awakened energy through his presence. I heard that once he was sitting in someone's living room, holding a ski cap in his lap; when he tossed the ski cap and it landed in a someone's hands, that person instantly fell into meditation–thus receiving the awakening literally "at the drop of a hat."

Ernest had been so kindled. He was a professional peer, solid and gracious, my father's age, with a kind face, intelligent eyes, and a gray goatee. He looked at legal issues with a deep caring for the ashram and its residents. He served as a caretaker and steward–protecting people and their sacred energies, rather than their financial assets–and thus served as a role model in my search for a new way to be a lawyer and a seeker. Over coffee, I confided to him that I felt stymied in my search for God.

Although I had had many meditation experiences, inwardly, I felt I did not know God, did not know spiritual surrender. In some ways, despite my repertoire of inner revelations, I still felt dry; there were some spontaneous experiences of love, and bliss, and contentment, but still this great split between the ashram and the world, and still this feeling that I had never dived all the way down, into the place where the immanent God truly resides in my heart; nor had I swum to the farthest shore, the place the transcendental God of all universes dwells. I mourned this gulf between myself and God, this great bridge that could never, it seemed, be crossed, no matter how many tools from how many religious traditions: Judaism, Catholicism, Buddhism, Gurdjieff, Krishnamurti, yoga, prodigious meditation, others.

Ernest offered to bring me up to my spiritual teacher and make an introduction. He seemed to think this would be the answer. I judged this naïve, like many of the suggestions of ashram residents and visitors that seemed over-enthusiastic or at least improperly ascribing magical properties to the path. Doubtless, the ashram had great spiritual power–a power I believed came through the lineage of teachers, was supercharged by its ability to awaken kundalini, and was reinforced by the loving care and attention to detail by those who offered *seva* at the ashram. Doubtless, this power had awakened or at the least explosively fueled an innate capacity for inner experience within me. But did I believe that "the Guru" was the answer to everything?

Again, I resisted superimposing one set of orthodoxies on another. As much as I loved being at the ashram, I sometimes found its lingua franca too glib, too easy, too unwilling to confront the significant emotional and physical hurdles of daily life. And this criticism was by no means unique to this spiritual place; it characterized many spiritual paths; and, to the credit of the community in which I was beginning to find a healthy locus for my spirituality, became a critique with which members of the ashram would come to constructively grapple. There is a fine line between seeing "Trust in God" or "trust in Jesus," or "trust in the Guru," as a healthy spiritual practice and truism, and using it as a cliché to bypass emotional responsibility and wisdom. And so I resisted Ernest's suggestion. In addition, my response to Ernest was that I had already met my teacher during my first weekend at the ashram; I had waited in the long line, come up, had someone say my name, respectfully bowed, and received a brush of the peacock feathers. At that time, she personally greeted each newcomer to the retreat center. In fact, we had met more informally–perhaps more transcendentally, since shaking hands is not necessary for an energetic introduction–during my first visit in 1992, when I stood in the front of the room, mentally asking "who are you" to the woman in an orange robe, as thousands of people chanted, swaying from side to side, arms levitating with spontaneous bliss.

But Ernest persisted, and ultimately, I accepted his offer for a more personalized moment: how could another it hurt?

Ernest and I sat together through a program of chanting, meditation, and a talk. I adjusted myself on the meditation cushion and sat in absorption. A part of my mind was watching how my whole being was engaged in the talk. It wasn't just that the person in the chair at the front of the room was a good speaker. I had heard captivating speakers, those with winning personalities and those with complex and intriguing ideas. But this spiritual teacher had the ability to invest each word with meaning, the kind of meaning that unfolded and exploded from the inside. When she spoke of the Self, she was in the state of the Self, and conveyed that state to others—certainly to me, and perhaps to thousands of listeners. It was not her personality that was of interest, it was what we call her "state:" the place of consciousness behind the verbal information, a place of consciousness with which I could be become aligned in a cloud of ease, arising, again, from within.

The fruit of the talk was the direct experience of the content of the talk: the Self, a sense of the vast oneness, compassion, and presence of the Infinite. And unlike my experiences with Nick, the ferry here was internal, delicious, authentic, true.

My teacher's prime statement was this: *God dwells within you, as you, for you.* My experience during the talk was of silent communion with this truth. And I understand the word "guru," so maligned in our culture, as its literal meaning: that which brings light to darkness. It referred to the inner guru—God within—not to the outer person sitting in a chair giving teachings, except to the extent that being embodied the sprouting of the seed within each of us.

After the program, she was sitting on her chair, legs crossed, sipping water from a silver cup from time to time, greeting a seemingly endless line of people. Ernest and I waited off to the side. Meanwhile, I prayed over and over: "Please, God, let me know you." This prayer had a particular force—the force of longing of lifetimes.

I did not know whether knowing God was an experience this spiritual teacher in orange robes could facilitate in a private moment apart from the talk—in fact I doubted it; but I sensed that grace flowed through the lineage and through her, and could touch me through this simple practice of an introduction. As I prayed, longing arose from the deepest part of my being. I knew, as I watched my teacher greet thousands of people, that she could sense my prayers, though I stood some distance from her. I sensed she was aware, and aware that I was aware that she was aware. I started to see lights and colors around her, and beautiful beacons of light shining from her heart to mine, while I waited from a distance.

When we finally came up, Ernest made a little speech about how he and I had met and the fact that I, too, was trained as a lawyer.

After this introduction, he made as if to conclude: "And so I brought him to you." But instead, my teacher looked right through my eyes, and said, "Yes, I brought him to you."

As she said those words, the truth of her statement permeated me. I sensed that she had, indeed, brought me to Ernest, to the center, to this path, to presence with her in this moment of seamless connection, through lifetimes, eons, from the primordial beginning. I recognized her. The recognition was profound and total: I had known her (or whomever she was behind the immediate personality of this Indian-looking swami in orange robes) since the beginning of time, and that we were completely connected in the Godhead. The fact that she and I were one came through with a pulsation of recognition, not as words, in a meditative state of awareness in which I could read the present moment, Michael and this person known as the head of lineage of swamis, and also as many other meetings.

In that moment, my entire being welled up with gratitude, and as my hands made the sign of *Namaste*, I walked backwards, feeling her blessing, and the blessings of the many that stood behind her, the blessings of a swarm of swamis, rabbis, priests, ET's, conglomerates of angels, multinational/multiethnic/multigalactic all holy ones. My body began trembling. I felt the energy rush in. Technically, I had completed the introduction and was moving backward, as a long line of people moved in to fill the space; physically, my body was separating from the zone of contact one normally associates with the seventh layer of the human energy field. But now some huge energy was moving through my body, awakening like a roar through my spine, skin, fingers, muscles, everything trembling and awakened like all the samskaras or old karmic sludge being cleared out all at once, an immense waterfall of light pouring through my crown and simultaneously rising from the earth and stirring from all sides. I walked all the way to the back of the hall, where I sensed my teacher, curiously, in contact with me from her chair and yet right beside me.

It was, I later read, a classic kundalini awakening: the roar of supercharged energy scrambling through my spinal pathways, physiological and in the other bodies: Shakti, the feminine aspect of the divine, coursing through the central corridor, liquid luminosity pulsing.

All the perfected beings were there with me. Supercharged energy ran through my body while I sat, and then lay supine on the marble, hands in the air. I felt my spirit move beyond earth, beyond time and space, beyond creation, my being leaving its karma far behind. I was in a plane beyond birth and death. I went far, far from the physical realm, not knowing in what vehicle I was traveling; beyond "my" and "mine," beyond "I," beyond this world, beyond duality; through the tunnel of time and space, cascading even beyond notions of time and space, beyond any sense of finitude or even of infinity. There was no body, nor even really a mind located anywhere from which to regard the body, nor really any bodies anywhere.

Nothing like this had ever occurred, and no memory remained in my consciousness. I was completely absent from time and space, but the new geography that had no geography was so unfamiliar that I lacked any orientation, even to an "I" that might have orientation.

In a corner of the intelligence that was my mind, I grew afraid: what if I didn't come back?

At that moment, with that thought, in an instant, I came back to this plane.

It was like the moment when the Jewish mystics arrive, through mystical practice, at the gates of Paradise (*pardes*, the Garden), and one cries out "water, water!" Then suddenly the garden disappears, and they are drawn back to this world. In an instant, the "I" returned as did the sense of having a body and karma.

But something had changed. I realized that I was not this limited identity that called itself, "Michael." I was the very energy that permeates everything; only a thin veil of identification separated this awareness from ordinary awareness. I realized, too, that everyone in the room was this all-pervasive energy (which they call Shiva), only nobody else seemed to realize their true identity. I was in bliss.

I remained in this state for a long time. As I remained in this state of total unity with the *Ain Sof*—that which is without end—which we the ashram called Shiva, whatever perception was my consciousness noticed that everyone else too was Shiva. Shiva, the exalted universal consciousness, was everything, had become everything and everyone. Inexplicably, every other Shiva in the room had chosen to *contract* its awareness to the limited consciousness of an *I*, lost in specific tasks—deciding what to eat for dinner, for example, or figuring out how much money was in the wallet.

Ernest consulted a swami. I was lying supine on the marble with my hands outstretched in the air, the delicious energy bouncing between my fingers. I might have appeared catatonic, but my awareness was absorbed in observing the energy move from one channel to another—the Indian scriptures say we have seventy million such channels, *nadis*, and I could feel the energy traversing new routes like a kid enchanted with a new ski slope. My hands remained aloft of their own, deliciously enjoying new sensations. The swami came back with a present from my spiritual teacher: a banana and some sugary cookies, to help me arise and walk.

Ernest and I walked the Silent Path toward a dorm room where I would be able to sleep and rebalance my system. The stars, trees, insects, everything looked intensely alive, as if I had never noticed before, but had been imprisoned in my own limited thoughts. Consciousness appeared to dwell in *everything*.

Ernest broke the silence to recall some special experiences he had had with his teacher, and part of me listened, the other part unbounded. I could barely speak. Finally, we reached the dorm room. I lay down, only something much larger and more universal was buzzing around the space that my physical body occupied.

All night I remained feeling 'dancing Shiva,' the energy racing through my body, liquid light pouring into every channel, cascading with an intense sweetness into all remote pockets of awareness. Everyone was in this universal energy, and everyone was this universal energy, yet nobody realized it; each lived in the delusion of being what Alan Watts called "an ego encased in a bag of skin." And my realization of this fact was TOTAL: not mental, not even spiritual, really, but as real and dynamic as waiting for the traffic for the light to change. And that traffic light was the hope that everyone else could break into this new perception of consciousness, and that it would last forever (if even such a thing as forever existed).

A few days later, I took the ashram course on Fear. The point of the course was how fear of any kind, of all kinds, blocked us from a deeper experience of ineffable love at the core. Swami J led the course. At the break, I asked if I could speak with her. We sat on a wooden bench in the immaculate lobby, decorated with paintings and statues of Indian deities. I described my experience to her.

Swami J asked me: "How do you feel about your experience?"

I searched and said: "Nothing."

She looked at me intensely, as if patiently waiting for more, and then replied: "The feeling of 'nothing' is just a fear of getting deeper into your true feelings."

"Okay," I said. "The experience of expansion to infinity was *terrifying*. I had to come back."

"Of course," she replied, with recognition. "You had a glimpse of your true Self. We can't get these experiences on demand; they happen through grace. They're beautiful when they happen: terrifying at first, but eventually you contain them."

Swami J, a former professor, briefly told me some of her own experiences, and how she had to pull back, initially, from their enormity. She, too, initially had been too secure in her limited identity to embrace these tastes of the infinite; in fact, to cognitively begin to contextualize her experiences, she had read a book entitled, *From the Finite to the Infinite*. She suggested that perhaps I was not yet sufficiently grounded to hold the experience I had tasted. She pointed to our spiritual teacher's picture. "She lives in that state, but she can also walk through the lobby and notice a missing light bulb."

That image stuck with me: I had always imagined that a person living on the transcendental planes would be too absorbed in the infinite to notice the finite.

Swami J continued. "The experience is scary because you realize you're not just Michael; you're much more than you think you are. And now you're ready for *years* of spiritual practice." She put emphasis on the word "years," to let me know that just because I had glimpsed the Eternal did not mean I was ripe for Liberation. Rather, I was to accept this grace humbly and continue doing daily practice. Just like the rest of us mortals.

She reported on our conversation in the afternoon session—keeping my name anonymous—to the entire group. "It's one thing to experience that state," she said, "another to hold it. For this, we cultivate egolessness, detachment, surrender of the little self to the Great Self." She added: "Once you've had an experience like this, you never forget it, because you've had a glimpse of ultimate reality. The kundalini, the Supreme Energy, purifies our mind and emotions, and ultimately frees us from fear by setting us on the battlefield of life. Sooner or later, we meet our worst enemies, which are all internal, and

Michael H. Cohen

God is with us from beginning to end. The more you do spiritual practice," she concluded, "the more you realize you are not this little physical body. You are the great energy that is working inside you. You are That."

In meditation, I experienced myself as Christ on the cross. I wept with love for the soldiers, for humanity. These words flashed in my consciousness: "O unspeakable love!" It seemed that the kundalini was projecting my consciousness in moments of meditation or deep relaxation into these different settings and modes of awareness. The "I" of Michael would simply drop away, and I would become anything: an insect, a ghost, a deity. Consciousness was much more fluid than "I" had realized. Gurdjieff had written of the various *I*s competing for supremacy, and about development of an 'objective, permanent *I*.' What was happening inside was a broadening of the number of *I*s competing in the screen of my mind, a loosening of the psychic floodgates. Someone else may have been overloaded or overwhelmed--or wondered about psychosis; but I felt comfortable in the exploration–reminding myself that they say that the kundalini is an intelligent energy, self-guiding toward Self-Realization. The metaphor given is that kundalini rises up the spine until it, in the form of Shiva (Supreme Consciousness) merges with Shakti (its divine, 'female' element or consort). Once this unification is complete, Liberation occurs. The discomfort of the shifting *I*s was merely the release of *samskaras*, old psychic grooves–a process Barbara Brennan termed 'releasing frozen psychic time conglomerates.' (For better or for worse, 'conglomerates' reminded me of Wall Street).

I considered offering full-time service in the legal department of the spiritual center. In meditation, I asked: "Is this a wise choice?" The response: "Consider future lifetimes as well." This is not something one ordinarily considers on making a career move, and I realized that not only are our prayers heard, but that we are listened to deeply, intently–every thought. They say that "karma" is nothing but the principle of action and reaction: *every* action, including a thought, generates a reaction.

I recalled that Bob's take on worrying about karma was a semi-humorous remark: "If you think like that, you'll never get out of bed in the morning!" To which I had replied: "If you think there *is* no karma (are no reactions), you'll never get out of bed in the morning, either." Bob was right in articulating one arm of the paradox: you could not be paralyzed by inaction, worrying about the laws of karma. In the *Bhagavad-Gita*, Krishna himself had articulated this to Arjuna, observing that a person cannot *avoid* action–one *must* act in this world. Krishna followed this with the famous quotation, better to do one's own dharma than to follow someone else's. The other hand of the paradox was that action inexorably triggered reaction.

The fact that every thought and action had consequences first meant accountability for each choice–every action rebounded. Second it meant that we are paid attention to and cared for, much more deeply than we realize. Our actions and thoughts and awareness are recorded and transmuted into a chain of effects that teach us what we have created, manifested, triggered. Third, if only we knew how our thoughts ricocheted out into all the universes, we might guard the prize of our minds more carefully. Certainly we would not allow something like Nielsen ratings to dictate the violence and junk we send out on the radio and airwaves to all beings across all galaxies.

I was reminded of a story told of someone who asked my teacher, "Do you read minds?" To which the reply had been: "Why would I want to read junk?"

Just as shuttling to the ashram was uplifting, returning to the law school again presented institutionalized torture in the form of the usual psychic beatings, humiliation, degradation, competition, envy, jealousy, stupidity, and other norms of academic life. I lived duality: the spiritual path was sublime in geometric multiples; the academic environment an ugly conglomeration of snakes and toads (and a few genuine, similarly oppressed, friends–one of whom struggled with his own spontaneous 'kundalini awakening' through Christian mysticism).

Unrelated to the professional issues, I began to experience clearing in meditation in the form of unexpected total body jerking movements. I learned these are known as *kriyas*, movements by which samskaras and negative energies are expelled by the rising kundalini.

Returning for a weekend at the ashram, I meditated in a special room reserved for those who go into kriyas. Common ones involve making lion roars and other animal sounds (I had a phase during which I would wake myself up in the middle of the night spontaneously making these sounds). In the kriya meditation room—which was otherwise empty—I went through several boxes of tissues as I cried out God-knows-what. Then, as I continued in meditation, I began vocalizing what turned out to be demonic howls.

The vocalization intensified as I simply allowed whatever was coming through to be channeled, not shutting off the experience through judgments and thoughts. I watched as a series of demons actually fled from my body. I watched in witness state, and could not name them or specify to what they referred—e.g., Lust, Greed—except that very plainly these were demons, emanating from my body, not the physical body only but the body housing the soul of Michael over many ages. One by one they fled my body as I continued repeating the mantra in my mind and vocalizing the howls with my breath. As I sat cross-legged, the demons staggered out and, as if pushed by an invisible hand, stumbled toward the photograph of the guru in meditation at the front of the room. When they reached the photo, they did a *pranam*, a respectful bow. They then were absorbed into him.

When the exodus of the demons was completed, I felt tremendously cleansed. I had the sense that I had carried these demons for many eons, now released through grace. Why the release came through this path and another was unclear—perhaps because of the power of the awakened energy, a power greater than dogma or belief. Jesus, of course, has a famous incident in which he confronts a man whose name is "Legion," because he contains a legion of demons. Jesus expels the demons. Literalist readers of the gospels find in this "proof" of the special status, origins, and powers of Jesus.

After my experience in the kriya "cave," I wondered how many of us are carrying Legion. I felt that I had been purified, that grace had unlocked a prison of millennia; that just as worms and parasites exist in the body, so many humans house many demons. Perhaps psychological phenomena such as projection literally involve a movement of these demons on an astral level—here is a research arena in which mental health researchers and energy healers with high sense perception can collaborate. It would be interesting, I thought, if federally funded research were to move beyond scientific or religious dogma and into the kind of spiritual perception that can recognize and report on these phenomena.

Years later I would have Rolfing, a form of deep massage over the fascia that can be extremely painful. The Rolfer explained: "The pain is *in* your body. It *has* to come out." It was a nice reframing of the assumption that the Rolfer was the one causing me the pain. And in a similar way, the *exodus of the demons* had to occur. I was lucky it occurred in meditation.

I would be leaving my down-sized law school and looking for another teaching position in an upsizing location. I went to the ashram's main sanctuary, the Temple, to ask for blessings. At the center of the temple is a statue of the head of the lineage. This statue has been "enlivened," meaning that a ritual had been performed "installing" the deity or guru in the statue, investing stone with consciousness, the notion being that conscious intention could saturate an inanimate object with potent awareness.

Sometimes I would hear direct guidance; otherwise, the silence would be an instruction to stay with whatever was troubling me, as the answers would be revealed through experience. I heard: "Ask for the *highest* blessings" (rather than anything specific). I continued to meditate, following this instruction. After a while, I heard: "You've been asking this, and that, and this, and that ... so many deep, essential questions;" then, I heard the lines from the *Bhagavad-Gita*, spoken by Krishna: "Meditate on Me ... in this way, you will surely come to Me."

Our teacher had been clear that the whole world was an ashram–that Liberation could, and would for most individuals, come in mundane existence, not in the shelter of an ashram or cave. Our teacher had encouraged some to take the *shakti* or divine energy awakened in meditation out into the world: a kind of social activism emanating from awareness of the divinity within everyone. This instruction was for me, too. As much as part of me wanted to stay at the ashram forever, soaking in holiness that emanated as much from the carefully scrubbed tiles of the bathroom as it did from the Temple, I had to return to the world.

I was completing healing school. A difficult lesson involved relationships. While learning to recognize divinity in everyone, I still got hooked by infatuation. I tried to draw inspiration from Ramakrishna, an Indian saint who would gaze at a statue of the Divine Mother and fall into ecstatic trance; he saw the whole world as a living manifestation of the Divine Mother. I picked up the *Gospel of Sri Ramakrishna* and opened a page at random, finding the following story: Two hookers were brought before Ramakrishna to tempt him. Seeing them, he saw the Divine Mother in them, and immediately fell into *Samadhi*.

Much as I endeavored to imitate Ramakrishna, there were many temptresses in healing school and at the spiritual center–tempting because they embodied the goddess, radiant with potentiated awareness, and still carrying (and projecting) unresolved very human wounds. These wounds somehow exactly matched whatever unconscious baggage I was carrying, so that we did a quick dance that, in its own way, brought lurking issues to the surface and expelled old projections and fears.

One temptress was a beautiful actress who had a part on a popular soap opera filmed in New York City. She was sitting a few tables away in the lunchroom of the hotel where Brennan held classes. The actress shot a rose arrow across the tables and I was hooked. She motioned and I came. In a lilting voice she said, "I see the Holy Spirit in your eyes."

Who could resist such a charming entrée? Her gaze, voice, words, body and language were as powerful as any arrow of Cupid–energetic arrows, they pierced my loneliness and desire for human company. I was instantly infatuated; but nothing developed; in fact, the reverse: as soon as I was 'hooked,' she walked away and decided thereafter to ignore me. I felt seduced and abandoned, my holy hopes dashed with a sprinkling of flirtation. The grappling hook only succeeded because I had a receptor site in my psyche that provided perfect aperture, and perfectly accepted the seductive overture. Yet there still was a hook.

Bob, with whom I continued to do telephone therapy from Pennsylvania, empathized and offered counsel: "It's tough being Ulysses. You have to see her strutting her stuff, doing the dance of the seven veils, only she does it with *ashram*-speak, and you have to remain centered, recognize the pirouetting. It's really outrageous, disenchanting and depressing– people using this stuff, pick up a few words and misuse it to act out their old, tired, seducing methods. It you want beauty, put a picture of Mother Theresa on your mantle."

I already had had a picture of Theresa in meditation but as a man, having company in the Spirit was not the same as having it in the flesh. I admired the mystics who could become 'brides' and 'grooms' of 'Christ,' and thereby banish the need for a physical bride or groom; but we are social creatures, and though Aquarian, I found my personality desirous of social contact and greatly enhanced by such exchange. Spirits were no substitute for friendship in this realm, though friendship with them could greatly enhance the experience of this world.

Another issue was the difficulty in maintaining psychological boundaries in an environment in which we learned to transverse boundaries. In healing school, we interacted with each other not only on the physical level but also on energetic levels, learning to "read" energy fields, not only kinesthetically but also visually. Thus, the phenomenon of "strangers locking eyes across the room" would be multiplied by the ability to actually see (or feel) cords of energy making rosy arcs across the ceiling and landing in the heart (or genitals, depending on the interaction; heat is heat and fire is fire). Sitting together in the hotel Jacuzzi was particularly bonding: our chakras mingling in the swirling waters, love energy everywhere.

The more I learned about balance, the more it threw me off balance. On one hand, I was having these transcendental experiences at the ashram and on the other, experiencing psychic openings and heart openings in healing school; added was the cold, unfeeling, unsafe environment of the law school; and on top, a deep desire for intimate connection; and all the wounds of childhood were surfacing and swirling for all of us in healing school as we refined our intuitive abilities. We were becoming healers; but we did not live in a culture in which these kinds of 'invisible' connections were openly acknowledged, other than metaphorically. We had no models in the world, only friends in the healing vessel that school provided. Like many classmates, I could traverse universes in meditation, allow God's love to course through me, and feel shakti dancing on my fingertips, yet there were lessons to be learned in the realm of relationship in human love.

During junior year of healing school, one of the teachers was featured on Oprah: Peter. His namesake in the gospels had been the "rock" on whom Jesus would build his church; this Peter now was lucidly explaining to Oprah how one evening he had been 'abducted by aliens.' He had worked with psychiatrist John Mack from Harvard (later a professional colleague) and had gone into hypnotic states to uncover the trail of abuse, trauma, and revelation that accompanied his journey.

Before a national audience, Peter described his encounters with the aliens, the experiments they performed on him. These encounters included human-alien breeding. He admitted to having several "hybrid" children. The experiences initially were traumatic, but they had opened him up to a kind of inter-cultural (interspecies) dialogue that, he believed, humanity was being ripened for experiencing.

Peter had courage in disclosing his inner life. He was a good-looking, ordinary guy who married and practiced acupuncture, yet had the experience that he had "soul-mates" on other dimensions of consciousness, and that what had begun as a terrifying experience of invasion, mellowed into a wisdom and knowledge of other worlds. He saw his appearance on national television, in a sensationalized subject area, not as a means to fame (or infamy), but rather as a mission, to help teach the world about our connection with other beings, other worlds; he felt that this was helping prepare humanity for a contact that might not necessarily be physical (in flying saucers), but would primarily be accessed from within, through mental and spiritual technology. He risked great ridicule in the process—and the effect of verbal abuse, on a national scale, on his professional life and marriage.

I had a lot of respect for Peter as a pioneer, willing to risk his reputation by coming forward with experiences that the vast majority of peers would dismiss, distort, and deride. As a teacher, Peter helped me with a specific learning skill at healing school: how to connect points of blue light on the first layer of the field.

He was teaching me in many ways. We found ourselves alone in the hotel's elevator after class. The usual elevator attendant was gone. I looked at the panel of elevator buttons and asked Peter: "Permission?" He replied: "Power."

Even friends in healing school were frightened of his experiences: we could mingle with guides, angels, disincarnate entities, even demons, but *aliens*, they were scary, misunderstood. Peter was the only one who showed no fear—he simply accepted that this was his path, to convey the information about "ET" (or extraterrestrial) contact to others. In addition to admiring him, I was curious about my own connection, ever since the mention in Nick's channeling sessions that I was "Starseed," and the information about the "Ashtar command."

I did not have abduction experiences; rather, from experiences in healing school, I was beginning to feel as comfortable with ET's as with guides and other spiritual teachers. Indeed, I welcomed the connection, and intuitively felt it was a part of me: that on some level, I *was* an ET, with part of my consciousness tied up in this human vessel called

"Michael." In fact, I could hold this other awareness intact, together with my professional identity as a lawyer—both identities at once.

Apparently I was not alone: at least one other classmate felt there were cords running from her temples up to the "ships;" in fact, there were three or four of us with some kind of dual "passport to the cosmos" (as John Mack, MD would entitle his second book about the "alien" experience). Some were frightened. But the notion of alien cords was not too strange for me since, after all, we learned that we had cords running to each other, to our loved ones, to deceased persons, ancestors, guides, deceased pets--cords perceived through high sense perception.

Peter, in the hallway of the hotel, sensed my distress about navigating this multi-faceted identity and having to return to a faculty environment that was difficult if not sadistic. He tenderly said: "Michael, you're just learning to connect your head, your body, and your heart." As he said this, I could feel energetic connections between made between these different parts of my being. "Once you've done this, you'll be a model for others," he added. Peter combined a lot of healing power with gentleness, sensitivity, and respect.

I was able to confide in him that I, too, had my own ET Connection: sublime and not invasive. The summer between first and second year of law teaching, I had visited the Cleveland Clinic as a faculty scholar in the Medical Institute for Law Faculty run by Cleveland-Marshall School of Law. This Institute afforded participating faculty the opportunity to interact with physicians and, among other things, attend surgery.

While we chatted with surgeons about medical and legal issues, I was sensing kinesthetically the effect of the conversation on the energy fields of the anesthetized patient (who was out-of-body). I would see the patient's etheric body, which appears as bluish. I would perceive the outer, seventh layer of the energy field and even fields around the surgical instruments. I also perceived various deceased relatives, guides and angelic beings around the patients. Light-green healing energy emanated from my field, and heat from my hands. (I wrote about this visit, omitting details about light-streams and the ET encounter, in an article entitled, *Toward a Bioethics of Compassion*, and later in *Beyond Complementary Medicine* (2000)).

I was in my hotel room after a long day visiting Intensive Care. Suddenly I felt as though an etheric net had been put over my body, and my consciousness was being pulled out of my body. The experience was intense, and I asked for some relief. As I returned to my body, I detected a light being in the corner of my room, female. She looked like an icon of Mary, with a burgundy form-fitting suit that covered her scalp as well. She was quite beautiful and at the same time quite other; she communicated telepathically and seemed to be enjoying a great, respectful friendship with me. Her eyes were piercingly intelligent, and glittered with knowledge; she was conversing mentally like an old friend. I had no fear; I realized: she *is* an old friend. She just comes from another star system. These ET's are my brothers and sisters, part of the humanitarian mission as much as earth brothers and sisters. They and I are one.

Peter talked about the mission of these beings. Their intelligence is so constructed that they do not completely understand emotions. Some of them are, in effect, scientists who research human emotions by joining human energy fields.

According to Peter, there were several different races of aliens, though people usually. Among these, the Grays were the ones known for abducting humans and conducting experiments without their consent; the Blues and Whites were of a higher evolutionary order. The beings with whom I interacted were tall and striking, benevolent—Blues perhaps. After talking with Peter and checking my own experience, I concluded that I might be something of a voluntary participant in intergalactic research. I experienced my emotions and experiences almost being recorded and playing back, as if on some reel of film somewhere.

It seemed I had contracted with these beings to come into a human body and be kind of research subject—much like the research subjects my group would later recruit for NIH trials.

A Friend of All Faiths

The notion of contracting, prior to birth, was not too far-fetched to my legal thinking, once I accepted the notion that souls could exist prior to birth as well as after death, and thus make legally binding arrangements in the in-between. For the many who would ridicule these beliefs (yet accept, for example, that 2,000 years ago a child of God walked on water) or that prior to that someone parted the Red Sea with a rod, consider that more people in fact believe in aliens than believe in the principles of modern scientists (according to astrobiologist David Grinspoon in *Lonely Planets* (HarperCollins, 2003), p. 331)–an idea that is not "*inconsistent* with science, only *unverifiable* by science." Some believe souls choose bodies, others that genes (or hormones) choose mates.

Peter felt he, too, served in part as a camera for the ETs: "I'm a probe. They look at the world through my eyes, and if you look into my eyes, you'll see them." His eyes were warm and intelligent–caring, he was a sane guy who mowed the lawn and loved to ride a motorcycle. And there was also this hint of an observer or witness from far way–not a faraway look, but a sense of another presence with whom you could connect through the eyes. "Everything I see is recorded and goes to them for research," Peter said.

"What is the purpose of the research?" I asked him. Later I would learn to justify my grants to the National Institutes of Health in terms of "specific aims."

"To help heal our multidimensional reality," Peter responded.

I began to realize that I was having a similar experience of other wise beings looking through my eyes, of having details recorded and fed to a video on one of those ships. My night travels included visiting the ships. I reflected that others, too from the prophet Ezekiel to Swedenbourg, had recorded voyages, traveling perhaps through the cords up to some other realm, though they may not have conceptualized such journeys as visits to "ET's" or "ships." My visits were instantaneous, not bound by the speed of light: one moment I was lying in bed, trying to fall asleep, the next moment my consciousness whisked to another dimension. The more I opened myself to healing school, the more these energies became accessible in a non-threatening, loving manner that made me realize more of my own innate wholeness as a creature 'made in God's image.'

I began to sense the ET intelligence while doing healings: much of that intelligence was vast, networked, more analytic than emotional, more akin to higher mathematics than opera, and containing a fascination with human experience. This idea of connecting instantaneously to the world wide intelligent web, and without visible wires, may have seemed preposterous in 1995; ten years later, it has become the norm through the medium of silicon chips and wireless signals, rather than through the thought-waves of consciousness, though we are now beginning to experiment (successfully) with machines that can help paralyzed individuals by translating mental impulses (commands) into movement.

My visit to the Cleveland Clinic was only several years after the term "alternative medicine" had been introduced to the American public; the medical profession had high skepticism that even something such as acupuncture might be anything more than placebo. Once I opened to these many different levels of consciousness, I found such medical dogmatism not only unconvincing, but also uninteresting. I was reminded of the statement in the *Upanishads* that "those who think they know, don't know; those who know they don't know, know."

My profound energetic encounters at the Cleveland Clinic were at the human, as well as extraterrestrial, level. I finally found one or two nurses who had heard of therapeutic touch, but kept their skills closeted. Later, I met a physician who had the reputation of initiating medical board investigations against doctors who recommended alternative therapies to their patients. "Are you a quack buster?" I asked him, perhaps naively in light of his notorious reputation.

"No," he said. "I'm interested in patient protection."

I could read that he sincerely believed this, even though he was alleged to have gotten

Michael H. Cohen

honest physicians in trouble with the authorities. Because of the genuineness in his reply, my heart connected with his. I asked him what he thought of therapeutic touch.

"You can't heal someone from six feet away," he said dismissively.

Nonetheless, as he walked away, I could see the outer edge of his energy field and connect to it kinesthetically. Healing energy drifted from my thoughts and positive intentions toward this man into his field. At the same time, I thought: in five minutes, I could have taught him how to sense energy for himself. All that energy packed into resentment, dismissal, arrogance, judgment, presuming to *know*, explanations substituting for knowledge, when had he been a little more open, he might have explored experientially, and then returned to cognitive processing of the experience. When, some years later, I read in a newsletter that he had died, I thought of the trouble he was said to have caused many physicians; but I also recollected our brief encounter with warmth and fondness. Perhaps I had not entirely learned to "love your enemies," but I did get to *see the love* and in some small way, transcend the definition of enemy; I knew on some level that all of us our bound by cords, and by the ancient law of action-reaction that churns events.

Senior year in healing school I presented a client healing. Since my profession was legal academe, I did not have regular clients. I decided to focus my presentation on someone I knew. I was involved with a woman whose husband had died rather young and unexpectedly. The relationship plunged me into all the intricacies and uncertainties of psychological and spiritual frontier work that Bob had warned against: questionable boundaries, mixing of realms, contradictory impulses of longing and fear, repressed grieving, and a host of unhealthy dynamics. In some ways, I felt more connected to the deceased husband than to the woman, and felt some responsibility for helping the children; thus adopting a savior role and justifying that through what I perceived through expanded perception. In short, I was functioning highly in healing skills, and poorly in psychological self-awareness.

I found myself doing a healing on the entire family, without realizing the cost to my own clarity; yet, the healings seemed to have a beneficial effect. Only later, recognizing the craziness into which I had voluntarily plunged, did I realize that energy healing had a long way to go to develop as a profession; that healers and therapists had much to talk about. Healers moved in the realm of the unbounded, while therapists had strict boundaries; and beyond ethical guidelines for energy healing, and more work on such rudimentary foundations as transference and counter-transference, there had to be a dialogue about the ways psychological and spiritual frontier could both mesh and collide. In this way, my personal stumbles during training as a healer propelled a professional interest in the relationship between energy healing as an emerging profession and insights from the mental health professions.

In the meanwhile, I did healing work with Kristin, the eleven-year-old daughter of my amorous interest, and focused my "case" around these sessions. Kristin was a fair, delicate girl, highly intelligent and intuitive, who found herself bullied by classmates because of her tendency to withdraw socially. In the first healing, I cleared what I perceived as "etheric mucous" in the chest and lungs; shortly thereafter, she was diagnosed with a rare autoimmune disease and put on medication. She asked me to continue working with her to help strengthen her resources and reduce dependency on medication.

In the second healing, I saw the room dissolve into purple light and then saw her deceased father next to her. I then saw her in her late teens and early twenties, and felt the support for her from the other realms. I felt my connection to the earth, and received guidance that I was holding a space of safety for Kristin, to come into her body and feel the strength, wisdom and love of those supporting her from the other realms. After the healing, Kristin's back chakras were more open. Her heart and throat needed more work, but were more open and her whole face was radiant.

In a third healing, Kristin lay down on the healing table, holding her stuffed, flying white unicorn, and kept her eyes open; she seemed to communicate with the guides during the healing. I saw Kristin as a wise crone whom I had known many times. It occurred to me that there were energetic links between the autoimmune disease and the way Kristin was handling (or not handling) her grief around her father's early death; Kristin's body, one could argue (or see metaphorically), was attacking itself because Kristin had not been able to process her feelings about suddenly losing her father. As I continued working with Kristin, her mother began, finally, to tap into feelings of rage against her deceased husband for leaving them.

I could feel the husband in the room. "He can't hear me!" she screamed.

"Yes he can," I responded.

"I am with her always," I heard.

Somehow, this facilitated a conversation between them in which she was able to acknowledge and release some of her held-back feelings. I was crossing multiple lines here, being involved as a boyfriend and healer, and ultimately this was disastrous, but it taught me a much-needed lesson, not only about boundaries, but also about containing my healing energies and knowledge, and using these wisely.

I realized during my case that I had been the client all along: visiting the family, a house of grief, triggered my own grief, which needed to be healed. In many ways, I had been in mourning: there was the separation from Natasha; the loss of my paternal grandfather when I was sixteen, which I never properly grieved; and the loss of parts of myself in work as a lawyer and law professor. Kristin had a beautiful face and smile, but also a deep sadness; she was a lonely child who felt isolated and tended to stay in her head or her will, sometimes lashing out with sarcasm. I noted that Kristin's sole support system was her mother, yet Kristin was growing and asserting her independence from her mother, and needed a safe place to express all her feelings. I knew I could not be the vehicle for this, but that Kristin needed another healer or therapist, who was not so intertwined with the family.

Being a medium does not protect us from our grief around those we love who pass on. And, while perceiving the spirit world enriches my emotional life, it does not diminish the pain I feel when someone I love leaves the body.

My neighbor down the thousand-foot driveway in Lykens, Pennsylvania was Hermann. He lived in a small house with his wife Evelyn (we shared the bottom part of the driveway and took turns at the commercial snow blower during the winter months). Hermann was old enough to remember parachuting onto the beaches of Normandy during his World War II service. He also used to take care of stray cats.

One day a beautiful kitten wandered across the driveway and into his barn. We noticed that the kitten had an eye infection, and was growing sickly. It was snowy wintertime. I tried to catch the kitten, to take him to the vet, but the little guy was elusive. I spoke to the kitten, aloud and telepathically: "Please let me catch you get you proper care, I only want to help you." The kitten was too fast, dodging all attempts at capture. Once or twice I brushed by the kitten's tail; or we looked at each other from across a bale of hay. In this way we made contact; I started developing feelings for this kitten and, I think, the kitten for me.

The winter was fierce, and I saw the kitten huddled and shivering under piles of newspaper in Hermann's barn. But I could not catch the kitten and bring it to a vet. Each time I approached, tenderly and slowly, he scampered. Did he know what was coming? Was there a reason he resisted arrest, was he willfully bound for *olam ha-bah*, the next world? Surely he was suffering in the wind and ice.

Several days later, I saw the kitten, frozen stiff. His paws were outstretched. He lay on his side, eyes open. I felt so much grief, so much love for this little being. Hermann's wife, Evelyn, and I, buried the kitten beneath some bales of hay. There was so much ice and snow we were unable to reach the earth and make a proper grave, so we made a hole in the snow and moved some hay over the cover the kitten for a makeshift place of rest. We said some prayers together.

Evelyn was aging, and soon would be helping Hermann through a terminal cancer, struggling through his illness and what Medicare would pay for and what they had to do on their own, as well as the limitations of the body, feeding him ice cubes to keep him hydrated; and I would be using my skills to run energy and make some attempt to help him feel a little more comfortable, and little more prepared, if such a thing could be. And so we prayed. These sessions also made me late for mandatory faculty meetings about downsizing; and I was chastised while holding within an energetic connection to the kitten's fate.

Brennan told us that the being continues to hover around the body and relatives for three full days after physical death, hence the tradition in many religions about not moving the body during that time. This is a transitional period during which a person comes to his or her own funeral, hears accountings of his or her life from relatives, and actually helps those grieving to let go. These first three days are an especially important time, therefore, for prayerful connection, assisting the person's soul to move toward the next destination.

I remained close to the kitten's spirit, while the dean droned on about who might be downsized first. He responded to questions with charming wisecracks. It was difficult to tell from the information given just how far the downsizing would spread down the ranks. I read control and fear behind the words: domination and aggression. He hinted that faculty evaluations of each other might have an effect on who would be terminated; at the same time, his smooth words told, we were to keep a "collegial" environment. This was a sure way to promote insanity. Whatever small amount of trust and camaraderie existed under this administrative regime evaporated. Fear was the administration's best ally, beating submission. I doubted the capacity of my profession to produce compassion, empathy, and true wisdom; saw how the surface gliding of words could actually increase dissimulation and destruction; and felt more than ever how important were "high sense perception" and other tools of expanded awareness, so that human beings 'could call each on their stuff,' communicate truthfully, and access the heart.

The Devil was not in the details; nor did he sport red horns and a tail. He lived in the lies that ordinary people told each other to protect their jobs. He lived in the lies they told to hide their hides, their lies; he resided in voice and the breath, in language and thought; in body, speech and mind; he was not so much "the Adversary" as an archetypical adversary, personalized in the choice in every moment to hide in fear or to shine in one's own truth, power, and light. He was falsity incarnate, and lived among us, hidden even from those who gave him shelter.

Some of the faculty cultivated ties with dean by playing tennis or having private lunches. Shifting alliances kept the sea of lies afloat. Meanwhile, the programmed "downsizing" proceeded through a stream of invective about "teaching" or "scholarship" used to justify cuts. I was on one such review committee, which aimed to skewer a colleague who was up for promotion to Associate Professor. I found the calumnies unbearable. By taking a position, however, I knew I would likely be targeted. And truth did not penetrate these hardened hearts. We were to teach our students "law;" yet collectively, displayed nothing of knowledge of laws of the heart. It was difficult to reconcile the disappointment, betrayal, and anger I was feeling with the spiritual teachings of the ashram.

"Don't be attached to results," I heard inside while trying to figure out a way to manage the chaos of my career within the school in which I had put my trust.

At first, I did not listen to this advice. I drafted an angry letter for the dean, and then sat in meditation. Immediately the advice I received was: "don't send it." I tore up the letter— venting it by writing had been therapeutic, but I did not need to enmesh myself further in this cycle of attack and counter-attack. The letter would have added fuel to the karmic fire, multiplying the present ugliness by adding my own negativity. I had learned just a little bit of restraint. There are times when it is appropriate and necessary to send such a letter, and other times when it is more helpful to know that "what goes around, comes around," to withdraw emotionally and energetically, and let the situation unwind without throwing more cords into the equation.

After realizing this, I had a meditation in which I saw all the faculty in my school in another lifetime; they (we) had thrown this dean down a well, as in the story of Joseph and his brothers. Now he was wreaking his revenge, only it was not really revenge, but rather a balancing of karma, the law of action and reaction. He was just exacting a pay-off, divinely arranged, for the injustice of centuries earlier. Of course, one could interpret my meditation image psychologically as a wish-fulfillment: a desire for revenge—part of me unconsciously *hoped* the faculty would rid itself of this evil influence by throwing him thrown down a well like the biblical Joseph (not that I would ever act out the unconscious fantasy). So: was the image a past life or wish fulfillment—spiritual clarity or ego blockage? Or was it both at once? The question of psychological and spiritual integration may be a koan that mental health disciplines and spiritual teachers may have to collectively resolve.

Returning from one of these insufferable faculty meetings, which seemed nothing more than thin veils for degradation and humiliation of 'colleagues,' I received a call from my mother. She told me right away that Zaydie had had a cerebral hemorrhage and was on life support. I told her I wanted to be with him, that I could immediately fly to Detroit; but by the time I would arrive, it would probably be too late.

It was time to focus all my emotional energy on the present situation and to offer what I could to uplift it. I immediately went into prayer. First I recited all my Indian mantras to lift Zaydie to the highest possible plane. Then I chanted the Hebrew evening service. I stood on my back porch, facing the forest, as the night sky descended and stars appeared. I chanted to the wise trees; to the rocks; to the animals; to the God of Israel, who was everywhere.

Each word of the service had meaning; I realized this would be the last time I would chant these sacred phrases while my Zaydie, who had been responsible for teaching them to me, was alive.

My mother phoned again to tell me that the family was around Zaydie, and that they had made a decision to disconnect the life support. I asked her at exactly what time this would occur and prepared accordingly.

At the appointed hour, I wrapped myself in an enormous *tallit*, the ritual fringes, and recited the Kaddish, addressing the forest behind the house. Simultaneously, my great-uncle Sol, one of Zaydie's brothers, was reciting the Kaddish into Zaydie's ear. This was for transport to *olam-habah*, the next world, the incantation that would maximize the presence of the divine in his ferry-ride through the cosmos. Alone in my cedar mountain house, I continued to meditate and pray. And grieve. And to connect with Zaydie's spirit as it moved through various planes of existence.

That week, I received a call from a Congressional staffer on issues concerning alternative medicine. The politics never interested me much; but the spirit behind the politics engaged me deeply. The staffer invited me to serve on the board of her organization. I accepted. In my heart, I dedicated my service on this board to Zaydie. A prayer arose from that place:

> There is no liberation without group liberation; no enlightenment, until all of humanity is enlightened. Therefore one must incarnate again and again, in human form, to help alleviate suffering, until the last human being is liberated.

With all my struggles on the physical plane, with all my desire to transcend once and for all, end my karma, and move on the realm of the enlightened Masters, this heartfelt prayer engraved itself on my consciousness: to return again and again, as many time as necessary, to give everything for all beings, everywhere. It was a prayer born of immense love; the love for God, the love of the Buddhas, and my love for Zaydie, all merged into one.

When Barbara Brennan described her first experience of a Jewish funeral, she reported that the rabbi says something in Hebrew and all these angelic beings appear and lead the spirit, out of the grave, through successively higher dimensions toward the Godhead. She continued, half-jokingly, that during the English translation, nothing happens; then the rabbi chants again in Hebrew, and all these angelic things start happening. Barbara was testifying to the power inherent in sacred language, in words chanted with intentionality. The translation is a copy, has power but not the same vibrational quotient.

Barbara's report echoed my own multidimensional experience in my Zaydie's funeral. First, I was asked to lead the service. I was aware of my voice and the power of the Hebrew words. Then, below the surface of this role, I felt my own feelings, the feelings of boy toward his beloved grandfather. At the same time, I aware of others' feelings, a group energy, and the effect the prayers seemed to have on my family, releasing love through the grief. Finally, I had the experience my healing teacher was describing, of sensing an effect of the various Hebrew phrases and parts of the service on my Zaydie. There was an energetic completion, a moving forward, and for the living, a launching of the grieving process and preparation for our life without him on the physical plane.

Zaydie was more than a zaydie to me: he radiated spirit, connection to the ancestors, caring, warmth, learning, purpose and direction; *ahava* (the Hebrew word for love). He was the unbroken link from Eastern Europe, and through that back into the centuries, to Moses and Abraham, and before that, to the still morning before morning had even been created, when God said, "Let there Be." He was the link to the inexpressible longing to become human, to incarnate for the purpose of sitting in residence with one's loved ones throughout the ages, to be able to feed a child, share play with one's beloved, assimilate family in a human body.

When we went back to my Zaydie's house to sit *shiva* (the Jewish mourning custom), I took some time alone and circled around the house. Later, I learned that this is an ancient custom: to walk around the home of someone recently deceased as a way of paying respect to their spirit. Intuitively, I was honoring Zaydie's spirit. I was also letting go of his presence in the body and learning to connect with him in channels beyond the body. I could feel him filling the entire space with his love.

At one point, I found my Bobe (grandmother) "taking a nap" in one of the small bedrooms. I knocked on the door. She was holding her face between her hands. She had "held up" so magnificently so far, not showing any grief, being strong; perhaps she was afraid of being overwhelmed by the feelings, or of overwhelming others with the feelings. I knew what was present. I sat beside her. Gently we spoke for a few minutes. She recounted how she had brought Zaydie to the emergency room, and there were some delays. She blamed herself for not doing enough, for not acting fast enough - if only she had done such and such, she could have saved him.

So many of my loved ones had gone, and I remember feeling completely ignorant of any way to comfort them. Now I had all these tools: an understanding of relaxation therapy and trance, energy healing, intuitive abilities. I let myself be guided. I let Bobe know that she had done all she could, that there was nothing more she could have done, that God knew when to bring Zaydie close and exactly how to do so.

Bobe repeated some of these phrases; they seemed to bring her comfort. Still, her mind—understandably—was going around and around. I gave her a mantra to say to help anchor her in God. It was not Hindu, but Hebrew. *Ribbono shel olam*-Master of the Universe. My Bobe repeated: *Ribbono shel olam, ribbono shel olam, ribbono shel olam.* And finally, she slept.

Some months later, while sleeping, I astrally projected to my Zaydie's home. I saw a kindly presence looking over Bobe. I asked: "Who are you?" The spirit answered: *Moshe Rabeinu* (our teacher, Moses). I know now that Zaydie is always with her. He is always with me—something I did not know then. He visits regularly from some kind of transformed space—I cannot explain other than to convey the impression of awareness of his consciousness filling up the room and becoming one with everything. Freud's descendants

A Friend of All Faiths

might say that I have projected the internalized image of a warm, caring father (grandfather) onto the cosmos; Freud, after all, saw God as nothing more than a grand projection of the ideal father. But it does not *feel* like projection—it feels like Zaydie's consciousness has expanded in the after-death stages of the journey of his soul, and has united, like that of Arjuna and Krishna, with the One. My interpretation is different than the local Freud's, less reductive and perhaps more grandiose, but it is the one consistent with my experience.

In the week of Zaydie's death, I did not see him as a soul hovering in my room and one with everything: he was my Zaydie, and I was a boy who had lost someone he loved. I had so much grief. I called my best friend from healing school. I told her that as people were sitting around the sofa, remembering Zaydie, and sometimes crying, I could see Zaydie, in his golden body, in the middle of the room. He was so busy! Trying to comfort everybody occupied him joyfully, although I sensed he had his own work to do in making the transition. I told my friend about my feelings for him, and asked how I could help him. What was he doing there in the middle of the living room, I asked her, when he should be journeying toward one of the heavens?

"He's there because everybody needs him so much," she said. "You can help him the most by *letting go.*" But how could I let go of Zaydie? I loved him so much; he had just died; my grief was so fresh. "Allow yourself to go through the grieving process," my friend said, "but know that the family's need is keeping him here. If you release him to God, he'll be able to continue on the next phase of his path."

I prayed over this; I took some quiet time, alone, in his study. There was the green couch on which I had snuggled on so many stay-overs; the bookcases with Zaydie's favorite books—Hebrew novels and readable books about science; a pillow embroidered by my aunt with an elephantine design; a copy of her children's book, *My Father's Moustache*; the pull-down shade with a hint of sunlight streaming through.

Mentally, I sent him whatever energy I could release for him to move on. I called my friend again, to verify that he was receiving all the blessings he could receive. As I looked down to dial on his old-fashioned, black rotary phone, I noticed his calendar. It was open, and his handwriting during the final weeks of his life was distinct. There were some tasks and responsibilities, a few notes. I turned back a week or two and zeroed in on one day for which there was a single entry.

Zaydie had written: "Michael called."

The floodgates of my heart opened yet further, and I wept with love.

Michael H. Cohen

HEBREW SCHOOL

(DETROIT, BUENOS AIRES, AND JERUSALEM, 1962-1979)

At Hillel
(the day school in Michigan:
not the astral being).

In the Desert

Esoterica tells us that we choose our parents.

Destiny then selected a lifelong involvement in health care and medicine. Information about the structure of organic compounds, the nature of mitochondria and the steps of the Krebs cycle filtered into the amniotic sac along with basic nutrients, as I spent nine months as a soul hovering around two finely chosen parents, both in university.

With one hand on her abdomen, the other on the pathology textbook, my mother insisted on finishing her senior-year exam at the University of Michigan School of Medicine. States away, my father was a soldier, drafted into the United States Reserve and stationed in Georgia. It was 1962: John F. Kennedy was President; ahead were Vietnam, humans on the Moon, and huge social changes. If I timed things right, I would have a great astrological forecast and the perfect karmic cards to transform my consciousness, do some good for the planet, and go for *jivanmukti*. And I had chosen a family steeped in learning and appreciative of education, which meant that I could fulfill a scholar's dream of absorbing just about everything, since we practically lived in a library.

Everything was ready and right, yet Mom was still creating black holes with her Number Two pencil. I was growing impatient. The word—words to come, the language of identity—would be flesh as biochemical and pharmacological formulas seeped into consciousness. She kept scribbling away, weaving equations like a reincarnated alchemist, hoping to placate anonymous examiners at the state medical board, while I began my martial arts maneuvers to let her know my soul was ready for incarnation. I kicked, prodded, tucked and rolled, displaying all the different martial arts styles I remembered from former births-while Mom sweated, scribbled, inscribed, put her hand to her stomach, and ... finally, succumbed. Taken by ambulance to the University hospital after the last abstruse medical question had been masterfully answered, she recited some choice verses of Torah in praise of the birth process as tiny feet protruded from their previous lodging. Inhale, exhale, just like all the yoga I had learned in previous life-times. Someone slaps my buttocks and I cry.

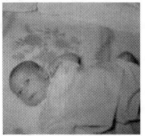

"Kwa! Kwa!" a spiritual teacher wrote; the baby cries, "I am this, I am this!" It is the cry of a little ego, whereas the enlightened soul cries, "Ham-Sa! Ham-Sa!" meaning: "I am That! I am That!" At birth we plunge into ego-awareness, a contraction of the great unity consciousness we enjoyed before birth. The Jewish Midrash concurs, relating that just before birth, an angel presses a coal to our lips, extinguishing our memory of the pre-birth state. That way, we can move through our karma with enthusiasm and abandon: hating having to pay taxes, struggling with our emotions, learning to perfect ourselves by swimming upstream against the currents of life.

Even though Dad was away because humans on this planet still needed armies to fight wars, and even though Mom, a super and superb achiever, moving through med school as one of twenty women in a class of 210, was still writing her exam, I wanted entrance in to Earth, *karma bumi*, the world of karma; I wanted in *now*.

On January 29, a date astrologically steeped in esotericism, I was later informed by one astrological practitioner or another, at 6:18 pm, a time of Aquarius rising, Aquarius dawning in the month and Age of Aquarius, I came into the present physical body on this plane.

Jacob held onto the heel of Esau as the twins came through the womb; why should I not recall the same? This life is a transit between birth and death; the afterlife and before-life are of deep interest; and how do we know what we know or do not know? God asks Job: "where you there when I created the Leviathan?" When it comes to his karma, Job is clueless; he goes through the five stages of death, finally emerging with acceptance. My birth and life are miraculous and freighted with conversations with God as those of every human being ever born or to be born on this planet; like Tevye in Fiddler on the Roof, praising and protesting and thanking and questioning all at once; demanding entrance too soon but never arriving too early or too late; always in step with the divine plan and constantly wanting to see more of the blueprint faster than it rolls off the giant Torah scroll in the sky; and always learning the details only as they occur, unhealthy egotism being crushed, the flames of healthy heart-love being fanned, the full karmic blueprint withheld from intruding queries for my own good and that of the creation.

My father's name, Perry, is biblical; Peretz means "to burst forth" and was an ancestor in B'raisheet (Genesis; "In the Beginning"). Margo is the name of a flower in Israel; Zaydie drew inspiration for the name from a poem from a modern Hebrew poet named Schneyer. Perry and Margo begat Michael, Daniel, Jonathan: we all had biblical names. Later, I also identified with Archangel Michael, with his flaming sword, emblem of truth, integrity, healing, faithfulness, justice, *dharma*. The Torah says: "*Zedek, zedek, tirdoph*:" you shall *run* after righteousness. So Michael symbolized to me. Daniel, the

great Hebrew prophet, literally means, "God is my judge;" and Jonathan means "God's gift to me." The "el" in Michael and Jonathan is *El*, a name for Yahweh; so is the "jo" in Jonathan, standing for *Yud-Hei*, the "ya" in "Yahweh."

Kindergarten was at Hillel Day School of Metropolitan Detroit, and Shabbat services at Shaarey Zedek, the synagogue my Zaydie's mother, Rebecca Panush Saks, had joined on arriving in the Detroit area from Poland. In that space, generations of our family worshipped and served God and my parents were married. I still have dreams about traveling through the painted, cinderblock corridors and on the grassy knoll that held its playground. Hillel was housed on the ground of the first schoolhouse in the state. I studied Jewish holidays, learned Jewish history, and by first grade, was well on my way to the rabbinate or to become a cantor.

Even in kindergarten, the Hebrew alphabet intrigued me. The kabbalists say that every letter has significance: the Torah contains codes within codes; the letters carry numerological meanings; and the spaces around the letters (white fire on black fire) contain the secrets of God. When we held services, and the Ark was opened, it was like an interdimensional portal though which I connected to all the cosmos, to the angels, to previous and future births, to lives on other planes, to my brothers and sisters in other dimensions of existence, the essence of divine love, *Shaddayi*--God.

Early on I learned to traverse worlds. One of my earliest memories involves a collision on my tricycle with an illegally kept go-cart in the neighborhood. At three-and-a-half, I fell and the axle of a motorized wheel ground against the flesh of my face. I was covered in blood; my parents bathed me in a towel and transported me to the hospital. The scar bisected my forehead, ran between the eyes (I was extremely lucky to have kept both intact), continued down the nose and around the mouth, wound past the chin, and finally ended all the way down the throat.

A Friend of All Faiths

My face had been bisected, literally and visually. Already I was divided between worlds. I can remember learning in college about the character Raskalnikov, the "divided man" in Dostoevsky's *Crime and Punishment* and thinking, "that's me, the divided man," and although his tendencies were vicious the metaphor stuck. Eventually, by ninth grade, I would have plastic surgery. Through the efforts of a talented plastic surgeon, the scar would be made almost invisible. And yet the memory of the scar lingered. The perpetrator was named Paul–not the one of the gospels. Years later I was preparing for the plastic surgery during which I also had the sensation of cross-world transverse (my mother claims that the anesthetic, ketamine, was hallucinogenic, so that the mechanisms of spiritual travel could have been biologically meditated). I remember waking up from the morphine to the third volume of JRR Tolkien's "Lord of the Rings" trilogy.

Classmates would ask about the accident and invariably end with a ringing: "did you sue?" My relationship to litigation as a lawyer since has been freighted with ambivalence. I might have been a successful courtroom lawyer; I have written many briefs, helped coach clients through litigation processes, clerked for a trial court judge, and taught a course about litigation strategy (civil procedure). And later I would be involved, tangential, in litigation consultation and review. But I would not become a courtroom lawyer. I would turn toward corporate law practice as a kind of uniting objectives with language; and prefer mediation, negotiation, and other forms of 'alternative dispute resolution' to litigation, and wishing there were ways to come to resolution in a less violent karmic balancing than the drama of the courtroom. I might have sued Paul (or rather my parents might have paid a lawyer to do this) but I have no memory of the litigation; it is hardly worth mentioning, except perhaps as a trigger for ambivalence around the whole concept of a lawsuit, a sense that this serves only as a surrogate for our innate ability to agree, another symptom of the broken vessels of divine consciousness in the light of which, when healed, everything would be made whole.

Following the accident, an event occurred that would set the stage not only for a philosophical predisposition toward religious pluralism and mystical adventure, but also future interest in medicine and healing: the consequences of a classmate's mental lapse involving the phrase, "can I go to the bathroom," in Hebrew. I watched his distress increase exponentially each time the teacher tried to tease out the correct words. Finally helpless, frustrated, outmaneuvered, he let his bladder leak out onto the floor. I watched the yellow dribble accumulate into a substantial puddle. When the prodigious flow subsided, I responded. Either prodded by the teacher or volunteering out of simple remembrance of some vow taken lifetimes earlier as a *bodhisattva*, one who takes birth again and again to alleviate human suffering, I fetched some paper towels to help clean up the mess.

This simple action linked my consciousness to his; in some corner of my mind, I identified with his involuntary release, a shameful and public contraction of his essence. It was first-grade Hebrew school that alerted me to the need for a health care system beyond what Western orthodoxy, or any too-disciplined system, could offer. My baptism in complementary medicine had begun.

Following first grade at Hillel, we moved to Buenos Aires, Argentina for three years. I attended *Tarbut* (literally, culture), a school that taught in three languages (Spanish, English, and Hebrew) and in which my Jewish education continued.

We lived in a large house, inexpensive by American standards, with several helpers (maids), while my mother pursued her Ph.D. in biochemistry at the University of Buenos Aires and my father worked for Chrysler Ferve Argentina. I learned to play the guitar and sang patriotic Argentine tunes about the founding of the Republic and its ideals. I knew more about Manuel Belgrano than George Washington, and my English was coated with a Spanish accent. The advertisement jingoes were in Spanish ("Ford puede, y major"); my dreams were in Spanish; and the *bodhisattva* ideals that originated in Judaism found impetus in the passionate Latin American patriotism that I was daily imbibing from our maids and in school.

Time in Argentina was full of mystery: a foreign land, exotic yet familiar. Some traumatic incidents occurred despite my parents' best intentions to shield me from the ugliness in this world. I had many friends. Yet children can be cruel, aggressive, and violent; one child was jealous of the expensive crayon set I had brought from the U.S. He punched me in the mouth; I fell to the ground, cracking a front tooth that is still missing a tiny corner today.

There was also time to play Zorro with my brothers, bouncing around the gardens in a black cape, swirling my toy sword and mock fencing with Spanish taunts to my assailants.

The year 1969 disappeared.

I am certain that my parents have a memory of me in 1969, but I was convinced in 1970, and remain convinced today, that I was somewhere other than on Earth. I have a memory of one day at Tarbut: the ground was full of slugs. It was awful, because you could not step without your foot landing on a slug, and that being would be squashed, and there would be an awful crunch and dual sense of guilt and inevitability. The night before, a few slugs were out; somehow they had multiplied. I would later do my seventh-grade science project on genetics and the Russian monk Gregor Mendel, thinking I might someday become a genetic scientist; in Buenos Aires, I was amazed that these few creatures could multiply so quickly.

I climbed into a tree, with a female friend, and our favorite books. Mine was *King Solomon's Mines* by H. Rider Haggard. That book propelled me into another world, one equally real to the study at Tarbut. I was wearing the Tarbut uniform: white shirt, blue tie, blue shorts, white socks, nice shoes. I had curled up on a branch, high above the slugs and teachers and classmates.

When I came down, it was 1970. The preceding year had disappeared.

Was I abducted by aliens? Was my consciousness replaced by some other intelligence, one that shared a kinship with Michael but was *other than* nonetheless? I would have been seven years old in 1969. I remembered the year disappearing long before Nick channeled that I was "Starseed:"

The vividness of those impressions are embossed in the consciousness of old. For Starseed has been born within you at age seven. The mask of many will begin to take form in the consciousness to help you develop.

What exactly happened that year? Where did I go? Who came into "me" in "my" place? What was identity, anyway? No wonder I would be so drawn to Gurdjieff Work, with its theory of the many shifting /s. In truth, Gurdjieff loomed large; as did Nick, and other teachers, because history catalytically propelled me toward a future I had always known inside. Since my earliest years, I had been absorbed in the quest to find God, to understand: from first-grade drawings of Israelites pulling bricks for the Egyptian pyramids and a man on his knees, crying out, "O Lord what have I done;" to poems such as "The Aftermath of World War Three;" to the out-of-body experiences in John Jay Hall, freshman year at Columbia University, to inhaling the white smoke with the Monk at the Iowa Writers' Workshop, my soul was primed for mystical experience.

Today, when I see snails after a rain, I am reminded of being taken up out of the body.

Returning to the U.S. and assimilating back into Hillel was like confronting a foreign culture. My accent was Argentine; I wore glasses; I was more comfortable with soccer than baseball; I used a knife and fork like Europeans (holding one in each hand); and once again found myself bridging worlds. Yet, through Hillel and Shaarey Zedek, Judaism was wrapping my early life in its protective cloak, a garment of love and nurturing from the ancients, stemming back through Moses and Adam, indeed back as the Greek Professor in Iowa had said to the Primordial Father. I learned all the holidays, and sat with Zaydie in synagogue on Saturdays.

Every morning, before class, our headmaster got on the intercom to read the daily psalm in Hebrew. I participated. Each one starts with: "This is the psalm which the Levites would recite in the Temple" (on such-and-such a day of the week). Perhaps I was connecting to a time in the Temple as a priest.

My favorite teacher at Hillel was Rabbi P. He taught the Talmud in Aramaic: Mishna, a commentary on the Torah, Gemara, a commentary on the Mishna, and various commentaries on the commentaries. Rabbi P insisted that since Adam, "the generations are getting weaker," that we are further and further from our connection with God. Later this would resonate with the Hindu notion of *kali yuga*, the idea that we are living in a cosmic age of unrighteousness, a cycle of time in which everything is upturned, and *adharma* (the opposite of *dharma*) prevails. The Talmudic texts wove logic with dream, legend, psychological interpretation, scholarly debate, and myth--all good preparation for law school.

We studied the ancestors, using Kabalistic interpretations of their actions and even their names, since names embody the sacred, and language is a code pointing toward divine truths. We looked at Adam, for example, the original man. The "A" (or *aleph)* is the first letter in the Hebrew alphabet--primordial, oozing, the cosmic soup; "*dam*" means "blood." Thus, Adam, the first human being, is the entire divine energy of the creation condensed into a vessel of flesh and blood. *Ish*, "man," has the same letters as *esh*, "fire" (in the Torah, the vowels are omitted); *isha*, "woman," has the same letters with the letter "hey" added (which stands for the feminine principle in God-consciousness).

Thus, the symbolism came alive through the letters. Since we have moved further from the original union with God in our continuing experience of expulsion from Eden, our task on earth, Rabbi P imparted, was to "repair the broken vessels" of Light that had been the original breach in which we lost contact with our divine essence. I still have the original Hebrew and Aramaic notes taken from fourth grade.

Rabbi P was delighted that my family had planned a trip to Israel. For me it would become a place where each square foot of land held generational memories. Although back then, I could not "read" energy fields, did not "tune in" to the land for guidance, could not "see" past lives and battles enacted in meditation, I nonetheless would be able to appreciate the land from a historical and emotional standpoint, as well as our deep connection to the topography of our heritage.

Prior to travel, Rabbi P had asked if I would hand-carry a special package on the plane to his relatives in Jerusalem; the package, he told me, consisted of extremely important items not available in Israel. I accepted, knowing how sacred was the mission entrusted. I then persuaded my parents to hand-carry these heavy packages through the airport and onto the plane. Through customs, we were subjected to a rigorous search. Our packages from Rabbi P turned out to be American diapers which he had me wanted to bolster supplies of his cousins in Israel. It was at stage I began developing serious authority issues. Rabbi P had initiated me into mysteries of Torah, but he was also fallible--his clay feet showed, even as he interpreted divine authority. The contradiction prompted an inner impulse to find my own synthetic truth, even though I revered the tradition, the history, and the longing expressed by the language of the heritage into which I had been brought.

By seventh grade, I was alternating between a career interest rabbinical school, and a career in genetic engineering: both promised to reveal the ultimate mysteries of the universe. I was following the maternal lineage, since Mom was a doctor and Zaydie a high school chemistry teacher, and then principal. My father, an economics major and CPA, was working for Chrysler Corporation in finance, and his father had worked in sales. (My paternal grandfather had attended law school in Detroit but, during the Depression, could not get a job, because there was discrimination against Jews. My maternal grandmother or Bobe had attended three years of law school in Detroit.)

I had these twin passions: religion (Judaism) and science. There was no conflict: both led to unbroken contact with God, the union that concepts such as *jivanmukti* and *bodhisattva* would later promise. Beyond Rabbi P, and subsequent teachers of Torah and Talmud (including a teacher who led us in Hebrew through the Desert and into the

Michael H. Cohen

Revelation and up and until the point where Moses, on Mount Nebo, watches the Israelites cross into the Promised Land), there was my science teacher, Mr. P, who also helped me start a stamp collection. Each stamp represented a portal to another world, another country, another dimension; each mini-scene conveyed new dimensions of consciousness, new friends, travel, portals and doorways and staircases and gateways. My favorite childhood game, appropriately enough, was "Chutes and Ladders," an epigrammatic diagram of travel from one world to the next, a metaphorical predictor of the kind of consciousness-switching travel in which I would embark as a passenger later in life.

Mr. P led our class through a famous experiment involving *thanitol*, a colored liquid we concocted in a test tube in which we were told that within minutes, we would begin sensing a specific smell that emanated from its substrates. Everyone smelled this on cue; and after, Mr. P informed us that thanitol was nothing but colored water, and that the experiment was really about the power of suggestion.

Mr. P had managed to show how our desperate desire to please could even make us mistake the false for the real. Privately, I had many conversations in fifth, sixth, and seventh grade with Mr. P. He told that time travel was possible, but one had to use the Kabala, the teachings of mystical Judaism. However, it was forbidden to study Kabala if a man was under the age of forty, because the teachings were so deep, he might go insane.

So I read science fiction instead. And wrote my own stories, such as *The Aftermath of World War Three* ("A lonely blue planet floats silently through space; The stars from above try to keep up the pace; they gloat, laugh at its people–yes; laugh at those who made such a mess"), and poems, such as *The Death of Sir Henry the Bold, Sir Henry the Brave* (I rhymed "brave" with "grave"). The fertile crescent of my childhood led to a fertile imagination, filled with archetype, metaphor, symbology, and speculation around the future of the human species in light of our post-exilic condition and efforts to make peace with our Creator.

Robert Heinlein, Isaac Asimov, and other writers transported me to worlds where robots and extraterrestrials controlled humanity, telepathy was common, and people could leave

their bodies and travel anywhere, instantly. These realms of imagination seemed extravagant and delicious; I could little imagine, while reading the Haftorah at my bar mitzvah, that multidimensional reality someday would be a regular feature of mundane life. (Here I am at my Bar Mitzvah.) I would visit my three great-grandmothers after judo class; each spoke mostly Yiddish. learned a few phrases, such as *tsurus* (troubles). While the nursing home attendants struggled to meet different bodily needs, my aunt gesticulated: "English, Ma, English!" The nursing home was a land of sorrow for me at that age, a place of physical breakdown and disrepair, a life spent, an agony of barriers to communication. Early grief and sorrow lodged here, as did the seeds of interest in healing.

My great-grandmothers were present at my bar mitzvah, an event that bound me to my lineage and ancestors. Some moments of the service had particular power-my uncle, holding up the Torah scroll for the congregation; my grandparents, coming up to read the blessings before the Torah reading; and the biblical portions I read-the Torah portion contained the giving of the Ten Commandments on Sinai, and the Haftorah, a vision of the prophet Isaiah:

> In the year of King Uzziah's death, I saw the Lord seated on a high throne; his Presence filled the sanctuary; above him stood seraphs, each with six wings: two to cover its face, two to cover its fee and two for flying. And they cried to one another: 'Holy, holy, holy is the Lord of Hosts; His glory fills the whole earth.'

The reading continued with Isaiah's fright and dismay at his own uncleanliness; the angels touched his lips with a live coal, which purged his iniquity; thereafter, Isaiah heard the voice of the Lord saying, "*Whom shall I send? Who will be our messenger.*" To which Isaiah replied: "*Here I am. Send me.*" I read significance in this divine assignation of the Torah and Haftorah portion: on one hand, highlighting the Ten Commandments, Judaism's ethical imperatives from God; on the other hand, drawing attention to the personal mystical experience of the prophet.

Judaism and Jewish learning were significant in my parents' household, with two sets of plates (*milchik* and *fleishik*), regular attendance on *Shabbat* morning services, and a *kiddush* on Friday nights. The house was full of books about Israel and Jewish philosophy. As the oldest, I would regularly recite the *kiddush,* in Hebrew, after my mother lit the Sabbath candles.

A Talmudic passage taught that two ministering angels escort us home on Sabbath Eve- one an angel for good, the other, for evil. If the candles are lit, the table is set, and all is prepared for a festive Sabbath, the good angel, seeing the love and goodness in the family, says: "May it always be so." And the evil angel is compelled to answer, "Amen." On the other hand, in dysfunctional families, the evil angel says, "may it always be so," to which the good angel is compelled to answer, "Amen." When I recited the kiddush, my youngest brother would play with flipping the *yarmulke* over his head so that he appeared bald. I would retaliate by tying the fringes of his *tallis* (prayer shawl) to the *siddur* (prayer book) while he slept during the rabbi's sermon in synagogue. We would giggle surreptitiously at our play. And both angels would say: "May it always be so." It still is, to this day.

One of my favorite activities was reading the Torah for the congregation, standing with the cantor, holding the pointer to the scroll and chanting the calligraphic letters (the vowels were not written in, so they had to be memorized). I studied for the National Bible Contest, memorizing perhaps a hundred biblical passages, in Hebrew. One summer, I wore *tzitzis* (ritual fringes) under my shirt, and followed the Talmudic laws regarding the Sabbath strictly (no writing, no tearing paper, no "creation" during this sacred time). I kept the laws of *kashrut* (kosher). My middle brother and I each wore a *yarmulke* daily; he developed a business knitting personalized, multicolored yarmulkes emblazoned with designs.

Hillel provided a relatively sheltered environment in which to learn and play. With my best friend, I created an elaborate fort outside, made of branches, stones, and earth, and in it we imagined many scenes. My Zaydie had donated books for the library. Classmates were safe, raised in progressive environments that valued education and decent behavior.

I left Hebrew school after seventh grade in order to "broaden my horizons." For some reason this was the phrase I used in persuading Mom and Dad of my need to leave Hillel. Little did I realize that the new horizons would turn out to narrower, not broader, or broader only in the sense of bearing witness to a distasteful range of activities including petty theft, brass knuckles and parking-lot hazing, "lawn-jobs," and other misdemeanors.

One of the teachers in the public school used to respond by "dusting" students; this involved throwing a chalky eraser at them. Like others, I was exposed to the violence of the world through these 'broadened horizons.' I was back in the secular world, a world that seemed to exist without values. I continued Jewish studies by afternoon at a local Hebrew high school, and in a regional synagogue group. I still believed in God, but was losing faith in the power of the adult world to impose control on the chaos of other humans.

The strong chord of Jewish lore, and reverence for learning, in my family, reverberated particularly through my relationship with Zaydie. Whether reciting mantras potentiated by Siddhas ("perfected beings"), chanting Buddhist sutras, or experiencing the Christed self, my identity as a spiritual being flowed from Jewish religion, culture and identity through Zaydie, whose Hebrew name is *aryeh*, lion.

I knew, as I grew up, that he was born in Szcuszcyn, a town in Poland, in 1910. At eighteen he grew a moustache, to disguise his age so he could avoid the Polish draft (Jewish boys were sent to the front lines). He told us the moustache--which remained throughout adulthood--existed to "hide the pink elephants." I had no idea why pink elephants were hiding there, but I believed him. Perhaps it was a metaphor for Jewish life in his home village. Zaydie came from a lineage of rabbis, and he, too, had begun studies toward the rabbinate. Together with his parents and three brothers, Zaydie fled Polish anti-Semitism in the twenties. Those that remained behind were killed by their own townspeople when the Nazis invaded. Zaydie received a letter, after the war, documenting the way each Panush was individually murdered.

Zaydie frequently took me to Shaarey Zedek. During the rabbi's sermon, he would surreptitiously read Hebrew novels, tucked between the pages of his *siddur*. He could find connection to God in this way—reading a Hebrew novel and connecting to the language of our ancestors *was* spiritual to him, more so than listening to a sermon on some contemporary political subject.

One time, we both picked up some dead branches and used them as canes, imitating Moses crossing the Red Sea. Zaydie was a link to the ancients, a connection to Abraham, Isaac, and Jacob. Later in life, as a vigorous eighty-year-old, Zaydie no doubt was puzzled to see me suspending a pendulum over my brother's chakras, measuring their diameter and rotation, yet he accepted the interest in energy healing. Zaydie was a link not only to God, but also to Eastern European Jewry, and thus to the devastation of the Holocaust, the question of evil and the search for the presence of God in human history and in life.

Age sixteen was the summer of threats, and "summer of the three rabbis."

Between eleventh and twelfth grades, something has shifted. I am coming into manhood: I can no longer indulge in summers playing tennis, but must prove my earning capacity in the real world. My uncle, in the construction business, owns apartments in Southfield, Michigan. I meet the maintenance supervisor who offers me summer work on the maintenance crew. Our duties include picking up trash around the property, circling with a garbage truck, and collecting the garbage bags off the curbside and taking them to the large compactor at the back.

My fellow employee, Jim, a decade or more senior to me, is tough. We ride the top of the garbage truck and heave the bags over our shoulders. We talk about many things. One day I make some casual, innocent remark about the Vietnam War that offends him. I try to retract the comment, but he does not allow it; he responds with physical threats. I watch him carefully. He pours out his rage against all those who misunderstood him, diminished him; pours forth about his war buddies, the dead ... and directs all this intensity against me, as if I am responsible, holding in my being the collective wrong-doing. My comment has become an assault on the sacrifice he and his dead brethren have made. He tells me I am privileged, elite, arrogant, and ungrateful. I keep some distance between us on top of the truck and stare warily as he fiddles with one of the shovels we have used to scoop up loose trash garbage.

As soon as the shift ends, I see the manager and resign from the job.

I then take a job at a Jewish summer camp. Here the three rabbis appear. Together, they teach me something about the limitations of religious clergy, the limitations of religious knowledge, the humanity behind our shared divinity.

The first rabbi is a twenty-five year old scholar who is distraught because his fiancé broke off an engagement. We bond and talk about God, Israel, love, everything. Meanwhile I become infatuated with a much older woman who is running the summer acting program; hearing her sing tunes from "Rocky Horror Picture Show" in Hebrew only deepens my enthrallment. I confess my infatuation to my rabbinical friend. Ultimately, it turns out that the light of my attention illuminates the woman's perfection to his mind, shining a beacon that resuscitates him from the abyss of loss. Six months later I visit them in his apartment; she sits on his lap, one arm around his shoulders, the other resting on the copy of the

Egyptian Book of the Dead on his lap. They marry.

My crush has ended and his new life begun.

The second rabbi is psychologically disturbed. We share charge of a group of unruly adolescents. One of the campers sexually threatens a bunk-mate; when I offer to bring the matter before the camp's administration, this second rabbi threatens me: again a threat–he knows karate. Ultimately I disclose the incident and he is expelled, along with the abusive camper.

The third rabbi is known as the "Gaon" or genius of his generation–a Talmud scholar who is so brilliant that the apocryphal tale is true: open the Talmud to a page, put a pin through a word, tell him how many pages the pin is going through, and he will tell you the word on the other side of the pin. He gives a lecture, after which I ask him for a walk around the lake. In private, I ask him how God could have let the Holocaust happen. The quickness of his brilliance is legendary. But he does not have an immediate answer. We walk and walk in silence.

"The question," he finally replies, "is how humanity could have let it occur."

The summer between high school and college, I made another trip to Israel, this time on my own. I walked out to the desert, alone, and watched the sun set. I thought if prayed hard enough in Hebrew, I might catch a glimpse of God-or at least, His back, which was all that Moses, less privileged (and less terrified) than Arjuna in the Bhagavad-Gita, was allowed to glimpse. I was in a settlement close to the Green Line, a triangle of trees that mysteriously appeared in the desert and served to separate Israel from Jordan. I imagined the biblical prophet Balaam, standing on the hillsides; he set out to curse the Israelites but was intercepted by an angel, and ended up blessing the people. I saw the sun slowly descend, and imagined the Sabbath Bride sweeping over the hills.

I waited for a sign.

Nothing came, and I was profoundly disappointed. I thought that if I asked hard enough, a sign would appear. In biblical times, God had appeared to the people of Israel as a cloud by day, and a pillar of fire by night. I did not know at the time about "high sense perception," about clairaudient messages, kinesthetic sensing, or clairvoyance ("clear seeing"). I only knew the Jewish traditions of my ancestors, as filtered through my education at Hillel and in the United Hebrew High School. Signs seemed abundant in the Torah, to the Prophets, but messages failed to reach me in this protected time and space.

I wandered back to the settlement.

Despite my disappointment at lack of a personal message from God, I felt illumined by the joy of the people in the settlement. The *Shabbat* services were ecstatic: singing, clapping, jumping in place, dancing in a circle. People hugged and kissed "*Shabbat shalom.*" Everyone had biblical names. A man named Abraham, told me: "We're living in God's time, so there's no generation gap. We're connecting to something that has no time. " This Abraham used to be a Big-Eight accountant and moved to the settlement after a huge audit on Union Carbide.

Our focus was on biblical text, manifestation of God's will for the community, for a good life. Abraham and I studied Ishbish, a commentator on the Torah, together. Abraham said: "You could spend weeks understanding just one letter." He started with the first two words: *b'raisheet barah-*"in the beginning, [God] created." "What does this mean," he asked. "Not 'in the beginning,' but 'with beginnings, God created heaven and earth.' This means that God is constantly creating new beginnings. How can you be sad, knowing everything comes from God? If you're in the pits, you can still create a new beginning." He then showed me his Hebrew calligraphy. "None of the letters can touch each other; do you know why? Each letter in the Torah contains one of the souls of Israel; each can stand alone

Michael H. Cohen

without leaning on its neighbors. Also, each must stand alone so that each knows its place-no single one is supreme or more important than its neighbors."

I met his children; their names were mystical: *Kadosh* (Sacred), *Tipheret* (Glory), *Malcha* (Queen), *Simcha* (Happiness)-all kabalistic names for attributes of God. And I thought: "I have a soul. I cannot die. I am not limited to this body." Although I had not had the mystical experience I had sought as a Hebrew in the desert, the thought was comforting. It did not occur to me at the time to inquire into the source of this thought "inside" my head.

I took several trips to Israel during childhood and high school. Terrorism then was not the constant concern it became. One could walk in the marketplace and not fear that some child or pregnant woman would be strapped with a bomb. I could experience the holy sites with reverence and appreciation for the meeting places of different faiths, and particularly, at that time, with connection to my ancestral lineage in this incarnation. There was another sense in which my identity was evolving, though: I found some aspects of Jewish identity restrictive, too doctrinaire. On one trip to Israel with my synagogue group, I received a list of statements concerning Jewish identity. The form gave space with which to agree or disagree. Usually I disagreed. For example: "A Jew is one whom others consider a Jew" (I wrote: *Clothes don't make the man*); "Being Jewish requires actions as well as belief" (*Actions make the identification believable*); "Each of us has an obligation toward the continuing existence of the Jewish people" (*Possibly, but too negative an approach*); A Jew who keeps the *mitzvot* (commandments) ensures the continuous existence of the Jewish people more than one who does not (*Misdirected: Judaism exists for Jews, not the reverse; for many Jews, the mitzvot are far from central*); The danger in changing Jewish law lies not in the additions but in the subtractions (*There is no danger in adaptation or evolution; the danger lies in orthodox rigidity on one hand and revisionist zealotry on the other*); There is no inconsistency between loyalty to the country in which one lives and loyalty to the Israel (*one can disagree with foreign policy yet retain allegiance to one's birth homeland*). I rebelled against black-and-white statements that backed the reader into an intellectual corner. Suspicion of authority and dogmatism was deeply engrained.

On the other hand, I had few other venues to express the longing for God. And in disputing or negating the traditional forms of expression around me, I was armed with reason rather than revelation. Other than sensing something extraordinary in the language, the rituals, and holy sites we visited, I had not discovered the mystical element in Judaism; had not found teachers and resources to connect me with inner spiritual experience. What I had, though, was passion: a strong emotional connection to the land, the people, the literature, and the sense that somehow, through all this, the living presence of God had flowed into my life.

My Jewish identity was not free from anti-Semitic incidents and memories. Most profoundly was our history's constant reminder of our isolation from other tribes in the world, and the visual detail offered by the Nazi documentaries shown at Hillel to give us a sense of the enormous suffering during the Holocaust. There was also an incident in which someone pushed me to the ground just because I wore a yarmulke. There were other subtle reminders, such as someone in the public school lunchroom saying she thought I was "damned for killing Christ;" or a popular teacher in high school opining that the Jews "made too much of the Holocaust," since other peoples also suffered; he was fond of repeating over and over that "the Jews went like sheep to slaughter;" another teacher insisted, "Jewish students use Rosh Hashanah to go home and play cards."

If I had an affinity for Christianity, concretized in attending some early Catechism classes (albeit partly to accompany an elusive love interest), and focused perhaps from early contact with Argentine maids, this affinity was not returned by the world; the experience of alienation, isolation, oppression, persecution was embedded as an ancestral memory deep in my subconscious.

One incident stands out from the high school's closing months: one teacher, a former missionary to the Congo, had put a giant cross in the classroom to celebrate Christmas. Some students were uncomfortable, and asked me to register an objection on their behalf with the principal. Doing some preliminary legal research, I determined that the cross, an obviously religious symbol, was not the same as a crèche. The U.S. Supreme Court had allowed the crèche to appear in publicly funded places as not inconsistent with the Constitutional ban on separation of church and state. I articulated this argument, but the principal, a smooth-tongued bureaucrat, had little patience for our objections. He dismissed our concerns and defended the cross. He also called a faculty meeting. Later in private conversation, my English teacher, in tears, described the meeting as, "looking under a rock and seeing all the ugly insects you'd never before noticed."

Clearly the insects were buzzing: someone called the local television news crew. In a brief interview with the adult interviewers, I defended the principle of separation of church and state, seemingly an objective proposition. I watched the broadcast a few hours later. To my surprise, the newscaster was shown standing in front of a brightly lit Christmas tree, not the actual cross from the classroom.

"I am standing in the principal's office at this local high school," he said in a soothing voice, "where a couple of *Jews* voiced their objections to *Christmas*." The camera left the newscaster and panned the tree, the little wrapped presents underneath, the jingling decorations on the tree, the harmless chocolate Santa.

He had the story all wrong: the objection came from a diverse group of students from different religious traditions; and the objection was not to Christmas, but to the presentation of a religious symbol in a public school classroom. But distorting the story, he had framed the incident in an inflammatory way, casting "the Jews" in the role of the Grinch who stole Christmas. This version had innuendos and repercussions: how could Jews be so insensitive as to try to crush the Christians' celebration of Christ's death on the cross, his sacrifice of eternal love? Why was it *the Jews* again, spoiling someone else's joy? Could it be the "Jewish nose" for others' business? The story seemed yet another version of the 'blood libel,' the slander propagated in Europe that spoke of Jews sacrificing Christian boys and baking their blood into matzah, thus provoking many pogroms, spreading hatred via religious fervor. The news station had done the story a disservice by framing it in terms of a conflict between religious groups, instead of between religious zealots and students adverse to public establishment of a particular religion.

The camera panned back to the newscaster who continued to spin the story of Jews opposed to Christmas; Jews versus Christmas. Each time he seemed to drag out the "ew" in "Jews," an ugly little mannerism.

My interview came on the broadcast: "A secular symbol is permissible but a religious symbol is illegal," I said. But the interviewer surrounded my words with other meaning. Someone suggested I contact the American Civil Liberties Union, but I had no interest in a formal, legal fight and declined the invitation.

Years later, I ran into a former high school friend in California. We had dated briefly, during high school, before the Christmas incident. I have a hazy memory of an evening on the couch in the basement; where I had once seen God. Although I had been at the center of the debate over principles, she had been more immersed in the group "buzz," the negative gossip that surrounded the event. That had a more lasting impact. She told me that found in our contemporary conversation about those events a kind of reconciliation for her residual conflicted feelings for me, which had been tainted by the buzz. Those feelings, she said, had been locked up since high school. "I never hated Jews so much as then," she admitted. The newscaster had done his work, all right.

But then she softened, bringing herself back to the present. We let the incident go, to enjoy ourselves rock-climbing in Mexico.

Michael H. Cohen

COLLEGE AND FEDERAL COURT

(NEW YORK CITY, 1979-1983, 86-87)

BENCHING AND BY THE BENCH

Thoughts of entering the rabbinate at the Jewish Theological Seminary drew me to New York for college. I initially thought of the combined BA at Columbia University and a BHL (Bachelor's in Hebrew Literature) at JTS, though later, I felt satisfied with a course or two at JTS, focusing on my secular studies at Columbia.

Always the question of life purpose stood prominent. In fifth grade, I had learned that my name embodied a spiritual call; in Hebrew, *Michael* meant, "who is like God?" And *kohen* was the segment within the Levites, the tribe of priests, that attended to the Temple. My middle initial H symbolically wove a bridge between two pillars. Later, in meditation, I saw that the two pillars stood for *law* and *healing*. Factually and not metaphorically the H stood for Howard, after my great-grandfather Harry; in Hebrew, *Tzvi*, which means "Deer." I was intended to be a swift-footed servant of the priestly tradition. When called for an *aliyah*, the blessing before the Torah reading, it was always, *ya-amod* (please stand) *mi-cha-el ben peretz ha-cohen*, Michael son of Perry *the* Cohen, the priest. In this way, even when dressed in narrow Italian shoes at the Wall Street law firm and inhaling the cherry smoke from a partner's tobacco pipe while negotiating silence with Japanese partners, or while meeting behind the eyes of a blissed-out monk backstage during a talk by the Dalai Lama, the name reminded me that I never could forget a deeper identity, one given before birth, the one sealed while I was still in the womb.

As God lovingly had told Jeremiah, "I knew you while you were still in the womb," so the name reflected an intimate association before the forgetful passage through the birth canal. We were all intimately associated with God; I had a name that would not let me forget that I had other interests to pursue beyond the texts of college.

And there were mystics in our lineage.

I knew this from Bobe, who did not find anything strange about receiving auditory guidance from the spirit world. Her maiden name was Lipshitz, and she always believed there a connection to an artist by a similar name; who knew what other forces and influences were encoded within the genes? Bobe's letters always gave full approval to my mystical explorations and hinted at an intuitive understanding of what they portended; in some ways she, my mother's mother, knew. Notably, receptiveness to such guidance may

have skipped a generation, with my mother standing solidly in the modern "scientific" tradition, believing that dreams were merely 'random firings of neurons.' So it goes, this tension between "religion" and "science," the play of duality, the poles of opposites. Our family embodied the union of the opposites, as it embraced many sides of the spectrum from orthodoxy to reform to conservative Judaism; science to mysticism; business to spirituality and back. On my father's side, his great-grandfather and grandfather were orthodox Jews in the "old country," but his own father "rebelled," and became Reform; my father eventually found an intellectual home in Reconstructionism, a kind of humanistic Judaism with an appreciation for the historical and cultural gifts of Judaism "as a civilization" (in the words of Mordecai Kaplan) and an overlay of spiritual impulses.

Years later, I would hear Marianne Williamson, the popular exponent of *A Course on Miracles*, acknowledge during a public talk that she came from a lineage of rabbis. As she said this, standing at the high lectern in Boston's Unitarian Church, I noted a line of rabbinic energy over her left shoulder. I then understood the mysterious way in which a lineage of Jewish rabbis, ancestors, could help Marianne, a marvelous orator, channel wisdom in the tradition of the *Course*, a book that reportedly was dictated by Jesus to a Jewish psychologist named Helen Schuman during her tenure at Columbia's medical school. The rabbis surrounding Marianne were not concerned with whether her message was "Jewish" or "Christian;" just as Marianne, in her talk, emphasized the need to bring perennial wisdom to the political sphere; just as the Tao Te Ching had put it, "the Tao that can be named is not the real Tao."

Consideration of the rabbinate intensified toward the end of high school. I was deeply involved in United Synagogue Youth (U.S.Y., you-es-why), as vice president for religious programming at Junior Congregation in Shaarey Zedek, and regionally. Our weekend retreats were filled with ecstatic chanting of Hebrew songs and bits of prayers (*Shema Yisrael*, Hear O Israel), as well as stories from the Midrash (the Jewish legends and lore) and readings from mystical thinkers such as A.J. Heschel ("to have more is not to be more," he wrote in his classic book, *The Sabbath*). The heritage of my childhood was being complimented by this more mature investigation of its rich intellectual, emotional, and spiritual possibilities, expanding beyond study of Talmud to these other sources of learning.

I led one weekend for our Junior Congregation (J.C.). It was a time of being filled with heart connections with friends and with our shared spirituality. Our advisor wrote that J.C. also stood for Jewish Community. He complimented my leadership of the group and urged me to extend this path of service in future studies. It was indeed a magical weekend, and I felt that extending caring in social directions marked a high note of happiness and satisfaction. I was in my essence, filling (or more accurately, being filled with) the archetype of priest: not so much as ritual shaman, but as minister to the need for love and community in all our hearts. This filled place within me, serving in community, was one I would not rediscover again until past the alienated feel of law school, business school, judicial clerkship, and Wall Street; it would not resurface until exploration of Ericksonian hypnotherapy; a sense of ministry initially with Nick; hands-on healing with children victims of Chernobyl radiation; energy healing at the Barbara Brennan School; and professional affiliations in the complementary medicine field.

Following the J.C. weekend, I investigated a joint program between Columbia University and the Jewish Theological Seminary, in which candidates can simultaneously earn a B.A. and a B.H.L. (Batchelor of Hebrew Literature). I also visited JTS: it was perched at the top of a hill, bordering the gateway to Harlem, and within its red-bricked courtyard were some of the greatest scholars of Jewish learning. These same scholars had, with ferocious intensity, separated myth from fact, contributing to the dismemberment of the childhood illusion that God or Moses had written the Torah. They did so through rigorous analysis of biblical and historical texts, including separating the strands of various writers (J, the Yahwist; E, the Elohist; P, the Priestly writer; and D, the writer of Deuteronomy).

Like Harold Bloom, whose *Book of J* argues that the Yahweh of the Torah is a literary figure, conceptualized by a brilliant Jewish writer with access to ancient Babylonian, Persian, Egyptian, and other myths, these scholars maintained a passionate love for Jewish lore while instilling rigorous criticism into the naïve mythologies that had sustained my childhood. Their love was particularly palpable during the Friday night *erev Shabbat* service, when they lovingly chanted the *lecha dodi*, the song to the Sabbath bride, and a seemingly infinite number of melodies converged and separated, dancing along the wave of divine consciousness as we collectively greeted this white-robed messenger from God.

In some ways, the joint program would have been a healthy choice, intellectually stimulating and spiritually enriching. Yet, paradoxically, I rejected this option, just as I had chosen to leave Hillel Day School after seventh grade. The universal impulse was strong. Though my roots were in Judaism, I felt both nourished and simultaneously stifled by living in one paradigm. Among other things, I was finding adherence to the laws of *kashrut*, which I had kept through childhood and into high school, increasingly difficult to justify for myself, as they seemed to separate me from others as I moved into a broader world than Hebrew school, synagogue, junior congregation. Columbia had a "kosher dining room," but this meant that one mingled only with Jewish students; further, these students had in common certain cultural assumptions that defined contemporary Jewish experience in some superficial ways but did not necessarily bind us to God; and I found Columbia already too fragmented along ethnic, cultural, and religious lines.

I was increasingly interested in international affairs, this probably the legacy of innumerable childhood dinners participating in the family debate around what Israel should do politically, in the face of world complicity in the hatred generally directed against her, and in vows by multiple Arab states to "push the Jews into the Sea." Columbia had a school for international affairs and keeping to one dining room felt parochial to me in the face of a more global consciousness.

Ambivalence—a strong passion for both sides of a choice--is said to characterize Aquarius, my birth sign, represented by the Roman god Janus who has one face toward the past, the other toward the future. Janus also embodies the union of opposites, as in the symbol for yin and yang. Consistent with this, I like Walt Whitman's question: "Do I contradict myself? Very well then I contradict myself. (I am large, I contain multitudes.)" Whitman accepts his innate contradictions, and goes further, beautifying them as emblematic of his insistence on non-conformity. He celebrates the kaleidoscope of his multi-faceted being. Whitman, a direct poetic ancestor of Allen Ginsberg, celebrates the all, the holy holiness of the Ain Sof embodied in the human.

Visiting the dorms at the Seminary I had experienced the beauty of *zmirot* (chanting) during the Sabbath meal; and the transporting elegance of the morning and evening prayers, filled with melodious harmonies and paeans to God. At the same time, I felt limited by the rule-bound aspect of the religious impulse and drawn by my interest in other cultures and traditions while remaining rooted in my own. Meanwhile, Columbia University, with its Italian Renaissance architecture and Core Curriculum, offered a doorway into multidimensional exploration of the human heritage. If Bob thought that Divine Mother represented an archetype of the child's wish for a perfect mother, he would have loved Columbia, "dear old Columbia," also known as Alma Mater, Our Mother who Art on Earth. She resided in her earthly state as the statue of a beautiful woman with an owl perched on her shoulder, emblematic of wisdom. She was stationary, seated comfortably while wrapped in her flowing gown, on the steps of Low Library, holding the energy for the concentrated learning of thousands. She had seen generations of students, all moving through the same Core Curriculum, a series of courses aimed to explore the intellectual heritage of the planet, from literature to art and music. Since the curriculum had been initiated, every student at Columbia started Contemporary Civilizations with Plato's *Republic*, and moved through the masterpieces.

Some blocks away, the Jewish Theological Seminary provided spiritual refuge and the companionship of daring intellectuals who were applying scholarly tools to Judaism's most basic assumptions. I studied with a brilliant professor who, among other things, insisted on reading the seductive scene between David and Batsheba in the inflection of a Japanese Noh play. Over paper bag lunches, he would continue the performance in different languages. I would wax on Jung's notion of the collective unconscious and Nietzsche's theory on the different between the plastic Apollonian arts and orgasmic Dionysian frenzy. Somehow, these discussions would help alleviate symptoms of involuntary trembling and grunting his body would experience from Parkinson's disease, as his arms uncontrollably jutted up into the air. His condition was degenerative, yet somehow we seemed to form a unique bond. Some recognition arose in this tender relationship, in which both of us completely lacked any self-consciousness; he seemed to see past my naïveté (and perhaps grandiosity) as a college freshman, while I saw past his illness, through the watery eyes that sometimes praised and sometimes rebuked God, to the sweetness of his heart. At times, I helped him retrieve the pills from his shirt pocket, which alleviated some symptoms when his trembling arms could not maneuver toward the pills. This was one of my first experiences of unconditional love.

Michael H. Cohen

Every college student chooses extracurricular activities and devotes such energy to these outside experiences that they seem to shape a destiny in perhaps more far-reaching and subtle ways than the academic encounter. One of my choices was Columbia Glee Club. I waited in line while various former high school musical stars did their Rogers & Hammerstein best. When my turn came, I sang a few lines by heart from my *bar mitzvah* portion; this was the only music I knew. The conductor, a multiple award winner from Julliard, smiled and admitted me.

Much of the Glee Club dealt with wild parties on visits to women's colleges. As Columbia at the time admitted only males, and Barnard females were gated, the deprivation of an outlet for our collective testosterone was somewhat cured by these events. But on a spiritual level, I learned from the Glee Club about other forms of sacred music. We sang gospel pieces, and, of course, masses. This required me to overcome a childhood anathema to Jesus by invoking such phrases as *kyrie eleison*. I could sing "Christ is the Son" without having to buy into it. I was especially moved by the Brahms *Requiem*. To my surprise, I found as much ecstasy singing masses in a group as I had found chanting Torah in synagogue. It was another doorway to universality; in a subtle way, I was connecting to the consciousness of universal love, which some call Christ consciousness.

During freshman year, I also received a job, through JTS, as a cantor to lead a congregation in New Jersey for the High Holiday services. The melody for these services is particular soulful, even mournful during Yom Kippur. Again I was typecast in the archetype of the priest. As I was leaving the synagogue, a child approached and grasped my hand.

"Rabbi," he asked, "is it okay to eat a cheeseburger?"

What Plato's *Republic* particularly impressed upon me, other than it being a foundational document for many of our ideas about government, was Plato's metaphor of the cave, the idea that most people are caught up in the shadows on the wall, refusing to look toward the light. The metaphor caught the mass delusion that inspired any kind of narrow thinking, including fundamentalism. But it still was difficult to study the Torah of my childhood critically. In one class, a debate arose as to biblical authorship, with the professor introducing the idea of these different editors J, E, P and D. This was the first time I serious considered the idea that it was not God who wrote the Torah. The notion that different human authors had compiled this sacred text blew apart any dogmatic notions that remained from the teachings of my childhood. This could not fail to affect other parts of my faith in residual truisms from Hebrew school, or to increase my personal commitment to the principle enshrined in a popular bumper sticker: *Question Authority*.

Moving from the Torah to *Timothy*, there was also the residue of anti-Semitism in the gospels to confront. I came to understand that much of this verbiage had to do with the incipient separation between these two camps at a certain period in history in which Christianity had not been institutionalized; and during which the two were competing sects *within Judaism*. My professor analyzed the development of the 'cult of Christ' as the aftermath of a failed revolution; the followers of Jesus expected him, as the "Messiah," to overthrow the Roman government, but since he was captured and killed, they had to re-interpret his death in cosmologically significant terms, re-working his kingdom as one "not of this earth." This interpretation was as controversial to the "Christians" as J, E, P and D had been to the orthodox Jews; it separated the classroom into those who read the "Bible" literally and those who saw it all as metaphor. And yet, the professor pitted scholarship and reasoning against belief and faith; critical thinking against uncritical swallowing of dogmas and doctrines. Polarization ensued.

How language separates and appropriates! In his introduction to *The Book of J*, Harold Blooms notes how pejorative it is to label the Torah the "Old Testament." Bloom argues that this is a revisionist molding of Jewish heritage into Christian pre-figuration, an attempt to supersede rather respect Judaism, through the "replacement fallacy," the notion that

A Friend of All Faiths

Christianity teaches love while Judaism's God only emblemizes violence. And in classes subsequent, we also had occasion to learn how this fundamental negative stance in the gospels against Jewish leaders directly formed the basis for so much medieval anti-Semitism, finding its capstone in doctrine propagated by the Nazis. It was difficult to ignore the profound effect of these distortions compounded through history and resulting in genocide and justification of that genocide by countless religious and political leaders. It was hard to separate a legitimate acknowledgment of these different historical connections from venomous undercurrents of prejudice and misperception in the microcosm of a global community represented by our college class.

Over two years, I moved through various college departments, rejecting each, refusing to be pinned down, mastering eclecticism: the requirements for an English major were too laborious, the pre-med majors required too much memorization; philosophy was too abstruse and focused on semantic coherence; economics felt too complex and abstract a description of human motivations and affairs. In addition to courses from anthropology to creative writing, I took a course on Jewish Mysticism. Something about trance, ritual, peyote, and Ezekiel's journey to the heavenly realms appealed. But as junior year approached, I was in need of a major. I did not have aptitude in biology to move on to organic chemistry and become pre-med. I settled on political science as a kind of applied philosophy, a way to move beyond the linguistic games of philosophical discussion and make a change in this world. Our charge as humans, according to the Kabala, was to "repair the broken vessels of Light," to help God heal the world, and political science seemed to offer tools to do so.

Some of my professors were Marxists, and for a time, I found comfort in this view of the world, tossing off phrases such as "exploitation by the periphery of the core." One professor taught a course called World Order, which was a visionary attempt to remake the world according to key global values such as peace, justice, and economic security. One course, taught by a former aide to President Kennedy, focused on the Cuban missile crisis. For my senior thesis, I studied nuclear war doctrines, including "mutual assured destruction" (MAD), analyzing the number of warheads it would take to launch a preemptive strike against Russia. It seemed, perhaps, an unlikely tack for a later interest in energy healing, spirituality, and consciousness. I was interested in developing a joint BA-MIA program between Columbia College and the School of Public and International Affairs. I ended up instead in law school, and then spending time an ashram, and then returning to political science through interest in negotiation and international diplomacy during time at Harvard. Somehow all these paths converge. Whether one tries to bring heaven to earth or transport oneself from earth to heaven, the journey is still one of mediating worlds: no matter how you slice it, it comes up healing.

During college summers, I worked in a lab in the Department of Pharmacology at the Wayne State University School of Medicine in Detroit, where my mother had a faculty appointment. My job involved "sacrificing" rats and then pulverizing their livers so we could measure levels of glucagon in response to various chemicals.

If there is any single action I regret in my life, it is the taking of rat lives.

This is how much science is done: we measure things in "animal models" before applying them to humans. In academic papers, we say that so many rats were "sacrificed." We do not say that they were killed or murdered. This is interesting, because we and not they have made the choice to sacrifice them; unless one wishes to say that 'at a higher level,' their spirit has chosen this. There is no doubt in my mind whatsoever that these beings suffer and experience their suffering; if one looks in their eyes, at their tiny bodies, one can read the fear, the intensity of anxiety, the foreboding about what may come. One does not need any kind of psychic mumbo-jumbo or expanded awareness nor even any religious doctrine to realize that this creature, like you, knows what is about to happen and

Michael H. Cohen

dreads it. You know what it feels like to wait in the doctor's office; now this rat is waiting for be guillotined, or to be experimented upon while alive.

As a legal scholar I know how our rules about informed consent have come from the Nuremberg Trials, which exposed Nazi experimentation on human beings and emphasized the need for informed consent. And yet can one be a friend to all creatures who have faiths, including dogs, cats, spiders, and rats? Children who grieve for their pet hamsters know this intuitively; only adults require volumes of philosophy to justify their feelings. What bothers me is the seeing of animals in terms of their body parts, the assumption of species superiority—that we have the right to discard of their lives and use them for our purposes like mechanical parts in car. There is a presumption that human needs are of a higher order.

Even with NIH guidelines for "ethical" treatment of animal subjects, various presumptions are taken for granted: that animals do not feel pain, or that their pain does not matter because it is in service of alleviating human pain, or that their pain is irrelevant because they cannot verbalize the way humans do. There is a kind of implied consent, a grotesque fiction we perpetrate on our animal companions.

Pursuant to this myth, the lab assistants and I did our work: we first placed the rats in a smooth-bladed guillotine and, like executioners (except that we did not invite our victims for a last chance to address Heaven), we chopped them on the neck with a blunt blade to stun them. Once stunned, they lay helpless, staring up into our eyes, as we injected them with anesthetic. The rats, *still visibly conscious* but immobilized, would then be placed on the operating table. It was important that they be kept alive. We opened their bodies, watching to ensure their hearts kept beating; we dissected them, injected them full of chemicals, and removed their livers. All this occurred with full, conscious "cooperation" by the sentient rat being. While the rats were suffering—"sacrificed" not voluntarily--we used sophisticated machinery to measure various chemical reactions going on in their bodies, as well as in the pulverized livers. The most difficult part was using pipettes to measure out portions of liquid liver, trying to avoid getting raw liver into the mouth.

By the end of the operation the rat—or what was left of its body—was discarded. The rat would have been alive and aware during the operation until pain, an accidental disconnection of a vital blood vessel, too much damage to an organ, or a fatal injection, allowed its spirit to leave the body and rejoin its heavenly Father.

Some years later, I would encounter these rats in meditation. During the meditation experience, I connected with their experience on the sacrificial altar of progress. The cascade of emotions (horror; remorse; grief; loathing) was strong as my consciousness alternated between theirs and mine. Stunningly, in *Saved by the Light*, Dannion Brinkley writes of his experience after being struck by lightning, twice: Brinkley went through the 'tunnel of light' and had some strong near-death experiences. He writes vividly of the life review, a process during which he not only had a movie-like review of his entire life, but also of his life in every encounter *from the perspective of every other person in that encounter.* By literally sitting in their experience, he was able to see with absolute clarity the effect of his thoughts and actions on their lives. Brinkley notes that there is no judge. Rather, one experiences the effects of one's own conduct with others. In fact, a person experiences his or her own karma fully. This was my experience in meditation with the rats.

Another strong experience during these summer jobs involved visiting the medical school basement. There, the faculty kept various creatures for experimentation, many larger than rats, including rabbits and dogs. When I entered the room housing the rabbit cages, the rabbits all stopped breathing, and aligned their heads in the same direction. Fear was palpable. I could not bear the room with the dogs, with their fearful howls.

The different basement rooms I visited were out of a B-movie. Perhaps the most horrifying was the gross anatomy room: corpses in plastic bags, tagged organs, the smell of formaldehyde. The detached, analytical study of it all unnerved me. This was where we ended up, the sum of our days.

I raised the subject with my father, as he dropped me off for my night job, which was bussing dishes at Machus Red Fox, a local restaurant. My dad found the subject too grim for discussion. I had no answers, only a deep aversion to probing life in formaldehyde. Medical school was out.

By the third summer, I stayed in New York. At this time, my father moved to New York, changing careers from finance at Chrysler in Detroit to risk arbitrage on Wall Street. It was a courageous move, both geographically and professionally; my mother would follow a year later, leaving Wayne State for another medical school and eventually founding Exocell, Inc., an entrepreneurial company devoted to diabetes diagnostics and therapeutics. My father's appearance in New York gave us opportunity to have dinner together on a frequent basis.

During this time I was working the Marxism out of my system. My father had worked for what I termed an "imperialist, capitalistic, multi-national corporation" but he was not part of the exploitative evildoers; on the contrary, like Adam Smith, he saw the increasingly efficient production of goods and services as augmenting individual wealth, thus enhancing personal freedom. He suffered my Marxism patiently, a fervent phase that had emerged from the pricey college education for which he was paying. I would guess that being a father (or mother) is one of the more difficult jobs in the world, calling on all one's bodhisattva potentialities.

I landed a summer job as a secretary, and then a paralegal at one of the world's top law firms, Cravath, Swaine & Moore. This crème-de-la-crème firm had lush carpeting, exquisite furniture, long, spacious halls, a sense of aged dignity and a history of having birthed and nurtured some of the most pre-eminent corporations in history (such as IBM). I was in the Blue Sky department, which involved getting securities offerings through the maze of state regulation, and was named for the fact that those involved in securities swindles were like selling pieces of blue sky to investor-victims. I liked the intricacy of these regulations—they reminded me of the layers on layers of text and commentary in the Mishna and Gemara of the Talmud. I also enjoyed the firm's hallowed halls, although I did not see much evidence of happiness in the associates I came to know, other than in total dedication at all hours of day and night to their work. Curiously, the experience did not turn me off to law firms or to Wall Street. On one level, I saw law firm practice as a bridge to public service, to the work I might eventually do in international affairs. And perhaps on an equivalent scale, spirituality at this particular moment was suppressed as a more worldly part took over, the priestly part temporarily anesthetized.

At that time in New York the dance clubs were becoming more popular. I spent a lot of time at the legendary Studio 54. There I blended into the anonymous crowd of gyrating post-teens, dancing until three or four in the morning. Another favorite hang-out was Danceteria in the Village. There I met Roland, who became my best friend: somehow his name, with its hint of medieval French something epic, suggested a carefree attitude, the ability to be anybody in the club. We spent weekends jogging together, making pasta, and clubbing.

After graduating from Columbia a semester early, I took a job as Assistant Investment Officer at the Municipal Assistance Corporation for the City of New York. I help manage the investment portfolio this quasi-governmental entity, learning a lot about the market for overnight securities. The firm was located on the 89th floor of one of the World Trade Center towers.

I would not return to New York until after graduating law school, when I received an offer as a law clerk to a federal judge in the Southern District of New York.

The judicial clerkship is a law students' dream-job *par excellence*. It involves participating in discussions with the judge in chambers, and then sitting in court, in a little desk beneath the judge's elbow, and helping to draft opinions on the case. As a judicial law clerk, one sees the best lawyers and the worst; partners in the top firms try to please the clerks, who at the ground level control many subtle aspects of the proceedings and, as those who give the judge feedback about the case and take a first crack at the judicial opinion, have a great influence on the ultimate outcome. Many groundbreaking cases came through S.D.N.Y., and at the trial level, I had the opportunity to see both civil litigation and criminal cases. The courthouse was surrounded by a little park that commemorates the spot where Thomas Paine used to hand out his leaflet entitled "Common Sense." I called the stone building and tower the "Temple of Justice," the title for a book of short stories I eventually developed as a thesis for the Workshop. The judge for whom I clerked was a tall, lanky man with a gaunt face that looked severe until he cracked a smile. By reputation, he was idiosyncratic, temperamental, always brilliant and frequently challenging for lawyers. His "bullshit detector" was quite sensitive, and when distrust was aroused, he would rarely let an attorney finish a sentence. He was what they called a "hot bench:" not sitting passively through hours of proceedings, not wading through mounds of paper, but rather interrupting constantly with questions, and directing the highly- priced 'hired guns' to move quickly, as Shakespeare put it in *Hamlet* with "more matter and less art." In short, he tended to cut through jargon and arguments to get to the emotional conflict at the heart of the case.

This was his gift: most of time, he coached (or use his authority to almost coerce) the parties to settle the case, thus saving precious trial and juror time. With a huge backlog of cases and the time and expense of trials, he helped manage the docket by bringing about negotiation rather than litigation. He despised "motion practice," the way in which lawyers eat up client time and money by making procedural maneuvers. His methods reduced a lot of useless spinning behind the scenes and helped the parties talk about the things that really bothered them. The Judge's style and temperament offered instruction in conflict resolution, the notion that many disputes could be solved with greater ease and less cost than through a trial. Many were simply human conflicts, not legal conflicts—disagreements and could be solved at a lower level of engagement once parties owned up to their disappointment and anger with one another.

In this particular case, the plaintiff stood in the back of the courtroom, increasingly red faced while yelling at the other litigant. The judge refused to hear the case and told the litigant to "simmer down" and get calm, lest he have a heart attack." In this sometimes heavy-handed way, the Judge frequently told lawyers that he would not allow their cases to go to trial; or he would privately tell each side he thought the case was worth very little; he did this to force them to "step outside the courtroom" into the Robing Room, a small chamber to the side of the main courtroom where I would gently help him into his black robe. There, he often got them to settle. Attorneys both respected and dreaded him. They respected his ability to settle cases and feared his immediacy, his thunder. "No you may *not* approach the bench!" was one of his favorite expressions; it rolled like thunder while he held up his right hand in unconscious adoption of the Hindu *mudra* or hand-gesture of fearlessness (and American for "back off, Jack!").

In one of his most famous cases, the Judge presided over a libel suit involving a food critic who had written a devastating critique of a particular chef. Rather than "decide the cases on the papers," which could consume an enormous amount of time, the Judge invited the chef into the courtroom to cook the meal about which the critic had written. He then had the jury taste the food to see whether the bread was indeed as "hard as leather" or whatever the critic had written. He was pragmatic.

Because of his pragmatism, he served as a model of "holism" as a lawyer; although he could be angry and irascible, he did cut down on wasted time, and got to the heart of disputes without elaborate word-games. His style and philosophy responded to the growing sense I had developed in law school that too much abstraction and intellectualization tended to obfuscate rather than clarify, and that many lawyers, in the name of reason, had moved too far into posturing and away from basic communication and conflict resolution skills.

Apart from the judge's preference for settling cases, many of the cases that we saw at the federal district court level never required trial, and could be resolved "on the papers" because they involved appeals from other courts under special procedural and substantive rules. These included constitutional appeals of civil rights cases.

> *On September X, 19XX, plaintiff, an inmate at Y Correctional Facility, was eating dinner at the mess hall when Officer D told him to leave. Plaintiff rose from his chair and said to the officer, "Fuckhead, you're crazy." Plaintiff alleges he then was punched from behind; defendants claim plaintiff threw a punch, whereupon the mess hall became riotous and plaintiff had to be restrained.*
>
> *Plaintiff was taken to the hospital, his only injury a cut lip. A nurse examined plaintiff and told him he would be all right. Plaintiff claims he was given inadequate medical treatment, that the nurse told him 'sarcastically,' 'you'll survive,' and that the incident violated his right to be free from cruel and unusual punishment.*
>
> *Plaintiff claims a host of injuries including: 'muscle spasms, nausea, vomiting, headaches, insomnia, diarrhea, and excessive autoerotic stimulation to relieve untreated anxiety.' Defendant argues that even if prison staff were inattentive to plaintiff's needs, their neglect was benign and usually explained by other legitimate demands on their resources.*
>
> *The standards for determining whether an alleged beating violated a prisoner's constitutional rights are set forth in* Johnson v. Glick: *'Not every push or shove, even if it may later seem unnecessary in the peace of a judge's chambers, violates a prisoner's constitutional rights.... A court must look to such factors as the need for the application of force, the relationship between the need and the amount of force that was used, the extent of the injury inflicted, and whether force was applied in a good faith effort to maintain or restore discipline or maliciously and sadistically for the very purpose of causing harm.' The majority of cases upholding a plaintiff's constitutional claims involve either severe beating or systematic beatings.*
>
> *Even if plaintiff's version of the facts is accepted, plaintiff was examined by a nurse, with the only visible injury being a cut lip. Plaintiff has received regular psychiatric treatment for his other injuries. He must allege more than an actionable state law claim for assault or battery; the conduct was be so extreme as to 'shock the conscience' and offend even 'hardened sensibilities.' Defendants' motion for summary judgment should be granted.*

Who could tell exactly what happened in the prison mess hall that night? There I was, very young and very far from the kind of environment the prisoner was experiencing. I could not drop into the minds of the prisoner-plaintiff or officer-defendant. I could only read the papers, and only decide based on the facts presented, and the law given in prior opinions by the U.S. Supreme Court and other courts. It was an enormous responsibility. And yet, the process was not arbitrary: it was governed by standards, set down in lucid language, crafted precisely to help govern situations like this. *Not every push or shove* could be actionable ... courts had to consider *such factors as the need for the application of force* ... the *amount of force that was used* ... the entire context in which force had been applied. All this had to be done carefully, based on what was presented; and although the presence of the Second Circuit Court of Appeals above offered a corrective avenue should our judgment go awry, this escape hatch did not release the responsibility of mediating the rights of these two parties and ensuring (in the form of a draft written opinion for the judge) that justice, justice, was pursued.

This next part is about a case that on re-reading years later, I feel awkward having had to contend with. At the time, the mental hoops were expected, but now conscience presents the case in different light:

> *This is an action brought under Section 205 of the Social Security Act, to review a final determination of the Secretary of Health and Human Services denying*

plaintiff's application for disability insurance benefits. Plaintiff, a forty-four year old woman, had surgery on her wrist to remove a ganglion; she re-injured her wrist while working as a nurse's aid and had surgery on the right radial nerve. The Administrative Law Judge accepted the medical testimony that she is now precluded from performing any work involving her dominant right extremity.

I was at several layers of remove from reality: first, reading "the papers." Second, I was writing about reality as evidenced by someone else--the medical doctor who had been a witness, as such evidence had been accepted by another person, the Administrative Law Judge (ALJ). Third, the language seemed have to come from Mars: the plaintiff was *precluded from performing any work involving her dominant right extremity*--in plain English, she couldn't use her right hand. This was her story, re-written as judicial opinion "for the purpose of" (everything had to be "for the purpose of") deciding whether she could get Social Security benefits.

The ALJ also noted that plaintiff is obese and has a history of hypertension.

This was simply noted. Her condition seemed dire, but the language of the opinion had to move on to the question of whether she was entitled by law to the benefits. The first question was whether plaintiff had *engaged in substantial gainful activity since the alleged onset date*. The ALJ had found that plaintiff was *not disabled within the meaning of the Social Security Act*.

The Act defined "disability" as *inability to engage in any substantial gainful activity by reason of any medically determinable physical or mental impairment which can be expected to result in death or has lasted or can be expected to last for a continuous period of not less than twelve months...* But under regulations promulgated by the Secretary, a claimant could be considered disabled if suffering from any impairment listed in 20 C.F.R. Part 404, Subpart P, Appendix 1; or, cannot do any work he or she has done in the past because of a severe impairment and cannot do other work considering his or her residual functional capacity and age, education and past work experience. Appendix 2 provided rules using data about jobs that exist in the national economy to make such a determination of disability.

The ALJ found that plaintiff fit none of these categories: *although plaintiff's additional nonexertional limitations do not allow her to perform the full range of sedentary work, using the above-cited rules there are a significant number of jobs in the national economy which plaintiff could perform.* One wonders how the plaintiff--let's give her a name, Sally--would react when reading this sentence. She is sitting in a darkened apartment, depressed, perhaps watching television, on painkillers, clutching her right arm. She is unable to button up her shirt or tie her shoelaces. She gets no exercise and is, as the ALJ has noted, obese--obesity rising past that recorded in the medical testimony presented to the ALJ, as that was some months earlier.

I am sitting in the judge's chambers, fit at twenty-four, eating a chicken salad sandwich, reading. *The ALJ listed examples of such jobs as: solder dipper, sorter, inspection of small items, coil finisher, pneumatic press operator, and riveting machine operator.*

I have graduated from one of the nation's top law schools, and before that an Ivy League college; I have every opportunity open to me; partners from world-class law firms are groveling because I am a federal judge's law clerk; and I note, trying respectfully not to drip my chicken-salad sandwich on Sally's case, that all is not lost for her--she can be a one-armed solder dipper. This is also known as *residual functional capacity for a limited range of sedentary work.* And the federal government cannot possibly pay every claimant for these benefits.

At the federal district court level, we have a standard for review; we cannot simply second-guess the ALJ. *This court must affirm the determination of the ALJ that plaintiff is not disabled if the decision is supported by substantial evidence.* The term "substantial evidence," like "beyond a reasonable doubt," functions as our standard by which we are bound to judge the case. What, then, is the evidence for Sally? First we need to know if plaintiff is in fact "obese" sufficient to meet the definition of impairment listed in Section 10.10 of Appendix 1, requiring a finding that she is in act disabled. Plaintiff claims that ALJ improperly based his determination of her height on a measurement taken with shoes. If she is 70 inches without shoes and weighs 306 pounds, she is obese. She was measured by her doctor at 71-1/2 inches, a measurement she claims was taken with shoes; she says she is only 70 inches. At one point, she weighed in at 326 lbs., and testified that before the wrist injury she was 260 lbs. What is the role of compassion in reading about this misery?

I summarize the evidence: the various physicians, the various dates, the various weights. Several paragraphs described Sally's growing obesity. Can you imagine? What would go through Sally's mind reading this summary of her ballooning by a federal judge? But we, I, had to summarize the evidence. The case is about the law and the evidence. So it is and so it goes. At 70 inches and 306 pounds she is disabled; at 71 inches and 309 pounds, she falls short of the requirements of the table. And she must have the requisite height and weight before a certain date, *the last date on which she met the insured status requirements of the Act.* See Koss v. Schwieker ("*We do not subscribe to the view of some courts that a person may receive benefits if he had a condition during a period of eligibility which later became sufficiently severe to be called a disability within the meaning of the Act*"). Saint Peter, give me a break! Let me in to the pearly gates!

"We do not subscribe to the view....."

Can you fit through the door if you were not in a state of grace before the specified date but came into grace, through deeds, thoughts, or God's compassion after a specific date? Will Saint Peter let you in?

I am reminded of Kafka's *Before the Law.* A man stands before a door, hoping to gain entry into the court of justice or perhaps to see the emperor, where the man will receive redemption or what he is urgently seeking; a gatekeeper stands, holding the man at bay for what seems forever; finally the man gains entry and there is another door, with a similar gatekeeper, with a similar eternal holding period; and so on, until finally he reaches the last door. But after again a long wait, this door does eventually open, and the man can see the judge, or emperor, or whomever. It then abruptly closes only to swing shut for all eternity. The gatekeeper informs the man that the door was made only for him.

Sally is before the last door.

But after all this wrangling, even if Sally meets the height and weight requirements of the table, *the record does not establish that she has one of the five associated conditions necessary for a finding of obesity.* This included some horrific things, such as *history of pain and limitation of motion in any weight-bearing joint or spine associated with x-ray evidence of arthritis ... hypertension with diastolic blood pressure persistently in excess of 100 mm. Hg measured with appropriate size cuff... chronic venous insufficiency with superficial varicosities in a lower extremity with pain on weight-bearing and persistent edema...*

The nightmare goes on. Sally tells us that she–no, that *the records shows she*–has arthritic leg pains, hypertension with diastolic blood pressure *persistently* in excess of 10 mm. Hg, and *severe* venous varicosities of *both legs*. She is not in good shape. *However*– everything and not just a red wheelbarrow depends on this 'however'–the *only evidence of arthritis in the record* is a report by a certain medical doctor ... which offers no x-ray evidence but only a *mere characterization of the kind of pain plaintiff claimed to experience*. I wrote these words. *In fact, there is no indication that this is an objective medical finding as opposed to a record of plaintiff's subjective report of pain.*

On Yom Kippur, tradition tells us, we do not receive automatic forgiveness from God merely following atonement; rather, we are commanded to ask each person we might have offended for forgiveness of our transgressions. Sally, I hope you read this book. Forgive me, Sally ... and all those similarly situated. I shudder to think what went through your mind as you read the judge's opinion denying the benefits you needed to survive. I understand that somewhere we must define "disability," must have rules determining who shall and shall not receive these benefits, must find some rational way to distribute government funds to

Michael H. Cohen

those in needs. And yet, as I read this language—this mind, gifted with language, moving words this way and that in denial of something small for the taxpayer, large for you—I wonder how you might have felt pursuing this appeal. Let's see. You are somewhere between 70 inches and 306 pounds, and 71 inches and 309 pounds, or you were when you were weighed; you might have put on more weight after the no doubt depressing and humiliating decision you received from the ALJ, and thereafter, our decision.

And you do not know my height and weight though I know yours.

I managed to find all the little holes in the evidence: you were not really obese; you did not really have hypertension (there were only four occasions on which your blood pressure was at the requisite level, and eight in which it was not!), or let's just say that maybe you did have hypertension but it was not "persistent" where it should have been to get you the benefits; I also pointed out your doctor's opinion that—shame on you—your hypertension was *poorly controlled, partially due to poor compliance with medications.* I found out enough to know that venous varicosity *means the veins are abnormally and irregularly swollen or dilated.* One of your doctors found you had this. Sally, do you know the old joke? A woman goes to a psychiatrist who tells her, "I think you're crazy." She says: "I want a second opinion." He says: "Okay, you're ugly too." How is that for black humor? Your doctors knew your legs were ugly, swollen, filled with edema, *an abnormal accumulation of fluid in cells, tissues, or cavities in the body, resulting in swelling.*

However! Again the however comes to deprive you of your benefits. You have no benefits, you obese Sally, non-compliant with hypertension medication, with ugly swollen legs. No doubt you are suffering—*however, this does not indicate that the varicosity is chronic, as required by Section 10.10D.*

I am sorry.

Nor does it show that the edema is persistent, as required by the rule, as opposed to trace, which means a barely persistent amount. Truly, now, the apology is real and not a literary flash of irony. Could I claim allegiance to language? I was bound to these words, words like *persistent.* I persisted in following the rules given me. Am I making an excuse? I was bound, don't you see, by law, language, airtight reasoning. And I had the ALJ before me; I could not simply overturn him (for there seems to be a gender element here; all the doctors are male, I am male, the judge is male, all the rules are male as they speak of *he* and *him,* only you are the fat ugly female—forgive me, but this statement is supported by the evidence—condemned to battle alone against the human as well as natural elements afflicting your body, mind and spirit. Do you not recall what I wrote a few pages back? *This court must affirm the determination of the ALJ that plaintiff is not disabled if the decision is supported by substantial evidence.*

The evidence shows you're screwed. The ALJ summed up your situation like this:

The medical evidence establishes that the claimant (that's you, Sally) has severe obesity (aha, he admits you have not only obesity but severe obesity, you are very fat indeed, though as you will see a few words down the pike not fat enough to get the benefits), hypertension, arthritis, and residuals post surgery for excision of neuromatous tissue on the right radial nerve of her dominant right extremity (it's bleak indeed, the ALJ seems to get that all right), but that she (you, Sally) does not have an impairment or combination of impairments listed in, or medically equal to one listed in Appendix 1, Subpart P, Regulations No. 4 (in other words, goodbye).

If I were you right now, I might be thinking, *fuck Appendix 1, Subpart P.* But forget I have said this—it is heresy; I have taken an oath to defend the laws and the Constitutions of these United States; indeed, I cried when I took this oath, because inside, I recognized my love for this place, this life, this incarnation, this family called Earth, this system of rules and cords that binds us to on another, and my own pledge to uphold, support, defend, and be an active, positive part of our common destiny. But there you are, perhaps alone in your apartment; you do not care about my oath, my commitment, my earnest erstwhile promise to

- 161 -

defend and protect. I have been too, too literal, and you are screwed. I am just like the ALJ. Did either one of us ever visit you in your apartment? Do he or I know the pattern on the lampshade? Do either of us see you fumbling, agonizing one-handed with the buttons on your shirt? Can we really see you as a one-armed solder dipper? No matter: I have sealed your fate. *The above review of the record demonstrates*—it is plain for all to see—*that this finding is supported by substantial evidence*. The Government wins; you lose.

You should read Kafka, Sally.

In one footnote alone, for example—imagine, dispensing with this ugly reality in a footnote—you argue that *there is no basis in the record to infer that plaintiff's obesity is remediable*. In other words, you recognize you are doomed to a life of obesity, with all its attendant medical dangers: there is no remedy. Your next stop is Peter. Perhaps in the heavenly body there is a remedy: you return much lighter, freed from all this fat—all this weight. The weight is at once a physical reality and a metaphor; I feel it, blubbering through all this language to get your claim right.

Do you recall Gurdjieff's Law of Opposites? Nothing can exist without its opposite, and everything turns in time into its opposite. Since you have an argument so does defendant. Is it not curious how a P can become an upside-down D? Defendant is quick to point out that *case law recognizes that obesity is a remediable disease and hence is not considered disabling*. Oh, low blow! The judges—probably males—have written, and thus enshrined as truth, that your blubber is not a disease, it can be controlled, just as you could have controlled your hypertension, Sally. You got yourself into this mess.

Admittedly, the ganglion on the wrist was not your fault; we all have our karma. But after that ... you really shouldn't have bought those full-fat potato chips, should not have had that Super-sized shake or burger. At twenty-four my metabolism is so great I can have as many as I want...I am the elect, the chosen, a law clerk to a federal judge, but you ... save your calories, Sally. Adam's mistake was to eat the apple and yours to not take your medication. He was expelled from Eden, and you from our Social Security benefits plan for disability. But I am getting off-track: let me go back to Section 201.00(h), which is much safer.

You are not disabled if you can perform sedentary work as listed in these rules. What about the solder dipping? Regionally, existing jobs for you are numerous: solder dipper (2,000); coil finisher (1,800); assembly press operator (3,000); inspector-examiner (10,000); sorter (4,000); riveting machine operator (3,500); and machine tender (1,500). I have catalogued these meticulously, following the testimony of the vocational expert before the ALJ. Do you need a third opinion? It seems you are not only fat and ugly (considering the swollen legs) but lazy, too. Why did you not apply for one of the 1,800 jobs as a coil finisher instead of applying for these benefits? *The vocational expert described precisely the tasks involved in each job and the manner in which a person with one operational hand could perform the job*. Accordingly—a kind of analogue to the awful however—*I find that this constitutes substantial evidence*, etcetera.

But, you argue, the vocational expert failed to take into account your pain, drowsiness, and inability to work. To which I inexorably respond: *The claim has no merit*. Do you get it? Not only are you fat, ugly, and possibly lazy, but you bring to the court a claim that has no merit. It is true, I note, that upon cross-examination by your attorney, the vocational expert admitted that pain, drowsiness, and lack of concentration could affect each of these jobs. Would I want to dip solder under these conditions? No way! *But*, I write—oh, the nightmarish *however* disguised in terms of the *but* word—*but anyone could testify that such hypothetical impairments could affect the performance of nearly any job*. And so we pit your *subjective testimony*, which lacks any validity since anyone could whimper and complain, against the ALJ's finding which has to be upheld if supported by substantial evidence. The ALJ found your assertions *not credible*. Which suggests to Us that you also may have a propensity to lie. I will admit: you do have a neuroma in your right arm. Ever the clever law school graduate, I know that neuroma *is a tumor derived from nervous tissue, consisting of cells and fibers*. That is the bad news: you are not only fat, ugly, lazy, a progenitor of unmeritorious claims, and possibly a liar—*but also* you have a tumor, too. It does get worse after all. But this condition elicits no empathy. Quickly, I manage to squeeze in another *however. however, the neuromatous tissue was surgically excised.* And the hospital report notes that you 'tolerated the procedure well.'

Okay, so you do not have a tumor after all; you had one but it was surgically excised and you did just fine. You were in fact discharged the day of the operation! So how can you claim all this pain? The attending doctor noted that although you whined about the pain—I forgot to add this to the list (fat, ugly, whining....)—you could make a fist, *ambulate without difficulty*—do you know what this means? Translation: you walked. You could get dressed and undressed, and get on and off the examination table. I am sure now that you wanted to get on and off without assistance, even at 360-some pounds, not realizing that this small movement of remaining independence would someday be used against you.

There is no indication whatsoever—I can really bring the point home when I want to—*that any pain plaintiff experiences or claims to experience in her right arm, wrist or hand is sufficiently severe to preclude her from any kind of work.*

I suppose the Egyptian rulers used the same logic when they enslaved the ancient Israelites and forced them to build the pyramids. You can solder dip, all right, claims of pain notwithstanding; don't look to the government for a free lunch.

Now there is the matter of your testimony that you take Tylenol with codeine. I have taken it myself, an excellent narcotic after dental work. You have asked us—the Judge and I—to take judicial notice of a medical publication that states that this product *"may cause drowsiness" (emphasis added).* Boy, can I drive a point home: do you like the parenthetical? *May* is simply not good enough, that is why I have added emphasis. I write: *This is not of much weight.* This means that I give no credit to your argument. Ironic, how the whole issue is about your weight, and I am constantly subverting your claim to disability benefits with these subtle, perhaps snickering references to the fact that you, at 360 pounds, more than twice my physical weight, are making claims that literally have *no weight*.

To make my point, I quote the testimony in the record:

Q: Does the Tylenol with codeine have any effect on your ability to function?
A: I sleep—I sleep a lot, you know.

At forty-two I understand everything that this question and answer portends. I know what it is to sleep, and sleep, and sleep. I have developed compassion and life experience. The body is what it is until it dissolves, and it does dissolve, inevitably, invariably, giving no record to rank or status, accounting not a whit for clerkships and honors. When disease and deterioration strike they strike equally; we each are humbled. We can fall prey to physical dissolution and mental depression. "Sleep, death's counterfeit," as Shakespeare called it, comes quickly, without warning.

The humility is missing from my razor-sharp, razor's-edge analysis.

I am compelled, *however,* at twenty-four to write that this Q&A *provides no indication as to the degree of drowsiness plaintiff experiences or*—and now the zinger again—*claims to experience*. My life experience now tells me you are in pain much of the time; you take a lot of this codeine medicine; it makes you very drowsy; you sleep a lot, live in a fog, not sure where to turn. You have pain on all levels. And you are probably intensely lonely and rightly fearful of what is to come. My life experience now can fill in the gaps of your testimony. Perhaps a more astute lawyer at the time would have better prepared you, coached you to answer these trick questions in a fuller way so as to bring out all the dimensions of your pain. If Buddha's First Noble Truth is that life is suffering, his second truth—had he been a plaintiff's lawyer—would be: Document it Fully.

You have not shown that *such drowsiness, if any*—oh the zinger again, the implication that you are making all this up—*is sufficient to preclude* you from performing any of the jobs listed by the vocational expert. You have a few remaining arguments to dispose of. I take these one by one and show that they have *no weight* (pardon the pun); *no merit.*

It is true, I must admit, that *an insubstantial number of jobs identified by the vocational expert* exist in your county. Read that again? Of the 2,000 jobs for solder dippers in the national economy, very few if any are within driving distance from your house. With all your physical and emotional burdens, you would probably have to move to another state to get one of these jobs. *However*–yet again–*the statutory standard for disability refers to inability to engage in substantial gainful work in the national economy.* And to quote another one of my favorite phrases, *it is not relevant.* It is not relevant *whether such work exists locally, or a job vacancy exists, or whether the claimant would be hired if he*–there is that "he" again, though we know you, Sally, are a "she"–*applied for the job.*

Who is kidding whom? It is highly relevant to you!

In any event–another favorite–*there is no evidence in the record, apart from plaintiff's testimony that she has difficulty walking* (I waited the entire opinion to mention this detail), *that plaintiff is unable to travel to work outside her locality.* Sally, why are you complaining? You could take that solder-dipper job in Alaska. *Indeed, plaintiff's testimony at the hearing was that she has current license to drive.* You have a license, my logic goes, therefore you must be able to drive as long as it takes for one of these jobs, even though you might have difficulty walking from your car to the place where the solder is kept liquid and aflame.

For the above reasons, the decision of the ALJ should be affirmed and the action dismissed. The door has clanged shut, forever.

The most difficult part of the clerkship was making recommendations to the Judge for sentencing defendants who had been criminally convicted. At that time there were no federal sentencing guidelines, and the Judge was free to fashion his own based on the evidence in the case. He also took the defendant's expression of remorse (or failure to express remorse) at the sentencing hearing into account.

The Judge insisted that everything had to be decided based on the law and the evidence, not on the emotions or intuition. In short, my "read" of a person meant nothing. And in this insistence the Judge probably was right: that was his responsibility; emotions were untrustworthy, while the record provided an objective basis to perform his function as impartial arbiter. The Judge was simply doing his part to avoid "passion" and "prejudice." Yet how could I exclude passion from the calculus?

In part, this imbalance provided an impetus to write stories about the cases during the clerkship. I had thought these stories were destined for publication in a law journal, but instead, found them expanding beyond legal analysis to the human stories behind the cases. These stories eventually wound up as part of the application to the Iowa Writers' Workshop. On the surface, Sally's case was a dry appeal for benefits from the Social Security administration; it becomes rich only in reflection on the split between head and heart that her situation elicited. But when I found a nugget, I polished it, and continued to work on these stories as I returned to Berkeley for the final year of my M.B.A. program. The clerkship catapulted me from a career focus on law toward one more geared toward writing and creative pursuits–built in a desire for spaciousness in which exploration could continue.

At this time, my business school classmates were heading toward lucrative jobs in real estate, investment banking, marketing, and finance. Part of me resonated with this drive, while another part knew I could not follow it. Our business school graduation speaker was the famous mergers and acquisitions baron, Ivan Boesky (before his conviction). It was in this forum that Boesky gave his famous "greed is good" speech, memorialized in the film, *Wall Street.* It would not hurt to take my place on Wall Street, and capitalize on my educational advantages by spending some years in a firm.

So I was surprised when I received an acceptance letter from the Workshop. My decision to attend added a year and a half to the time between graduating from law school, and joining a law firm, a hiatus that put me off the normal law firm track and helped set up a continuing sense of having left a 'normal' legal career.

HERE AND HEREAFTER

(SOUTHERN CALIFORNIA, 1996-99)

Wheel

(yoga teacher training, 1999)

CHECKERBOARD SQUARES

Plato conceived of soul mates as two halves of a whole. He also believed in the transmigration of souls, the notion that souls reincarnate again and again in different bodies—some human, others animal. In Contemporary Civilizations, a required freshman course at Columbia University, we had learned that "all philosophy is a footnote to Plato," and thoroughly studied Plato's *Republic.* Plato's theories on government received approval while his ideas on the soul were derided. More recently, psychiatrists have begun investigating 'recall' of 'past lives' by patients under hypnosis. Whether a phenomenon of soul incarnation, collective archetypes, or "merely" biological memories encoded in DNA, the notion of past lives requires that one stop identifying solely with the body and mind and gains awareness of a soul. Stripped of dogma, some things are the product of experience in meditation and cannot be rationalized. Although at first I denied these experiences, I began having so many experiences not only of recognizing a connection with certain people, but of our mutually finding the same locus for that connection. For example, my friend saw herself as a soldier in the Civil War during the healing in which I had the same vision.

Of course, we might have shared a delusion, if one adopted a reductionistic interpretation. But I trusted my experience, as the other parts of my life were fully sane. Except for relationships. By the time of my move to California to join a second law faculty, I was wondering whether that one and only person existed who would be the second half of my soul with whom I could form the perfect relationship on Earth. At the same time, I was gaining a mature wisdom that no relationship drops magically from the sky, and that healing our childhood misconceptions, learning to negotiate feelings, and creating new patterns to nurture and be nurtured was part of the learning experience of relationship.

I also learned that some people with whom we have transient connections may be part of a larger 'soul family.' I had a male friend in healing school. When I was giving the healing and he lay on the table, I saw his face dissolve into light and transform into this little Japanese boy, my son, whom I had lost to disease or war many centuries ago. Experiencing the connection and the loss of that time, I cried vigorously during the healing. He had little contact with me after the program ended, and in this lifetime, we are unlikely to spend much time together. I learned to simply acknowledge the soul cords from other dimensions, and let go.

I had to hold both the psychological and the spiritual realities at once. Discernment was required. For example, with soft brown hair, warm eyes, an understanding voice, and intelligent hands that knew how to help heal the body's alignment, Athena was easy to like. I sat in meditation and saw her in medieval Spain, as my wife in that lifetime. But in this lifetime, she was married and therefore off-limits. In the next meditation I saw her in her modern-day clothing, wearing a silk, yellow blazer; she had her back to me, but turned her head my way and said: "We won't be partners in this lifetime, but love will always be present."

Eventually we became close friends, an unspoken trust between us. In fact, she entrusted me with being her healer as she became pregnant with her first child. As my hands moved above her energy body, I became aware of many levels of contact: hands on skin or over clothes; intelligence meeting emotion; past meeting present and future; reaching the being inside her. Respect magnified with this intergenerational soul contact.

The Buddhists say that every person you see may have been your mother in another lifetime: therefore regard all beings with compassion. This is the way I experienced Athena: not holding on to the life that was, but not neglecting it either.

Some claim that delving into 'past lives' is spiritually regressive, as it takes one out of the present moment where the most important lessons are to be learned. Why go back to the lifetime as a member of Attila the Hun's attack force, when you could be meditating on compassion today? Why draw on all those memories and thought-forms of violence, when you are practicing non-violence today? Who wants karmic regression, when the balance sheet of karma is steadily clearing? In one sense, past relationships are simply the past, while the present commitment offers the container for grace in moving together toward liberation. Yet, some of the beautiful, and even wretched, experiences can serve, through contemplation, as exemplars of lessons on the path from A to Z. California provided a period of experimentation. I had a friend named Dave, a former actor turned manual laborer and psychic. He commented: "God is playing checkers with you, Michael. I went through this for two years before meeting my wife. You leap over potential partners like checkerboard squares. First one, then another, closer and closer, and finally, he brings you to the one he wants for you."

God may not play dice with the universe, but he or she does play checkers.

A is for alcoholism. I attended a singles event: within a few hours, the room dissolved into an alcoholic haze. Alice flirted in the underground parking garage after the event. With her curvy body, Alice exuded confidence, but she volunteered that she "felt fat," was "between jobs," and was staying at her aunt's. For our first get-together, she showed up in a red convertible that she told me she had "borrowed" from her cousins. She was withdrawn until we went to the beach, during which she unexpectedly stripped down to a provocative blue bra. This contradictory pattern of standoffishness and exhibitionism, seductiveness and hostility, showed up over several dates, and had I had my DSM-IV handy, I might have understood that I was about to enter a deeply pathological dance. I later learned that her father had killed himself with a shotgun; that her ex-husband had beaten her repeatedly and had tried to throw her out of a moving car; that her last view of him was his being dragged off by the police at a party; and that her belongings were still in his house. Her troubled nature was difficult to resist; full of new confidence as a healer, I was unconsciously eager to care for someone wounded and needy. What I lacked in healing training was the kind of insight that clinical training in psychotherapy might have provided.

Though Dave explained the fiasco in terms of our past karma: she and I had been married before, always ending disastrously, as the relationship this time would end. His interpretation appealed: but only after I had plunged into chaotic binding did I receive intuitive guidance. I was holding her in my arms on the couch, feeling nothing but tenderness, when all of a sudden I clearly heard an inner voice: "*Stay away: she's full of darkness.*" I paused: had I heard this correctly? I looked down and saw her face, child-like, angelic; yet the message was direct. Why now, after I had taken the emotional plunge? I heard: "*It's her darkness, not yours.*"

We drove that afternoon to lunch. In the car, I started singing a particular song. Alice began to cry: it was the song her father used to sing to her when she was a little girl. How could I have known? The song had just come to me. I felt validated as a healer; yet psychologically, was struggling with relationship and with the vortex of unhealed emotions, unhealthy transference, and acting out. I had drawn someone recovering from cruelty and violence, who did not know how to escape the cycle.

Dave warned me time and again to leave before things ended darkly: with her history of repeated physical abuse, he said, Alice tended to "recreate" that abuse in her relationships.

A Friend of All Faiths

"This is not to 'blame the victim,'" Dave told me, "as she has surely been victimized by a bastard. But energetically, you have to know that Alice has a pattern with men, and that is to be extremely provocative, drawing out their darkest sides through teasing and then sadistically withdrawing."

I was certain I could disregard Dave's warning. After all, I was a healer with an allergy to violence; had I not been drawn to Alice in this healing role? Had I not channeled her loving, deceased father (whom, Dave reminded me, also had ended his life in self-inflicted violence; and who knew what more was in Alice's past that she had not told me?). But sure enough, there came a time when Alice began to draw me in more deeply than before and suddenly withdraw completely. The episodes of reunion and separation became increasingly traumatic. No doubt I too played into this unhealthy pattern. I felt hurt and humiliated, frustrated and pushed to limits. I responded to one insult with another during a final episode of escalating taunts, then--wisely--left the apartment.

Two blocks away, I immediately called from a payphone with an apology.

I knew though I would never return.

Alice responded to the apology with warnings and threats. She told me she had called the police, reporting yet another tale of "abuse" by a male perpetrator—with who knew what details real or imagined. I stayed away.

Three years later, I befriended a gay man who invited me to attend a "spiritual meeting" with him. This turned out to be a "twelve steps" group for "love and sex addicts." As individuals around the circle began to share, I heard a familiar story: the speaker was involved, once again, with an unavailable man ... married ... her past several boyfriends had been physically abusive....I looked up. Her face was red, her skin flaked and rough, perhaps, I wondered, from excessive consumption of alcohol. She was barely recognizable. The beauty and softness I had seen three years earlier were gone; she had gone, I gathered from her self-disclosure, on a rampage of continued self-destruction and destructive relationships.

She did not recognize me. I told her that I had done something terrible that hurt her at the time, and that I was deeply sorry for what I had done. I asked her to forgive me. She stared ahead blankly and seemed to have no recollection.

B is for Bea: beaconed; beckoned. I was standing with Dave at a supermarket check-out counter. My eyes drifted to an attractive woman a lane away. "Stay away!" Dave barked. "Remember Alice. Don't you read karma?"

Terrified of abandonment on one hand and of domination, on the other, they oscillate between extremes of clinging and withdrawal, between abject submissiveness and furious rebellion.... Extreme sadism and murderous violence were the rule rather than the exception in these dreadful histories.

Dave had given me Judith Herman, *Trauma and Recovery* (Perseus Books, 1997, pp. 124-5). True, I reasoned, trauma survivors needed healing relationships on the path to recovery, but as conscious contracts, with commitment to mutual respect, and a frank confronting of the survivor's unhealed rage and fragmentation. Had I continued to frame my encounter with the Alices of the world as offering a healer's compassion to persons in need, I would have neglected the destructive toll of such a relationship on my own health. I would have placed myself in the heroic role of rescuer rather than acknowledging my part in an unhealthy dynamic. I would have ignored Alice's need for counseling from a real therapist, not a lover.

My teacher told of a seeker who, filled with light and love, tried to pet a vicious dog. The seeker was so surprised when, after seeing the dog as Ram or Krishna, he was bitten on the hand! "But how can this be," he exclaimed, "since after the Intensive, I see the whole world as filled with Ram and Krishna!" To which his spiritual teacher calmly replied: "The dog has not taken the Intensive."

Bea, in turned, was a regular visitor to the meditation room that I frequented. From the outside, she had all the qualities that intrigued; the truth was that I knew little about her except my projections of holiness. In meditation, I saw a possible future with her...specifics, details. Could this have been something possible for us had she been attracted and ready? Or was I was only augmenting my own delusion, a projection of my own mistaken consciousness fueled by the rising kundalini so as to expel the deepest confusion from my system?

Bea dismissed my wooing. She let me down with a compliment. "You're so handsome. However, you need to reach inside for the love you're seeking outside. Find your own wholeness instead of projecting it onto me or anyone else."

Two years later, Bea, who by then was serving full-time in the ashram, shared chai with me and we had a profound conversation about our spiritual paths. I was seeing myself as a *sanyansin*, a renunciant in orange robes, in meditation. Bea took me up to my spiritual teacher and flawlessly outlined the experiences I had shared. I received a blessing with a wave of the peacock feathers. In meditation, I received guidance that through her clarity, Bea had given a long-lasting spiritual boon, far greater than she might have offered through a marital bond this lifetime.

Dave called Bea a "near-miss." On the next retreat, Bea seemed to taking steps to avoid me. Her behavior hurt, and seemed incongruent with the holiness I had projected on her. Dave suggested: "Like many others, for whatever reason, you weren't ready for them, or they weren't ready for you." Years later, I would see Bea in person at the ashram, still lovely, still remote, focused on the path before her. And then again, in meditation: the same vision of closeness on some level.

Dave reminded me that this could all be idealization—"not a reliable guide" to reality. These were snippets of images of the lovely Beatrice: the flowing brown hair, the clear eyes, a smile, her silence on the way to the Temple, her clear language before my spiritual teacher; the evidence of behavior, though, included her pushing me away verbally and non-verbally.

Dave summarized in his usual aphoristic style: "Her lack of interest spared you perhaps a greater tragedy that would have come had you connected. Disaster would have manifested more permanently had the nail of confusion driven infatuation into the coffin of remorse."

Chrissie introduced herself at a professional meeting. Before long we seemed to know each other well. On return I received a message of electronic flirtation. The promise of this message was not fulfilled in real life; on the contrary, new barriers seemed to have been erected as quickly as old ones had been taken down. We did have a chance to visit the Thomas Jefferson Memorial together at night—lying on a mound and together experiencing Jefferson as a fine intelligence or collection of intelligences far beyond regular Earth knowledge. Jefferson seemed a portal, not to early American history, but to the stars—his guides came from somewhere else. Perhaps our combination was a key to a particular opening, fitting into the lock of the exact location where we rested our heads; perhaps our meeting was about that experience, and not about a possible relationship. I did not form significant heart-cords with her; although I could reach back through consciousness and detect a kind of priestly alliance, and a closeness from some other time and place.

Months later she quit her job and married her 'usual type:' much older than her, wealthy. I could still read her, sense her from afar: that kinship present, like a distant cousin with whom one can always rekindle a connection. At some level love lives in the awareness that we may be united by shared karma over millions of years, that behind a flitting "date" may lie millennia of exchange. And simultaneous with this recognition is the knowledge that moving on means letting go while remembering the unity consciousness in which we are friends.

Debbie was doing a double master's in ethnography and filmmaking, documenting a particular tribal culture. Was God black or red, and when you got to the other side, did you get two checkers instead of one? She (Debbie) shot footage of me channeling. After we broke up, I received a video: "One day I had the opportunity to sit somewhere in a desert mountain, with a very special man. We climbed up to a perfect rock that was fully exposed to the hot sun. He sat there as she focused the camera onto his kind face, his hands, then she heard: *Reach up to the Father. For He is the light around you; and He is the one who will guide you in all these activities. I am the light of all beings and providing a firm foundation for your work. The bride and groom you saw today are symbolic of the union within. Hold yourself steady within the om consciousness. Be prepared to accept the mantle thrust upon you for there is work to be done, clearing and cleansing through various lifetimes now coming to completion. Give yourself as fully as possible to each lecture as the radiant divinity shines before you. Recognize it is I speaking through you with the crystal voice of clarity you need.*

Did I channel that? We had traveled together to a shaman. I wrote about it in *Beyond Complementary Medicine*. The lodgings he suggested were a six-by-six mud box with an iron gate that had to be locked at night to keep out brigands. What I omitted from the published narrative was a series of incidents involving clawing neediness, verbal insults from her family, and my hasty retreat from a no-win situation.

Eve had slept with many leaders in the field. One of the keynote speakers had slipped her his hotel room key, begging her to visit.

There is a Jungian archetype of the Demon Lover, wrought beautifully in a book called *On the Way to the Wedding*. The book offers a psychological analogue to the notion of checkerboard squares: just before marriage, we meet a series of archetypical lovers, ones who—through the flaws and failures they both present, and invoke—heal us from our childhood wounds and thus prepare us for marriage with the right partner. Among these, the Demon Lover becomes a magnet who draws us into the depths of delusion.

Before meeting the likes of this archetype, I should have read the *Upanishads* on discipline and the senses: *what at first tastes like poison eventually becomes nectar; what at first tastes like nectar eventually becomes poison.* But it was the Weesak, celebration of Buddha's birthday. Eve and I looked into each others' eyes and found in them tunnels by which we could transport ourselves to other planes.

We accessed a unique portal to other beings by connecting in this way. I have never repeated that kind of cord; perhaps it is like a highly conductive telephone line, one between here and a part of the planet that can only be accessed through a particular network and operator. In terms of romantic connection, though, the line was frayed, and relations subsequent to the conference steadily deteriorated.

Dave called a few months later to let me know that after I had declined Eve's invitation for a visit, she had invited another man instead. Dave commented: "If she was a man, she'd be a womanizer." In meditation, I experienced Eve using her spirit guides to *spy* on me, an abuse of spiritual power. About a year later I heard from her: "Do you remember me? We almost had a relationship a year ago." In fact, our 'relationship' seemed to go much further back, and tinged with negative as well as positive elements.

"Francine is a master at playing with sexual energy and not revealing herself.... Her maneuvers are confusing." This was the highly charged dynamic with a professional dynamo who was simultaneously inviting me in and spitting me out.

On our first get-together she invited me into her sauna naked. But I had developed terrible diarrhea. Embarrassing gaseous supernovae discharged at an alarming rate from my intestinal archives. Dave called this "a grace from God."

We sat in a coffee shop digesting the experience, Dave reiterated: "You were spared." Clutching my stomach that fateful evening, I had indeed wondered how many men had climbed naked into the sauna, and actually saw some of her lovers in meditation (not a pleasant vision). Despite these 'red flags,' I still idealized her, because of her accomplishments and that combination of seductiveness and spirituality.

Dave admonished: "You're not seeing her realistically; she's trouble: backing away during kissing, acting out the anger, circling the wagons around her at the party, rejecting you; being seductive and inconsistent; beware." Years later I again saw her at a conference, during which she, now married, tried to sneak a kiss in my ear, then pulled away leaving only the warm breath.

Gina somehow found me through a web of connections and called my home. She claimed to know me intimately from the very start. The very lack of boundaries that made instant intimacy so possible in energy healing was a warning side therapeutically; I knew that this duality had to be bridged, that I had a professional commitment to help build such bridges—once I sorted them out in my own life, and that task was not at all easy. In our next call, Gina claimed to have an orgasm over the telephone just by my 'energy.' So much for boundaries; but instead of attending to the proverbial 'red flag,' I charged ahead. When we got together I noticed she had brought roses for me. Putting the roses in one of my hands, she grabbed the other. I started seeing what I had gotten myself into.

She suddenly pulled away: "I'm afraid I'm too fat for you."

I tried to reassure her regarding her figure.

She grabbed both of my wrists and announced: "you love to fuck, don't you."

The comment took me aback, and I gently tried to extricate myself. She whirled around with a few choice words. Later that day, Dave suggested I call and say "I am sorry if in any way I offended you." That, he said, would rebalance the karma and leave the incident clean. A few nights later I called and she pretended not to recognize my name, telling me I had the wrong number.

Helga claimed to have healed herself from a car accident and a bad marriage through yoga. Her singing of Indian chants was mellifluous and identified her in my mind as a future saint. I was amazed at how much spiritual energy she could channel, the way she lovingly put incense to all the Krishna statues in her house.

But, Dave pointed out, always counter-balancing my desire to seize the slightest promise of intimacy and jump right in, Helga had manifested a few destructive behaviors already. Said Dave: "She is narcissistic and unavailable, other than to be adored and admired and held up on a pedestal where she can reign over many men." The seductiveness and spirituality, two opposite messages, confused me, and I found myself on spin cycle again. And again I was spared as within a year Helga had moved through two different new marriages.

Ida: having had my fill of sexually and spiritually intense checkerboard squares from Eastern religion, I somehow bonded with a fundamentalist Christian. She had intense green eyes, and seemed to be gazing at everything through her open third eye. Although she did not believe in a "third eye;" all she could talk about was her "relationship with the Lord." And, though we seemed opposite when it came to religion (her fundamentalism versus my experimentation with all these forbidden practices), we related in our love for the divine. The heart connection was pure; it was the Earth connection that was all screwed up. In observing that 'ignorance of the law is no defense,' courts acknowledge that 'an open heart and an empty mind' are not helpful to a defendant; similarly, an open fourth chakra without the discernment, discrimination and psychological maturity elsewhere offer the requisite 'poor boundaries' that lure a seeker of relationship into destruction.

Once, Ida had a vision of God "calling, calling, calling" me—as, she told me He had called the biblical prophets, that was the stature of my work. Flattery does not hurt, in the early stages of a relationship. She told me she could see angels as well as demons around people; an ex-boyfriend or ex-husband tried to strangle her. This should have been a red flag, but again, to me it only promised what I needed. Of course, she only saw angels and holiness around me, which seemed perfectly appropriate. But there were other signals.

She was intensely sexually charged and felt guilty about it, giving her contradictory impulses of sexual aggression followed by instantaneously calling off the charge, followed by remorseful prayer. There was a sense of being whipsawed between these extremes. Finally, she told me she was scared because we were growing closer, which brought up the fact that the last time she had loved, she had been choked, almost to death. As well, she was "good about self-restraint" but it was growing more difficult, she coyly admitted.

As Dave predicted, she quickly vanished back into her problems. After spending some weeks healing my disappointment, I found the connection within. With no expectations for any further contact, I wrote to her: "I am sorry for all the things any man has ever done to hurt you...I hope with time God's love will lift these burdens. My blessings are always with you. When two people connect in the heart, they are always connected....May perfect love cast out all fear." I was able to connect the cords back into my own heart, and to release her with love.

June only dated billionaires. Bored, lonely, and frustrated, I had dropped into a dance club. The woman I danced with turned out to be the year's Ms. America. She gave me her telephone number.

"You're a star," Dave said, "that's the message of meeting her."

I may have been in Dave's mind, but in her mind, I was more likely just another contestant, as she left the subsequent call unreturned, indicating in her voicemail that she was away judging a Miss Universe contest.

Kat's first question: "Do you think I'm mentally ill?"

"No," I replied. "These are all spiritual experiences."

But inside the message flashed: "Warning: she is unstable and dangerous."

"What I appreciate is that you look at me with understanding, not the way other men look at me." The last person she had dated had slipped a drug in her drink.

This time, I listened to the warning bells.

Lisa played *Ave Maria* on the piano, but before she picked up the tune, I had heard it play inside my mind. It was amazing that the guides knew what she was going to play and conveyed it first. We ended up having dinner in an Indian restaurant whose owner had a guru. I looked at the guru's photograph and heard: "Look at her, not at us. You are with her now. See us through her." So the relationship was to be another vehicle for spiritual practice. But there were practical psychological realities. When the weekend ended, she claimed her "tank" was "empty." The conversation deteriorated, indicating a deeper torment.

"Maybe I'm beating up on you … I'm a difficult person to love …. I have nothing to give …. I am still in my cocoon phase."

She was divorced with a three-year-old, unwilling or unready to heal. It was difficult, she admitted, to connect just now. In meditation, I saw us married, in a past royal life; but I knew our paths this time were separating, and that was best.

Mona. I felt that by dedicating myself again and again to service to God, the sludge was arising to be cleared: this relationship stuff was, I was told, "the sludge of innumerable lifetimes." Mona was colorful, with her long, white-blond hair, milk-white skin, saucy exterior, and Polish accent. She had been damaged by some hurt: "I do not know whether it was the first or second husband, the life in Warsaw or Berlin," she said, but I felt tremendous love for her as for a sister. Yet I recognized the danger signals and the ambivalence. She canceled at least one date because she had "so much sewing to do," and warned: "I'm trouble." She was tender deep inside, even though in this life and body she seemed to be suffering a thousand agonies: around finances, her daughter, other things, and the strange remark about how she had had "a perfectly good husband, only he died."

Afterward, I wrote her: "You are a fine person. If you could let your heart stay open you will know you are safe. I do not know all that has happened to who has hurt or taken advantage of you. But I do recognize an inner strength and beauty, and know that friendship is the basis of love.... As much difficulty as you experience, I also experience you as light, and fun, and free. Know that. Trust that. Honor that. You *are* that: divine. You are my friend." I did not send the letter.

Around the time I met Mona, the law school where I served as part of the inaugural faculty started falling apart. Before my job interview in the California law school, I had told God I would be fully myself: no more hiding, no more split. I put "Graduate, Barbara Brennan School of Healing" on my curriculum vitae, right after the Ivy League college and Berkeley. As it turned out, the Dean of the new law school had spent his adolescence immersed in transcendental meditation. He told me during our job interview of his visits to the Maharishi. "I need you here," he insisted, and that was the offer. He then asked if I would do a healing on him.

I began to work on his mid-back area. Tuning to the fourth level of the human energy field, the astral level, I pulled an etheric knife from his back.

"Wow," I said, surprised at its size and depth. "Have you been betrayed very recently?"

He pushed his hand through his shock of hair. The week before, his fiancé had broken up with him ... abruptly and in great anger. He exhaled slowly. We looked at each other for a long while, acknowledging our powerful spirits. We then sent energy back and forth with our palms.

Gurdjieff's "law of opposites" would soon change the results of his visionary plan. Within two years, an atmosphere of love turned to one of fear. The inaugural dean had founded this new law school as a humanistic enterprise, an attempt to dispense with the kind of humiliation often dispensed with Socratic method, the brutality I had experienced my first day as a student in Civil Procedure a decade earlier, the day Ms. Irma Galapolis was reduced to tears because of her lack of facility with the facts of *Pennoyer v. Neff.* What I liked about him, in addition to our mutual interest in spirituality and healing, was his attempt to "restore dignity" to the law; this afforded a path to integrating my Brennan training with legal teaching and scholarship. Yet, there were financial and status pressures, and a student lawsuit against the school; the meager enrollment was declining still further, and once again, fear prevailed, the fear that the school would dissolve and its faculty become unemployed. And so, in a secret meeting, one faction of the inaugural faculty assembled by this dean launched a coup, and through certain maneuvers, achieved a vote to relieve him of his post.

We witnessed the expulsion from an Eden of mutual trust and support and subsequent devolution of our faculty community into a polarized field of informers and loyalists, of those who would vote against the old regime and those who would stay loyal; those who held power and those who did not; those who had long-term stability and those who depended on their good grace; and so on and so forth, the old Darwinian pattern repeated in a new academic institution, the good intentions behind the school's founding dissolved in a haze of hypocritical rant about the university's "mission," and the manipulation of people, events, documents, to oust those unsympathetic to those dominant in the power struggle.

"And there came a Pharaoh that did not know Joseph...." We know the story: the Jewish people were enslaved and embittered with hard labor, and so the pyramids were built; although the school gained accreditation, it lost its soul. I confronted a new person at the top of hierarchy, one whose auric field, to my perception, glowed one way when I showed him a brochure for the First International Congress on Tibetan Medicine where I would be speaking, and another when he was discussing faculty politics.

Nina, at thirty-nine with two young children, was toned from her daily yoga practice, a practice all the more impressive by the fact that one of her hands was withered. (Dave insisted that this was because Nina had killed someone with that arm in a past life, and now was suffering her soul's remorse. He also insisted she could grow her hand back if she reconciled with that past life.) Nina's husband had left her when she was pregnant. After one evening together, she failed to return two phone calls, and then called to say she was feeling too vulnerable, financially and emotionally for a relationship. Intuitively I received guidance not to pursue.

> Silk and lace, she represents the past. Iron and fire, these are the women of the future. In them you will see your destiny, in the warrior-goddess, reflection of your masculine warriorship. Be keen for the battle, it is the birth of your soul's longing and purpose of on this planet, and in this time and place is definite purpose to your struggle for soul emergence. You are victorious and in solitude is the divine amanuensis forged. Outer accomplishments are nothing; it is the inner alchemy the Christ is after. See him standing before you with sacred heart ablaze and rays of fiery love extending in all directions. Tears release old sufferings; shed them and be cleansed.

I had some conversations with her in dreams and meditation, but reporting them out only frightened and alienated the physical being in her fragile state.

Olga liked the fact that Philip Roth got a lot of mileage by perpetuating the archetype, in his book *Portnoy's Complaint*, of the "*shikse goddess*," the blond non-Jewish female. Olga was the archetype (or stereotype): a six-foot blonde who turned up in a California synagogue; I had gone one random Friday night to see whether the service might reinvigorate my spirituality, and found this woman by the Kiddush cup, hovering around the eligible men who might be suitors. What was she doing in a synagogue? "Meeting Jewish men," she replied–in other words, seeking her "MRS" degree. I fit the bill, or rather the archetype (or stereotype). In addition to her long, flowing blonde hair, which cascaded Rapunzel-like toward her waist, Olga had a chiseled face, marked by sadness; seemed physically awkward and uncertain, perhaps because of the height. By telephone, we had long conversations, read poetry to each other; she told me of her past failed love with a rich kid; she had a good relationship with his father, especially when he was dying. She struck me as very spiritual, emotionally intense. Her father had cheated on her mother and lived in Mexico, her mother was cruel to her during childhood; Olga remembered her mother stepping on a sandwich and forcing Olga to eat it.

Later, I would learn about the "borderline" personality type, with a childhood legacy of sadism and abuse; the title of a popular book, *I Hate You–Don't Leave Me*, would encapsulate what I could expect with such early disclosures of exhaustive trouble. Our first date was at a lovely hotel on the beach; Olga showed up with black gloves covering her hands and wrists. I inquired about the black gloves: did they show an enthusiasm for the popular singer, Madonna?

"No," Olga replied in a definitive voice. She told me she had cut herself on the way to our date and was in such haste, she put the gloves on, hoping they would stop the blood.

"Oh you should probably get a band-aid," I suggested, asking to see the cut, the healer in me triggered.

"No, that's okay," Olga replied shyly.

"Please," I insisted.

"No, that's a bad idea," Olga said again.

"Oh please," I asked, more insistent than might have been wise.

"Well all-right," she agreed, and proceeded to offer her wrist, while I proceeded to gently pry the black glove off her right hand, holding it tenderly over the pizza.

Suddenly, blood spurted from the vein into my face.

"Oh my God!" she cried out.

The spurting continued; my face and shirt were coated with blood; and it continued. I put the glove back on, hoping to stop the flow of blood, but blood soaked the glove. Olga began crying.

"Let's get you some help," I said. I helped her rise from the table and proceeded toward the hotel lobby. She faltered; blood spilled through the glove and dripped on the floor. Olga fell to the floor, unconscious. By now, someone had called an ambulance.

"Step away," the paramedics brusquely advised, as they put her on oxygen.

Olga came back to consciousness. She argued with the paramedics: "I'm not going that hospital, they're crooks." Finally she passed out again; they took her.

I did a healing on her hand in the emergency room, sewing up the bright blue lines on the first layer of the feeling after the doctor had sewn up the physical skin; the cut was much deeper and more extensive than I had anticipated. Had Olga simply torn her hand, brushing it against a broken car handle, as she reported? How could she have been so eager to have the date that she would simply cover over such a gash with a glove? Why had I been drawn to her? Why was it necessary for her to spill blood during our first encounter?

"Don't be a caretaker," Dave advised, as I called him from the payphone in the emergency room. "For all you know she mutilated herself." I had called him because when Olga had fainted, I could not be sure that she was not dying; I did not know how much blood she had lost. I also felt useless when the paramedics came, my healing skills brushed aside and relegated to non-importance when life-saving medical care was necessary. There was also the matter of Olga arguing with the paramedics, and then her insisting that she did not have a mother or father or friend anyone could call, even though she had told me her where her parents lived.

Dave admonished: "Your healing training may suggest you need to be there for her, but healthy psychological boundaries dictate a little separation. She got herself into the mess and you barely know her. You may think you have past-life love for her, but she's got to sort through her problems before she can have a healthy relationship with you." In the game of checkers, no square could be skipped.

Petra and I met first in meditation then in person. She was studying to become a therapist, but admitted that she was afraid to open up; her last lover turned out to be married; she had not dated in a while. The red flags again were waving loudly, but the attraction, a combination of biological response to seductiveness (in a mechanistic, physical sense) and past-life recognition (in a spiritual sense) kept me hooked. I noticed, though, that on a sunset date, she would not remove her sunglasses (warning: danger!). She reported how dysfunctional her mother was, and how sad she was about her father.

In healing programs, such disclosures could facilitate intimacy, as they were done within a supportive environment dedicated to empathy, compassion, and healing; but on a first or second date, prematurely revealing such wounding often signaled an unhealthy lack of boundaries and trouble to come. Sure enough, the requisite ambivalence showed up on her part, and consequent feelings of disappointment and betrayal on mine.

In meditation, my guides reported: "In the past, you were a magician and she was a student who abused the teachings; don't give her any power over you." That seemed consistent with a feeling of seductive manipulation in the present persona.

Queenie and I met at a party by my accidentally spilling wine on her, a move Dave later interpreted as re-enacting a past-life event involving a shooting between us. At dinner, Queenie seemed awkward and nervous and asked whether I thought she was "making good conversation." She also told me she "worked out obsessively." One of the comments she made was that she and I were "kin." Indeed, it felt that way. But as we got to know each other, she suddenly confided that she had another boyfriend.

As it turned out, she had "fled" one state to leave an ex, and now wanted to flee the state she was in: literally and figuratively. Dave was not surprised by her multiple identity with different boyfriends; according to him, she had been shot for infidelity during Civil War times in the South and died in my arms, during which time I was a doctor or perhaps her brother.

"Rosa, rosa," I had sung as a child in Buenos Aires, "tan maravillosa...."
Now I asked: "May I have your phone number?"
What was a saddhu like me, reincarnated as a law professor, a man who had chanted mantras and had shaken off demons in an ashram, and dedicated his life to God, a man of the cloth, a reverend, an energy healer, a burgeoning bodhisattva, a man who connected with Jesus, Mary, the Sabbath Bride, the guides and Masters, a man of deep faith, what was a man like me doing, asking a question like this to an attractive woman in a parking lot outside the county library? What was a man like this doing with his divinity?
But I was also a man: hormonally charged, driven to reproduce, alienated, existentially malcontent, feeling separate from God and from my fellow humans, lonely, wanting companionship, wanting fellowship, wanting harmony in my world and intimacy in my social circle and personal life. And there was this tall brunette in the parking lot....who knew what cords connected us or what hunger she might satisfy me or me in her. Thus I reasoned, or rather did not reason, but simply acted, asking for the cord of connection through telephonic exchange.
Rosa did not act surprised, but she did ask whether I was married.
"No, of course not," I chastised her.
"Well," she apologized, "my last lover was...a lot of men have used me for sex."
"Great!" I said. Just kidding. What I said, with true empathy, was, "I'm sorry."
What I should have thought was: RED FLAG, WARNING DANGER. It was time to take off the healing school hat and put on the WATCH OUT FOR POOR BOUNDARIES hat I was learning from my therapist. But of course I was needy, I was suffering from the crappy environment in my academic and professional environment, and I was looking for a "quick fix" in the form of a Southern California relationship. I truly was sorry that men had emotionally abused this beautiful being...and on a hidden level, wanted perhaps to rescue or fix it. RED FLAG, WARNING, SAVIOUR COMPLEX TRIGGERED. BACK OFF, DRIVE AWAY. But instead I put pen to paper and took her phone number.
I named the coffee shop where we would meet. She showed up awkward, immediately confessing that she had not dated in a while, and just as suddenly, held my hand and asked me to pretend that we knew each other well. After the coffee, Rosa confessed she was angry that I had not invited her to dinner, but only to coffee. Again, my healer's instincts, without the clinical training or perspective of psychotherapy, mislead me. I admired her openness about her feelings. The truth was that she was enraged: yet another man betraying and disappointing her; I was simply another projection in the lineage of failed or abusive partners.
Acquiescing to her demand rather than reading the signals, I agreed to up the ante and take her to dinner even though we had only agreed on a quick initial meeting for coffee. Dinner turned out to be an exercise in self-disclosure. Rosa told me that she was adopted and now engaged in a search for her real mother. Her adopted mother, she told me, used to beat her and her father did nothing; still, she got along fine with them now. She was twirling her pasta with her fork in this trendy, upscale restaurant while telling me the deepest details of her childhood.
I literally saw an angel, hovering around her as she was speaking and twirling her pasta. The image filled me with deep love. I felt the Christ energy, protecting Rosa. I said very little, silently offering blessings. Rosa's ready-made intimacy, demanding dinner and pretending we were already lovers, yielded no fruit. Within weeks she had a new boyfriend, and let me know two things: first, that without him, she was lonely; second, that until she met him, she "thought all men were scum."

Sandra, too, showed insecurity right away—and anger if not properly reassured. We had met in a meditation center, not a parking lot. But she, too, had a tale: her old boyfriend hit had her in the face with a gym bag, leaving a scar. She also told me she was a recovering heroin addict, and sometimes suffered from severe depression. There were further disclosures, right away, and then she invited me to come over and make chocolate strawberries; but when I showed up, the house was dark, and nobody answered the bell.

Tammy greeted me in line at the health food store; she was thirty-one, curly red hair, radiant but also withdrawn and fearful. She was one heck of a tennis player, she quickly moved in our telephone calls to using "we," a kind of create-a-relationship through language. But she alternated between seductiveness and ambivalence, showing a lot of lethargy when I returned phone calls; again the promises; again, the alternation between enthusiasm and withdrawal or hostility; again a cancelled date. When that happened, I asked why I should give her a second chance. She replied: "Because you want to." Not a compelling answer.

In meditation I saw her shoot me in the heart with a crossbow. Then, continuing the meditation I saw us married around the time of Atlantis, perhaps there in one embodiment; and in another vision, saw us elsewhere as mortal enemies. So the dynamic as both lovers and enemies was part of the history and it seemed to play out—an inexplicable push-pull, promises of intimacy followed by withdrawal. I also garnered in meditation that my destiny was to go to India, and that she could not come, because of the karma of her body, and disability, and that therefore it was best to separate me from her. The second chance was the same as the first: over-enthusiasm, followed by lethargy and ambivalence. She talked about wanting to play Ave Maria at her wedding and how much we had in common. Seductiveness now was going way beyond the physical, to the metaphysical; but then she gave me the cheek and a hug, along with references to weddings. The impression was one of intense avoidance combined with intense reeling-in.

We had only one more meeting after that. We sat on a rock and she took my hand, rubbed it, and said she was "numb," "still trying to figure out the last two relationships," sorry she had "nothing to give."

Within the hour, she had called again, stating how attentive and wonderful I was, how she had prayed to God for someone like me, and so on. She then told me she had an incurable disease and that when she told her last boyfriend, he cried, but she could not; she had to have surgery from time to time since the disease, which was not cancer, spread (but it's not cancer). I told her that I was going to spend my summer in the ashram. She said she hoped I would call before leaving, that she did not want to lose me and that she would be sad if I did not call (though, again manifesting the ambivalence, she also said it was good that I was going away for the summer). She added: "I'm not going anywhere. I want to come to you whole." That was the last time we spoke.

Uma sat by the pool in a bikini and invited me into her apartment where she had a pocket *Kama Sutra* on the living room table. She had been to India and claimed to have knowledge of exotic sexual techniques. We went to a Mexican restaurant for dinner and began to talk about our professional lives.

At the door, she said she found my report of work "negative," then gave me a hug, and said to call her sometime after tax season. It was three months away.

Dave had this to say: "Your heart is open, but hers is not. Whether through hysterical anger, neglect, lack of communication, or lapse of time, each candidate severs the cord of relationship abruptly, severely, and permanently. You must guard your heart against these wounded souls that flit about you with temptation."

Uma's friend was someone I dated for a while. But she became suspicious of my meditation practice, and thought I was in a "cult." I had a meditation about my connection to this woman; in it, she and I were back to back, our hands tied, at the stake. In that lifetime we were burned together for religious reasons. *No wonder she won't let me talk to her about embracing spirituality again.* The meditation image also accounted for the depth of

A Friend of All Faiths

the connection I felt–having ascended from the body together on the pyre–despite her "bad behavior" in this lifetime. It was so hard to let go; in the next meditation, I saw that even the grass was weeping.

Venus made her living belly dancing. She had married a man during a visit to Iran, but he tried to keep her there, as well as their son, now a teen-ager, who hovered around to make sure his mother "behaved." Venus's dog barked at me each time at the driveway, and nipped my heel as I entered the apartment. Her son stared, wondering when I would make my move. And I had difficulty watching men stuff dollar bills into her undergarment as she belly-danced for their pleasure.
"Good you exited. You averted a catastrophe," Dave congratulated.

Wanda wanted to talk about energy healing, but started off by letting me know that I had to "take charge of the conversation. " There was this curious mix of control by telling me to be in control. We walked by the ocean and spotted some dolphins in the water. But she was so guarded, it was hard to exult in the presence of these sea-friends. Her time was always uncertain, and I felt pressed into the safe spaces in her calendar. Ambivalence and hostility, the familiar trademarks, surfaced in several negotiations over get-together times.

Xena told me, over our first dinner, about the lifetime she got a spear through her chest in Africa, and in the next being a mobster in the U.S., and in this one, having two raging, alcoholic parents, and a long-term, severe depression. The next time I saw her was in a bookstore; she was staring at a postcard showing a man with a knife; she told me she planned to send the card to an ex-lover who had betrayed her. She could not speak with me because, she claimed, she was recovering from alcoholism. A few days later she sent me an email. I did not reply for four days, and because of that I received a hateful and accusatory letter by federal express. "You were spared," Dave enthused. "You chased this karma but again you were spared."

Yolanda: Dave asked if I would put up a "special friend" of his for two days. This was not a date, but I consider her a checkerboard square because she tested severely, and may have represented a check-box on the way to the wedding, something I had to handle to grow stronger. Unexpectedly, she turned out to be difficult and demanding in several surprising ways, and within a short time period, I felt unsafe with her in the house. Because of this feeling about safety that would not go away, I gently approached her after her first night's stay, and asked if she would mind staying in a hotel. I told her that I would foot the bill for her hotel stay.
I had no obligation to her, and due to her professional status she certainly had resources. She nonetheless had no appreciation for my financial offering. Instead, she accused me of "abusing her" by giving this suggestion, and by "not giving twenty-four-hour notice." As if my apartment were a hotel and she had "rights." Her voice rose higher and higher, until she finally locked herself in the second bedroom and refused to come out. At length I coaxed her out the bedroom and ushered her to the doorway, where she stood berating in a loud voice.
When I called and spoke to Dave about the incident, he merely said: "Oh, that's a shame, is she doing that again?"
That was the end of my friendship with Dave.
I ran into the woman a few years later at a conference. She sat cross-legged during my entire talk as if to absorb everything in meditation. Her face, however, looked anything but tranquil to me. After the talk she came up to see whether I remembered her. Indeed, I had. She then snapped: "If you ever do to me again what you did in California, I'll have you disbarred."
I made "prayer position" with my hands and gently backed away. Mercifully, I never

saw or heard from her again.

Zena: The potential partners were coming now as pairs of opposites. I wrote in a journal that one wanted human betrothal but did not understand my betrothal to God; the other understood betrothal to God but not the human betrothal (she spiritualized, avoiding intimacy). *The universe is presenting the extremes so I can learn to find the middle.*

I met Zena in the usual way-by flirting. She was serving muffins at the breakfast counter. I found her beautiful and said hello. In a short conversation over the muffins, I established that she was a Russian woman living in Germany who came to the retreat for three weeks and spoke little English. I figured that was the end of it.

A week later, after a meditation program, I was standing outside looking toward the sky. "What are you doing?" she asked.

"Watching the stars," I said.

A week later, she appeared before me by the pay phones. I told her she would find it easier to make an international call using a calling card. This became a pretext for me to drive her to the local gas station, which really was an excuse to take her down the road toward the mountains for a beautiful view. In the car, she asked whether I had a girlfriend. We were in this romantic setting, beneath the stars and mountains. She brushed by me; as I moved toward her, she moved away. That should have been a clue. How I was tormented by desire and despair! As another student of law, St. Augustine, had written: "I burned in the boiling cauldron of lust and despair" (until he found all the love he needed in God). Somewhere in the basement, I still have Augustine—or rather, the suppose piece of his bone that Nick had given me, tucked in a red cloth within a gold-filled reliquary. Yet Augustine's presence in my basement did not help with Zena. Later that night she and I wandered into a coffeehouse. We stared into each others' eyes in a bedazzled manner. Much was being exchanged: promises, mystery, hints. There was a checkerboard on the table. As we worked through the language barrier, we decided to play. For a time, I was winning, and I could sense her struggle with the notion that I might win the game. But then Zena got a queen. She moved her queen in an unknown zigzag that I had never seen, resulting in the elimination of my queen. I protested that this move was unknown—she was changing the rules. She insisted that that was the way she played. I said that if I had known, I never would have placed my queen in a position vulnerable to the move she was making.

I could feel the power shifting back and forth between us: it was a metaphor for the brief intense, bizarre drama, for the whole relationship. From my vantage, I let her win—but only for so long. Some evenings later, we hiked up a trail and got lost up the mountain. As night fell, we found ourselves disoriented among snowy trees; somehow, intuitively, I saw flashes of purple light shine in the woods, which literally guided me back to the trail. In contrast to this exalted experience, we also had horrendous encounters. These included her screaming about minor perceived infraction and then demanding to be taken to a hotel. The power struggle was endemic to this meeting of souls. But finally (going back to our checkers game) we agreed to call a stalemate. We wiped the checkerboard clean: we parted.

She would refuse to speak to me though we would cross paths many times months. Even years later, in the ashram, we sat in the same hall during a meditation retreat while our teacher said to the large crowd: "If there is anyone in this room with whom you are still angry...reconcile!" Yet she did not.

In an Indian scripture, the *Yoga Vashista*, the sage tells Ram:

> *I tell you, O Rama, if you cannot do without loving a form, love the form of an avatar of God, for you do become what you love and serve sincerely.*

The sage is not necessarily advocating celibacy, but he is, as I read it, urging a balance between seeking love in this world and keeping love of God foremost.

A Friend of All Faiths

THROUGH THE TUNNEL

Elephant-faced Ganesh, Remover of Obstacles and Destroyer of Sorrows, sat serenely on the dashboard, one leg resting on his opposite knee. The god's bronze body was just large enough to obscure the broken mileage meter below the speedometer; yet he exuded a powerful presence. Ganesh seemed pleased with the rose petals offered at his feet, and with the mantras chanted from behind the shoulder belts. His elephantine face, as always, was mysterious and radiant; his body shone with sun-spun gold, as he directed the forces of destiny from his contented perch on the dash.

Maya set her coffee cup down in the car seat holder as we rounded the bend. It was a special coffee with cardamom and delicate Indian spices. We were heading toward Maya's healing room, about a mile from the main building of the ashram where I was spending my summer off from law school teaching. I was on "summer staff," displaying a bright yellow tag showing a little square photo, with me smiling, and my name—I had not adopted an Indian name like Krishna, Arjuna, or Shiva but kept my own as "spiritual" nomenclature. It had been a satisfying eight or ten weeks, performing *seva* ("selfless service") with love and spending hours in the meditation cave. Now Maya had converted a basement apartment into sacred space, with a massage table, sofa, incense, phone, and pictures of various enlightened beings adorning the walls. The week before, Maya had done a healing on me, an intense experience in which I drifted into other times and places—it seemed in those "lives," if such they were, that my healership had challenged the authorities, and they in turn had wreaked such vengeful havoc that I still needed to heal the scars.

It was my turn to return the favor and do a healing on Maya.

As we rounded the corner and approached her makeshift temple, I noticed that an oncoming car was honing in on us. The car's movements seemed abrupt, absurd, weaving across the yellow dividing line. Maya veered left and then right, but the car followed, as if the driver had a death wish and was determined to ram into us. Maya continued adjusting to dodge the oncoming vehicle, but it was coming fast and heading directly into us. At the last moment, Maya veered onto the dirt shoulder. Then I heard her exclaim, "O my God, Michael."

Death smiled. His arms were folded, his body was exquisite, and he was draped in white. My time had expired: I was thirty-five. I had not accomplished all I wanted to accomplish; I had so much to learn and so much to give; it all seemed rather quick and premature; and this incarnation was over. I knew this with certainty: the appointed calendar for this physical body had been extinguished.

I had always prepared myself for the moment of death. I wanted my mind to be calm, lucid, and conscious. This was, in fact, the teaching of many spiritual traditions. Even in Judaism, the rabbis had said: "Repent the day before you die. But you do not know the day of your death; therefore, repent, turn to God, every day." I thought I had done so, but even so, the timing took me by surprise. Here, on a country road in upstate New York, Death had taken me unawares. It was like the parable of the man who runs away from death to the village of Samara, only to find Death there confirming: "We had an appointment today in Samara."

Spontaneously, as the oncoming car crashed toward us, I did the only thing I knew to do in the last breath of life: I uttered a mantra: *Om Namah Shivayah*. I bow to the Lord who dwells within me. With these words I hoped to propel myself to a more advanced state of consciousness. Simultaneously, I ducked.

I looked down to see if my legs were still attached to my body. I did not know if I was alive or dead. I half expected my spirit to fly out of my body. Or perhaps the life review would begin as I exited the body through my crown. I smelled something burning. In a corner of consciousness, I thought of the Holocaust.

Suddenly I said: "Maya, get out of the car!" I unbuckled my safety belt, took a breath, bolted out of the car, took refuge on the dirt shoulder, and waited for the car to explode. I

Michael H. Cohen

looked inside: the car did not explode; it seemed that Maya had already left her body; yet, my words were pulling her back to this plane: and with these words (she would later report), she realized she had a choice, to leave or stay. She crawled out and sat on the dirt shoulder.

The other driver staggered toward us. "Are you all right?"

I scanned his energy: dark, clogged. Perhaps he was drunk. I waved him on.

Maya screamed at the oncoming cars: "Get an ambulance!"

Her hand was shaking uncontrollably. Someone said: "She's going into shock."

I popped into witness consciousness. I was there, in my body, on the dirt, waiting for help; yet a part of me was observing. I felt a wave of bliss drench my being. I had been saved and protected: God was with me.

I held Maya's trembling hand.

Soon others started to come. I knew the whole drama would play itself out: we would be taken to the hospital; there would be x-rays, doctors, forms to fill out. I knew there would be no physical damage. I was in divine alignment.

Two residents from the ashram drove up and put their hands around us, "running energy" to help release the shock and clear our energy fields. Maya's whole body now was shaking. Someone went to her car and retrieved our bags, as well as the tiny Ganesh. It was just a small metal statue; but I knew that being was our friend, had saved our lives. I felt so grateful and so protected. I was in a spiritual bubble of gratitude and protection. I had been spared from death for a reason.

As the paramedics loaded my body on a stretcher, a stranger from the ashram came up and looked down into my eyes. Her face momentarily shielded me from the blinding sun. She uttered the same mantra I had spoken before the crash. "God is good," she said. "God is protecting you." I could feel the calm energy of my friends from the spiritual center, who were praying, sending energy, and aligning the healing on the higher planes.

The frenetic and uncaring physical plane was a contrast to the peace and bliss that had filled my being in the immediate aftermath of the accident. First and most immediate were the paramedics who took responsibility on the physical plane. I had always admired paramedics for their calm readiness to help save lives. But now, in my state of heightened awareness, I could easily read their nervous, anxious and fragmented energy. Their panic was palpable and distressing: I could read them clearly, but I was also in their care, and vulnerable, and protest was not an option. Nor would they understand a comment by an accident victim about their "energy." They would probably argue in response that their duty to save lives required them to be free from such psychological and spiritual mumbo-jumbo, that they were attentive to subtle physiological signals.

At the same time, they were, from my perspective, clueless—in the dark about consciousness, about anything other than the material, biological, chemical, electrical that was their stock in trade. They could not read where I was—deeply inward, immediately post-accident, and physically and emotionally fragile. They were masters of the physiological, the biomedical, the biochemical, but they had no spiritual sensitivity. Their handling was rough—apart from the care in lifting me into a stretcher, and they did not respect my stated wishes. For example, in the ambulance, they insisted on giving me oxygen though I insisted I did not need it and indeed found it distracting. They simply overrode my request, leaving me feeling powerless, whereas instants earlier I had felt the hand of grace.

Next, they asked a series of questions and studied carefully to see if I was responsive according to their criteria. It did not occur to them that I had just seen Him (Her), the Big Man Upstairs—had a kind of life review, saw it all flash. They asked for my address, and I answered in a quiet voice—it was still difficult to externalize, coming from such an inward place. They interpreted this quietude as an implication that I was losing consciousness. From their perspective, certain life-saving procedures might have been mandatory; yet from the perspective of my experience, their inability to tune in to what I was feeling, even in a rudimentary way, was unnecessarily destructive to my fragile state.

They insisted on speeding down a bumpy road even though I told them this was jarring a body that had already been traumatized, and feared another crash. There were no physical symptoms requiring this high-speed journey. I asked them to slow down to a reasonable speed, told them they had not detected any imminent damage in my body; and again found my wishes ignored. My transcendent bliss slid toward sadness as I realized I would have to deal with a bunch of mundane realities that were far from the tunnel of light: people with clipboards and insurance forms, lawyers, nurses, and doctors. Their voices were much louder than I could tolerate, and in the subtle space between life and the near-death experience, every nuance of unprocessed harshness in a voice seemed to penetrate my field. This had been my consistent experience as a witness to others in emergency rooms, and now I became keenly aware of how—as competent the medical staff may have been in its field of expertise—psychologically and spiritually unhealthy the energies were that permeated that treatment space. This embodied the split I had been facing in my life: between spirituality and healing, and the world of law and the mundane. There was little reconciliation as few in the mundane space of doctoring, checking insurance claim forms, administering, could also sit in the still space from which non-verbal communication effortlessly emanates. In coming days I would find myself alternating between the two polarities of our nature.

The x-ray revealed that nothing had been broken. As the x-ray was being taken, I could see the room being filled with a purple light. I felt protected: the same love that had kept me death or a maimed existence was now guiding recovery. Yet, the accident had not come without warning. Three days earlier, I was sitting in the ashram's main temple. The energy was so thick, intense, and scintillating I could barely sit; I felt waves of electricity coursing up my spine and engulfing my whole body in flames. As I moved into meditation, my meditation teacher appeared. I saw her rip a piece of clothing in two. In Jewish tradition, renting a garment is a sign of mourning; one tears one's clothing when one hears news of a loved one's death. Although my teacher is from India, I had a feeling she was using this Judaic ritual to get my attention. I heard her say: "This which has known itself as Michael Cohen...."

Then she disappeared.

Two days before the accident, I received another message. I was still wondering about the rent garment when I was sitting in the Temple, meditating. Obviously I had received a message that something major was going to happen in my life. Perhaps the symbol of mourning for death meant that I would experience a psychological death, perhaps the death of my ego, followed by complete enlightenment; or on a smaller scale, perhaps some troubling facet of my personality would dissolve, to be replaced by a lighter, freer self. I was hopeful.

Again my teacher entered my meditation. Rarely did she come in so strongly. I heard her ask: "What is the purpose of your life?" Her voice was insistent, urgent. Instinctively, my mind flashed back, in this telepathic dialogue, to a line from the morning chant: "Service to God. There is nothing higher."

A few minutes, eternities, passed. Again, the voice asked: "What is the purpose of your life?"

Again, I answered: "Service to God. There is nothing higher."

Again, silence; a third time, the voice flashed with the same question, and again, I answered: "Service to God; there is nothing higher."

When I returned to the Temple following the accident, I was so grateful for the body that allowed me to walk to this place and offer worship. I sat down and propped my head against the wall, my neck in a brace. I was grateful for my breath, for the ability to cross my legs and inhale, exhale; grateful for the ability to mentally repeat a mantra; to have arms

Michael H. Cohen

with which to embrace my friends; to have vocal cords, with which to speak and chant God's name. I was grateful for my digestive system, for my saliva, and hair. Every part of my body now seemed to vibrate with light. I experienced profound gratitude at every level.

This time, in meditation, my teacher came in again. She showed me a vision. I saw myself in my office. Above my door was emblazoned in fiery gold letters, the following logo: SERVICE TO GOD, SERVICE TO THE PLANET. Above that was my name.

The day after the accident, I took a meditation intensive with my teacher. My neck muscles were so weak that I sat slumped in my chair, my neck brace propped against the back of the chair. My father was taking this intensive with me. I had actually seen this in meditation some five years earlier. I felt flooded with feelings of love for him. I saw him in a white shawl, with a mantra inscribed around him. And I had heard: "He will come to me. I will bring him here."

During the intensive, I found my consciousness leaving through the top of my head (the crown chakra) and going through a white tunnel. It seemed as though I was being drawn up now for some meeting. I could see different beings laying out charts and blueprints and maps of the new world–the new plan for my life. Various options were discussed and missions described. I floated in and out of awareness in the intensive. Though my body was in the chair, my spirit was "up there."

I had various reconstructive healings following the accident: a lot of chiropractic, massage and acupuncture, for example, to help with residual whiplash that seems to have lasted through the present. During one chiropractic session, I went through all the feelings of fear that had been suppressed during the moment of trauma; as the chiropractor applied pressure to various parts of my body, I felt these feelings arise and be expelled. We felt the "death energy" leave, accompanied by trembling, lights, and other phenomena.

The night before the accident, Maya and I had met by the lake. We had grown close. We felt a little guilty for this meeting, as the purpose of an ashram was not to engage in stealth romantic encounters. But we wanted to explore the potential.

As we walked around the walk, repeating our mantras, I received a message. This was unusual: this experience of hearing God in the first person, but it came from everywhere outside as well as inside me. "I am separating the two of you."

Consciously, the message made no sense. Had we done something wrong by meeting by the lake? It was clear that God, for reasons I could not understand, was going to separate us. I could not possibly have imagined the mechanism. And then God's voice came from the lake. "Remember, I have made you a priest."

I told one of the swamis: "Just after the accident, I felt like a saint. There was so much love radiating into my being and out into the hospital. I don't want to come back to mundane reality."

We sat at a table in the dining hall, a wooden structure filled with portraits of Indian saints from times past. The swami ate slowly, chewing every morsel at least fifty times. He spooned some brown rice and reassured me: "You *are* a saint. It's your destiny, as it is the destiny of every person who places love of God foremost." In our brief conversation in between slow-chewing bites, I told him I was amazed that I had emerged relatively unscathed, given the intensity of the impact. He replied that he was not surprised at the intervention of grace. He paused, and added: "You were saved for a purpose. There's more work for you here."

I returned to the law school. The psychological shift required was from focusing on the meaning of all that had happened, and a weekend of silence–immersion in ecstatic states of being after being saved from a near-death experience–to the politics and, indeed, paranoia of a faculty in trouble. Student lawsuits were continuing, accreditation could be in jeopardy, jobs could be lost, and so on. A discussion of "image" and whether we should hire a public relations firm occupied center stage. I was barely back in my body, barely returned to this life from a near-death experience. I was having experiences of conversing with Great Beings about the most profound aspects of reality I knew. And all this surface talk seemed to be about covering up the school's deficiencies through a little bit of PR—as though the bandage of public opinion was the salve for academic leprosy.

At night, I began to prepare a stir-fry for the wok. I was still deeply connected to the wisdom of my meditation experience and the purity of its silence, yet also processing the crazy intrigue of the work environment. And so, I began to chop the garlic with haste— perhaps even rudeness and anger. Chop, chop—and thoughts continued about the various events of the day. I heard a voice: "Stop! You're hurting me!" Nobody was about; I lived on cedar mountain house, alone on the hill.

The message seemed to be coming from the garlic. Indeed, everything is conscious— God dwells in everything. Even Moses was chastised for hitting a rock. The auditory frequency seemed to be a response to my brusque movements and uncaring movements, unappreciative that at least this form of consciousness had sacrificed its life to serve as food. I immediately apologized, and softened my peeling and chopping, adopting gratitude, and recognizing in that moment the unification of being, my connection to my food, the cycle of life.

Almost exactly a year after the accident, I found myself back in the meditation center for a weeklong retreat. The day I arrived, I forced myself to revisit all the places where I had experienced trauma: here was the table under the tree where Maya and I had coffee, ten minutes before the accident; there I had staggered, hovering between euphoria and depression, some hours after the crash.

I sat down under the tree and entered a meditative state. I melted into bliss. A being of light descended from heaven on a golden ray. "I am your very Self," he said, "your innermost nature. I am the bliss you attain by garnering meditation energy. I am You, and You are That." I merged into stillness. Nothing could disturb this place of pure peace. A few minutes later, a voice said: "Go to Ganesh."

As I walked toward the Ganesh statue, in the corner of my eye, I saw Maya, sitting on a stone bench, surrounded by Sanskrit inscriptions. We had not spoken in months, since she had sent a postcard saying that she was unready for a relationship and committed to an undisclosed long-term, intensive therapy.

I smiled and sat next to her. "Hello, Maya."

For a moment, her eyes were blank, as if she did not recognize me. Finally, she said: "Oh, yes, from last summer."

The casualness of the recognition startled me. But I was feeling happy from my meditation. I looked at her tenderly; the veil of amnesia seemed to be lifting.

"How are you doing?" I asked.

Her eyes narrowed with anger. "Still fighting with insurers ... and *lawyers*." She rose. "With no support from old *friends*." The word *friends* had a bite to it. I realized that was the end of the conversation, and that I was not expected to reply. Had I been able to read the future, I would have seen myself back in almost the same place, three years later—Maya, still refusing to speak to me, even at this late stage, walking through the same hallowed halls in which we shared the same sacred meditation energy.

But for now, I looked at Ganesh, the Remover of Obstacles, as Maya got up and walked out of my life. I had prayed many times for clarity in my relationships—but that clarity could only be granted if I assumed it myself, by no longer idealizing the female other, and letting go of responsibility for bad behavior on the part of others. Perhaps the obstacles were inner even more than outer, and they were being removed one by one.

All the rounds were complete. Having completed the game of checkers, God was about to grant me a queen.

THE OLD WORLD

(POLAND AND RUSSIA, 1800's)

This Generation (photo taken September 9, 2001, South of France)
&
Some of Our Ancestors

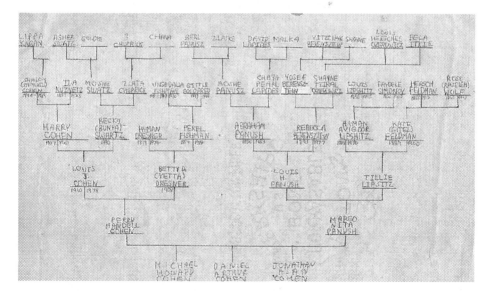

In addition to seeking our soul mate, marrying by choice or through family or tribal alliance, we humans tend to seek to locate ourselves through lineage and ancestry. People do this, even using genetic snips to locate part of their ancestry. Truly, we are all part of each other, but for the purpose of locating this body in time and space through the lineage of Judaism, I like to go back to Aaron: he begat several sons, but two made an unlawful offering and were consumed. Aaron's surviving children begat others, thus passing on the lineage of the *cohen* or priest within the tribe of Levi; and through the centuries the begetting continued.

My great-great-uncle Frank, whom I interviewed in 1973, told me of Lippa Kagan, my paternal ancestor. He begat Shalom (Samuel) Kagan (1848-1939), who married Ida Kuznetz (1855-1923). Their son, Harry Cohen (1887-1961), my paternal great-grandfather, emigrated with Becky (Bunya) Swartz and their three-year-old son, my grandfather, Louis J (1910-1976), in steerage of a steamship.

Once settled in Detroit, my grandfather Louis studied law but could not, as a Jew, find work with a law firm; instead he worked as a salesman for Frank Tea & Spice. I remember him with a big cigar, enjoying backgammon and bridge, and always magically making a penny disappear and reappear from my ear. He loved life, and spent much time playing with me.

He was also the first person I loved who ever got sick, visibly weakening from cancer as I was turning a teenager. I remember my father gently lowering Grandpa into the bed, this unknown melancholy descending over the house as something incomprehensible to my adolescent mind was taking over our lives: the gradual deterioration of my grandfather's body and movement of his spirit to another plane, leaving emptiness that had been filled with his generous laughter.

My grandfather had married Betty (Yetta) Dresner, giving birth to my father, Perry Mandell Cohen. My Grandma loved to read novels. She had an active mind and a great heart for us. She also loved to travel. She spent hours creating the container for great play and delight among the cousins and larger family. During my later teens, I became aware that my grandmother lived in the shadow of widowhood, a loneliness that seeped into our family consciousness. She expressed her love by cooking for us and hosting us, and delighting in the many grandchildren she had.

The encounter with my grandmother's widowhood was encounter with suffering; as a young prince, the Buddha had seen an old man, a sick man, a dead man, and therein realized his first "noble truth:" that life is suffering, that all beings go through these phases of existence, that he too was bound to experience these things. Such a realization was bound to generate compassion for all beings. But it also launched his journey, an all-consuming drive to understand and ideally transcend the psychic imprint of these difficult encounters. My grandmother's death was traumatic. I remember my father ordering delicatessen food during *shiva*, the mourning period; while I sat in the bathroom, closed the door, and wept.

My father followed his father's footsteps in the business world, studying accounting and then finance, and for years serving Chrysler's finance department in Detroit, before moving to New York to join the Wall Street investment community. From my father's professional journey, a bumpy ride, I learned persistence: the hard-earned foraging bequeathed to humanity from Adam's fall could be reframed, not as Yahweh's punishment for eating the wrong apple, but as a heroic encounter with challenges including bad bosses, jealous colleagues, financial straits. I helped my father fold his curriculum vitae and licking dozens of envelopes in the basement of our suburban, Michigan home. He was not interested in squeezing others, not cheating or wheedling or wheezing, he held a line of integrity, to my eyes. He simply did the work, and was sometimes rewarded, other times not; he picked himself up, though, and carried on: moving forward, moving forward.

Michael H. Cohen

As a teenager, my father had a milk route. His partner, another teenager, cheated him of his summer's profits; my father realized that knowledge of accounting could help place the requisite checks on fraudulent behavior. Later, he found in economics a useful policy tool to help cure international disorder; and firmly believed in capitalism as a vehicle for expanding personal wealth, and thus alleviating suffering. In some ways, he came to Buddha's commitment to alleviate the suffering of all beings from a different angle: from the charts and graphs of macroeconomics. This was, perhaps, an influence behind my studying political science (and economics at Columbia's international affairs school), and movement from philosophy to an interest in government. My father too, though, was deeply mystical, and in a very private way. He used to go for *Shabbat* weekends with Lubavitcher (Hassidic) families. The influence is there: every progenitor a strand. And so it is, as our longing sweeps us as a species till the final moment through time.

While ostensibly studying at the University of Michigan library, my father Perry, true to his Hebrew name Peretz (to burst), burst forth by sending a hand-written love poem to the "golden-haired beauty" across the green banker's lamp. This would be my mother Margo Nita Panush. The poem is still extant on parchment, archived permanently in her purse. Some months later, my father lent his car, which she unfortunately crashed, totaled, destroyed. This led to separation. But some months later she asked if he would give her a ride to his fraternity party, FIJI. He agreed, though he had also offered another woman a ride. On the way home, "Margo sat in the middle and insisted that I drop the other woman off first." The rest, as they say, is history.

Perry and Margo begat us: Michael, Daniel, and Jonathan.

On my mother's side, so far I traced the lineage back to my great-great-great grandfather, Beryl Panusz in Poland, although my great-uncle Sol says that he was named after Beryl's father Zalman. The origin of Panusz is unknown, though perhaps it means "little sir." Beryl and Zlatke gave birth to Moshe who, together with Chaya Perl Lapides (daughter of David and Malka Lapides) gave birth to my great-grandfather Avraham (1885-1953).

Avraham married Rebecca Berenzstein (1891-1977), my great-grandmother, also known as Bobe Rive (for *Rivke*, Hebrew for Rebecca). I have always liked the name Rebecca. She was the one who had the foresight to emigrate, even though she had to send her husband and son Louis Panush (my Zaydie) in the early 1920's, and wait until they could make enough money to bring her and her other three sons. She came from a family of thirteen children; her father owned a hat factory in Poland. She was the first to join Shaarey Zedek; my wife looked up her name on the memorial list during a visit to Detroit.

Three of my great-grandmothers had come to my Bar Mitzvah: Grandma Cohen (my father's paternal grandmother); Grandma Dresner (my father's maternal step-grandmother, as his grandfather Hyman Dresner, who I knew in childhood and visited in his Florida apartment, had remarried); and Bobe Rive.

I remember visiting Grandma Cohen in the nursing home; I was around ten. She spoke only Yiddish and kissed me profusely by sucking on my cheek. I felt the tender bond, though at that age could not well understand (as I do at forty-two) the immense love of the ancestors for the enormity of the ties between the generations, how we are all bound in one unbroken chain. This was an old person, in an awful place of tubes and nurses in white; I could not comprehend that this was once a young person like me, and that someday we would be trading places, in the great cycle of incarnation and being. What I knew was: this was Grandma Cohen, who came from the old country, and that somehow what I was learning at Hillel and what I would become had something to do with this unknown language, Yiddish, and a culture gone by.

I visited Bobe Rive many times in the Federation apartments where she lived in the Detroit suburbs. I had judo practice nearby and would often come by to see her. I do not remember what we talked about, only that she had enormous confidence, a straight back, a joy about her, keen intelligence, and spiritual depth. She had a *siddur* or Jewish prayer

A Friend of All Faiths

book on her table, one she had brought from the old country; it was her comfort and sustenance. She was proud of us, proud of her family, proud of her identity: a proud person in the best sense, proud to be alive in God's care. There were these different strands of spirituality, of religious depth, of divine connection and expression in my family, and she represented another strand.

There was the Yiddish of Grandma Cohen; the cerebral and hidden mystical affinity of my father for Judaism; my grandfather's rebelling against his father's orthodoxy yet the love of Jewish customs evident in his home; the rich education of Hillel Day School; my Zaydie tucking Hebrew novels in between his prayer book and reading during the rabbi's sermon at Shaarey Zedek; the Kashrut in our house; and my Bobe Rive's siddur, somehow connecting it all.

I come back, through Judaism, to my teacher's question: what is an ashram? An ashram is home: the interior castle of consciousness in which one's inmost divinity dwells, the access point to one's heart. Whether I am chanting *Hare Krishna* at the ashram in upstate New York; following the cantor's mournful recitation of our sins during Yom Kippur services; hearing the glistening calls to Allah bouncing off the minaret; embracing the frankincense wafted over my head by the swinging drone of a Russian Orthodox priest; kissing an icon of Mary or sprinkling holy water on my forehead at the entrance to a church; or sitting in meditative contemplation before a statue of the Buddha; all roads lead me, through Bobe Rive's siddur, back to the Source: to the one great crier, the great cantor of our blessedness and struggle, the One who dwells in the hearts of all.

This is my longing: to experience the ashram everywhere. The same love of the ancestors resonates in every being. Whether it is the curly green worm lovingly lifted on an index finger off our car seat and gently placed on the grass (*al kahn-fei nesharim*, "on eagle's wings" I will carry you, Yahweh said to the Israelites; *be-etzbah elohim*, "with the finger of God" the tablets were written; "with a mighty hand and an outstretched arm" were we lead in exodus from slavery), or my grandfather winking and retrieving a penny from my ear, or my great-grandmother sucking my cheek and exclaiming in Yiddish, the same love binds me to all creatures, all beings, all peoples. That love goes beyond form: it is not dependent on the face I see. The bluish-white hue of the first layer of the auric field still shines, no matter what the person's "identification" by way of things such as gender, race, age, or even mood.

In Brennan's system, among others, we each have seven major chakras, and cords of relationship; but on a broader scale, we have infinite chakras and cords, all connected to one another, to all beings who have ever lived, to the godhead.

I recall sitting stiffly as a faculty member, in a row of stiff faculty members, during a compulsory drill for Martin Luther King Day. So many hollow speeches were made; discrimination was an important subject, yet so many of the speakers lacked the discrimination (in a spiritual sense) to discern fullness from emptiness, truth from hollowness, authenticity from falsity, intention from games of faculty politics. As I was sitting in that room, I did not see in black and white. I did not need language ("no discrimination on the basis of race, gender, sexual orientation, age...."). As a lawyer and professional wordsmith, I honor the capacity of words to heal, clarify, set boundaries, discriminate between helpful and hurtful, the permissible and the impermissible, the legally sanctioned and the prohibited.

But looking at the soul, I saw a sea of spirits: blacks who had been whites; whites who had been Native American; Native American students who had been Asian. I questioned the check-boxes on application forms, the myriad of words hurled in misunderstanding, heaped upon one another with the stated intention of healing, and just as often carrying more confusion. Civil rights and other liberties were important concepts, and yet the consciousness behind them could be elevated. When love resides in the heart, one does needs no words. Laws protect those who suffer from beings who fail to heed the law of love. "Love one another as I have loved you," Jesus summed up; as did Hillel when asked to summarize the whole Torah while standing on one foot: "Love your neighbor as yourself." Rights are necessary to protect us when others do not heed the true heart. When the U.S. Supreme Court said that "separate is *not* equal," these were necessary words; and yet, we must transcend the need to impose such statements. As the *Tao Te Ching* puts it, "the Tao that can be spoken is not the real Tao."

Zaydie married Bobe (Tillie Lipsitz, daughter of Hyman Avigdor Lipsitz (1888-1940) and Kate (Gitel) Feldman (1889-1960)). Bobe attended law school in Detroit, but apparently sacrificed law school to raise a family. She also had a healthy will and ability to call people on their crap. She did so with the law school dean, resulting in her diploma being denied. This quality of Bobe's was apparently one I inherited—the inability to tolerate an injustice and remain silent. Once her father sent her to retrieve money he had loaned to a Mr. X. X's widow still lived high on the hog, fancy clothes, expensive habits. This woman dismissively told Bobe that any financial questions could be handled by the attorney. Bobe, who was nineteen, responded: If a man dies, his family should to anything to clear his name, even if requires settling debts. Bobe's father forgave the debt, and laughed on hearing the story—he admired her standing for principle, it was more important than the money. That made an impression on her for life.

Bobe told me a little about her side of the family history, when my wife Elaine and I visited her in Detroit in 2003. We took her to a Starbucks and introduced her to the joys of gourmet hot chocolate amid the Motown music.

Bobe told us that her mother, Kate (Gitel) Feldman, emigrated from Russia in 1902; her family worked in the business advising the Czars, until anti-Semitism required resettlement. When Kate had Parkinson's disease, she asked Bobe to read *Paradise Lost* aloud. One line stood out: "plain living and high thinking."

Bobe's grandfather, Louis Lipsitz, sold jewelry all over Russia. Even though he traveled extensively to make a living, he was always back home before Shabbos. On one trip, he was infected with gangrene. The village "doctor" amputated the leg on the kitchen table. His son Hyman, who was only eight at the time, heard the screams; thereafter he always hated hospitals and medical things.

Hyman emigrated in 1908. He was a good horseman. In the old country, he had tutored wealthy children in algebra. Unlike many contemporaries, he was educated. The Russians allowed him to sit in the back of the school because he was handsome and he "didn't look Jewish." Hyman spoke Serbian; when he came to Detroit, he sold watches to people in the "countryside:" in his day, Fourteen Mile road, where my parents later built a suburban home, was unpaved, horse-ridden, and considered the country. For a time he went to Alabama, but he said everyone there was constantly perspiring, so he returned to Detroit to make his way.

In the 1970s, my parents would buy a house on Normanhurst off Fourteen Mile Road, the same area in which my great-grandfather would sell watches on horseback. If time does not exist, these two events are contemporaneous: Louis Lipsitz galloping down a dirt road, displaying his watches and speaking Serbian to expatriate immigrants; my brothers and I, playing "fort" behind a large rock.

I have a recurring dream that I am in my childhood bedroom on Normanhurst, searching through the closet: we are moving, but there are books left behind. Curious, because we are known as the People of the Book, and nothing in my life is as sacred, profound, or exciting as the written word. Perhaps the books I am longing to discover in my old closet are the parchments on which the lives of my ancestors are written, and behind them, the scrolls on which the lives of all ancestors are written. These, in turn, may be the earthly representations of the so-called Akashic Records, the divine and angelically-mediated blueprints for our lives, composed and then stored in the great architectural firm in the ethers that I was privileged to glimpse during my journey through the tunnel following the head-on car collision.

When the wife of Zaydie's brother Sol passed away, I at first neglected to send a sympathy card. But while I was visiting Bobe in Detroit, Sylvia appeared to me and gently chastised me for failing to send the card. She repeated her appearance several times. On return to Boston, I intuitively wrote some words on a piece of paper and sent them to my great-uncle. I do not remember what they were, because they were channeled. I received a letter saying that his heart been greatly touched. My uncle Sol had been one of the "Flying Tigers" in Burma in WWII, invented many processes for color in the automotive industry, and, I later learned, written a book entitled "An Ode to Love: The Afterlife of My Darling Sylvia." He appreciated remembrance and verbal testimony to his beloved. I was glad I heeded Sylvia's advice.

In our trip to Detroit, we visited Bobe and Zaydie's old house.

That house held more than memories—it held the energies of Jewish learning and beyond, the love of the ancestors. The smallest nuances had meaning: the red, white, and black brick pattern that framed the outside of the house; the chandelier in the lobby, beneath which Bobe and Zaydie had greeted us regularly as we grew to adolescence and then manhood; the small kitchen with the yellow half-curtains at the window, and that folding table, sometimes covered with Bobe's steaming meatloaf, at other times filled with stacks of letters to the editor Zaydie had written on behalf of ZOD, the Zionist Organization of Detroit, where he served for decades, directing Public Affairs; the jars of herring he would eat, reminiscent of the Old Country, next to the matzahs, under the record player in the corner; beyond that, the kitchen sink where I used to help Bobe dry the dishes, and the pantry in the corner, where I would sneak chocolate almonds; the sunken living room, with a baby grand piano at which I spent hours, playing classical tunes and show music; one step above that, the dining table, where our Passover Seders connected us through the ages to all who had made a similar exodus to freedom; the less formal living room, almost a large study, with a lazy-boy chair by a grandfather clock, a sofa covered with hand-knit pillows, a charcoal drawing of my mother in her teens (looking studious diagonally across the frame); and a built-in bookshelf filled with volumes on science or Judaism, as well as, somewhere tucked inside, some of Zaydie's writings, such as his dissertation back in the 1930's on the need for a Jewish state, or his commentary on the Torah.

On the other side of the kitchen, a corridor led to a bathroom, where I used to find small toothbrushes (Zaydie tended to buy in bulk as it saved money) for my frequent stay-overs; the small study where Zaydie composed his writings and made his phone calls on the rotary phone; and then the bedrooms, the children's one, still covered by the bedspread that Aunt Naomi used growing up, and the master bedroom, with circular windows opening up to the yard, and a polished wood bedroom set, with drawers stuffed full of matches they saved from every restaurant they had ever visited.

The neighborhood apparently had changed since we had sat shiva for Zaydie, and Bobe had sold the house. As I gazed through the kitchen window, I was flooded with many beautiful memories: spreading butter on the matzah; flipping through Zaydie's Time-Life science books; leaning back in the lazy-boy or playing the piano for my aunts. Now, someone else was enjoying the space. It was hard to imagine: this permanence of the structure, and the impermanence of so much that had been significant; the fact that the bricks had outlived us, that our memories of love were of lives lived, that everything flowed, sooner or later, into the spirit realm. On the one hand, by this point in my life, I felt so connected to the spirit world, there hardly seemed any separation at all; yet still, as an embodied being, I grieved, mourned the loss of what physically was, noticed the abiding sweetness of each memory.

As we turned the corner, I noticed a sign on the driveway: "This house is protected by the blood of Jesus." It was as if one religion had been supplanted by another, and the memories of connection through our rich heritage discarded. I felt the new occupants as intruders on my precious memories. I knew this was irrational, but nonetheless, the feelings held sway. I mentioned this to my wife. She responded by noting the continuity of religious connection, and that the relationship with Spirit is universal, no matter what its specific expression. The new owners were honoring God in their way as we had in ours.

Bobe reminded me that when I was a child, I enjoyed helping her cook tomatoes by engaging in the "tomato wars:" I would pretend that we were boiling the enemy. It is hard to believe that I would use such a gruesome metaphor. I have some colored drawings I made in second-grade: one series shows people bent over in two dragging the pyramids into place; another drawing shows a person on his knees, saying: "O Lord, what I have done?" Throughout grade school, I read everything I could about the Holocaust, preoccupied with the problem of good and evil.

A Native American myth states that all the creatures of the Earth got together to decide where to hide God, since they knew that humans, being inclined to destroy everything in nature around them, would be likely to apply this same destructive tendency to the divinity. Finally, a wise one said: "let's hide God within the human heart, within the heart of the two-legged, since that way they will never find him." This is a sad but funnily wise commentary on our shared dilemma: this secret hiding place is where we need to find political wisdom, not in words but in the experience whose fruit is the unconditional love for all beings of which so many religious traditions ultimately speak.

The ancestors, the deceased, those linked to us through family and love, speak through us, live through and alongside us. In achieving, we honor them as well as ourselves. We dedicate our merits to their continuing evolution in the spiral of *teshuva*, return to God. I sense them around me, around all of us, assisting and also benefiting. This sensing is visual as well as kinesthetic and frequently auditory. They are present in the moment. Sol gave us his autobiography as a wedding gift, and in it I learned more about my ancestral heritage. Uncle Sol writes:

Although I was only nine years old when departing Poland for America, the depth of my birthplace image as perpetually Jew hating and nothing more than a killing field as far as Jews were concerned, was deeply ingrained in my memory.

At Easter, he had to hide, because the "agitated" non-Jews "rushed into our backyard," fueled by the blood libel. The story is painful familiar to Jewish identity, and to identity as a human in the cosmos: Cain versus Abel, a history of murderous adversity repeated again and again in cycles of massacres across peoples and places. Sol writes that eighty-three of ninety relatives were killed in the Holocaust. He takes us through the burning and destruction of Sczuszczyn, the village where our family grew up.

Sol writes that according to other teachers in the village, Avraham's grandfather Zalman was the greatest scholar of Szscusczyn. Zalman, "with his snow-white hair and the white beard that shrouded him," recited the Shema (Hear O Israel) as he died. In telling our family's story, he adds idiosyncratic detail—for example, that his grandmother "always had many cats in her house." He writes of the journey to the new country. Bobe Rive sent her husband to the U.S.:

With four boys to raise, and no source of income, strong-willed, visionary Ma insisted that her gentle husband, a Hebrew teacher and scholar, set off on a journey to the 'promised land' so that their family could escape the tribulations, present and future, in treacherous Poland. Pa used his meager savings to clear boat passage and with only the clothes on his back and a small 'peckel' (a large handkerchief draped around dried bread), a bar of soap, comb, toothbrush and siddur (prayer book), Tanah (Hebrew Bible), he began his epic journey.

God had told Abraham: *lech lecha me-artzecha asher yadata ahser noladeticha*. Go you, leave your land, which you have known, which gave you birth; the poetic repetition in the

A Friend of All Faiths

Hebrew gives poignancy to Abraham's leave-taking of everything he has known. Avraham, my great-grandfather, left his birth-land with almost no personal possessions, yet carried the books of his faith.

Two years later my Zaydie came; and three years later, the rest of the family. Sol and brothers arrived in the United States with *no* money; his mother had at most five dollars. Sol's father, my great-grandfather Avraham ("Pa") worked as Hebrew schoolteacher for United Hebrew School of Detroit (where I later studied Talmud) and lived on script issued by the city during the Depression. My Zaydie and his brother Beryl were teaching in Wilkes-Barre, Pennsylvania (I later had a house not too far from there in rural Pennsylvania).

"Pa," Sol writes, became an "author, teacher, playwright, both in verse and music" and organized the first Hebrew library in Michigan. Sol quotes my great-grandfather Avraham as saying: "Everything was created in God's image—this is our awareness." This quotation resonated; how I loved the quotation over the gateway to the ashram—"see God in each other;" and how the few recorded words of my great-grandfather jibe with this universal vision.

Bobe Rive ("Ma") also was instrumental in establishing the library for the United Hebrew Schools; during the Depression, she sold toilet paper from door to door to raise funds for

this cause. According to Sol, she had "abiding faith in the world beyond the grave." She spoke Yiddish, Hebrew, English, Polish, and Russian; "God was her companion and friend."

Bobe Rive apparently was quite astute in her politics: she ran a small hardware store in Sczusczyn, where:

She would turn the large photo on the wall so the czar would be seen, for on the flip side was the Kaiser, to be displayed whenever the Germans would recapture the village.... To fight with guile without being slaughtered was survival and Ma was a survivor.

She was also a prolific writer, keeping notes in Yiddish on scraps of paper and on the side of a cardboard carton. After Bobe Rive's death, my Zaydie and Sol found among her papers a letter dated August 30, 1945, in Yiddish from a relative who had survived the Holocaust and fled to Alemlo, Holland. The letter chronicles the deaths of the Panushes and other villagers.

Zaydie (picture above) wrote:

Although I translated this letter primarily for my children and grandchildren to read and remember, I felt that it should be read by others, Jews and non-Jews, for whom the Holocaust is a tragic period in Jewish history, but which now, decades later—some think—perhaps should be gradually forgotten. As I translated the letter I remembered the small town with its 3000 Jews, the streets, the buildings, the stores, and old and new shuls, the people ... all of them gone, all of them brutally down away with...May their memory be blessed!

In 1993 I traveled to Byelorussia to help with hands-on healing for children who had suffered radiation from Chernobyl. The journey opened yet another channel to the ancestors in the form of auditory guidance. The guidance poured in as I connected powerfully to the children whose lives had been shattered by nuclear radiation. Many were speaking: ancestors, guides, and various healers from the past. I felt I was making a sort of reparation to the land, bringing healing where many of my family had been murdered: a gift offering of love where we had experienced hatred. The physical visit was also a psychical encounter.

Sol had visited Bialystock (where Sczusczyn is located) in 1988. One of the places he visited was his high school, Tarbut Hebrew High School. I was curious to see the name, since I also attended a Hebrew school called Tarbut, in Buenos Aires, Argentina. Sol's visit included the old grounds were his family members were murdered, now covered over with grass; included Treblinka, about two hours southwest of Bialystok.

Bobe Rive's parents, Joseph and Shayne Tzirl Bernshtein, wrote a letter to their daughter on September 16, 1929. As recorded in Sol's book, they wrote as their daughter prepared to emigrate to the U.S., knowing they would likely never see her again. They spoke of their grief, and encouraged her to raise her children through Judaism; to have them put on their phylacteries (tefillin) each day, to say the Shema, to keep the Sabbath.

Do not think that your mother is an ordinary woman. God listens to me when I beseech him.... When one is true to God, then God is true to man.... A person does not live forever. One needs to give an accounting to God. Man's worldliness is not eternal. He does not take away with him what he eats or drinks—only the good deeds which he has performed.

And so it was, and so it is—a longing for God that began long before this writer came into this world, and that will persist long after his departure.

HARVARD TO ATLANTIS

(CAMBRIDGE AND THE BAHAMAS,
2000-04)

Contemplating the existence of God on a pink sand
beach in the Bahamas (above) and during a
Fellowship at the Center for the Study of World
Religions, Harvard Divinity School (below).

Finding God in nature while visiting
the island of Eleuthera, in the Bahamas.

SANCTUARY

I am standing on the Mount of Olives, overlooking the old city of Jerusalem. The sweeping vista suggests the confluence of at least three major faiths. Perhaps even more faiths are represented, if it is true that between ages twelve and thirty, Jesus visited the East and integrated influences from Buddhism, Hinduism, and other religions into his teachings. Layers of history unfold before the gaze. Immediately below—a road paved by invading Arab armies from the desecrated tombstones of Jewish settlers; further down, churches that sprang up in places where Jesus was supposed to have preached; also remnants of ancient synagogues and ancestral burial places.

At sixteen, I am wearing a yarmulke that is attached via bobby pin to my head. I stand on holy ground in the desert heat with a dozen classmates and a guide. It is 1978, a year of long hair and bell-bottoms. I have an "afro," curly hair that I maintain with a metal pick in my pocket, and decidedly unstylish clashing clothing. Standing on the Mount of Olives, the yarmulke perches effortlessly on my head, as much a part of my anatomy as the cell-phone is in today's world. But while the cell-phone reminds us of horizontal connections (to other humans), the yarmulke reminds of connection to God. Re-minds. *Da liphne mi atah omed*, the text admonishes: know before Whom you stand.

Now, I am still standing on the Mount of Olives. Only the setting is a tea bar in Cambridge. Carved wooden masks adorn the walls; bamboo and bonsai trees, the tables. Eclectic music filters through the speakers—Bob Marley, trance chant, gospel and blues, jazz fusion, sacred music. It is an easy place to write about God, Yahweh, Jesus, Buddha Self, Gurdjieff's Self-Remembering, Plato, the commandment to Remember, Awaken, Know the Self. The year is 2004; I have shorter hair—no yarmulke; Birkenstocks, or maybe comfortable "Earth shoes," no socks; a buttoned-down Oxford shirt. Here I blend into anonymity, catching snippets of conversation and watching auras. Rising to order another cup of green tea, I still try to recall before Whom I stand.

Peter, stirring the tea leaves beside me, reminds me of this statement:

On the spiritual path, first you realize you're Nobody.
Then you begin to think you're Somebody.
And finally, you recognize that you are Everybody.

One of the gifts I receive from my friend Peter is learning how to integrate the sublime and the mundane—how to incorporate spiritual experience alongside the ordinary. Peter can relate to experiences of traveling among different realms of consciousness, yet we just as easily talk about daily struggles—mowing the lawn, taking out the trash, dealing with "alternate side of the street parking" in Boston, figuring out logistics, conflict resolution on the job and in marriage, the realities of running a business, and other facts of life in this body.

And, as men who work hard for a living, and are never sure whether today's income will arrive in as fair a portion tomorrow, we talk a lot about money.

I entered the new millennium in debt, just a few thousand short of clearing my negative balance—and that small gap in credit felt like an enormous spiritual deficit. Not so for nations or individuals who find being indebted a way of life; not so for those who *expect* Social Security to be bankrupt. But debt, I knew, exists on a spiritual as well as material level—it needs to be cleared completely, lest we have to undertake birth again to repay it.

I had worked hard to pay off the "negative balance." But a new client had just cheated me of payment due. Now I was on spiritual retreat, studying scriptures about bliss being the ultimate nature of reality, but psychologically, I was consumed with anger against this individual. This anger became thief of my inner resources—my own mind thieving against itself by not letting go of the anger.

In meditation, I received these words:

You've become a healer to the nations. Endure the finance charges. See God's

hand in everything you do. Then you will attain Liberation.
The phrase *healer to the nations* did not swell my head with visions of power and authority–it was merely recognition that the direction my work as a healer had taken since graduating from healing school involved law and policy, working at the level of institutions rather than individuals. And I was being guided to *endure*.
The rest of the message counseled not getting caught up in temporary balances, but rather in continuing to 'run the race,' as Paul would put it, all the way to the end:
Daily you scrape off the karmic residue–accumulated crusts of lifetimes.... Wise man, be a fool for God's love. Stoke the fire of Liberation. Your longing isn't strong enough till you are thoroughly disgusted with the rapture of the world. Its false icons consume mad hopes and dash their brains to the rocks of folly. Like sunflower seeds their vital energies scatter through the window. Praise the indwelling Lord, Reckoner of hearts. You know him well enough by now. He certainly knows you–the noose around your temporal neck and the choke-hold your ministerial duties exert and afflict. He will release you in time from your groaning if only you let him. Let go, proud warrior. Be not ashamed to eat a beggar's feast. To toast the new millennium with a pauper's eye. You will be handsomely paid in God's coin minted in His image. He will stamp His impression on you so powerfully you will never forget your eternal union.
By reminding myself of my ultimate purpose on spiritual retreat, I might release the contracted feelings around money issues.
Eternal bliss is your divine birthright. Earthly treasures can neither augment nor decrease it. This bliss does not wax and wane like your finances–like your mind does....
To bear one's little cross with equanimity is a high achievement–difficult in practice. Infallibly, like clockwork, being short at the end of the month was dogging me. And there was a nagging discomfort in this: it does no good to achieve supreme enlightenment and then have something due on the MasterCard or Visa–instead of escaping the wheel of death and rebirth, one incarnates to pay off the mortgage. I despised debt: it had become my sworn enemy, and I *will* defeat it, I thought. Then again, *willing* something rarely brings wholeness.
Seeking solutions, some would argue: why not apply the divine solvent of spiritual practice to manifesting money? Surely, I could pray for money; why not? People pray for lesser things, such as parking spaces on a crowded street (and I sometimes wonder how God can look for a parking space when She is busy stopping wars; is this not overloading a divine consciousness already crazily multi-tasking?)
A friend at the Workshop did pray for money, and then it turned out that someone he loved died, and left him a pile of money–he felt incredibly guilty, and decided never again to pray for something material. And did Jesus not say that person "cannot worship both God and Mammon"... "it is easier for a camel to go through the eye of a needle..." I did not pray for money. But my reaction to the untidy situation shifted from minor annoyance to degradation and humiliation. I wondered: Do angels have credit cards, or do they pay everything up front? Or, as angels, are they freed from the concept of payment–merely cogs in the divine machine, giving freely because they are commanded to do so, because that is their programming; while we, cursed as well as blessed with free will, struggle bravely onward, chained to the ledger of debit and credit? Welcome to the human race.

In meditation on the year 2000, I received this guidance:
Remember, Michael, the purpose of your birth is to write about these things–you are amanuensis–a universal translator of God's teachings on different planets and systems of knowledge.
The guidance firmly reminded me that bridging worlds–medicine and healing, law and spirituality, religious tradition and mystical experience–were ultimately important; that while

Michael H. Cohen

balancing my checkbook counted, the spiritual journey was primary. Such reminders have grown constant. When my head hits the pillow each night, the "my" completely disappears. My vision is engulfed by a brilliant purple light; my awareness grows initially beyond my body to the outer layers of the aura. I feel a swirling, electric energy–the kundalini–moving not just around my spine, but around this entire, egg-shaped, luminous structure, that is somehow "me." I am not identified with my thoughts, feelings, or body, as my awareness of what is "me" is now much larger. I do "see" movies on the screen of my mind–things that have happened and the larger spiritual energies and forces around them; things that are to come; things that might come or might be averted through awareness and practice. Cognitively, this all makes sense: "we fight not against the flesh, but against principalities of darkness...."

There are angels as well as demons; the experiences are vivid, authentic, living history in one plane or another, and it becomes difficult to differentiate "dream" from "vision" from "meditation" from "journey." Adam named the animals, but they are what they are independent of the name; and so pure awareness exists, independent of what I call its object. Patanjali differentiated different kinds of *Samadhi*, the unbounded awareness, and included both awareness of an object in its totality and pure awareness. My consciousness seems to shift of its own accord–moved by the intelligent, supreme consciousness of the kundalini–through these various kinds of levels.

At some point, the movie simply *is*–and the "I" watching is no more; my awareness has expanded beyond the purple, egg-shaped aura and to something larger. Sometimes that becomes a group of people, an event, or even the planet or galaxy or entire universe. And just as quickly, I can plunge back into worrying about my tax return or the laundry or tomorrow's meeting or something equally mundane. I travel, I travel: I am carried to other lands.

This book weaves together many different strands of my own contemporary spirituality, including my appreciation both for the heritage of the ancestors I carry in this birth and for universal heritage of humankind. Nick provided one (humanly flawed) doorway to a rich path bejeweled with many other experiences. And I have been drawn at various times to various paths and beings–during the time with Nick, to Mary; at other times, to Krishna; at other times, to the Jewish mystics, the Sabbath bride, the Torah, and the Hebrew melodies. Just as one drifts through a museum–drawn now to the Impressionists, then to contemporary art–so I have been drawn to different expressions of the same universal truths. In moving through different spiritual traditions, I have been integrating and adapting teachings to my individual journey, bringing the universal, home.

Cambridge, Massachusetts: "a shining intellectual center for the planet," I thought, while admiring the ancient intelligences beaming through the red bricks. Walking through the campus with Peter, we could feel the souls who had passed through these portals. I was glad to have been drawn to this place.

Ten years earlier I had left the world of New York law firms and interviewed for positions as a law school faculty member, I stood at Georgetown University where the interviews were held, staring at the adjacent medical school building and asking: *Haven't You made a mistake? Aren't I supposed to be there, across the street, at the med school rather than law school?*

By a chain of events over seven years, I ended up as a faculty member at Harvard, specifically within the medical school, where I learned to re-tool my legal skills as a medical academic by writing grants, publishing, and lecturing on medico-legal topics related to the integration of complementary and alternative medical therapies into conventional hospitals.

My professional path had evolved considerably over these years around building a legal structure to support holistic health care. The inquiry had begun in 1992–the same year Congress established an Office of Unconventional Medical Practices at the National Institutes of Health--as a two-page memo and research and writing assignment of similar

HARVARD TO ATLANTIS

(CAMBRIDGE AND THE BAHAMAS,
2000-04)

Contemplating the existence of God on a pink sand beach in the Bahamas (above) and during a Fellowship at the Center for the Study of World Religions, Harvard Divinity School (below).

Finding God in nature while visiting
the island of Eleuthera, in the Bahamas.

Michael H. Cohen

the underlying dynamics the auras represented, and by naming the dynamic, to create safety and opportunity for learning.

I flew back to Southern California, my old home, for the final session of the Institute of Medicine's Committee on Public Use of Complementary and Alternative Medicine. Struggles persisted. Here I was consulting on legal matters, in my essence as lawyer-healer, fully empowered, sitting on a prestigious committee with medical luminaries, and staying at a luxury palace of a hotel. At the same time, I had overdrawn my account and gotten myself in a fix the machines and after-hours clerks could not resolve. Consequently, after an exhausting flight and bus ride to one car rental agency, I was re- shuffled via courtesy van to another rental agency and waited again in a two-hour line. When I finally made it to a live human clerk, my credit card was declined, which meant I had to wait for the rental car courtesy bus and take it all the way back to Los Angeles Airport. I had just enough cash to take a Super Shuttle down to Orange County. The Shuttle circled the airport so long, looking for extra passengers, made so many stops, bumpety-bump, that when it arrived at the Four Seasons, I staggered out, dehydrated and dizzy, and nearly vomited on one of my esteemed colleagues who stood, radiant in a suit, holding his wife's hand, on the marbled entranceway, greeting me with enthusiasm while elegantly dressed staff were opening the hotel door to chime, "Welcome!"

A little discombobulation is good for the soul, and I had asked for it. "Please God, take away my ego. I'm not asking for riches, or fame, or worldly glory, just burn my ego in the fire." I had jumped into the sacred fire pit (it was dry, no fire was burning) sometime in eternal time back in the ashram, and made my plea. So here I was, burning in the sacred fire, nearly puking on my esteemed medical colleagues due to divinely ordained, humanly requested, severe disorientation. Consider the *Bhagavad-Gita*, quoted in commentary to a translation of Patanjali's *Yoga Sutras* by Swami Prabhavananda and Christopher Isherwood (p. 110):

Thinking about sense-objects will attract you to sense-objects; Grow attached, and you become addicted; Thwart your addiction, it turns to anger; Be angry, and you confuse your mind; Confuse your mind, you forget the lesson of experience; Forget experience, you lose discrimination; Lose discrimination, you miss life's only purpose.

I had underlined it, read it a thousand times. But in practice....And there were new anxieties, primarily having to do with surviving through grant cycles and the search for philanthropy at Harvard: descent into degradation, humiliation, dissimulation alongside the ecstasy of intellectual discovery.

Again, the two parts of my being combine: Lawyer and Healer, West and East, rational and intuitive, whatever archetypes you may choose.

I am sitting with a colleague who has been hired as a consultant to help us plan our integrative care clinic. We are discussing the liability and financial issues around building the clinic. She is five months pregnant. In the middle of our conversation, I hear the child in her womb: "I can't wait to be born!" I continue our discussion of business issues, acting nonchalant, and meanwhile feel such an excitement from this being about incarnating. My whole field is buzzing. My eyes grow brighter and I feel more enlivened as I carry on two conversations, one with my colleague and the other with her unborn child. That day, the head of a government committee to study and propose acupuncture regulation calls and asks for comment on a draft report: should acupuncture scope of practice be tied to efficacy? Why should consumers have access to "unproven therapies?"

I am reminded in meditation and in dreams of the density of the inner life, compared to which the outer world seems a shell. I was having viscous experiences in dreamland about the Jewish contours of my childhood: the beauty of the sacred biblical language, that I lived, that I breathed, studying for the Hebrew Bible Contest, memorizing endless passages from Jeremiah. *I loved you while you were still in the womb.* And: *lechtech acharai bamidbar be-eretz lo zruyah* (you followed Me in the desert in a land that had not yet been sown). Standing at the *bimah* (the 'podium') in synagogue, holding the *yad* (literally the 'hand,' the pointer for the Torah), chanting the calligraphic letters, white fire on black fire, written by the finger of God, Cantor Rube standing at my side, following with his eyes, facing rows and rows of worshippers in the congregation over the sight path of the parchment scroll. Sitting in synagogue with my Zaydie, playing with the fringes of my *tallis*, reading the commentators in the *siddur* or prayerbook ... visiting his mother, my great-grandmother, Bobe Rive, at the Federation Apartment in Detroit, as she prayed out of the same *siddur* she used as a child in Poland ... watching my brother Daniel sow new designs for yarmulkes, which he embossed with classmates' names ... teaching him songs learned in United Synagogue Youth....

As God is One, so it is one spirituality that issues forth: the same spirituality that fed Talmud and Torah into my heart and mind resonates in the upcoming trip to India; speaks to me in the white shadows that line the walls as I tune into my guides.

There are visions and meditations and many voices that have come and continue to infiltrate this seemingly solid reality. I have selected snippets of events that influenced this path, and for reasons of space omitted many layers of stories that deserve telling and may be told elsewhere (they say each person contains universes). I have written *A Question of Time* on Ericksonian hypnotherapy and learning the language of trance, of the unconscious mind; and *Healing Nuclear Absurdity: A Memoir of Children in Chernobyl* to describe the visit to Byelorussia. Those and this memoir are linked by the quest for God, the Self, Realization, wisdom, via multidimensional experience. And the journey is ongoing: Earth school.

Within the classroom, the notion of karma is rather like the links on a Web page: you *click* on this event or that one, and are led to another page explaining more, giving background and updates; you click on a link on that page and are led to another Page of Your Life History, of Your Karmic History going back through infinity to the "Big Bang" when the One Great Soul split into millions of fragments—a terrible accident, Jewish mystical scriptures assert, when the "vessels of light" were broken; a great boon, other traditions claim, since God split Himself and Herself into all of us. It is comforting to know that even God has karma. Comforting to know, to believe—are they the same thing?

Even God has to reckon with action-reaction, with the principle that thought precedes manifestation. Back in fifth grade, I wrote these lines in poem:

God was lonely, so He said I think can
Create another being—and I'll call it Man.

Readers will, I hope, forgive the gender-based reference of 1970.

The other day I cut my foot. I was thinking rather than being—going over a busy "to do" in mind head while rushing toward a talk I was scheduled to give at Massachusetts General Hospital (MGH). I tripped over my folders and into the radiator—an open piece of metal that we should have repaired earlier sliced into my second toe. Suddenly blood was dripping onto the carpet; tiny pools of blood fell onto the hardwood floors. Whenever blood flows, I pay attention. What had I done? Why this, now? I could not tune in as I had to get to MGH. Fortunately, the department in which I was speaking was just past and above the emergency room, so when I dropped in to the ER to ask for some Neosporin and a band-aid, the triage nurse examined the wound and said I would need stitches.

Promptly after the talk, I checked in for the minor surgery.

In a flash I exchanged one status for another: the Harvard faculty member, wearing his best tie to share knowledge with docs at one of *the* elite world hospitals, to a guy in the ER, bleeding, waiting in the visitors' area with the rank-and-file, oppressed by the blaring news about war overhead on the screen. Truly we are all made of the same stuff—we all bleed, we all have bodies; it reminds me of a Talmudic exchange about whether it is ever ethical to

Michael H. Cohen

kill another person, to which one of the rabbis replies that you should never kill another human being, "for who is to say that your blood is redder than someone else's?" Truly in the ER all blood was the same red, whether from a Boston Brahmin blueblood or someone from a "lesser caste." *File away*: great movie title–Children of a Lesser Caste. Starring William Hurt, perhaps. One of the psalms describes how God can humble mighty princes (and princesses), and raise the low to a mighty stature. In the ER, I felt gratitude that this blood-soaked event was so small, that again I had been spared something more difficult. And yet, even this injury to this toe reminded me of how vulnerable we are in the body–even though so many of us identify ourselves almost entirely with the body, most of the time.

I have to acknowledge the efficiency, care, and dedication of the MGH ER staff–and realized I had written in *Future Medicine* about my prior ER encounter, which was obnoxious and antithetical to any notion of "healing." *Disclosure*: I own no stock in MGH and presently receive no consulting fees whatsoever or research grant from the institution. So I can praise the care received without any conflict-of-interest. In any event, the individual who cared for me (with the intermittent supervision of the attending physician) was a third-year medical student.

Small, focused, and kind, she immediately connected with me as a person.

From this drama of blood and sewing was that I was able to witness the procedure consciously–I watched everything, from injection of the anesthetic into the top of my toe to the suturing. I had always had a fear of surgery, but watching the student concentrate I felt reassured. I admired her total focus–and also had a sense of many guides around her, watching, encouraging, and assisting in the process.

When the anesthetic first went in, I felt the pain shoot up my leg with such intensity I thought I might pass out. Moments later, the toe was so numb I could not feel it pricked with a long needle. I remarked on the rapidity and intensity of the pain and its equally rapid disappearance; asked about the mechanism of action, and learned that pain resulted from the rapidity of nerve firings (the anesthetic slowed these firings down). We both remarked on how "spiritual" medicine could be. If meditation involved slowing down the nerve firings, great synaptic leapfrogging, and undulating sodium-potassium-intra-ionic meanderings of the mind, then there was a great correlation between this process and at least one form of medical treatment on the physiological, intracellular level, for pain.

Also, if our nerves were so sensitive that a tiny injection could alter my consciousness so much in either direction (almost to blacking out on one hand, and to numbness on another), then surely they were equally sensitive to detecting other realms through altered states of consciousness; meaning that it was entirely plausible, to me, that we could make connections with other worlds. We have a kind of DSL or fiber optical line to other galaxies, other gods and goddesses or aspects of the One God, other parts of ourselves, and those who have gone before. Surely we could have these cables and cords, invisible now except through high-sense perception, just as we have black holes that drop us through space-time and Ethernet cables (interesting name: that invisible substance, ether) to communicate with humans across the oceans.

And just as surely, I mused while watching the sewing, we can use our nerves to overload our attention and focus on tasks, connecting to fellow humans through electronic media rather than body-to-body exchange with all its visual, behavioral, and energetic cues. Spending all day typing messages to people across space and time has an effect on my nerves; I much prefer the one-on-one. To "see God in each other" I like to "practice the presence of God" by actually being in someone's presence. If I was having serious surgery, I would not send an email to God and ask for an email back–I would want to see God right there, by the surgeon, in the room. (A colleague routinely sat through meetings with both thumbs fully engaged on two 'Blackberries,' typing messages through space and time to contacts and minions–in this truly a hybrid, Cyborg, half-machine, multi-tasking beyond previously understood human-machine limits.)

Our nerves could bring pleasure or pain, contact with many different kinds of experience,

A Friend of All Faiths

and they could fire at different speeds, sending information appropriate to a given experience. Metaphorically, the nerves expressed, the choice was ours: we could connect to any form of consciousness, human, machine, animal, spirit, ghost, and on and on. They would be steady servants of the Ultimate Message selected for transmission.

Once my nerve-firings of pain had slowed to an imperceptible point, I could attune more readily to the room rather than the perception of pain. Shreya (the student surgeon) expressed appreciation for our conversation as she focused on prepping the area with iodine, keeping a sterile field, sorting out the instruments, applying the anesthetic, testing its effect, and suturing up the wound. She next confessed her skepticism about "all this waste"–she would be discarding so many gloves, instruments, paper, cloth, after the procedure; whereas in India, they would re-use a rubber glove again and again. Standards of care and resources were very different in her birth country.

As we talked, she seemed pleasantly surprised that I, the patient, was not rushing her–pressuring her to move more quickly so that I could get to my next important cell phone call or email. I was amazed that she was being conditioned to receive this from patients. After all, she was the caregiver and I the one being taken care of; did I not owe her a lifetime debt of gratitude for her great care in mending my broken body? (Or perhaps I had sutured her on some battlefield, and the debt was being repaid).

I had written so much on efforts to reverse paternalism in medicine and the need to emphasize the ethical value of patient autonomy–and yet, from the perspective of this medical student, many patients were more than autonomous: they were bullying, so much so that she had come to expect it.

I watched the creative and focused suturing proceed, admiring the care and single-pointed attention that Patanjali had also characterized as a form of Samadhi. As she finished up her labor of love, I asked: "Doesn't *shreya* mean 'the good'? Don't the *Upanishads* speak of *shreya* and *preya*?"

"The good and the pleasurable," she nodded, smiling. "You sure know your stuff."

"Well, you never know who your caretaker will be."

The *Upanishads* inform that in every moment we have a choice between the good and the pleasurable–the latter brings an instantaneous feeling of benefit but has long-term consequences, while the former may require discipline but brings lasting benefit. In some sense the sages knew what economists do–that you cannot go around forever piling up debt (K-Debt, Karmic Debt, not just National Debt), accumulating pleasures; cannot trade your long-term future for short-term gain. Thus *Shreya*, the Good, stands for choosing what is ultimately beneficial.

The Buddhists say that you should regard every being as your mother in a former life. Transference aside, I would say this profound realization marked the exchange. I left filled with appreciation and a sense that I wanted to offer to be helpful if ever I could professionally. As I got off the table, I told her my website–keeping an appropriate boundary as the patient–in case, I said, she ever was to build and run three charitable hospitals in India and one for-profit here.

"Especially the former!" she exclaimed as she removed her rubber gloves and disposed of the remaining iodine prep in the trashcan. With that affirmation, she embodied her name. What a great attitude for a third-year Harvard Medical School student. What a *mahatma*.

That night, sure enough, I had a dream: an Indian woman told me that her father had esoteric knowledge about two principles in the scriptures, *Panna* and *Ranni*.

On awakening, I reflected on the meaning of the dream. Clearly the Indian woman was an archetypal image raised by my encounter with Shreya. For Shreya, an embodied being, was more to my psyche than simply some nice medical student who sewed up my toe. She like all women was an embodiment of Parvati, just as all men were an embodiment of Shiva–all made in the image of God, all humans within whose hearts God, in Her and His totality, dwelt. Now from an objective, 'scientific' perspective, we could dismiss any heart on

Michael H. Cohen

my part as attraction toward a twenty-something-year-old, albeit just engaged to another medical student. And honesty, integrity requires that psychological dynamics not be buried in spiritual talk.

But I would submit that a deeper, more eternal, more divine love was exchanged in that encounter, and that I am able to distinguish emotions from energies on a soul or transcendental level–that a deeper level of psychological and spiritual maturity is available to us than that presented by the caricature of spiritual teachers who act out through boundary violations. I submit that the appreciation that flowed between us was set in the mature realization that we each were playing out our karmically-assigned roles; that in *this* lifetime, this encounter, she might be the doctor and I the patient, but that in other realms of consciousness, we might have other identities. Who know who was paying whom, for what?

Payback time comes, we do not always know the rules; we only know to pay or be paid with detachment. I use the word love–divine love–knowing that I am completely detached as to whether I will ever see this being again in this lifetime. Just as I am aware that my contact with Athena, who may have been my spouse ages ago, may be sporadic and fleeting in the incarnation we now inhabit. Love from a place of detachment is very different from the stuff that fills the garbage-can of contemporary books and films: namely, the obsessive, violating behavior that inevitably damages individuals and families.

In my dream, whatever Shreya represented to the psyche became simply: an Indian woman. Since I am not in relationship with this human, I do not know what she is like in ordinary exchange: whether she gets angry when the toothpaste cap is not screwed on, or the toilet seat kept up, or other mundane details in embodied existence. I do not idealize her, put her on a pedestal, psychologically; but in my dream she becomes an archetype. That, too, is part of her identity, as it is in mine–we archetypes exchange energy in the surgery ward as in the coffeehouse.

Curiously, the topic of Shreya's father never arose during our conversations–thus, he too was something my psyche lifted from our brief exchange. *Panna* was the name of a woman associated with my spiritual teacher. So I conflated the heart-connection with my spiritual teacher with conversations with Shreya about the *Upanishads* during suturing. *Ranni* stood for Ronny, my uncle Ronald who died of colon cancer. My mother had mentioned Ronny during our dinner that night (she and my father happened–once again–to come to town the very day I had a physical accident, this one involving a cut to my foot and not a car). I was close to Ronny–someone once 'channeled' that he and I had been brothers. Somehow my unconscious mind selected this one detail out of the entire dinner with my parents, and elevated Ronny into a symbol of secret knowledge from the *Upanishads*. In a way, he was. That is the greatness of heart-cords with those we love.

India: as of 2002, it is still a journey to come.

While meditating on an upcoming trip with my wife to study yoga in Southern India, I had a curious experience in meditation: I began to see faces, a few at first and then hundreds– faces of people I would meet on the street, in restaurants, temples, mosques, trains, rickshaws, everywhere. Each one is God. And yet, in my meditation, I could see Zaydie's essence in the eyes of a particular five-year-old India boy.

Will that boy, I wondered, someone we will meet in India, be a being in whom Zaydie, or part of his Oversoul, is reincarnated? Are we to come into deep contact with that boy, or just a casual encounter on the street? Did I see Zaydie's essence enter into more than one figure in the meditation-dream? I am not sure. Is this symbolic or psychic and literal? I do have a sense that Zaydie's essence can freely permeate different beings at different times– that bodies are permeable, and souls can pass through them. Curiously, that night my friend L called to tell me she kept seeing the letter "Z" over my body and was wondering what it meant. I knew it did not stand for "Zorro."

They say that in India there are horoscopes written thousand of years ago for each of us

- 203 -

in tiny script on palm leaves. A swami from the ashram told me he had traveled to India and seen palm leaves where his present-day American name had been written ages ago. I live professionally at the crossroads of health law, ethics, and policy: not all Ps are Qs but some Ps are; not all psychic forecasting is fraudulent and invalid but it is not all accurate either. Unfortunately our mental apparatus lacks the objective criteria of scientific method, so we have to rely on more nebulous but equally vital concepts such as discernment. And clearly my bias is in favor of opening the psychic instrument–to expansion of consciousness. There are those who would argue against this, and in favor of skepticism, based on our collective history of abusing religion, perpetuating crimes in the name of God. This is the price of free will, I would reply, and it cuts across technologies, whether the warfare be on material or subtle planes.

Past, present, and future are a mystery; all our worlds intersect. On falling asleep to these thoughts I recently heard: "Get ready for interstellar travel." I shifted, 'buckled up,' prepared myself–but there was no journey along the dimension of time; I simply *was* there, traveling among the stars, while simultaneously being in my bed, falling asleep. *No separation.* It is all one, I realized, occurring simultaneously in an omnipresent awareness of eternal being.

In these other dimensions of knowing, contact occurs telepathically. As some human beings are gifted with musical instruments and others with painting, and still others with dance, so it may be that beings from other galaxies have non-verbal awareness that match or surpass gifts of our yogis, but lack the color of emotions that humans still carry; or perhaps their brains have shed the primitive, animalistic portions and different forms of intelligence have evolved. As astrobiologist David Grinspoon suggests in *Lonely Planets*, why do we assume that the way our logical minds work will determine how races with thousands of millions of years greater technological and spiritual evolution than humans might behave? A Hebrew proverb says: the whole world is a narrow bridge, and the main thing is not to be afraid. *Kol haolam gesher tsar mei-od, ve-ha-icar lo lephached.*

In the early days of the Web, I put up my own website. Because of a glitch in Microsoft technology, the photograph of me had a bar going straight across the forehead, covering my third eye. This was less than pleasing. But a healer friend commented: "Your third eye is not ready to be shown publicly; there's too much power and information there, it has to be veiled." And so for a while I left the technological "glitch" sent by the "No-Coincidences Department" above.

My friend Jake, a psychiatrist affiliated with a top medical school, is concerned that people will misunderstand this manuscript–that my 'reputation' may suffer. Indeed, he is correct: I am on impeccable ground as a scholar and on shaky ground when revealing personal biases. The mask of objectivity is good protector, usually, so why should a professor, whose job it is to "profess" objective knowledge, turn the object of study on oneself? At worst, this can be narcissism or even grandiosity disguised as self-inquiry, and at best, will lend itself to multiple misinterpretations. Everything can be distorted: even mentioning a childhood influence such as Zionism can, in this world, lead to multiple innuendos.

I do not think I am grandiose; I still take out the cat litter and poop-scoop my dog. The ET, Jesus, Mary, Kwan Yin and Moses do not do this for me (though they may from time to time manifest a parking space when they're not otherwise engaged healing the planet from human ignorance). I do pay attention to my unconscious–following a tradition of great healing masters (let's say medical doctors and psychologists, and also yogis and others) who have done the same. And I am aware that parallel with the physical and mental life that I cherish, that seems so prominent, there is another life–one I dimly understand, that only few individuals (notably Gopi Krishna) have chronicled: the energetic awakening known in Indian religious traditions as kundalini, and sometimes ascribed to parallels in other religious paths. I am not entirely satisfied with this book, as it is uneven–telling stories in some places, telescoping events in others and narrating conclusions in yet others; some important details are entirely omitted and others given too much prominence. It is impossible to write a memoir of four decades in so few pages–equally impossible not to select according to themes; and I have probably overemphasized the triumph, or at least importance, of spiritual over material reality, whereas in truth these different worlds intersect, some back-grounded and others fore-grounded depending on the circumstances.

Jake's concern is also a compliment, since it suggests that someone may actually pay attention to my work in health care law and policy and find reason to critique the personality underlying the scholar's work. His concern additionally raises a question: does attending to inner voices and images diminish credibility?

Does it depend on whether one makes one's livelihood as a "spiritual teacher" or as a professor or professional? From another perspective, when one considers the pervasive nature of *maya*, cosmic delusion, and the pervasiveness of misunderstanding, loss, hostility, violence in this world, is there anything wrong with seeking illumination, with sharing as honestly as possible one's moments of realization, both as to spiritual successes and mistakes? Is it not the nature of contemplation and writing to attempt to emulate the divine eye? I offer myself in all my contradictions, in hopes of illuminating the personal paths of others.

And being as risk averse as any other, I asked my wife about Jake's concern.

She concurred that there is careful balance between too much disclosure and too much withholding; and remarked: "Maybe they'll be ready for it when you're an old man." By then I might view the whole thing differently–or have greater illumination, at least through experience in this world as the kundalini continues to rise and unfold. I do admire my wife's ability to peer beyond the present and see timelessness in any decision, to conflate time past and time future, to love me as I am, already knowing that we walk the journey of this physical body toward its ultimate dissolution.

I have written mindful of a reader, yet striving for authenticity. The journey I have taken, no doubt others will take, along individualized paths. As we become more and more connected to machines, and–with the advent of email, cell-phones, robots, nanotechnology, and on and on–less able to hold silence, it becomes even more important to dwell within; paradoxically, as the outer frontiers of science become increasingly accessible, it becomes increasingly important to explore what lies within. One of the frontiers toward which I hope this book will generate energy involves deeper psychological and spiritual synthesis, and the impact of this synthesis on all disciplines. For example, since all of our laws are premised on a three-dimensional view of the human being, what would happen we accounted for human energy fields when we regulated foods and drugs? The old philosophical question of mind-body dualism resurfaces–and whether we dwell in one, the other, or both, the contents of consciousness remain elusively enchanting.

I am speaking at a medical school conference. A moment before the talk I have stage fright; but once at the podium, a quiet, calm confidence takes over. The talk works its own magic with intelligence and humor. All the personal struggles are out of the arena, only a loving humor pervades my field. I am channeling the talk from a higher place of wisdom.

Someone asks: given the importance of the therapeutic relationship, if you know you've made a clinical mistake, should you apologize to the patient? There is a balance, I respond, between absolute truth telling and prudence. I wonder whether to tell the story of the "dog who did not take the Intensive," but tune in to my guides and take another tack. Hitting a few spiritual points seems to lift the audience–not so much as to raise hackles, but enough to raise the frequency.

Afterward I see an old friend, an acupuncturist whose steady gaze and deep, reassuring contact reminds me that we can connect at an essence level, that I need not wear such heavy armoring. Leading, healing, ministering, responding to questions individually, these are blessings, empowering not draining. My friend reminds me that law represents a pivot point in this field. She then asks how I have been and we share our struggles.

"It seems that everyone else is getting more armored," I say, "staring into their cell-phone visors and turning more to selfish pursuits; while I feel more and more vulnerable, the more turmoil I encounter. Why can't it get a little easier; why do I have to keep going in this direction?"

My friend smiles in gentle affirmation. "Because that's where the Power is." She points to her heart as she says the word "Power."

I watch the Boston rain flow, a perpetually suspended spring in a gray overcast. Castor and Pollux sit on the windowsill, perhaps tuning in to the guides. Are they thinking? Castor stares into space. I tune in.

I am here for you, Michael. Call on me when you need me. I am a spirit guide you do not yet know by name, but I hover around Castor and protect you when your grief grows too immense. It is the longing of centuries....Never doubt your love for any of the persons in your life; though on a mental and emotional level you feel depleted and drained and tired of these experiences, they do support and stimulate your growth....How beautifully you hold fragmented beings who cannot help but feel your longing for God....Divine timing will heal all the afflictions of your heart.

Jake had built an integrative care center that served thousands of patients over ten years. The center was a "Buddha sphere," a place of light, where love was palpable; he structured "seven levels of healing" to help patients move through all the levels of care, from chemotherapy to self-awareness, from physical disease management, to family healing and facing death, to deciding their goals during remaining moments of life. Ultimately the center proved too difficult to sustain financially, and after much anguish, he "pulled the plug." He told me this; we sat in a whirlpool after yoga during his visit to Cambridge on a snowy day of delayed spring. Through the spa windows, we watched the Charles River drift by, past the Kennedy School (dedicated to John F.). I was reminded of the John F. Kennedy library—recently it had displayed his doodles during the Cuban Missile Crisis. With all respect for rationality (in the face of the ultimate irrationality—destruction of the planet) and political strategy, I thought, *thank God for those doodles. They expressed the unconscious—he probably needed to access that, the place where wisdom resides (and then of course channel it through his rational mind).*

The doodles that saved the world.

Jake had some scheduled meetings regarding a databank he had collected during his years at the center. "In two months I will either declare bankruptcy or find myself wealthy. I could either find myself working twelve-hour days in biotech or going to India and meditating the rest of my days." In his tailored strip of a bathing suit, Jake could have been wearing a loincloth. He had traveled to India and age twenty and entered an ashram; he later went to medical school and became his guru's doctor; he then met another holy man in India who became his true teacher in Silence. As we shared our professional struggles and where we were, he was teaching me a profound level of letting go.

Those who work for selfish ends sink into the ocean of world existence, but a knower of truth knows all action to be non-action.

These words come from a chant. The sacred syllables of the chant always themselves reveal new truths to my being; I sit, and chant, and receive the sweetest, purest reality, allowing it to pour through me as the sounds continue emanating from the throat center. Jake was teaching me to live these words.

In August of 2001, we took a family vacation to France. My niece was only a year old, and we had also bonded around playtime with her. In addition, I had some unusual experiences—one involved seeing chakras in animals at the zoo; I could read their sadness

Michael H. Cohen

at being caged, and the expansion in their heart centers when nuzzling together. One of my brothers commented on one of the animals, half-humorously: "They made the head too large." Inside, I heard: "That's how I made them, Jonathan."

The other experience was a visit to the grave of painter Marc Chagall. Many visitors had placed small stones on his grave, as a token of respect; when I did so, I immediately heard: *Shalom*.

We returned on September 10, 2001. After thanking my father for the gift of this time and space together, I heard (for the first and only time) guidance in the little French I knew: *vous choisie le bon mot pour vos parents.* Was it from Chagall?

That night, my girlfriend at the time (later my wife) and I went to the restaurant at the top of Boston's Prudential Center. I kept focusing on the airplanes, blinking into existence from the night sky and swerving by our building before landing. I pointed out the planes. That night, I had a dream of a disturbing man on the beach, contemptuously throwing peanuts at people to get them to buy—sowing darkness. I heard:

Let him be, bless him; he is filled with demons. Don't partake in his karma by adding to his darkness. Love the Light in him—though he is far from it, I dwell in his heart. See him Realized—and some day he will realize My presence in him.

That same night, my friend Athena dreamed that she was in a plane with her husband. The plane crashed between two towers, and they could not reach each other or move. My girlfriend that same night dreamed that 9/11 was a code: the 11 stood for two towers, and the zero for a building (turned out to be the Pentagon).

September 11, 2001: My father and sister-in-law ran into each other on the streets of downtown New York, close to where I had worked on Wall street, and together saw the towers fall. Someone ran into my office, announcing that the U.S. was under attack. Later that day, the images played over and over on the news.

For a while the theory was pitched about an apocalyptic conflict between 'Western' religions and Islam, although subsequently the picture became more complicated. Somewhere, vaguely, there were memories of lives in the Arabic world—perhaps a mathematician, an astronomer, or maybe nobody at all.

Trauma and Recovery makes the observation (p. 242) that "entire communities can display symptoms of PTSD, trapped in alternating cycles of numbing and intrusion, silence and reenactment;" also (p. 32) that when post-traumatic stress disorder was first included in the diagnostic manual, the American Psychiatric Association described traumatic events as "'outside the range of usual human experience,'" whereas now, "sadly, this definition has proved to be inaccurate;" rather, "trauma, too, must be considered a common part of human experience; only the fortunate find it unusual." The whole world now was in PTSD.

I felt the negative power of the event lodged in my gut. I meditated to "unplug" from the swirling hatred, violence, and ugliness that was swirling as the media played and replayed the images of the towers falling.

In meditation, I heard my name in Arabic, followed by *Allah es Akbar*—Allah is Great. I then followed the thread of information from my guides:

Beware any negative thoughts about Muslims or Islam that might be a subtext on the news. Do not wish harm on anyone. They are also you, as well are all One, and God speaks to you from the inside also as Allah, Christ, Adonai.

I went to Boston Museum's of Fine Arts and sat in the temple exhibit, before the Buddha statues. I spoke to them telepathically. They in turn greeted me and wished me peace. I felt filled with peace. I moved into the room of the Pharaohs, then to Egyptian hieroglyphics. Again, here, I felt home.

Some days later, my girlfriend and I traveled to the ashram, where we chanted and meditated to uplift all humanity. My spiritual teacher was present. She spoke of how important it was to give one's best, one's highest. She emphasized that blessings *do* make a different, do uplift others. She stated that this was a war of ignorance—people ignorant of their true nature, of their own inner Light. She urged no blame, but rather responsibility—the

A Friend of All Faiths

ability to respond by serving with love.

At lunch the next day, I ate a burrito without blessing it.
That afternoon, I realized I had damaged my third chakra—the imbalanced vibrations of those who had prepared the burrito were still with me. I tuned in and learned it was important to bless food and thereby remove any karmic residue or impurities. Whether the blessing went to Allah, Christ, Adonai, Buddha, it was the blessing that mattered. I contemplated my teacher's talk.
In meditation, I saw my children, yet to be born, as my teachers: highly evolved and intelligent, with me on the inner planes. I also saw how my niece, less than a year old, was in her own way ministering to the family. In such a dark time, she provided joy, playfulness, lightness, humor. In her own child awareness, she was just being. But on a higher level, I sensed her as a wise teacher, healing the family, spreading joy, ministering to grief by reminding us of the love that existed within.

I heard many theories from friends of the 'karma' of 9/11. One said: "The concept of sacrificing one's body out of love is correct—as Jesus did it; the distortion is doing so from hate." Another: "The mental frequency is distorted when people think suicide bombing pleases God. These distortions are ancient; the thought-forms go back at least to the Crusades." And: "Some of them hate 'America' because they are reincarnations of Native American Indians who were oppressed." Then: "The best strategy is to become Liberated. Then the energy field of war that is gripping everyone's heart, both oppressor and oppressed, will not touch you." Finally: "Honoring America—the liberties—is appropriate, as the outer freedoms facilitate the inner freedoms. It is more difficult in a land with no tolerance. Toleration for religious pluralism was one of America's great gifts."
I felt my deceased grandfather, grandmother, and uncle send their love. I heard Buddha say: "Only Love Can Dissolve Illusion." I felt the love of Jesus as the nails dug into his skin. "Love all, bless all. You have the choice to bless or curse—therefore bless. I ask God to soften hearts and bring His mercy; at a soul level, beings realize we are all equal in God." More guidance: "Keep sending heart energy." I worked on this, my own small contribution to correct the disturbance.
As I drifted to sleep, my consciousness went 'behind enemy lines' and spread blessings—thus disabling offenses. My guides informed me that this was a usable "Defense Department" strategy—that practicing "love them that hate you" (when you were able to do so) in fact dispersed hostile mental energies. Many times I went in my dreams to a war-zone, sometimes terrified and under fire, and other times able to send blessings from a protected transcendental plane.
The spaceship returns to my dreams. In meditation I go down through my hara line into the Earth—and come out into a space docking station. This is my base. Atlantean priests and scholars give me a six inch, golden key to the future of Humanity. "Open the door," I hear. I am a guardian, a steward, one among many. The human race is not ready to receive it. But 2030 is an important year for rediscovery of this knowledge. I will be 68 in the year 2030.

Am I an ET after all? Am I Starseed? A hybrid? Is that incompatible with a university faculty position and work as a lawyer? During the memorial service for John Mack, one of his sons defined courage as doing what it takes to move ahead, in spite of fear for consequences. We lead despite our fears, not out of immunity from them. Similarly, David Grinspoon writes of the "ridicule" factor, and the fact that many only felt comfortable pursuing an interest in SETI (search for extraterrestrial intelligence) once the academics married the fields of astronomy and biology to create a new field called astrobiology.
In 2001, I received this inner message:
Only the spiritual realms are real. The material is an illusion. There are millions

of life-forms on different planets—they seek alliances with humans toward Liberation, because humans have universal knowledge, as they experience karma in different bodies, different lifetimes; whereas other beings, being made of consciousness, have only one body and do not know death. You are of that hybrid nature, being human married to the divine and expressive of many different collections of life-forms from various systems. That is why you experience everything multi-dimensionally. And so all affiliates on local channels are seeing the Blue Pearl and expanding consciousness through shaktipat.

It feels so freeing to acknowledge this. I can fully acknowledge my humanness, as Michael who struggled through law firms and various unhealthy relationships; who gained some limited acknowledgment for legal scholarship and taught at Harvard; who went to Hebrew school and later got these other degrees; and also this being whose consciousness can soar to the divine and intermingle with colleagues and friends on other planes of existence. I am a prototype of sorts, whose grounded professional life may encourage others to let themselves fully experience the risk of spiritual opening, learning in the process to trust the unexpected components that are part of the path.

In marriage I learned to expand my interest in spiritual universality, by embracing many different kinds of practice in a shared experience. I began learning to release some ego accompanying accomplishment, and to trust the universal forces that are guiding, frequently pushing, always with love and humor, always with grace. I began to learn to integrate the pulsating experiences of liquid light manifested by the blazing kundalini, and encounters and trials, with the daily highs and lows. Here in this benign humdrum and not beyond it, God dwells.

Elaine and I found a marriage location that would reflect the universality of our spiritual passion: the Bahamas, the sky for our canopy, the sea for our witness. We invited our families to the island. We wrote our own ceremony, acknowledging nature, and including many religious traditions without expressly naming them.

We drew a sacred circle in the sand and surrounded it with conch, then lit incense and blessed the space. We embraced unity through the contradictions of multiplicity, bringing in all the traditions. My best friend, a fundamentalist Christian, gave a reading from the book of Genesis (*Braisheet*) about how the man and woman knew they were naked and not ashamed. Peter officiated, connecting everything energetically, making sure we slowed down, physically and psychically, as we approached and entered the sacred circle.

In the end, everyone who participated felt the power of the ceremony, the uniting of all good forces in the universe toward our sacred union. The light was incredible, and shines through our photographs like a divine beacon, blessing the union. We stated our vows intuitively, letting them pour through us, from the sky and ground and through our voices, as our deepest essence spoke. When Peter joined our hands and blessed us "by a power greater than any of us here," we felt that power course through his body, through his arms and hands, and into ours. Words that might be spoken in wedding ceremonies in synagogues, churches, mosques, and other temples came alive in the spontaneity of the moment. After, my uncle Sol, fittingly gave a Hebrew blessing, and my wife's father gave a toast.

We celebrated and danced, including the requisite *hava nagilah* while up in the air in chairs, on the pillars of my brothers' and other guests' shoulders.

A Friend of All Faiths

I brought my wife a pair of gloves for the winter. She slipped one on her left hand and instantly removed it. "Are these made with rabbit fur?" We looked at the tag. "I can't wear this being's skin," she said.

The profound truth of her statement suddenly struck me—and that I, who considered myself to be so aware, had been so ignorant. Would I want a rabbit to wear *my skin* for the winter?

The consciousness of that being still resided in the fur, still could be accessed through high sense perception. Maybe during the Ice Age our cave forbearers used animal skins for survival, and, like Job, I was not around when God created the Leviathan, so I cannot tamper with the logic of what was. All I know is that I have a choice; that these rabbits probably were treated without compassion; that these beings in life were conscious of suffering, and probably more: conscious that the only purpose of their breath was for the profit of their captors. I could not bear to live in cahoots with those who had greedily put them to death.

There is a story in India scriptures about a king who has studied all the scriptures and is in search of a guru. His wife tells him he can become enlightened right there, in meditation, and continue to serve his royal duties. But he disagrees.

He abandons his kingdom, leaves his wife, and wanders through the forests searching for wisdom. Now the king does not know that his wife is already Self-Realized. Unbeknown to him, she slips out and tracks him. Eventually he meets a hermit in the woods who tells him there is a great guru in the next village, yonder. He travels and receives initiation from this great teacher. He becomes Self-Realized. The teacher tells him: go back, and now fulfill your royal duties with detachment. He returns to tell his wife the whole story, only to learn out that she already knows: it was she who had been traveling to the village and become its guru, and none other than she who had initiated him.

The other night it was raining, and without the least bit of awareness, I trod past some earthworms who were struggling across the concrete pavement; I was still absorbed in analyzing the movie we had just seen. It was only when my wife paused and suddenly drew my attention that I recognized that our Cambridge neighborhood pavements were the killing fields for them. More of our fellows crawled across the concrete into the street, where they would stiffen and die, or be mowed down by humans. One by one, my wife lifted up the earthworms. They curled around her fingers; she gently placed these beings back into the mud.

Brushing my teeth later that evening, I reflected with remorse: to how many beings would I have to account, on leaving this earth? How many worms of the Earth had suffered under my heel? Would I like to be in their shoes and they, literally, in mine? I had been so eager to arrive on this plane that I "prematurely" birthed into *karma bumi*, the land of Karma, crying: Kwa! Kwa! I am "I!" I am "I!" And for this privilege, this body leapt onto the Wheel of Samsara, birth and death, and endless suffering, repercussions from innocent actions changing the balance of the life and death in the cosmos. Cause—effect; action—reaction.

Because we live in the city, this pile of rubber and concrete and steel, the simple cleansing rain of the earth results in so much desolation. Do I make a "mountain" out of a "molehill"—an earthworm hill? The Talmud says "he who saves a life has saved an entire world." My wife lovingly picked up each earthworm, recognizing in each a being as worthy as herself to the gift of life. She did so without drama; dharma simply *is*; as Paul said, "love does not put on airs; it is not snobbish... Love never fails." Buddhist lore is full of stories of noble humans who helped fish, ants, other creatures escape Death and thereby gained merit; these creatures often reincarnate as our intimate fellows (e.g., the fish as Buddha's disciples). *Prophecies will cease, tongues will be silent, knowledge will pass away. Our knowledge is imperfect and our prophesizing is imperfect. When the perfect comes, the imperfect will pass away.*

Paul's quotation reminds me of a Sanskrit mantra:
Om purnamidan, purnaat, purnam udachyate,
Purnasya, purnamadaya, purnam evavshisyate.
Om (the primordial sound). This is perfect, that is perfect.
When the perfect is taken from the perfect, only the perfect remains.

The perfect, it seems to me, is that divine love that dwells within the human heart. Or, in the form I learned the teaching: *God dwells within you, for you, as you.* Hillel and Jesus had phrased it like this: *Love your neighbor as yourself.* Not to love the neighbor *as if* he or she were you, but to love your neighbor because he or she *is* you. That core love appears to me as extant in all paths; thus we can aspire all to be friends of all faiths. This book, then, is not only about a "me" and "my" path, with its eccentric twists, turns, and seeming aberrations, but also where we may be headed collectively, as a species, as stewards of the planet. Together, may be we friends of all faiths, and in this way, of one another.

IN MY DREAM

I have this recurring dream: am back in our Normanhurst house, in the bedroom of my childhood. White-painted bookshelves line the walls, filled with a combination of my childhood science fiction and astronomy paperbacks, and fiction from my parents' collection. My desk is crammed with diaries, notes, assorted papers, telephone numbers, and mementos. Two windows, for cross-ventilation, one giving view of a large oak, and then the neighbor's house, the other our back yard: the sandbox containing early memories, a swingset, a picnic table on our stone patio–the one I once thought to paint as an Israeli flag.

I used to see a face in the window some nights, on drifting to sleep–was it my face? Was it God's? Was the intruder all-knowing, friendly, or threatening to my subconscious? At the other end of the room loomed the closet: an object of inquiry–what was it I had left behind? It was always filled with files; my seventh-grade science project, a poster on the genetic experiments of Gregor Mendel; assorted knick-knacks, correspondence with childhood girlfriends, notes on everything–God, humanity, depletion of the ozone layer, exploration of space, old math tests, an old copy of *Lord of the Flies* or *I, Robot*.

I am always exploring that closet in the dream, collecting books and files for transport to the next locale.

That seems to be my life–collecting books and files for the inevitable move to the next phase of the journey. I have the same dream about my house in Lykens, Pennsylvania–gathering things left behind–only the staircase is missing some wooden planks.

Professional interests move from Harvard to Atlantis and beyond as geographical and professional touchstones–Cambridge and the Bahamas. Yet I still dream of Normanhurst.

"Passover: Our apartment in New York, 2005: near Central Park, my room giving a rear window view to the apartment across the way. A room so reminiscent of many others. On the wall–lithographs we picked up in Israel, showing the world of Shalom Aleichem's stories: the shtetl marketplace, a young boy selling juice, a woman carrying her duck to market, goats, bone-thin horses drawing carriages; a bearded sage; a Chagall poster of the Fiddler on the Roof; my home-made Matisse cut-out, and adolescent paintings (replicas of van Gogh's *Room at Arles*, which I had styled as *Room at Columbia*; the cover for Robert F. Heinlein's *Tunnel in the Sky*; Monets; abstract alien landscapes, full of fiery orange-reds and soothing sea blue-greens). A photo of my father from high school, pensive and bright; my brother dancing with his fiancée at Princeton; a Passover with our second cousins, Panushes from Israel; sitting with hands on knees, in sports coat and tie, in first grade at Tarbut Hebrew School in Buenos Aires; a blow-up of a story from the *New York Observer* ("Lawyer Who Writes Offers Advice for Those Who Might"); the ad for a fiction reading I once gave in Manhattan; photos from law school graduation; a collection of clay artifacts made in pottery class in Buenos Aires–a chess queen, blue and purple and yellow, a blue and yellow horse, some decorative pock-marked piece in green and brown, an orange pig.

Then there is the book collection, an endless library that wraps around this room and continues in wrap-around bookcases in every room of the apartment–and spirals therefrom into the infinite beyond–like my Zaydie's library, the one that housed his collection of Hebrew novels and Judaica, science books, and papers. In this collection on Central Park West, my books and Daniel's and Jonathan's and those of my parents mingle freely. Some of theirs: the unforgettable collection of Winston Churchill's memoirs–*Hinge of Fate, Closing the Door*, and other titles embossed on my childhood memory; books about Israel and the Jewish people and prospects for peace in the Middle East; *The Roots of War*, my father's *Foreign Affairs* pile; books on philosophy and history and science; Carl Sandburg's biography of Lincoln; books about the stock market, about management and investing. A collection of books on world religion: Buddhism, Hinduism, Catholicism, Protestantism, Judaism, and Islam.

Michael H. Cohen

Old Dr. Seuss books. Daniel's philosophy books. Harrison's *Principles of Internal Medicine* and my mother's anatomy and other medical school textbooks. Her German and Russian language books, poetry and fiction. Plenty of dictionaries. *Catch-22* and endless rows of fiction. *You Can Negotiate Anything.*

Then my books begin to slip in: *On Death and Dying.* My college poli-sci books: *The Conduct of Foreign Policy. Macroeconomics.* Books on Wall Street.

Then finally the eclectic array of books on religion and consciousness: *Major Trends in Jewish Mysticism* next to *The Coming of the Cosmic Christ,* right by *The Aquarian Conspiracy, Mind Body Therapy,* Don Juan books, Gurdjieff books, kundalini books, books on Kashmir Shaivism, Kabbala, meditation, *The Golden Bough, Autobiography of a Yogi;* then again here is Brezinski's *The Soviet Bloc, Jewish Worship, The Enneagram, Padre Pio, Tales of the Dervishes,* Joseph Campbell, Freud and Jung, *Small is Beautiful, Primitive Classification* by Durkheim and Mauss, *The Peyote Dance, The Nature of Personal Reality* by Jane Roberts, more dictionaries, and *The Jungian Dreamwork Manual.*

Someday I will give these books to a library—I have incorporated them, they are all part of me—to see them is to witness one's self externalized; and yet to bring the balance between giving and receiving, they are to be shared.

I grew up believing that books created immortality—to write was to secure forever—and we were, after all, known commonly as the People of the Book; later experience taught me the importance of the present moment, of timelessness and weightlessness in space and time, of meditation. Books matter but so does presence—and writing only partly explicates reality. Somehow it is the dance of conscious and the unconscious that informs my journey—like Kennedy's doodles, combined with his analysts' recommendations.

When the purple light comes, engulfing and extinguishing my small self and plunging my consciousness into an awareness beyond the confines of the body—any body—the destiny of eternity is revealed: respected in print and expressed through the mind yet transcendent of both. To the glory of that infinite journey, the one that surpasses understanding, this book is one offering of experience.

A Friend of All Faiths

This book is also for Castor and Pollux, Wizards of Love, spiritual teachers with whom the clear heart connection resonates eternally. I found them on a farm in Pennsylvania, as their mother jumped into the back of my neighbor Hermann's pick-up truck and found her way into his heart. There were four in the litter, two left: I had to take both home since the brothers belonged together. I learned over the years how much unconditional love we share with the animal incarnates of our soul family. Truly, these are enlightened beings who are teaching in every moment. Great souls sometimes come in the form of animal friends. Below, Pollux is pictured meditating on the Absolute, after having completed the Primary Series of Ashtanga Yoga and having memorized the sun salutation (background). Castor, pioneering the use of props, perambulates a chair as he envisions

different ways to perform supported Chair Pose; he is also Self-Remembering, as indicated by the engaged gaze and alert nostrils. Castor is completing an open-eyed meditation, allowing the full awareness of Being to flow through his body, while Pollux is in *shambhavi mudra*, the inner-directed awareness. Both are modeling different forms of Samadhi (one-pointed consciousness) described in Patanjali's *Yoga Sutras*.

These photos allow only a crude representation of the depth of awareness residing in each of these beings. For their faces, too, dissolve in white light into the appearances of family representatives past and future.

The next time around, I am told, they may be human, if not higher than that. I certainly believe the love of individuals for their pets lasts forever, and that we are reunited on the subtle planes. Indeed, this was my one meditation of heaven: the brilliant light; then, come the beloveds: pets first—the most visible heart-connection; then guides and family and friends and teachers and other people.

Michael H. Cohen

So many contribute to the unfolding of a life, and not all are in bodies. As to those incarnate beings I must thank included are those special people who read the manuscript and offered helpful comments. First my wife Elaine reads every word and has a keen eye for detail. Without her clear vision the page is amiss. Next, I thank my friends, Linnea Larson, MSW, and James Lake, MD, whose clear and generous comments provided support and encouragement. I also am grateful to Wayne Jonas, MD, both for reading this manuscript and for critiquing others, and for conversations in unusual places: a parking garage after shaking the Dalai Lama's hand following the First International Congress on Tibetan Medicine; a living room after healers departed; a freeway in Alexandria. Thanks also to Midge Murphy, JD and Laura Stevens for reading and offering comments, and to Linnea Larson for thoughts on "About the Reader." My appreciation goes to Will Bueche for the cover design, and Kathi Kemper, MD for the blurb. Margo P. Cohen, MD, generously devoted three eight-hour days to reading and offering detailed comments. Her contribution was generous and insightful. For friends and family, the gratitude is great: may we recognize each other through time and space and find a heart space to acknowledge love beyond roles. As this book was wrapping up, Ujayi came into our lives and has been bringing his paws for wisdom regularly to our experience.

I also thank all those who have been my teachers, many of whom may appear in slightly disguised form as characters in the book. You are all amazing. Whether our paths have converged briefly or fully, in satisfaction or bewilderment, I celebrate this meeting. I have learned from each of you, no matter how strenuous the encounter. I am human, you are human, and between us are cords of love and forgiveness.

"Sid," your words have touched me, and I appreciate your reading this manuscript and responding from the heart.

I thank all beings, visible and invisible, who are part of this journey. I thank the ancestors, for they are closer than the breath; and the children to come, as they are part of this conversation as they ignite the journey within. May those who read this work in future ages, in form physical or otherwise, derive blessings therein.

To the peoples of all faiths, I extend my love. May we meet in the One Great Heart that binds all. As we say at the conclusion of practicing yoga: *Namaste*–I bow to the divinity within you.

A Friend of All Faiths

An ancient meditation vehicle is to quiet the mind and ask: "who am I?" As each response arises, it also gently fades away with the realization "not this, not that," leading back again to the question. By continuing to ask, the one who meditates sequentially realizes: *I am not this body; not this mind; not these shifting emotions; not my accomplishments, nor my failures either. I am not what I think I am, nor what others think of me. I am not my worries, nor am I my plans. I am neither the future nor the past.* All identifications cease, leading to a direct awareness of the spaciousness of being. The term "spaciousness" like many mystical phrases may seem simultaneously empty and full, portending possibly everything or nothing. It is like the old joke: *what did one Zen monk say to another?* Answer: *Nothing.*

Instead of "About the Author," this section concerns the question probed here: identity—as Zen teachers ask, "what is the face you had before you were born?"

It is difficult to write about the spiritual path. There are many risks, including the lack of adequate language. Most of us lack the language to write about experiences that take place outside consensus boundaries of what is 'ordinary,' 'normal,' or 'real'—labels, really—and so we rely on terms such as 'non-ordinary' simply to demarcate arenas of consciousness outside the things that tend to preoccupy the mind on a more mundane (or even heightened emotional) basis. There is little agreement between mystics or even scholars in different paths on the content of experiences denoted by terms such as 'numinous.'

Further, skeptics automatically tend to dismiss spiritual experiences as lacking credibility, while adherents—just as reflexively—tend to embrace such tales as inherently authentic.

It is even difficult to define spirituality: what makes one experience "spiritual" versus another? Is falling to one's knees in a temple in a swell of blistering intra-dimensional light more spiritual than doing laundry? How do we orient ourselves in a world where the ordinary can—with the right eye—become extraordinary; and where experiences considered by many to be extraordinary (or non-ordinary) are for some, regular?

Yet another danger presents itself: what is the line between physical and/or psychological pathology, and genuine mystical experience? By describing inner experience, one risks being ridiculed. Particularly when such experience crosses the line of what is culturally acceptable (for example, encounters with 'extra-terrestrial' beings versus feeling the Holy Spirit during Sunday worship). I am a lawyer and writer, and seminarian, and healer, by training, not a philosopher or mental healthcare professional. Assuming these identification cards, labels, carry meaning. They do and they do not; everything is riddled with paradox. Perhaps this is why the Zen monks are silent. Yet a writer must engage verbally. My training does not qualify me to draw a firm analytical line between these different regions of experience—only to describe my experience.

But even if I could draw the right analytical boundaries, yet another risk presents itself. By exposing one's secret liaison with God, one risks a charge of arrogance. Why share what is private? Why claim grace landed here (and by implication not there)—or even mark grace's landing?

Still another risk is the possible accusation of blasphemy or heresy. After all, the scriptures assert such and such; St. Augustine says this; Aristotle put it that way; the Rabbis said X; this sage tells us; the guru told us; only through Me; this is the only way; those who don't believe; only these are saved; have you thought about where you will spend eternity; pagans and infidels; and so on.

The list of potential contraindications goes on. Writing a spiritual memoir is no small matter. And even if language existed to describe spiritual capacity and experience, and the requisite training was in place, there is the ridicule factor to consider. One person's miracle can be a self-proclaimed skeptic's proving ground.

When a friend provided an interview with a psychology journal about his inner journeys with ETs, in the genuine spirit of hoping to inform and assist others with similar experiences, he found a sensationalized write-up of "sex with aliens." This became the butt of jokes among those in his community. John Mack conceptualized a range of "extraordinary experiences" rather than simply "ET experiences;" the former being more inclusive and less open to academic predators. If gossip and titter are all we have achieved after thousands of years up the chain from Cro-Magnon, we have a long way to go. By describing encounters with ETs or figures such as Moses, Jesus and Mary, Allah, Buddha, or Kwan Yin, one risks alienating one segment or another of the readership, either skeptics of one sort or adherents of another; and worse, by detailing a rich array of inner experience, one risks enduring ridicule by those whose tools of rationalism also provide the sharp edge of language to cut down what might simply be a magnificent experiment in consciousness.

Yet, risk-taking is necessary. When considering the vast, recent increase of blinking lights, sounds, emails, computerized gismos, thumb-pressing button-pushing electron-peddling 'communication' rushing toward us—a whole lot of noise with little space between—I wonder how future generations will carve out space for inner experience, particularly if popular press and academics disrespect such experience. What has happened to stillness, to silence? The ancients went to forests and caves. Today, one can be in touch with the world via wireless "Ether" net and cell-phone even if meditating in a cave. Why not put in a satellite dish too, for the eight hundred stations, and order meals via the Web if fasting becomes too onerous? (After writing this book I came across a swami in a cave in India who did have a cellphone and, his own CD's).

You, the reader, must understand. You have responsibilities in the world, too. You speak to God in your own way, and hear back, receive guidance in your own way. Like me, you are a regular person with a professional identity and/or household life: an ordinary Joe, Kim, Chris, Tina, Doug, Sam, Jennifer, Terry. You have ups and downs, perhaps engage a psychotherapist, acupuncturist, chiropractor, or massage therapist from time to time or not; affiliate with a religious institution for worship or meditate and pray privately or not; have a rich interior life that you sometimes share with others or not; remember and record your dreams, some of which are magnificent and leave you breathlessly uplifted and exhilarated and others of which terrify you, or not; find modern life's pace hectic yet seek time for introspection and contemplation or not; seek clues to your own life's purpose—the reason you are here in this body at this time, or not; make great discoveries as well as regretful mistakes, or not; learn about your vast potential as well as limitations, or perhaps not. You are uniquely gifted, brilliantly individual—yet share the same humdrum as we all have for eons; seek a way out as well as in. Like the sign on the door to my friend's acupuncture practice: *The way out is the way in.*

What I have done is describe a broad range of inner experience that may have some unique aspects, such as its inclusiveness vis-à-vis a variety of religious traditions, and its pervasive intensity. Such inclusiveness also parallels an educational and professional path that spans different disciplines, including law, medicine, ethics, business, and creative writing. This inclusive perspective no doubt will challenge boundaries and orthodoxies. I celebrate—and question—my experiences on Wall Street as well as in Seminary; life in law's cool as well as in the ashram. With humor, I hope, and the proper combination of doubt and faith.

Isaiah opens chapter 6 thus: "*In the year of King Uzziah's death, I saw the Lord seated on a high throne; his Presence filled the sanctuary; above him stood seraphs, each with six wings: two to cover its face, two to cover its feet and two for flying. And they cried to one another: 'Holy, holy, holy is the Lord of Hosts; His glory fills the whole earth.'*" He does not begin with a philosophical justification of human propensity for mystical encounter; does not validate his findings through scientific inquiry; does not subject his vision to rational inquiry. He simply notes the year and what he saw. One can conjure mystics in any tradition who do the same. Swedenbourg sat in his chair, fell into a state between waking and sleeping, and talked to non-corporeal beings. God regularly appeared to Moses.

In Hebrew school, I grew to believe a great gulf existed between me, and the heroic individuals I was studying—Moses, Isaiah, the biblical kings and prophets. This gulf simultaneously mystified them and separated me, an ordinary person, from the depth of their experience. This gulf may be an asset to humility, but it diminishes capacity for inner experience. Institutionalized religions typically have elevated their historic representatives and downplayed the ordinary individual's capacity for an unmediated encounter with the "burning bush" of the divine. Religious authorities historically have distrusted mystics, because mystics bridge the gulf between themselves and the Divine and require no intermediary. Writing this memoir is an affirmation of the divine interconnectivity with our lives. It is also empowering: if anyone can have the receptivity of an Isaiah, Moses, or even Swedenbourg, then the Church (read any religious authority into *Church*) has less control over the individual.

There is nothing so dangerous as a person who believes in the truth of his or her own experience. This statement is double-edged: it is a truism, yet we could also substitute the word "beautiful" for dangerous, and the statement also would have resonance. The point is: many of those comfortable with or in charge of an organized religion find personal, mystical experience inherently suspect. Many religious traditions have forbidden direct mystical experience to the majority of adherents or allowed such experiences only through supervised, controlled settings. Scientific critics have equally attempted to control permissible experience through their logic, maxims, and concepts.

Yet, experience need not be marginalized; nor should openness to experience necessarily portend grandiosity, superiority, a sense of special grace. Paul (and others from different traditions) warn against "boasting" about spiritual experiences, as therein lies the trap of ego. It is one thing to boast, another to describe and inform; one thing to use one's private "revelation" as a means to control others, to gain adherents and manipulate them through ideological warping, and another to simply state what is, without requirements.

I believe the ability to receive revelation is every human's birthright. While I cannot claim to begin to understand how divine grace might function, my study of energy healing teaches me that human receptivity and openness can greatly facilitate the extent to which information is poured into the channel. Nick was a 'channel,' I became a channel, and everyone is a channel. To claim otherwise is to limit revelation to the private you—many of those revered in our time as founders of religions or as saints were regarded as grandiose misfits of their day, to be hounded, shackled, tortured to confess, burned, or flayed. Some of those survived and some of these erected systems to promulgate their status as the elect.

Julian Jaynes of Princeton had a theory that the ancient Greeks actually "heard" what they interpreted as "the gods" speaking from one of the chambers in the "bichameral" brain to the other chamber. This theory eventually fell into disfavor. By contact with the divine, I am not referring to messages from one part of the brain to another. I am referring to contact with beings like you and me, only their bodies are different than ours, not the flesh and blood to which we are accustomed. By inner experience, I refer to the kind of clairaudient, clairvoyant and clairsentient experience to which I was once a stranger, and that I now welcome as 'second nature'—the ability to see, hear, and feel non-corporeal beings ranging from spiritual guides to angels to divinity in whatever form it appears to the seeker. Like us, I believe, they come as beggars and kings, kin and strangers, saints and goblins, and they have lineages and hierarchies, just as we do. (Why else do we conceptualize God as "King," "Sovereign," "Lord," "Master," "Ruler?") At the apex of this whole cosmic order of being is, I presume, no matter what the name, let's call Him, Her, It, All of the Above, the Name (in Hebrew, literally *Hashem*):

this ineffable/numinous/transcendent/immanent/overarching/supreme witnessing/all-pervasive/omniscient/omsentient presence whose shorthand is this three-letter word (sometimes two letters and a dash as in G-d).

There must be reasons why we, as a world culture, generally have closed down our

Michael H. Cohen

channel to the divine. Many would assert that a major reason is not only the general opposition of much of organized (institutionalized) religion to private mystical experience, but also the numbing that religious practice within some contemporary communities can have–ironically–on the direct, unmediated experience of God. Specifically, once mantras (sacred words) become rote, they cease becoming living vessels of embodied divine energy. Once rituals become obligatory, they lose their freshness as living mediators of Earth and Heaven. Once priests become the necessary mediators, individuals lose direct contact with a consciousness mighty enough to connect directly with their bodies and brains.

Some find beautiful, direct connection to their deities (or The Deity) through a church, temple, mosque, or other communal place of worship, though it is generally acknowledged that 'organized religion' does not always embrace the private mystical experience. We can have many other hypotheses as to why present human awareness typically denies inclusion of these other parts of our reality.   Other social and cultural professional reasons may include the following:

- Inner experiences can be scary and can threaten to overwhelm our psychic boundaries;
- The line between mystical experience and psychosis is not well understood or clearly delineated;
- The field of psychology is dismissed by some as a 'soft science,' and even within the field, study of the 'farther reaches of human nature' (to quote Maslow) is marginalized by many;
- Unlike cultures in which shamanistic experience is accepted, modern, 'Western' culture has split off non-cognitive experiences;
- Further, modern, 'Western' culture has split off 'scientifically validated' phenomena, which are deemed 'objective,' from inner experience, which is deemed 'subjective' and therefore unreliable;
- More than 'unreliable,' our consensus culture tends to judge such as experiences as inherently not credible, thus dividing audiences into skeptics and adherents.
- Our culture is profoundly materialistic, $e=mc^2$ notwithstanding, and fails to recognize 'energy' in an immediate, kinesthetic way.
- Our culture mystifies intuition as a 'sixth sense' and thereby fails to integrate innate human potential into everyday use and experience.

Finally, a pervasive concern is potential misuse of spiritual authority. (I have written about this subject, including its regulatory aspects, extensively in my academic writings.) I learned something about this with Nick: he was a brilliant and simultaneously distorted teacher. Perhaps this is why the book begins with him: he helped opened a channel I always had latent inside me, and also taught me (albeit through his destructive behavior) about the ethics of spiritual power. I learned that another major reason why most of us have not 'opened up our channel' is that:

- Psychological health and emotional maturity are prerequisites to the successful integration of mystical experience that marks genuine spiritual development.

Spiritual health requires psychological health–religious maturity, psychological maturity; that is why religious doctrine alone will never produce the best humanity has to offer; why religion and compassion or love are not necessarily synonymous; and why faiths and beliefs can differ, but the healthy qualities religious maturity can produce can be shared and described universally across religions (often through experiences of the mystics). As a corollary, it may be the reason most of us do not exercise our latent spiritual gifts is that collectively we are not sufficiently strong and mature to handle these experiences–a point easily made given the way we misuse "outer" technology (imagine if we would wreak equal destruction through mental power, not even having to 'press a button'). Einstein's equation–

like nuclear power--proves that Kali and Shiva are equal as metaphors for destruction and creation. We can bless or curse, enlighten or clog.

As one in a series of 'dark teachers' of spiritual power, Nick like Darth Vader in *Star Wars*, presented the one who has been lured by the 'dark side of the Force,' but whose face is sweet when finally able to rip off the mask. Without presuming to explain the origins of this darkness, it is sufficient to recognize it exists, a temptation lurking within spiritual power correlative to the dark side of ambition in political power. We all face the Dark Side. I can be one with God and at the same time, *when will the elevator arrive* might just be one thought darting across a frustrating afternoon. Like my gentle, already enlightened cats, I can have a "bad fur day." I not only have to recognize my shadow nature when it pops up, I also have to "eat" it. Only by acknowledging and assimilating back the dark power projected onto the world can we fully embody our light and be whole. Some call for sublimation of negative emotions, others for their cathartic release–in either event, recognizing one's shadow appears critical to psychological and religious maturity and avoidance of delusion of self and repression/oppression of others.

One of the negative experiences I report in this book is that of perceiving a demon speaking through one of my law school faculty colleagues. I hope the reader will resist the temptation to see this as projection or metaphor on my part (academic politics can't be that bad!), and consider the truth of experience. With our channel open, you, too, may someday–like Jesus–see a Legion of demons spilling out of someone nasty at work. But perhaps you do not want to. I can understand that. Believe me, personality dynamics in meetings can be quite sufficient for a day's work–Earth being *karma bumi*, the land of action-reaction; watching the ghosts and goblins (and angels and deities) fly across the mahogany table is not for the faint of stomach. Paradoxically, it takes a great deal of inner strength to allow one's self to be so vulnerable and sensitive.

Not all mystical explorers have admitted to the paradox of fiery strength and incalculable fragility. Indeed, many deny it. When surveying the mystical literature–both historical and contemporary–one typically finds two paradigmatic formulas for narrative structure, neither of which gives full credit to the experience of encountering the divine in all one's humanness. First is The Conversion Story. This is exemplified by Saul's journey on the road to Tarsus, and again by St. Augustine' *Confessions*. "I was an ordinary shmuck, but through grace–a blinding, divine light; a voice; a vision; whatever–I found You, and now I am healed/saved/redeemed/made whole." The modern version of this would be *Conversations with God* by Donald Neale Walsh. One day God simply spoke to him through a movement of his pen. Then everything changed.

Second is The Believer's Tale. This is written by someone already converted, someone who expresses mystical experience in the dense symbolic and metaphorical language of the individual's faith. I think of *Dark Night of the Soul* by John of the Cross or writings by Theresa of Avila. These works are rich with personal experiences of the 'inner castle,' the 'many mansions' of the body, mind, and soul in which Spirit is said to dwell. Today there are writings by channels and healers, who purport to bring messages from non-corporeal beings; these writers 'travel' out-of-body or receive transcendental messages in slightly altered trance states, echoing the mystical experiences of saints from different traditions. But then one wonders, to what are they already converted? To the persuasive stories of former doubting Thomases turned converts? To the holy accounts of authoritative scriptural texts, or perhaps to their own idiosyncratic formulas?

Perhaps it does not matter–their conversion is already a given. In any even, neither the Conversion Story nor the Believer's Tale are totally satisfying, if one is neither a Convert nor a Believer. These structures favor our penchant for duality–for splitting, between one extreme and another, and then flipping between the two. The first extreme: *One day I was this and then such-and-such happened and I became that, and believe me, that is the truth and you get can there too, just in a snap.* The second extreme: *This is true, this has always been the Truth, and here is my experience within that never-ending, never-beginning truth.*

Michael H. Cohen

My journey is neither a Conversion Story nor a Believer's Tale. I did not "convert" *from* a specified religious path *to* another specific path; nor can I identify a set of beliefs other than openness to trusting my experience and the mature ability to differentiate psychological projection, wish fulfillment, and other defense mechanisms from genuine metaphysical encounters. Mine is the story of a variety of religious experiences, accumulated over time and with different stripes and stars and accents, all intermingling, a smorgasbord, melting pot, palimpsest, whatever metaphor you choose. All these experiences have informed my scholarly work.

While the Conversion Story and the Believer's Tale seem simplistic from a literary perspective, they seem to form the bedrock of religious tradition. On the flip side, to non-believers, they are inherently suspect–if not ridiculous. As suggested, mental health care professions have not successfully sorted out creative psychological states involving out-of-body or mystical encounters from destructive, distorted ones. Arbitration is indeed difficult. William James, for example, laments the way "medical materialism" attempts to reduce such gems as the inner experience of St. Francis of Assisi to the fruit of an epileptic seizure.

As to the yardstick for discernment, the measure for healthy inner voyaging, the one James used–true to his pragmatic philosophy–was, "by their truth ye shall known them." Psychological states, or encounters 'beyond this dimension' that are healthy produce healthy results in this world. Of course, representatives of different religious traditions have their own 'tests of discernment,' corresponding with their religious ideology. My own test is love: have these experiences cultivated greater compassion, love for all beings, active works of compassion and love in the world? Is my heart more still, more full, more open than before? Or as Ronald Reagan used to ask when running for President: *Are you better off than you were four years ago?* Do spiritual experiences lend themselves to greater good works of compassion and caring of *all* peoples, not just those belonging to one or another "ism."

This is the test I use on myself. And I ensure that, while expanding consciousness in unusual ways, I remain grounded in my professional work and daily life. If I have floated off to some ethereal realm I have not remained there; on the contrary, I have struggled to integrate such flights with the mundane demands of regular existence. In other words, after enlightenment–the cat litter. There are few subjects more volatile than religion, but I have decided to tackle experience that crosses boundaries, religious and psychological, toward a new synthesis. Again, this story is as much about possibilities for you, the reader, as about nuances in my own family. Using the metaphor of the Chosen People, we are all Chosen People: each anointed, by the divine, elected for responsibility as well as grace. My journey is simply a perception from one vantage of expansion in consciousness, an expansion that embraces experiences from different religious traditions–whether labeled "East," West," "science," or even "New Age." I may be one prototype of an integrated approach to awareness that seeks to merge with the divine yet remain anchored in healthy psychological states, professional contribution, and a life rich in relationships with other human beings.

Now may that story unfold and resonate in its own way within a journey that is entirely yours.

The final word is from "Sid," who has placed this blessing on the book:
Many blessings for the success of this book: for the fulfillment of your intention for people to become open to their own Light, their own great Self, through your sharing.

Also by Michael H. Cohen

Creative Writing for Lawyers (Citadel Press, 1990)

Complementary and Alternative Medicine: Legal Boundaries & Regulatory Perspectives (Johns Hopkins University Press, 1998)

Beyond Complementary Medicine: Legal and Ethical Perspectives on Health Care and Human Evolution (University of Michigan Press, 2000)

Future Medicine: Ethical Dilemmas, Regulatory Challenges, and Therapeutic Pathways to Health and Healing in Human Evolution (University of Michigan Press, 2003)

Legal Issues in Integrative Medicine (NAF Publications, 2005)

Healing at the Borderland of Medicine and Religion (University of North Carolina Press, 2006)

With Mary Ruggie and Marc M icozzi:

Integrative Medicine: A Legal and Operational Guide (Springer, 2006)

About the Author

Michael H. Cohen currently lives in the Bahamas with his wife Elaine and their four-leggeds Castor, Pollux and Ujayi. He runs the Law Offices of Michael H. Cohen, teaches, writes, and knows Atlantis lies beneath the waves.

Printed in the United States
By Bookmasters